HISTORY
ON THE RUN

Duke University Press   *Durham and London*   2021

HISTORY ON THE RUN

SECRECY, FUGITIVITY, AND HMONG REFUGEE EPISTEMOLOGIES

MA VANG

© 2021 Duke University Press. All rights reserved.
Designed by Courtney Leigh Richardson
Typeset in Warnock Pro by Westchester Publishing Services

Library of Congress Cataloging-in-Publication Data
Names: Vang, Ma, [date] author.
Title: History on the run : secrecy, fugitivity, and Hmong refugee epistemologies / Ma Vang.
Description: Durham : Duke University Press, 2021. | Includes bibliographical references and index.
Identifiers: LCCN 2020029561 (print) | LCCN 2020029562 (ebook)
ISBN 9781478010272 (hardcover)
ISBN 9781478011316 (paperback)
ISBN 9781478012849 (ebook)
Subjects: LCSH: Hmong Americans—History. | Hmong Americans—Cultural assimilation. | Hmong (Asian people)—United States. | Refugees—United States.
Classification: LCC E184.H55 V364 2021 (print) | LCC E184.H55 (ebook) | DDC 305.895/972073—dc23
LC record available at https://lccn.loc.gov/2020029561
LC ebook record available at https://lccn.loc.gov/2020029562

Cover art: *Grandmother's Way*, 2018. 5′ × 3′. Ink and colored pencil on paper. © Hauntie. Courtesy of the artist.

For my mother and father,
MAI and VUE,
And my daughters,
KIA and PAKOU

CONTENTS

ACKNOWLEDGMENTS   IX

INTRODUCTION   1
The Lost Bag and the Refugee Archive

1. SECRECY AS KNOWLEDGE   27

2. MISSING THINGS   57
State Secrets and U.S. Cold War Policy toward Laos

3. THE REFUGEE SOLDIER   93
A Critique of Recognition and Citizenship in
the Hmong Veterans' Naturalization Act of 1997

4. THE TERRORIST ALLY   117
The Case against General Vang Pao

5. THE REFUGEE GRANDMOTHER   145
Silence as Presence in *The Latehomecomer* and *Gran Torino*

EPILOGUE   179
Geographic Stories for Refugee Return

NOTES   189
BIBLIOGRAPHY   231
INDEX   251

ACKNOWLEDGMENTS

Many generous people have carried this book in various ways, and I cannot thank them all or enough for their support. I thank my interlocuters whose knowledge and stories shaped this book: Sai Kua Thao, Nhia Kua Vang, Soua L. Lo, Youa Vang, Col. Wangyee Vang, Faiv Ntaaj Vaaj, Sua Cha, May Vang, Chang Vang, Yer Vang, Chang Vang Xiong, Kia Yang, Kia Vang, Palee Moua, Dan Moua, Tong Xeng Vang, Phong Lee, Jesse Fang, Charlie Vang, Pao Fang, Blong Xiong, Atary Xiong, and Cedric Lee.

I could not have written this book without the support of many generous mentors. The faculty in the Ethnic Studies department at UC San Diego provided an incredible space to think and build community. I am most grateful to have learned so much from Yến Lê Espiritu. Yến has been my biggest champion while I was a graduate student and even now as faculty. Her unmatched mentorship shaped this project in so many ways because she consistently challenges me to ground my ideas in refugee perspectives. Her thoughtful attention to my work, even at its messiest phases, strengthened this project to become more than I could imagine. I cherish our friendship and the many rejuvenating get-togethers over the years. Ross Frank has been a tremendous source of support. I can always count on him to ask me thought-provoking questions that I do not yet have answers to but that nonetheless challenge me to expand my horizon. Denise Ferreira da Silva changed what I thought I knew about race, power, and resistance. Her sharp interventions early in my graduate study challenged me to think deeper and broader to formulate thoughtful critiques as well as to think about the possibilities of the refugee figure. Denise continues to be a source of inspiration.

Adria Imada carefully read my writing at the dissertation stage and gave me valuable feedback to expand on my ideas. She generously gave her time and incisive professional advice, and I have learned from her how one can be in the institution but also not think like it. Shelley Streeby also meticulously read my chapters in the dissertation stage, generously encouraging me to find my voice as a writer. Jody Blanco helped me to see the overall argument and importance of my work outside of my interdiscipline. Thanks to Natalia Molina, K. Wayne Yang, Lisa Yoneyama, Takashi Fujitani, Lisa Lowe, and Nayan Shah for the support at UC San Diego.

My friends from the Ethnic Studies department at UC San Diego continue to be a source of tremendous support. I found a true friend in Maile Arvin who tirelessly read my work and offered companionship through those hard years in graduate school. She inspires me to be a thoughtful and rigorous researcher, and a kind human being. I am always learning from Ayako Sahara to fight for what I believe in. My graduate school cohort pushed me through the various stages of my career. Tomoko Tsuchiya and I became fast friends and roommates. She offered companionship and advice when I needed it most. Cathi Kozen's steady encouragement and sisterhood has been a source of strength; her commitment to ethnic studies is unmatched. I value Long Bui's friendship and his constant support as a conference buddy in graduate school and now as fellow UC colleague. And last but not least, Angie Morrill and I go way back to our undergraduate days. Your love and encouragement cushioned the difficulties of graduate school; thank you and Leroy for welcoming me into your home that first year, and for your lovely friendship always.

I have been fortunate to learn from mentors and peer mentors in Southeast Asian American studies and critical Hmong studies. My journey would not have been possible without Fiona I. B. Ngô who first introduced me to critical race theory and Southeast Asian American studies. She taught me the importance of research, that Hmong history and memory is a worthy research project, and encouraged me to go to graduate school. Lynn Fujiwara wrote me a letter for graduate school and nothing has been the same since. Mariam Beevi Lam's keen mentorship for the UC President's Postdoctoral Fellowship has made all the difference. She has been an early champion of my work and was instrumental with expanding my work to engage with Southeast Asian studies. Mimi Thi Nguyen has generously shared her work and supported my research. She has read the book manuscript several times, and her commitment to deepening my ideas has shaped so much of this book. I am so grateful for Davorn Sisavath, her brilliant research, and the joy she radiates. Chia Youyee Vang, Mai Na Lee, and Leena Her are role models in critical Hmong studies; thank you for the paths you paved. Aline Lo, Chong Moua, Kong Pha, and Mai See Thao are brilliant scholars and the best confidants; every moment with you is not enough. Bao Lo, Pa Der Vang, Yang Lor, and Seng Vang have offered much-needed comradery. Louisa Schein was also a part of the early critical Hmong studies gatherings and gave me important guidance.

I am lucky to work with colleagues at UC Merced who have enriched my life. I am inspired by the dedication and vision of my colleagues in the Department of History and Critical Race and Ethnic Studies: Mario Sifuentez, Sean Malloy, David Torres-Rouff, Romina Rulvacaba, Sabrina Smith, Maria Martin, Kit Myers, Sholeh Quinn, Susan Amussen, Myles Ali, Muey Saeteurn, Sapana Doshi, Christina Baker, Nicosia Shakes, and Kevin Dawson. Mario's vision and mentorship has made all the difference in valuing the work we do. David provided valuable feedback on the penultimate drafts of the introduction and chapter 1. The all-around fierceness of Anneeth Kaur Hundle, Whitney Pirtle, Dalia Magaña, Sora Kim, Sharla Alegria, and Zulema Valdez helped me finish writing the book and navigate the institutional obstacles for women of color. A very special thank you to Anneeth, Whitney, Dalia, and Sharla for our adventurous women-of-color writing group, and their extensive feedback on chapter 4. To commiserate with Nigel Hatton is the best gift; the humanity and poetics in everything he does is my source of inspiration. It has been a pleasure to work with and learn from May Yang, May Kao Xiong, Jamin Shih, Chia Xiong, Chia Thao, Kau Vue, Houa Vang, Neama Alamri, Amrit Deol, and other graduate students at UC Merced. I am thankful for all the conversations with Hmong American students (especially those from the Hmong Students Association at UC Merced, UC Riverside, UC Berkeley, and UC San Diego) who remind me of the urgency of this work.

Many Hmong communities have been a part of my journey. The Lao Hmong Family Association of San Diego and the families I have met through this organization offered home and community during graduate school. Thank you to Palee Moua and Dan Moua for their generosity and care as key anchors in the Hmong community in Merced. Thank you to the members of the Southeast Asian American Professionals Association who welcomed me upon my first arrival in Merced and continue to be pillars of support: Dr. Tru Chang, Dr. Wa Chong Yang, Judge Paul Lo, Tou Her, Dr. Kou Yang, Darryl Yang, Johnny Moua, Nini Lee, Dr. Kimiko Vang, Dr. Lesley Xiong, and Fong Xiong. Pos Moua is source of inspiration; thank you for your poetry and may you rest in peace. I am heartened by the visions and leadership of Sheng

Xiong, Lee Lor, Bousavanh Lor, Amy Hang, Mao Moua, Linda Xiong, Tsia Xiong, and See Lee to make Merced and the world a better place for us all. I have been fortunate to play a small role in the Hmongstory 40 Project to tell Hmong histories in California through the visionary work of Lar Yang, Misty Her, and Koua Franz. I am inspired by Hmong and Lao writers: May Lee-Yang, Kao Kalia Yang, Mai Der Vang, Mai Neng Moua, Andre Yang, Soul Vang, Saymoukda Vongsay, and Bryan Thao Worra.

The Anne Frank Southeast Asian Archive Award gave me the opportunity to spend time sifting through its Southeast Asian Archive collection at UC Irvine's Langson Library. The early research and writing of this book was also made possible by several small grants along with the Ford Dissertation Fellowship and the University of California President's Postdoctoral Fellowship Program (PPFP). The archivists at the following archives have offered tremendous support: the Southeast Asian Archive at UC Irvine, the Vietnam Archive, the President Lyndon B. Johnson Library and Archives, and the Immigration History and Research Center at the University of Minnesota. I thank Lisa Park and David Pellow along with Kim Park Nelson and Peter Park Nelson for opening their homes to me when I went to do research at the University of Minnesota's Immigration History and Research Center. My time at UC Riverside on the PPFP expanded my horizon in various ways. Mariam Lam, Jodi Kim, Debra Vargas, Tammy Ho, Christina Swinkel, and Sarita See offered valuable advice. I cherish the community with Sylvia Nam, Hun Kim, Ivan Small, and Sarah Grant, and the scholars in the Southeast Asian studies program (SEATRiP).

The Critical Refugee Studies Collective, of which I am privileged to be a part (along with Yến Lê Espiritu, Lan Duong, Khatharya Um, Victor Bascara, Nigel Hatton, Lila Sharif, and Mohamed Abumaye), has opened up the space to finish this work. Funding from UC Merced's Vice Provost for the Faculty supported writing group meetings toward the completion of this book. Courtney Berger at Duke University Press has been an early believer in this project; thank you for your thoughtful attention and clear direction. Thank you Susan Albury and the Duke editorial team for ushering this book through in its final stages in the midst of a global pandemic. I benefited from a manuscript review grant from UC Merced's Center for the Humanities and had the privilege to receive Mimi Thi Nguyen's and Lisa Yoneyama's thorough reading and feedback to shape the manuscript. I thank the anonymous reviewers for believing in this project. Your incisive feedback provided important guidance to sharpen the book's arguments. Mai-Linh Hong and Aline Lo's careful reading and thoughtful comments on chapter 5 refined its argument and ideas. Sara Wise provided valuable argument development support in the early stages of the manuscript. Peter Park Nelson's careful editorial skills helped greatly in preparing the manuscript for submission. May Kao Xiong's keen and thorough eye at the copyediting stage saved me. Thank you to May Yang for the beautiful book cover art.

I thank my family for their love and encouragement. My parents, Mai and Vue, continue to be my pillars of strength and sources of knowledge. My siblings, sisters-in-law, and brother-in-law—Yen and Pao Yee, Cha Lee and Mai Neng, Kor and Mao, Mai and John, and Thomas—are at the heart of this book's ideas as I think through the shape of our upbringing and lives. My nieces and nephews—Pao, Xee, James, Connie, Shania, Shinee, Sherry, Chelsea, Alec, Gracelyn, Lily, and Nora—bring me joy whenever I go home. I am grateful to my uncle Chong and aunt Xia for their belief in me, along with my cousins See, Xeng, Brian, and Frank. Kua is a one-of-a-kind aunt and I am so happy for her and Chris. I am so lucky for the love of grandmothers Lue Thao and La Xiong. Lynne and Doug never gave up on me as they witnessed me fight for love. I have found home in your light and love. Jen and Stefan are models for knowing how to do things (e.g., vacation, love, raising children), and Ryland and Everett are such thoughtful, caring nephews. I wish to one day have the adventures that Enid, Tim, and Eric are enjoying.

Most of all, I could not have done this without the love and devotion of Kit Myers. You're the perfect partner to build dreams with. Kia came into our lives so full of energy and with an intensity to play. PaKou has broken all of our best-made rules with more logical reasoning than any three-year-old child should possess. They both have taken such full command of our lives that I cannot remember a time before; their laughter makes all things right.

A significant portion of chapter 3 has been published as "The Refugee Soldier: A Critique of Recognition and Citizenship in the Hmong Veterans' Naturalization Act of 1997," in "Southeast Asian/American Studies," special issue, *positions: east asia cultures critique* 20, no. 3 (2012): 685–712.

INTRODUCTION

THE LOST BAG AND THE
REFUGEE ARCHIVE

While conducting research at the University of Minnesota's Immigration History and Research Center, I found a half-sheet document tucked into one Hmong family's file. It was between the resettlement application forms that were completed prior to resettlement and the cursory notes that tracked refugees' progress after arrival that was part of a paper trail of their journey to the United States.[1] This document was a lost baggage claim form filled out by (or on behalf of) a Hmong family after their arrival in St. Paul/Minneapolis in January 1980. It reported the loss of one checked bag and its contents en route from Bangkok, Thailand, to Okinawa, San Francisco, and finally the Twin Cities. The contents of the form give shape to the lost bag's narrative about loss and exile.[2]

Losing luggage is undoubtedly a nuisance; yet it is also a normal occurrence in travel and this form shows the effort to recover it. But the estimated

TABLE I.1. Missing Baggage Claim
Western Airlines Statement of Loss

1. This claim is filed covering loss of: Checked baggage (including contents)

2. Details of loss:
   Trip began at Bangkok, Thailand (Trans Inter Airline) to Okinawa
   then to San Francisco, California
   then to St. Paul & Minneapolis
   When and where last seen? Jan. 28, 1980 Bangkok, Thailand.
   When and where loss first reported? Jan. 29, 1980, St. Paul & Minneapolis
   Does claim check show property was checked to final destination? Yes
   Do you carry insurance against this loss? No

3. Baggage Information:
   Number of pieces of baggage checked: 3

DESCRIPTION OF ARTICLES	WHEN PURCHASED	WHERE PURCHASED	ORIGINAL COST (IN US DOLLARS)
1) 4 Blue Hmong dresses (skirt)	Self made	Thailand	1,000.00
2) 1 chain gold jewelry	1979	Thailand	500.00
3) 2 silver bars	1972	Laos	500.00
4) 1 Necklace jewelry (silver)	1979	Thailand	500.00
5) 1 Headdress	1978	Thailand	25.00
6) 1 Suit men custom dress	1976	Thailand	50.00
7) 1 Baby sling	1980	Thailand	15.00
8) 1 Hat	1980	Thailand	10.00

NOTE: Author representation of a missing baggage claim form from one Hmong refugee family's file as a remnant of their multiple flights from Laos to Thailand to the U.S.
SOURCE: Author duplication, Immigration History and Research Center at the University of Minnesota. Recorded by Ma Vang on March 3, 2010.

$3,000 worth of clothing and jewelry, made and acquired by this family between 1972 and 1980 in Laos and Thailand (shown in table 1.1), not only tells a story about the losses of personal belongings but also the underlying losses of country and of one's *ntsuj plig* (spirit) through a long history of forced displacements—being on the run. The story of loss that haunts this missing baggage claim form emphasizes three Hmong refugee realities. First, it reveals the journey of a Hmong refugee family who were a part of a large wave of Hmong refugees resettled in the U.S. in 1980, after escaping war violence in Laos to Thailand's refugee camps after the U.S. "secret war." Hmong refugees were dispersed throughout the U.S. under the federal government's refugee resettlement policy to avoid placing an undue burden on any single community.[3] These early groups that arrived in the Midwest, especially the Twin Cities of St. Paul and Minneapolis, were sponsored by charity agencies including the International Institute of Minnesota and by churches.

Second, the missing bag and its contents are artifacts important to and carried by Hmong women. The first item listed is four "self-made" Hmong dresses sewn and worn by the Hmong women in the family for New Year celebrations or other special occasions. The attributed value of $1,000 reveals not just the market price but the un-recuperated labor in making the dresses. The rest of the items shown as purchased—jewelry, the men's custom-made clothing, baby sling, and hat—represent the material cultural wealth accumulated by the family members since their displacement from Laos in 1975. In fact, the silver bars purchased in 1972 were the only items brought from Laos. The items such as the silver necklace and baby sling purchased between 1976 and 1980 would have been replacements for those lost in the escape from Laos across the Mekong River to Thailand. The silver necklace, in particular, would have been a dowry given to the Hmong woman, a treasured item that connected her to her mother.

Finally, this incomplete record of loss and its emphasis on the missing refugee remnants illuminates the spiritual presence of loss. The items lost on the journey to the U.S. were replacements for a previous loss in the flight across the Mekong, yet they also reflect the perpetual state of spiritual loss of Hmong who fled in haste and forgot to call upon their ntsuj plig to also make the journey.[4] In Hmong cosmology, ntsuj plig and the body coexist whereby it provides protection for one's physical and mental health.[5] The body is a host for seven to thirty-one ntsuj pligs, of which three play significant roles to support the life of the body.[6] Of these three ntsuj pligs: the shadow plig remains with the body in life and death until the body decomposes after burial, the reincarnating plig stays with the body until death at which point it leaves to reincarnate, and the dreaming plig (sometimes called the wandering plig) "can move about in the world, unrestricted by land or oceans to visit places and people."[7] The wandering plig returns in death to the spirit world to rejoin the ancestors, and as medical anthropologist Mai See Thao explains, to its origin of the "Hmong kingdom of the dead."[8] But, the wandering plig can become lost through wandering or fright from traumatic events such as displacement or an accident, leaving the body weak and prone to sickness. Indeed, the host/body's health and wellness is linked to maintaining unity with this ntsuj plig. A soul-calling ceremony is necessary to call the ntsuj plig back to its body.[9] It is a practice rooted in the belief that one's ntsuj plig can flee in the fright and chaos of violence, or might linger at the site of the trauma, which could cause physical illness, depression, and *ceeb* (fright). Hmong refugees believe that the violence and trauma that caused their escape from Laos, along with those they encountered in their flight, disrupted the spirit-body balance. Upon leaving each temporary place of refuge along their escape path, the refugees must remember to not only gather their bags but also gather spiritual strength by calling their ntsuj pligs to follow and ancestral spirits to protect their journey. Indeed, this lost bag carries with it missing things that exceed the record of its loss.

The lost bag has wandered from its charted course and is on the run like the family (and people) it was supposed to accompany. The form's questions about where each item originated, where the luggage was supposed to end up, and where it was last seen reveal how the missing baggage symbolizes that which remains unknowable except through the trace of its having once been there. These unrecoverable remains and the stories one is left to grapple with constitute the histories that run because they are carried by people who are on the run. Being on the run denotes the difficulty of combining the tasks of movement and carrying things and carrying knowledge. History on the run, this book's central concept, names Hmong on the run as an episteme, one that is fugitive because it eludes traditional archiving yet it tracks the presence of Hmong refugee epistemologies in place and time. Refugee epistemologies are ways of knowing embedded in stories and Hmong cosmology that are grounded in place. The concept is a feminist epistemological framework that articulates loss as presence (in place and time) by orienting the refugee within geography and history. Specifically, it articulates Hmong presence beyond the frameworks of soldiering and secrecy composed by U.S. liberal imperialism.

To be sure, the loss that the baggage signified was not the first indication of Hmong refugees and what they had lost in the war years, in the chaos of escape, or even once they had resettled in the U.S. By the time Hmong refugees showed up on the shores of the Mekong River, in the United States, in the historical record, and in ethnohistorical accounts, they were considered out of place and historical time. The first time that U.S. Americans and the Western world encountered Hmong refugees was through the Indochinese refugee resettlement project, in which they were primarily portrayed as a people transplanted from premodernity to modernity.[10] Left among the rent receipts and utility bills that showed refugees' daily struggles, the missing baggage form represents the problems of knowledge about Hmong refugees and about what became known to the U.S. American public and in academic discourses as the U.S. "secret war" in Laos (1961–75). The arrival of Hmong, Lao, and other refugees from Laos to the Thai side of the Mekong River, televised in news outlets and contested in the State Department's Task Force for Indochinese Refugees,[11] required U.S. Americans to confront the clandestine activities undertaken by the Central Intelligence Agency (CIA) under the direction of presidents Eisenhower, Kennedy, Johnson, and Nixon as well as the Pentagon.

Between 1961 and 1975, the United States waged a secret, unauthorized war in Laos and conscripted Hmong along with other ethnic and Indigenous groups such as Kha, Khmu, Mien, and Brao as proxy soldiers in order to aid its war efforts in Vietnam. This war for which Hmong fought, along with the soldiers and civilians who were forced to fight and flee, was kept secret because it directly violated the 1954 Geneva Accords that declared Laos along with Cambodia and Vietnam independent from France and stipulated that these former French Indochinese countries would remain neutral, free from foreign military intervention. To maintain this façade of neutrality, U.S. state records relating to the "secret war" were classified. News reports in the 1960s about the conflict in Laos during the Vietnam War began calling it "America's secret war" to emphasize its covert nature. The U.S. government deemed the war a "secret" primarily to conceal the U.S. covert bombing missions in Laos on enemy sites and to disrupt the North Vietnamese Army supply route, Ho Chi Minh Trail, which ran along Laos's eastern border. Flying these bombing missions were U.S. American pilots who were discharged and enrolled as "volunteers," Thai pilots, and Hmong pilots. They dropped more than 270 million bombs, amounting to 2 million tons of ordinance, on the country. The Hmong pilots, under the command of Hmong leader General Vang Pao, were part of the CIA-operated "secret army" in northeastern Laos to combat North Vietnamese troops operating in the region.[12] As one of the largest ever CIA clandestine operations of proxy soldiers, the "secret army" numbered more than thirty thousand soldiers at its peak, recruiting from Hmong, Mien, Khmu, Kha, and Lao groups. The "secret army" provided intelligence, engaged in armed combat, rescued U.S. American pilots, flew bombing missions, and took part in various other military duties.[13] In addition, Hmong participated in various aspects of the "secret war" as nurses, aid workers, U.S. embassy workers, and Royal Lao Police.[14]

Upon discovering the missing baggage declaration form, I immediately realized that this was an inscription of the violence that Hmong refugees experienced during and after the U.S. "secret war." I had learned through countless stories about how Hmong had run from war, such as the Hmong woman who recounted her leg being injured by "friendly" air fire while fleeing her village and the Hmong veterans who showed me their war wounds sustained from combat. But I had not expected to see the epistemic violence that erased the refugees' and soldiers' stories. I went to other archives—the Vietnam Center and Archive, presidential records of Kennedy and Johnson, CIA documents, and refugee resettlement records—to look for "official" records of the violence. In these records, I encountered the violence of ongoing erasure. When I examined the state archives of diplomatic and military activities and records of refugee resettlement to look for evidence of Hmong-U.S. relations in Southeast Asia, the declassified diplomatic collections revealed very little about Hmong during the war or their refugee experiences. Because these documents are categorized by nation-state, I eventually learned to ask the archivists for materials on Laos-U.S. relations or was directed to these collections when I inquired about Hmong history. At the archives on refugees, on the other hand, the collections focused on Hmong and other Southeast Asian refugees' integration into U.S. society, with minimal attention to the conflicts that had displaced Hmong from their homes in Southeast Asia. What I discovered were declassified U.S. records obscured with massive and countless redactions, and paper trails left by refugees like the missing baggage claim form. Chapter 2 examines these redacted records to demonstrate how the missing things and postcolonial Cold War strategies were manifestations of a specific function of bureaucratic archiving and the ways history is an incomplete project.

History on the Run: Secrecy, Fugitivity, and Hmong Refugee Epistemologies grapples with the problems with knowing about refugee histories that my encounters with the archives illuminated. Beyond constructions of the "good" or "bad" refugee construed by liberal nation-states and their history, the Hmong refugee emerged as a gendered racial formation composed at the intersections of fugitivity, secrecy, and refugee epistemology. The Hmong refugee is a "compositional subject" whose critical position against the violence of colonialism and war, state governance, and national belonging is configured through these very domains of power.[15] Yet, Hmong on the run as an episteme reveals the contradictory liberal/illiberal and good/bad figurations to orient the subject's ways of knowing as fugitive—constitutive of silences, refusals, and evasions—and imagine ways of being in but not of the nation-state and its "official" history. The lost baggage claim exposes the dilemma of using the archives to find some historical evidence of Hmong lives in a "secret war." The problems produced by the baggage claim and archives raise an important set of questions about the paper trails: Under what conditions did Hmong families make this journey in the late 1970s through the early 1990s? What about the families that never got to make the journey? But my driving questions for this book are: How do you recount a history that has systematically been kept secret? How would centering the refugee's repertoire of stories and refusals shift the telling beyond masculinized, recuperative narratives? Although the details of loss are clearly written here, the claim form makes legible Hmong refugees' absence and disappearance in the records where stories about how they survived and what they carried do not fit within a narrative about U.S. militarism, postcolonial nation-building, and humanitarianism.

History on the Run argues, first, that the supposed secrets about war institute secrecy as knowledge such that secrecy structures "official" knowledge formation and refugee knowledge-making. The lost bag was not an exception of war, displacement, the archive, and refugee movement, but rather it constituted the very basis of this imperial structure. The refugee as an artifact of U.S. liberal militarized empire and state governance is also a subject of secrecy whose absence in the archives demonstrates record-keeping as one such form of violence. Hence, the violence asserts its presence by virtue of being absented such as the missing baggage claim. The incomplete and missing records' absenting of violence poses a danger for accounts of Hmong refugee migration, as an example, by beginning Hmong refugee histories with the "secret war."[16] Secrecy, as I will theorize in chapter 1, operates in U.S. governance to produce the conditions for material and epistemological violence that occur through the subterfuge of U.S. pilots pretending to be volunteers and frames the redactions of the records about a "secret war" (chapter 2), recognition for the former soldiers (chapter 3), and arraignment of former soldiers as terrorists (chapter 4). The secrecy of U.S. governance produced the conditions for the refugee to emerge as a subject of empire through the soldier and former ally who could turn into a terrorist. These categories, in turn, are conditions of possibility for the refugee to illuminate the contradictions and crises of race-, war- and history-making.

Yet, Hmong refugee constructions of history encompass so much more than the secrecy of state governance. *History on the Run* tells a Hmong refugee story that articulates the loss as not really lost but refused or embodied, yet may evade recovery as knowledge. The book makes a second argument that the refugee is a site of knowledge, an epistemological subject that unravels the secrecy embedded in nation, race, war, and U.S. liberal militarized empire, and a subject who enacts secrets and silences. The refugee as a knowing subject shifts the frame of reference for understanding refugee histories and experiences from the state, anthropological, sociological, legal, humanitarian logics to that which is grounded in the refugees' fugitive history—that is, how they narrate their stories based on their patterns of movement. That histories are made and move because they are carried by the people who move is the central premise of *History on the Run*.

History on the run is fugitive history whose telling is still unfolding. This history is "fugitive knowledge" that does not remain still and cannot easily be found.[17] This knowledge hovers over geohistories, escaping the closure of being found/archived. History on the run constitutes what Ann Stoler calls "epistemological uncertainty," knowledge that "goes without saying but everyone knows or cannot yet be articulated or said."[18] History on the run suggests a mobility that has no fixed origin or referent (whether in a singular repository or nation-state) except as a way of knowing attached to fugitivity. Histories that run are embedded in stories and embodied practices that drag history as marginalized people are forced to migrate. As a Hmong refugee epistemology, history on the run makes room for refugee secrecy that is not the same kind of secrecy as state governance because its emergence threatens to expose what the state and public are not supposed to know about the violence of state-making. Relatedly, the refugee is a subject whose ways of knowing evade emergence as Truth and whose subjectivity complicates liberal subject formation. History on the run questions historiography as a "tool of and against the state" in which history can still be used to foreclose other stories.[19] In doing so, it links the transition from overt colonial domination, disruption of decolonization, and "secret war" with the postwar period of ongoing circulation of knowledge through state, public, and refugee narratives.

This book constitutes a feminist contribution that delineates the particularities of Hmong soldiering as situated at the imperial intersections of U.S. empire-building and Laos decolonial nation-building with U.S. colonial rescue/civilizing projects. As a people whose sovereignty is not tied to any particular nation-state, Hmong tenuously straddle the categories of stateless and Indigenous, and were seen as a malleable proxy defense force for U.S. militarism. Under the U.S. imperialist purview, Hmong were deemed not-yet-modern subjects who were outside of place and time such that their military service would facilitate their assimilation into the Lao national polity and emergence in imperial historical time. Indeed, clandestine military service has framed Hmong refugee subject formation primarily as the loyal refugee ally. Hmong soldiering comprised a civilizing and racial project within the moral authority of U.S. liberal militarized empire as an inclusive and liberating project.[20] Soldiering through empire, as historian Simeon Man explains, is an optic to view the imperial and racial politics of war for which Asians and Asian Americans played a central role, and a way for them to negotiate a relationship to the nation and imagine decolonization.[21] Soldiering for Hmong was a way of instituting a people who may not belong to any nation-state as its soldiers and allies, whose displacement as refugees required rescuing, and yet their supposed nonrecognized state status continues to unsettle that rescue because they can become terrorists, as shown in chapter 4 about General Vang Pao. Rather than being an isolated historical nonevent, the "secret war" was a postcolonial Cold War project of U.S. liberal militarized empire, which produced the Hmong refugee figure as a form of colonial baggage that had been "lost" to/in the archive and in transit.

History on the Run establishes that the U.S. "secret war" in Laos is a particular kind of archive different from the declared or overt wars, slavery, or colonialism that also contain missing information about gendered racial lives. The particularity relates to the question of secrecy embedded in the missing, not only in terms of redactions but because the very act(ion) being referenced is itself a secret.[22] Indeed, the lost baggage claim's representation of the war's epistemic violence illuminates how the "secret war" as a historical event is also a project of knowledge production.[23] Although there is no official "secret war" archive, I suggest that this war exists as an archive which produces knowledge through epistemic erasure and violence in its attempts to reproduce the traditional record about the war and refugees. In other words, what circulates as textual evidence signals that no archival evidence should exist because it was supposed to be kept secret. The Hmong refugee figure and the violence it embodies are multiply concealed and secreted because of the nature of this archive.

Instead, I stress that the Hmong repertoire of stories, refusals, and embodied knowledge exists within the purview of a refugee archive. This archive is constitutive of refugee knowledge and fugitivity, and it illuminates the refugee figure as the trace of the collision between refugee histories and archival records about and by refugees. This is a living archive for Hmong to actively negotiate what are considered state secrets as well-known experiences and stories to them. Secrets do not just belong to the state, they are also kept by Hmong who bear witness to the violence and seek to tell a particular version of history and to keep hidden information that is still sensitive or may be too traumatic to reveal. Rather than a repository, the refugee archive is a key method with which to emphasize the embodied and material aspects of histories that run and the spiritual dimension of forced displacement without recovering the loss.[24] It complements the reading method in the lost bag to look for the missing things in the traditional archive and show how refugee histories are not really lost, they are secreted. As an example, I saw in the missing baggage form a Hmong refugee family, and many more families, who arrived in the United States carrying bags and stories to anchor each other.

My critical task does not aim to rectify the problematic historical notion that Hmong "entered history" when they became involved in the "secret war," but rather to pose a historical critique that makes legible Hmong presence long before and after the event.[25] This undertaking joins the important rethinking of the refugee away from its legal definition and its sociological framing as a subject in need of rescue yet who is unable to adapt to resettlement,[26] toward the refugee as a figure that questions the established principles of citizenship, nation, and the state.[27] Within this framework, the refugee is both a critical idea and a social actor "whose life, when traced, illuminates the interconnections of colonization, war, and global social change."[28] The refugee, therefore, is a critical subject for understanding the human impact of our global order of unending wars and ongoing state repression. But the refugee is also an important concept for tracing liberalism and how it operates by bestowing the "gift of freedom" on the grateful refugee and figuring the refugee as a solution to racial politics and poverty in urban America.[29] History on the run, then, is a theory of refugee critique within the interstices of ethnic studies and postcolonial studies—specifically Asian American studies, American studies, and Cold War knowledge formation.

The remainder of this introduction, in three parts, will deepen history on the run as fugitive history that encompasses a longer history of Hmong on the run fleeing persecution in China that links with forced migrations during and after the "secret war." First, I explain how Hmong on the run from Chinese imperialism operate within refugee epistemology as a fugitive history that has eluded archiving and settling. I foreground the concepts of fugitivity and place to show how refugee stories carry the places of migration. Second, I explain history on the run as a spatiotemporal concept that orients Hmong presence against the modern episteme of Hmong as a stateless and timeless people. Third, I show how the refugee archive is constitutive of the fugitive history and presence as a repertoire of Hmong stories that also enact silences and refusals to defer history. The work in this introduction frames the investigation in chapter 1 to build the secrecy-as-knowledge argument around the particular context of the "secret war."

Fugitive History
HMONG ON THE RUN

Hmong trace their ancestral homeland to China, specifically the provinces of Yunnan, Guizhou, Sichuan, and Hunan.[30] They migrated to live in the highlands of Vietnam, Laos, Thailand, and Burma beginning in the early nineteenth century as they rebelled and fled from Chinese imperial Sinicization of minority kingdoms.[31] The earliest Hmong migration into Laos was in 1820–40 into Nong Het, the northern part of Laos that currently borders Vietnam and China.[32] Hmong oral stories recall this history in China and escaping Imperial Chinese conquests that pushed a large part of the group to Southeast Asia, while also eliminating the Hmong writing system as a method of colonization. Indeed, the loss of a Hmong homeland in China resulted in fleeing and constituted the loss of Hmong literacy and Hmong history. According to historian Mai Na Lee, the story of how Hmong lost their literacy has been passed down in *zaj qeej* (musical rhymes of the qeej, a bamboo instrument) between qeej and ritual practitioners. Lee explains that in a zaj qeej told to Yang Cheng Vang, a ritual master, the Han emperor ordered all the books burned and writing outlawed after the Hmong king was captured and killed. Only one book escaped the carnage with a Hmong scholar. Yet, no matter the hiding places, the ditch behind his house, the threshold of the door, or a wooden trunk, the book would eventually be chewed piece by piece by a pig, a cow, and mice, respectively. What was left was sewn into Hmong women's *paj ntaub* (embroidery) for safekeeping, and it is now transmitted through women's needlework. The characters of the Hmong script are specifically embedded in the embroidered intricate patterns of Hmong funeral clothes.[33] As I have noted elsewhere, carrying the Hmong script has been a Hmong women's rebellion. Yet, the script has become indecipherable. Hmong history on the run from place to place is intertwined with "writing on the run," and both are embedded in oral traditions like the *Qhuab Ke* (funerary ritual ballad), qeej, *kwv txhiaj* (courtship song), and stories.[34] These sources of history and knowledge about Hmong origins and patterns of migration are integral to daily life. Their ongoing use in cultural practice denote Hmong history on the run. The condition of being made landless over and again has rendered their history and writing fugitive. This longer Hmong history of colonialism and war in China appear intermittently in Chinese records such as a Chinese general's report in 1682 that he had been ambushed by Hmong in southern China.[35] There were few Chinese-produced historical accounts on Hmong, if any. According to Lee, those that exist are pieced together from different records, such as Vwj Zoov Tsheej's *Haiv Hmoob Li Xwm* (The Hmong History).[36]

As a people who were displaced internally and across geopolitical borders, Hmong moved to Southeast Asia as "a people without a country" and "refugees" fleeing from the conflicts with Chinese imperial armies in the mid-nineteenth century to live in the mountainous regions of Laos, Vietnam, Thailand, and Burma.[37] The oral traditions that record Hmong forced migrations and also give accounts of the erasure of the historical contexts for leaving underscore the dilemma of producing a history about Hmong refugee displacement. Since they were either latecomers to Southeast Asia or they occupied the nonplace, uninhabitable spaces of the mountainous regions, Hmong were then perceived as not having a connection to land and place. By extension, Hmong were considered to inhabit a different historical time than that of the modern nation-state. In the Asian colonial context, it is difficult to resolve the claim that some groups arrived before others. For groups like Hmong, Lisu, and Akha, relatively recent migration to the area allows national governments to deny their wishes for recognized land rights.[38]

Today, Hmong are one of the many ethnic groups in Southeast Asia that do not dominate any nation-state. As peoples who live across borders, these groups have been subjected to multiple overlapping forms of state governance and colonial administration—including Chinese, French, and U.S. intervention. The assertion that there are no Indigenous peoples in Asia because supposedly there is no ongoing settler colonial structure positions these groups as remote mountain dwellers who create trouble for the nation-state.[39] But as cultural geographer Ian Baird suggests in his essay on the Brao people of northeastern Cambodia and southern Laos, it is important to link Indigenous peoples with colonialism in order to position people in a relationship with others instead of essentializing their place of origin.[40] As a group that does not dominate any particular nation-state, Brao have historically endured and continue to endure various forms of colonialism, which have shaped Brao subject formation.[41] Brao colonial domination by the Khmer, Thai, Lao, French, and U.S., along with the ongoing colonial practices of the current Lao and Cambodian states, blurs the distinction between precolonial, colonial, and postcolonial.[42] For Hmong refugees, overlapping forms of Chinese imperialism, Lao and Vietnamese state governance, French colonialism, and U.S. liberal militarized empire shaped their displacement and emergence as refugees. Hence, from the perspective of marginalized peoples in Southeast Asia, colonialism and militarism are intertwined and ongoing gendered racial structures of existence.

The "secret war" compounded Hmong life on the run through material and soul loss. Palee Moua explains: "No one tells you that you won't return so you don't think about grabbing the valuable and memorable items that have meaning to you. . . . In the midst of a panic, while running and fearing for your life, you don't have time to call your spirit to go with you. It is not a peaceful way to leave. Barely escaping war and death, your spirit is severely weakened, if not lost."[43] This explanation Moua offers for the spiritual well-being of Hmong refugees after forced migration demonstrates how, in Hmong cosmological view, fugitive acts to escape colonial and militarized violence also disrupt the spiritual balance. Hence, the particular elusiveness for understanding Hmong historiography of movement and fugitivity is structured by the spirit such that histories that run are not lost, they linger and wander. In her work with Hmong American interlocuters with type II diabetes mellitus, Mai See Thao explains how Hmong refugees who experience diabetes seek a cure and healing on return trips to Laos, not in the U.S. The cure they seek is "temporary and place-specific" in the places they once lived, visiting with those left behind and returning to the same lifestyle. Those who have returned to health upon returning from Laos explained to Thao "how their bodies embodied the animacy of the land and weather; that their bodies 'fit' there in Laos while being out-of-place/displaced in the US."[44]

History on the run is a Hmong women's narration of history that explains Hmong lives as constantly being on the run.[45] While running from place to place characterized the Hmong refugees'/veterans' displacement experiences, it specifically captures how Hmong women's narrative patterns of telling their stories about war and its aftermath, as I have argued elsewhere, emphasize a nonlinear path of migration and rechronicle Hmong refugee histories to disrupt the U.S. liberal empire's project of militarism. The war's victims were not just the soldiers and those who supported the "secret army," such as the nurses and other aid workers. Because Hmong villages and farms were the very sites of guerrilla warfare traversed by U.S.-allied and Communist-allied military forces, Hmong civilians—including women, children, and the elderly—became victims of war. They were subjected to military aggression from both the enemy and friendly fire, and forced to flee their villages to stay ahead of the fighting. Escape, concealment, and safety are "geographic options."[46] These patterns of forced migration reflect the longer history of Hmong migratory movements and loss.[47]

History on the run suggests neither that Hmong do not have history nor that their historical knowledges are recent manifestations. Instead, it conveys the difficulties of encapsulating Hmong refugee histories. Hmong histories are still unfolding because they wrestle with how history is a "moveable" referent for Hmong refugees/Americans in which community politics rest on "competing interpretations of a moveable past."[48] Transnational feminist M. Jacqui Alexander calls this unfolding and motion "the movement of history."[49] History on the run constitutes a Hmong "historical geography" of their migration pattern of an unsettled history.[50] The concept asserts the long, deep, continuous, and always emerging Hmong history that challenges modern state knowledge formation and U.S. liberal militarized empire.

FUGITIVE KNOWLEDGE THROUGH PLACE

The movement in Hmong on the run is refugee geography and knowledge. Hmong refugee geography refutes a humanitarian teleological rendering of the refugee and epistemology that almost always assumes "settling" within a nation-state as well as their histories being "settled" within national history. Furthermore, movement constitutes what Stefano Harney and Fred Moten describe as flight, motion, and fugitivity, that can offer a way of being and thinking. Fugitivity, for them, is separate from "settling."[51] Harney and Moten conceptualize fugitivity, which is grounded in the Black radical tradition, to consider learning in but not of the university and its various structures of professionalization, debt, and governance. The university as a site of refuge and enlightened education already produces the fugitive subject whose life cannot be legible to the institution. It is "fugitive enlightenment" enacted in the undercommons, an underground of the university, where learning can occur to rupture the commons.[52] I borrow from their approach to fugitivity as a way of being and thinking within and outside the institutions of the university and archive, just to name a few, to assert a politics of evasion in movement/migration. Hmong fugitivity suggests the permanence of running for the refugee, even in refuge, such that the figure unsettles the nation-state, democracy, and liberal empire as well as knowledge formation. It expands on the pattern of unsettledness to assert that knowledge and history are unfixed and are unsettling for national history and modern state-centered epistemology. Hmong history on the run as an unsettled and elusive history is linked to fugitivity for marginalized peoples.[53]

Unsettling geopolitics and knowledge make up a decolonial feminist praxis to war and displacement. The field of refugee studies broadly has lacked a sustained postcolonial or feminist critique of the "hidden geographies of cultural politics and social negotiations" as well as the gendered and gendering work of refugee resettlement in the Global North.[54] Feminist refugee geographer Jennifer Hyndman, following Doreen Massey's (1993) theorizing that mobility is subject to power-geometry, makes a distinction between the empirical expression of migration as a "barometer of geopolitics and global economic conditions" and mobility as a "tracing [of] the geopolitical pathways of migrants, shaped by state policies, intra-state conflict, and other geographically inflected political processes." Mobility opens up an understanding of the different meanings of movement.[55] War-based displacement provides a specific "social reproduction" that underscores refugee lives as "radical acts" of life-making for social struggle and freedom.[56] Feminist refugee geopolitics enhance history on the run as theorizing feminist epistemologies that are connected to place.

History on the run carries stories about place in migration. Hmong refugee geopolitical matters are historical matters,[57] whereby Hmong historical patterns of migration complicate the elusive geopolitics of homeland and demarcate the refugee histories that move and are also fugitive. The interventions that Black feminist and Native feminist scholarship have made in the discipline of geography to unsettle "geographic domination"[58] in the structures of slavery and settler colonialism help me theorize history on the run in the context of liberal militarized empire through place and presence rather than through the loss and absence of home. Specifically, the works of Katherine McKittrick and Mishuana Goeman—whose ideas refute enslavement and colonial organizing of land and location, and instead theorize place and space around stories, resistance, and other ways of being—open up the possibilities of history on the run. In *Demonic Grounds*, McKittrick conceptualizes Black diasporic subjectivity, which has been rendered "ungeographic" in the displacement and movement across the Middle Passage through the ships of transatlantic slavery, as geographic because the spaces of domination during enslavement and even the very ships of transport expose a "meaningful struggle for freedom in place."[59] Privileging the legacy of Black women's geographies and geographic knowledge, McKittrick explains that the relationship between Black women and geography can be conceptually fruitful to imagine how the alterability of Black geographies makes possible social and cultural transformation.[60] Her theorizing of Black geographies as space, place, and location to assert the inseparability between space and Black women's subjugation and struggle for liberation opens the conceptual space to consider Hmong migration patterns as inseparable from geohistorical concerns and refugee subjectivity.

Histories that run, in addition to being inseparable from geography, carry place as knowledge. In *Mark My Words*, Native feminist scholar Mishuana Goeman theorizes Native women's encounters with space and acts of (re)mapping that acknowledge Native epistemologies to challenge the acceptance of "colonial spatialities" and the urban/reservation Native dichotomy.[61] Hence, she argues for focusing on Native peoples' stories and efforts as alternative spatialities to imagine ways of mapping and seeing the world beyond settler colonial and capitalist structures. Drawing from feminist geographer Doreen Massey, Goeman thinks through space as holding possibilities and comprising the meeting places that are not transparent on a map rather than an empty expanse of surface.[62] Thus, the meanings of place come through the "migratory patterns of movement" where place is more than a mappable point but carries epistemologies of being in the world to help Native peoples "navigate settler terrains" such that one place of belonging is connected to other places of belonging.[63] Goeman's interrogation of spatial decolonization for Native peoples helps consider Hmong migration in a pattern of movement from place to place where refugee geohistorical notions of home, migration, and self are place specific.

Hmong Presence: Rereading Statelessness and Timelessness
The following pages unpack the discussion above about history on the run as fugitive history that carries stories about place to interrogate the imperialist frame that Hmong are an ahistorical (outside-of-time) and nongeographic (out-of-place) people who do not belong anywhere. I suggest that history on the run animates Hmong presence in place and time. I employ Hmong presence to interrogate the particular categorization of Hmong as stateless made by ethnohistorical accounts and the Southeast Asian scholarship. Hmong statelessness signals the condition of not-yet-modern—the predicament of Hmong migration patterns, not having a political state, and living in the suspended sovereignty of Laos as a decolonizing state.[64] The idea that Hmong have not yet been incorporated into historical time and the nation-state precisely points to how they have not yet arrived in modernity. They are perpetually suspended in what Dipesh Chakrabarty calls the "waiting room of history."[65] As such, the Hmong refugee figure exposes the uneasy relationship between refugee and stateless status and charts the erasure of history and the violence of war and state-making. History on the run does not resolve this crisis for empire but leaves open the condition of possibilities for fugitivity to think across categories of the refugee, people without a country, and Indigenous.

Hmong presence in place and time expounds on how the spatiotemporal is constituted in history on the run. The Hmong collective lament of "Vim peb tsis muaj teb chaws [Because we do not have a country/homeland]," which emphasizes the longer history of migrations and a collective hardship of colonial subjection, articulates a way of being present on the run. As an example, Yawm Xaiv Kuam Thoj (Grandfather Sai Kua Thao) explained in an interview that he became an orphan at a young age, and he linked his life without parents with the Hmong condition as an orphan people without a country. He grew up with older brothers who also stood in as parents to raise him. Even as he lamented not having parents or a country, he talked profusely about surviving and becoming a member of General Vang Pao's judicial council during the "secret war."[66] Yawm Xaiv Kuam's connection of his experiences with the Hmong orientation about historiography and geopolitics asserts Hmong historical presence alongside the time frame of U.S. liberal militarized empire.[67]

That Hmong do not have a country should not be an issue of Hmong ontology but a problem of "modern time consciousness," that is, empty, homogeneous time.[68] Asserting Hmong historical and geographic presence requires investigating how the not-yet-modern subject is viewed as "unfree" in combination with the perceived anachronistic territories it inhabits. Theorizing the refugee figure as a subject of freedom, Mimi Thi Nguyen explains that "imperial time" encompasses the view of both people and territories as belonging to the past and both needing to be liberated so that the "gift of freedom" is a "gift of time: time for the subject of freedom to resemble or 'catch up to' the modern observer, to accomplish what can be anticipated in a preordained future."[69] Time functions as an instrument to "enclose racial, colonial others as *on the outside*."[70] Hmong not-yet-modern as a consignment outside is constituted in "imperial time" to position Hmong as rescuable subjects. Bliss Cua Lim explicates in her work on cinema and the supernatural the possibility of unthinking time as a singular translation of being. There are multiple times which cannot be dissolved into modern time, what she names as "immiscible times," revealing the existence of multiple temporalities that cannot be quantified by the clock and calendar.[71] Homogeneous time is not reality but a translation of what remains untranslatable.[72]

In the context of history on the run, "because we do not have a country" functions as a Hmong reference of place and time, and a position of being present. In *Beyond Settler Time*, Mark Rifkin exposes the problem of translating Indigenous temporal orientations into settler time frames, which are "divergent processes of becoming."[73] Rifkin argues that asserting the shared presentness of Natives and non-Natives casts Indigenous peoples as "being-in-time."[74] Rifkin, like Lim, understands time as plural because the multiplicity "facilitates Indigenous peoples' expressions of self-determination."[75] This "being-in-time" or presence and temporal orientation is crucial for articulating Hmong historical presence in movement and fugitivity. As such, that "we do not have a country" asserts presence alongside the translation of place as nation-state and time into a singular measurement.

Hmong presence in place and time disrupts the not-yet-modern spatiotemporal representation that Hmong are a stateless people—presuming that they are placeless and timeless subjects even before they became refugees. Statelessness in the context of Hmong history is at times conflated with nomadism in which Hmong are a people who wander and have no permanent home, and, even more insidiously, a primitive people who are a part of an anachronistic territory. For example, Christian Culas and Jean Michaud, scholars of the early Hmong diaspora, explain that Hmong were the most recent migrants to arrive south of the Southeast Asian Massif as early as the late eighteenth to early nineteenth centuries, and moving as far south as the seventeenth parallel in the second half of the nineteenth century.[76] This nomadic migration was explained by the Hmong reliance on swidden (slash-and-burn) agriculture that necessitates movement every six or so years. The nomadic frame overwhelmingly focuses on the imperial control over opium as a cash crop that both produced and compounded the political instability underlying the violent revolts and rebellions in the southern part of China in the second half of the nineteenth century as well as forced migration.[77] Even such ethnohistories about Hmong migration patterns are fragmented and fuzzy—on the run, if you will. To be sure, Hmong migrations were informed by their practice of swidden agriculture whereby they rotate between plots of farmable land every few years to allow for the land to regenerate. Historically, seeking new farming land may mean crossing geopolitical borders. Nonetheless, swidden agriculture cannot be simplistically understood as nomadism and premodernity, as anthropologists and historians have noted, or used to justify the unrootedness of Hmong movement patterns.

Hmong elders' stories about the generation who came from China to resettle in the Nong Het, Xieng Khuoang, and Luang Prabang regions of Laos recall conflicts over group sovereignty and a search for home. They also recount the oppressive colonial conditions and internal displacements under French colonialism and the formation of a Laotian geopolitical jurisdiction. A contentious relationship between Hmong and the state has been a part of how Hmong recount history. Hmong history on the run cannot discount the imperialist forces that pushed their migration or its colonial knowledge formation.[78]

Given the fugitivity of Hmong history, the few accounts about Hmong only began to appear after the group resettled in Southeast Asia and encountered simultaneous territorial/state oppression and French colonialism. These narratives were primarily ethnohistorical descriptions produced by Catholic missionary priests who also advanced the French colonial project. François Marie Savina, a French Catholic priest and anthropologist, published one of the first books on Hmong, entitled *Histoire des Miao*.[79] Savina worked among Hmong (1906–25) in Vietnam, Yunnan, and northern Laos as a missionary priest, learning about Hmong culture and society to spread Christianity. He also worked as an ethnographer for the French colonial project.[80] Father Yves Bertrais, another French Catholic priest anthropologist, continued where Savina left off (1950–2005). Fr. Bertrais arrived in Laos in 1948 and took up residence in a Hmong village called Roob Nyuj Qus (Gaurs Mountain) in Luang Prabang Province where he was said to have preserved Hmong culture, traditions, and history as well as contributed to their economic and social development.[81] He has been accorded a special place in the history of Hmong Christianity and the study of Hmong because he, along with linguistic anthropologists Linwood Barney and William A. Smalley, cocreated the Hmong Romanized Popular Alphabet (RPA) in 1952.[82] This development of a Westernized Hmong writing system gave rise to the oft-repeated assertion that "Hmong writing is a recent emergence." Accounts about Hmong since Savina and Bertrais were as much influenced by authors' encounters with Hmong as they were by the colonial constructions about who Hmong people are. This particular colonial epistemological context frames the knowledge produced about Hmong during the "secret war," I suggest, as a people that needed to be saved and brought into modernity through their recruitment as soldiers.

Asian and Southeast Asian scholarship broadly defines groups such as Hmong, Lisu, and Akha among others as "nonstate" peoples who are unrecognized and denied by the state as legal citizen-subjects.[83] Historian James C. Scott in particular has characterized the groups in the highlands of Southeast Asia based on their nomadic movements, as nonstate peoples who strategically attempt to elude state governance. Peoples who are not "fully incorporated into nation-states" have historically encountered subjugation to different forms of state violence including slavery, taxation, and warfare. In critiquing state-making, Scott affirms these groups' status as "those who got away" or who voluntarily go "over to the barbarians."[84] Scott explains that the central preoccupation of statecraft in the Southeast Asian region involved "rounding up people and concentrating them in a particular place."[85] Scott makes an important intervention in rethinking the positionality of "ungoverned" peoples as running away from state governance to show their agency in eluding the state's regulatory power. Yet, the idea of choosing barbarism problematically comprehends these groups within a binary context between the modern state and a "state of nature" (primitivism). For instance, their uncategorized position and ability to elude the nation-state's efforts to impose cultural and legal boundaries may suggest that they exist in a state of nature.

What has yet to be fully explored is the question of nonrecognized peoples like Hmong who because of their patterns of migration do not fit within the nation-state paradigm of territoriality and citizenship. Running away from state jurisdiction, from the perspective of Hmong presence, was as much about groups eluding state governance as it was about the colonial violence that pushed them toward border spaces and less fertile land. Nonrecognized status can also operate as a way for peoples without a state to claim connections to land through a distinct history of forced migrations.[86] As Lee argues in her work on the Hmong quest for legitimation in French Indochina, Hmong political leaders have alternately allied with and resisted state power in order to advance their goals of territorial and cultural autonomy.[87] U.S. colonialism and war complicate assumptions of time and space further by producing Hmong as refugees.

Statelessness and the Refugee

To be clear, not all refugees are deemed stateless and not all who are deemed stateless are diasporic. Because Hmong supposed statelessness is a problem of geopolitics and modernity, it does not easily fit into the refugee's statelessness which can be resolved through resettlement or repatriation, or the non-refugee's nonstate status which may not be about war-based displacement. In political theory, the refugee serves as a limit concept that calls into question the categories of the nation-state, the birth-nation link, and the rights of man and citizen. The refugee as a limit concept reveals how bare life is no longer an exception or separation either in the state order or human rights.[88] In Hannah Arendt's and Giorgio Agamben's works of the same title, "We Refugees," the refugee highlights the nation-state's tenuous relationship with the citizen and territory. Agamben argues that the refugee's status is always considered a temporary condition that should be resolved through either naturalization or repatriation because its permanence unhinges the national order.[89]

The refugee figure's condition of statelessness has been one lens through which to complicate the categories of the nation-state. Among the central dilemmas in the work on the stateless person is the difficulty of distinguishing the stateless from the refugee and the importance of determining how the refugee is stateless. The Convention Relating to the Status of Stateless Persons was drafted in 1951, the same year the United Nations adopted the Convention Relating to the Status of Refugees, but it was not ratified until 1954. It instituted a standard of treatment for stateless peoples similar to that of refugees as a way to provide protection for those who do not "enjoy" the benefits of citizenship in order to reduce future stateless populations.[90] While the significance of the convention on stateless peoples lies in its existence, its attempt to legally define this category within an international human rights regime paradoxically privileges nation-states as protectors of those who pose a threat to the national order.

Arendt asserts that stateless peoples produced through the liquidation of nation-states after World War I were not necessarily refugees. Additionally, refugees are not necessarily stateless because they can be repatriated and accepted by their country of origin; thus statelessness is not the essential quality of a refugee.[91] The dilemma of stateless peoples, for Arendt, is their "undeportability," in which neither the country of origin nor any other would agree to accept these groups.[92] At the same time, she contends that the core of statelessness is identical with the refugee question, and yet statelessness has been largely ignored.[93] This formulation invokes the questions, Are peoples with a "migratory pattern of movement" who make lives across multiple borders stateless? Is there a structure that can account for fugitive lives? A project that pays attention to how these two concepts inform each other is productive in calling into question the legitimacy of the nation-state and citizenship.

Specifically addressing stateless status, however, Arendt underscores its relation to the idea of the "inalienable rights of man," which have become alienable to noncitizens. Statelessness captures a condition of rightlessness wherein the "Rights of Man," defined as "inalienable rights" independent of governments, function only as citizens' rights.[94] Stateless status signifies the "criminal" and the "enemy alien" in times of war so that this figure, which remains undefinable but always already configured as a threat from within, has the potential to incite an ontological rupture.[95] This signification as a threat cannot be "renormalized" as nonthreatening.[96] Statelessness merely remains dormant until the "right" time for it to reemerge as threat. Hence, one can read General Vang Pao's arrest in 2007 on federal charges of attempting to overthrow the Laotian government (which I discuss in chapter 4) as a terrorist ally assemblage of Cold War strategies with the U.S. global war on terror and a composite for rethinking history, as a configuration of the stateless refugee who is an ally and U.S. citizen, but who can also transform into a criminal and "enemy alien." Perhaps the threat of his condition of statelessness is always already present, even when he becomes a U.S. citizen, because he cannot claim a history from which he soldiered and had been displaced through secrecy's erasure of historical knowledge.

Although helpful for politicizing the refugee figure, the consideration of statelessness within a European context of consolidating nation-states does not interrogate the colonial context that produced racialized others who are displaced and move outside of the normative boundaries of the political and modernity. Specifically, the categorization of Hmong as stateless has written them out of history and geography as not-yet-modern so they cannot be reconsolidated into national subjects. Indeed, how do colonial racialized peoples emerge as a threat to empire rather than its consolidation? History on the run, I suggest, underscores the ungraspability of Hmong statelessness when the group's historical knowledge and presence cannot be comprehended by the state. Furthermore, the erasure of imperial Hmong racial formation is that which posits Hmong as "uncivilized" and a threat to the state.[97]

The Refugee Archive: A Repertoire of Deferred Histories
The refugee archive encompasses how Hmong refugees tell their histories such that it illuminates their construction of history and production of knowledge to bring awareness to historical silencing. It negotiates the tension that Hmong refugee histories contradict the U.S. explanations for its involvement in Laos, yet these histories may also not be outwardly critical of U.S. liberal militarized empire. In fact, the various retellings of the conflict by state records, U.S. personnel, and Hmong refugees reveals the very problems of upholding a singular history about the "secret war." Although the refugee archive may signal a memory repository of "supposedly enduring materials" such as texts, documents, and monuments, I conceive it as a "repertoire" of embodied, living, and ephemeral knowledge and practice.[98] An archive forgets and archiving does not always mean moving "from the secret to the nonsecret."[99] The activity of forgetting is already embedded in the idea of the archive precisely when the erasure involves institutionalization supported by law and rights.[100] "Archival memory," Diana Taylor explains, sustains power

by separating the source of knowledge from the knower.[101] The repertoire is "nonreproducible knowledge" and requires presence for people to "participate in the production and reproduction of knowledge by 'being there,' being a part of the transmission."[102] The refugee archive as repertoire affirms Hmong presence in (re)producing and transmitting knowledge.

The refugee archive allows me to methodologically link two main concepts: the war's secrecy as a problem of knowledge because it structures both official and refugee histories and how refugee stories on the run elude the revelation of secrets. While the repertoire is mediated like the archive, its embodied knowledge exceeds the archive and requires performance as an embodied practice that opens up other ways of knowing, where performances are vital acts of transferring social knowledge, memory, and identity.[103] The refugee archive mediates the refugee's encounters with forgetting in the traditional archive as well as the refugee's repertoire of stories and embodied knowledge that may also enact their own silences, evasions, and refusals about history. While Hmong have insisted on telling their stories through war monuments, legislation for Hmong veterans such as citizenship and burial rights, and the presence of veterans in army fatigue at annual events such as the Hmong New Year celebrations, there are less spectacular everyday practices such as family dinners that transmit memories and knowledge or even the act of not telling. Reading the refugee archive, I show how Hmong disrupt their emergence in suspended historical time, where they are always in danger of not existing in national accounts.

Hmong histories are deferred and disavowed through textual knowledge and language's inability to convey, even when they do emerge through media and cultural representations, as in my discussion in chapter 5 about the Hmong grandmother in the film *Gran Torino* whose lines were unsubtitled and could not be legible as competing war stories to Clint Eastwood's character. These refugee histories complicate knowledge production as nation-based and privileging textual transmission. In her important work on the production of history and the politics of knowledge and community of Tibetan refugees, Carole McGranahan explains that Tibetan histories of resistance are "arrested" and postponed "for future use" because they clash with "official ways of explaining nation, community, and identity."[104] Her description of the process of "historical arrest" to delay a people's histories for future release helps explain how accounts of the Hmong involvement with the U.S. discursively lag in historical time, not only because they are yet to be told or written, but also because they have been forgotten and are left unclaimed. Hmong narratives of war and displacement have continually been missing from the archive and from national memory, and have been disavowed as not integral to the Vietnam War historiography in order to deny the illicit U.S. activities in Laos. Because of the historical erasure, Hmong refugees/Americans have sought to envision futures as displaced peoples that hinge on embodied knowledge, memory, and attachments to each other.

The refugee archive reckons with the question of how to engage with memory, the politics of our lack of knowledge about history, and the production of such knowledge. Lisa Yoneyama contends that "memory is understood as deeply embedded in and hopelessly complicitous with history in fashioning an official and authoritative account of the past."[105] Employing the concept of memory means that our investigations into the past must have an awareness that historical reality can only be made available to us through mediations in the present.[106] Critical projects that engage in how acts of remembering can fill the void of knowledge must reckon with the question: How can memories, once recuperated, remain self-critically unsettling?"[107] Yoneyama foregrounds the assertion that "the fleeting and fragmentary moments of sympathy for the dead produce coalitional social and cultural practices," suggesting that we remain open to engage in such moments to illuminate critical alliances.[108] My analysis of form and content, the archive and its silences, remains vigilant of the things that become knowable and looks for the not-yet-there possibilities.

Through the refugee archive, I enact a methodology to track a historiography of the "secret war" to interrogate how we come to know something as secret (the lost bag) and an ethnography of Hmong refugee histories that holds the said in tension with what has been silenced (the refugee archive). The book is neither an empirical study of who Hmong are nor does it uncover refugee secrets. It captures my incomplete comprehension and telling of Hmong refugee histories, which I have turned into theorizing a methodology for how to write about things we do not know—the gaps in our knowledge—because they are missing from the "official" archives or delayed in transmission. The book resists positivist research on Hmong refugees that objectifies their experiences and recuperates them as truth at the same time that it wrestles with a critical approach to conceptualize Hmong distinctiveness and the specificity of Hmong refugee epistemologies to offer a broader theory on refugees and peoples without a country. Its theorizing, instead, is grounded in a Hmong refugee/American perspective that is drawn from extensive interviews and archival research yet does not resolve the empirical evidence into secrets. What follows is an attempt to show rather than tell the presence of the past, the places in migration, and the memories in histories. Each chapter dwells in secrets and maps, an eclectic refugee repertoire of the places and stories that matter to a Hmong refugee sense of belonging. The very writing of this book contends with questions such as: Is it possible to know something that is itself constantly slipping away, fluctuating between history and memory or even imagination? How can you render material the elusive (on-the-run) and secrets as violence, and seek possible forms of justice in epistemic ruptures of the unwritten? And, how do you write so as not to tell everything (because not everything should be revealed)? In wrestling with writing about the presence of Venus, the emblematic figure of the enslaved woman in the Atlantic, in the archive of Atlantic slavery, Saidiya Hartman explains that it is an impossibility to represent the full picture of the captives' lives against the limits of the archive.[109] She has chosen to write "by performing the limits of writing history through the act of narration" and by embracing "the impossibility that conditions our knowledge of the past and animates our desire for a liberated future."[110] Although the "secret war" archive is different from that of the Atlantic slavery which Hartman investigates because the event itself was subject to secrecy, in these chapters I hope to perform a similar writing about the impossibilities of knowing about the past to imagine a present and future of refuge.

This work is not a general history of Hmong, Laos, and the "secret war." Instead, it charts refugee epistemology and Hmong presence through the refugee archive as a perspective for doing historical analysis to understand the past in relation to the present. Postcolonial scholar Panivong Norindr, in an essay that aims to critically reflect on the history of Laos under French colonialism and U.S. imperialism, uses family and official photographs as points of entry into a "complex and contested 'official' history." Although critical of employing photographs as indisputable testimonials, Norindr contends that photographs "are a pseudo-presence that reveals an absence that can also heighten our sense of loss." In doing so, photographs can help us remember, illuminate the dark corners, give meaning to a life, and point to the presence of the lacunae of our knowledge that can never be filled.[111] Norindr's critical reflections on how to tell a history of Laos during French occupation and U.S. intervention through photographs bring into sharp relief the methodological dilemma of telling a history that was kept secret. These photographs, however, constitute their own archive of knowledge to shed light on histories that have been erased from the official record. In this book, charting refugee histories disrupts the U.S. narrative that it was never present in Laos.

How to Read the Chapters

The book's chapters are organized around "counterintuitive figures" that register the refugee's unraveling of secrecy.[112] This organization sets up an understanding of how secrecy produces the overlap between historical process and our knowledge of it as well as how that knowledge circulates. This introduction and chapter 1, together, unpack secrecy as structuring state- and war-making as well as knowledge circulation. Therefore, secrecy structures the refugee as a subject of colonial excess and subject of knowledge. In doing so, chapter 2 argues that the archive is a site where things are missing rather than a place to retrieve knowledge.

After the first two chapters focus on secrets as structuring of the postcolonial context and the archive, chapters 3 and 4 emphasize how the refugee emerged from these conditions as a political and ethical dilemma as well as a terrorist threat. In other words, as a figure whose emergence has been structured by secrets, the refugee showed up in the U.S. context (through the archives of law and the media) as a shifting "compositional subject" who can simultaneously become a citizen and a foreign threat to national security.[113] Chapters 4 and 5 along with the epilogue fully showcase how history on the run operates in Hmong refugee epistemology as fugitive history and knowledge. History on the run reveals that not everything about Hmong refugee epistemology can be resolved under secrecy.

1. SECRECY AS KNOWLEDGE

Secrets have structured the narrative of the Hmong-U.S. relationship that was forged in Laos around military alliance during the 1961–75 "secret war," and they have marked Hmong presence in the U.S. Although the size of the Hmong population in the U.S. is significantly less than the Vietnamese, but comparable to the Cambodian and Lao refugee populations, it is no secret that among the various Southeast Asian refugee communities, Hmong seem to have a unique alliance with the U.S. government to the point that the Hmong soldier/veteran narrative overshadows even that of South Vietnamese soldiers. While this close relationship to the U.S. affords Hmong an "undeniable claim to refugee status" and reinforces the logic of rescue and liberation,[1] it is a narrative tied to illicit U.S. policies during the Cold War and one already mired in archival secrets. As such, secrets have structured knowledge circulation by maintaining historiographic gaps about the Cold War postcolonial condition in Laos and of peoples with historical patterns of migration like Hmong. Yet, the war was no secret to Hmong whose stories continue to teach us about how their consciousness was shaped by running away from war, and how they have always been refugees—orphans without a country.[2] Although many ethnic and Indigenous groups including Lao fought in various aspects of the "secret war," this chapter unpacks the particularly well-known relationship between Hmong and the CIA/U.S. to open up secrecy as a structure of the Cold War postcolonial conditions in Laos and of liberal militarized knowledge circulation.[3] Therefore, along with the question of how to write a history that has been kept secret, posed in the introduction, this chapter also asks: What was the postcolonial Cold War context in Laos that produced Laos's arrested decolonization and Hmong refugee racial formation? *History on the Run* reframes the "secret war" as an interimperial event of decolonization in Laos intersecting with the Cold War. The book also shows how Hmong refugees were produced as the excess of colonialism, as not-yet-modern state subjects who required civilizing governance through soldiering, forced migration, and rescue after the war. Soldiering shaped Hmong racial formation as subjects who can be killed or incorporated as national subjects, not as citizen-subjects. As the excess of colonialism and modernity, the Hmong refugee is linked to, but does not fit within, the political philosophical meaning of "soldiering" in which the soldier is the protocitizen whose sacrifice makes him a citizen-subject.[4] Instead, the figure emerged as a pathologized trope: fundamentally shaped by war and still grappling with life in the U.S. and yet delinked from the Cold War postcolonial war-making.

The formation of a Hmong racialized subject, as an expendable subject who could be saved through soldiering, was situated within the context of Laos's arrested decolonization and the U.S. conjuring of Laos as a "neutral yet available" space. The "secret war" was a U.S. liberal imperial strategy of militarization to promote decolonization and sovereignty at a time when the peoples of Asia, Africa, and Latin America struggled for emancipation from Western imperial powers. The covert military operations in Laos might look similar to U.S. interventions in Central America, where the U.S. either supported rural development in Mexico or backed military regimes and nationalist dictators in Guatemala and El Salvador to institute state repression including the torture and disappearance of Indigenous peoples, the rural and working classes, and students.[5] U.S. efforts in Laos, however, were coordinated to strengthen the Royal Lao Army to influence Laos's postcolonial nation-building toward the U.S./West while simultaneously fostering Lao nationalism among Hmong, Mien, Khmu, Brao, Kha, and other ethnic and Indigenous groups through a rural development strategy. This project is consistent with U.S. strategies of setting up military bases rather than instituting direct rule.[6] Hmong soldiering reveals the connections between decolonizing Laos and U.S. imperialism, because, as Simeon Man explains, "soldiers performed the tasks that sutured . . . [the postcolonial] nation to the vast needs of U.S. capitalism."[7] Soldiering linked colonialism to postcolonial militarization and, in the Hmong refugee perspective of history on the run, exposed the arrested decolonization of Laos along with Hmong assertions of political autonomy.

Yet, the U.S. liberal militarized empire's imagination of Laos as a territory empty of people and politically "neutral" conjoined settler colonial logics of land acquisition and conquest of primitivity with U.S. imperialist intervention. While U.S. policymakers did not intend to occupy Laos via a military base, they saw the country as available for political maneuvering and imagined Hmong as Natives to be saved. Arguing that settler colonial expansion operates against the backdrop of Indigenous dispossession and the "problem" of Asian migration in the North American context, Iyko Day clarifies the connections between settler colonialism and "postcolonial colonialism" in which the former is "immune to the process of decolonization."[8] Settler societies involve the transfer of power in the metropole to the periphery to "subvert a normative logic of colonialism" such that "becoming 'postcolonial'" did not significantly alter the colonial relationship between settlers and the Indigenous population.[9] I am not arguing that Laos was a settler colony, but Day's points facilitate my understanding of the country's suspended decolonization in two important ways. First, decolonizing Laos experienced sustained colonial relationships with foreign powers. For instance, the competing imperialist occupations by France and Japan and the interimperial confluences between the Soviet Union and the U.S., which resulted in direct military involvement from North Vietnam and Thailand, formed the unrelenting intervention in the country. Second, the overlapping colonial and imperial view about Hmong determined the group as an Indigenous force to be liberated yet also as expendable. Laos and Hmong served a different kind of capital accumulation within the colonial structure as spatial and human capital that expanded the war without expending additional U.S. American lives.

This chapter argues that the U.S. state justified military operations in Laos as being for the benefit of the Laotian state and Hmong liberation, and that this militarized configuration of decolonization was structured by secrecy. The U.S. military intervention in Laos's decolonization needs to be situated within the longue durée of interimperial struggles in Laos extending from the thirteenth century.[10] The intervention in Laos to institute indirect rule through the promotion of self-determination and autonomy calls to mind the work of anthropologists John D. Kelly and Martha Kaplan, who point out that decolonization, rather than being an end, was the superimposition of something else, and the U.S. was the "world's leader at decolonizing."[11] Along with building alliances with nationalist leaders, the U.S. de/colonial logic also targeted Indigenous and ethnic leaders for development globally. For instance, village-level development in Laos through the distribution of food and the building of infrastructure such as roads, bridges, and schools sought to encourage nationalism among the so-called scattered groups who lived far from the central government. Yet, U.S. militarism was organized around illusory decolonization and sovereignty for the decolonizing world and its peoples. The chapter shows that the secrecy of the "secret war" can be a paradigm for understanding three things: the function and structure of secrecy, the postcolonial Cold War condition in Laos, and Hmong soldiering. It examines, first, how secrecy comprises the rule which structures democracy, the public, history, and refugee histories. Second, the chapter discusses Hmong soldiering to name the specificity of the political struggles in Laos. Finally, it deploys secrecy as knowledge to explore decolonizing Laos as a site of interimperial struggles which produced its ambiguous post-WWII status as a "neutral yet available" space.

Secrecy Structures Knowledge
WAR AS AID

The "secret war" operated by the CIA and funded by the Pentagon constituted an extension of colonialism in which it was a post/colonial struggle in the supposed postcolonial moment. "Secret" has become a descriptor of the legal maneuvering through which the structures that were supposed to prevent war from happening actually facilitated it. This secret conflict was an unauthorized war managed by the White House and the Department of State but operated by the CIA and humanitarian and development agencies, namely the United States Agency for International Development (USAID). Most decisions for military, economic, and political operations were made between the CIA and USAID personnel on the ground with the oversight of the State Department and the president in Washington. The CIA and USAID do not cite a single decision to operate an unauthorized war, but explain the war as a "natural" process which began with U.S. economic and military support for Laos's development in 1950. U.S. expansion of its aid programs following the 1954 Geneva Conference required the CIA's transport airline to make supply drops in "remote" regions of Laos and to circumvent the conference's restrictions against military aid to Laos.[12] The records, which I explore in chapter 2, and the official government discourse maintain that Laos was an important place to make a stand against Communist expansion and a CIA success story that shaped the agency's role and its subsequent operations. Secrecy has been used to bolster the CIA's role, which further elides and makes irrelevant the interimperial stakes of the conflict. U.S. efforts to hide this war were very much about militarized epistemological maneuvering: enlisting a "secret army" that would not be a part of the U.S. military, discharging U.S. pilots so they could enroll as volunteers for the Royal Lao Armed Forces, of which the Royal Lao Army was a branch, re-marking CIA planes with Lao insignia, and naming correspondences and any U.S. policymakers and personnel activities pertaining to Laos as "secret." It is my contention, therefore, that secrets were constituted in the discursive naming and marking of records as secret for processing in the archive, which produced missing histories for refugees.

Although it has often been recounted as a war being fought in the "shadow of Vietnam," the conflict was primarily seen by policymakers and military strategists as a "secret American military aid program" that "fueled a unique and little-known war."[13] The secret military aid program began as early as 1955 in the form of money, weapons, food, rural development, and diplomatic political assistance to support CIA paramilitary activities to counter North Vietnamese and Soviet involvement in Laos. Similar to how the 1954 Accords did not curtail foreign military aid, these paramilitary activities were not covert, resulting in a second Geneva Agreement in 1962 to specifically prohibit foreign intervention in Laos. Ironically, it was after this second international agreement that the U.S. operated a full-fledged war that was fought from the air and on the ground.

Although the U.S. State Department, the Department of Defense, the CIA, and the White House collaborated to hide the bombings (1964–73), the "secret" air war has been the most documented through experiences of U.S. pilots and, recently, surviving Hmong T-28 pilots and their families.[14] The U.S. initially provided air support to the Souvanna government in August 1963 with six T-28 airplanes and a U.S. Air Force (USAF) Mobile Training Team. By March 1964, Project Waterpump had begun, with a detachment from the USAF Special Air Warfare Center at Eglin Air Force Base, to establish a

Secrecy as Knowledge 31

FIGURE 1.1. CIA planes repainted with the Lao insignia to hide U.S. military operations in supposedly neutral Laos. Source: Trojan Foundation.

T-28 maintenance facility at Udorn, Thailand, and train Thai and Lao pilots.[15] Hmong pilots began training in 1967 and flew bombing missions until the end of the war. This air war comprised daily bombing missions flown from Udorn into northeastern and southern Laos along the Ho Chi Minh Trail. U.S. pilots were able to fly bombing sorties and other missions in Laos after being discharged from the USAF and reenrolled as volunteers for the Royal Lao Armed Forces.[16] In addition, helicopters and planes from Air America, the nominally commercial airline operated by the CIA, were repainted with Lao insignia to provide the illusion that Lao planes were flying in Laotian airspace.[17] By 1970, a total of forty-two thousand sorties had been flown to bomb northern Laos. By the time the Paris peace agreement was reached in 1973, the weight of bombs dropped on Laos exceeded the total tonnage of all munitions used by the United States during World War II.[18] The bombings devastated the Laotian landscape, destroyed homes and villages, and killed or displaced thousands of civilians who became the war's "collateral damage."[19] Unexploded ordinance throughout Laos still endangers civilians today.[20]

On the ground, Hmong and other groups in Laos had to defend their homes because their villages constituted the front lines of the ground battles, or flee their villages to escape the ground and air military assault. Hmong leader General Vang Pao served in the Royal Lao Army with control over Military Region II, where most Hmong lived, and was recruited by the CIA to command the "secret army" to defend their homeland. Young Hmong men joined the "secret army" to protect their homes, but were in fact deployed as a proxy army to support the air bombings.

By structuring U.S. postcolonial war-making and knowledge formation, secrets do not reference some hidden knowledge and practices of Hmong refugees. Instead, my conceptualization of secrets builds on the growing body of Asian American critique of the hegemonic Cold War narrative that concerns the critical omissions and the emergent knowledge Asian Americans produced as conditions of possibility for contending with historical injustice.[21] Jodi Kim's work proposing this Asian American critique suggests that the Cold War not only enacted violence against "racialized peoples and terrains" but also produced racial knowledge to configure Asians and Asian Americans as gendered racial subjects.[22] Secrets structure the "secret war" as a part of the postcolonial Cold War militarization and the knowledge that circulates about it. Secrecy, as I frame it here for the rest of the book, constitutes the missing interimperial links in Laos and for Hmong refugees. Hmong migration history is rarely linked to the broader projects of French colonialism, Japanese imperialism, and U.S. imperialism in the Cold War postcolonial conditions in Southeast Asia. In the diaspora, Hmong still maintain their status as refugees without a country, in contrast to other Southeast Asian refugee groups. For Hmong refugees, that unending war has to do with the secrecy of their wartime experiences that continues to circulate even in the diaspora. Through the lens of history on the run, secrecy deals with the epistemological structure of U.S. liberal empire, and reframes the "secret war" as the intertextuality of historical violence and the ongoing secreting about that violence.

I use the term *secret war* as it is used in government and some popular references to the historical event, but also to demarcate its epistemological work for the war as a secret. "Secret war" is an unintended yet productive conjoining whereby the policies and practices that were meant to be kept secret constitute how we come to know about secrets, and the knowing constantly escapes our grasp. Hmong refugee stories about the war and forced migration underscore an awareness that "secret war" and the associated historiographies delineate Hmong missing histories. Hmong refugee epistemologies show how the war in Laos that was not publicly fought or contested, and which public and scholarly discourse tended to gloss over, reveals the U.S. liberal militarized strategies of colonial rescue with violence during the Cold War.

SECRECY'S EPISTEMOLOGICAL WORK

State secrets are not secret to refugees or those who survived the material violence enacted by policies of secrecy. I ask, who or which public are state secrets intended to be kept from and to protect? My interrogation of secrets does not aim to reveal them, but rather to make space for justice. Therefore,

I use secrecy as an epistemological lens to study how secrets circulate. I define secrets not just as the hidden content, but as the structure of militarized liberal epistemologies and refugee epistemologies. By structure, I do not suggest that secrets are a totalizing force that defines all aspects of militarized liberal empire or refugee knowledge. Instead, I mean that secrets are constitutive of the structure of the public, the politics of transparency, historical knowledge and the missing things in knowledge, and even how refugees tell their stories.

Jacques Derrida's various works on the secret offer an important way of thinking about it as a structure.[23] In *Geneses, Genealogies, Genres, and Genius: The Secrets of the Archive,* Derrida's discussion of literature, the archive, and secrets formulates the secret as a structure of the content rather than as a condition of the content. He writes:

> Never has anyone so well addressed a library's unconscious. In order to say that the secret it keeps is not secret merely because it itself cannot access it, or because this or that part of its contents is hidden, encrypted, forever hermetic, but also because the form of writing, the literature entrusted to it, is so structured as to seal off its secret and make it undecidable, less a matter of hidden contents all in all, than of a bifid structure which can keep in undecidable reserve the very thing it avows, shows, manifests, exhibits, endlessly displays.[24]

In interrogating the library as an archive of literature, he explains that secrecy is not about access or the hiddenness of content, but rather the form of writing that has sealed off how something can be known. Here, secret is a structure of undecidability. Derrida explains that giving a secret away may mean telling it but may also mean keeping it so "deeply in the crypt of a memory that we forget it is there or even cease to understand and have access to it."[25] In this way, the secret is neither the hiding nor the revealing, but both. The secret is a force, a power that structures the undecidability about the thing "it avows, shows, manifests, exhibits, endlessly displays." In other words, the secret informs what has been made public.

The secret as a force negotiates what to make public or keep hidden. Anthropologist Michael Taussig articulates the secret's coconstitution of the public as the "public secret" wherein secrets are generally known but cannot be easily articulated.[26] The "public secret" theorizes that "there is no such thing as a secret" because social institutions and social knowledge are informed by a sense of "shared secrets."[27] Social knowledge lies in "the labor of the negative" of "knowing what not to know," that is, in the awareness that something exists yet knowing not to talk about it.[28] For Elias Canetti and Taussig, public secrecy lies at the core of power.[29] Political scientists have examined the coconstitutiveness of secrecy with the public through the politics of transparency, explaining that both transparency and secrecy form democracy. The secret, Jodi Dean explains, is publicity's limit and opens up the possibility to question the notion of a singular democratic public.[30] Clare Birchall astutely demonstrates the ways in which secrecy is not in opposition to transparency, but rather exists as a part of the same structure of democracy. Discussing contemporary U.S. politics, Birchall questions the assumed "false choice" between secrecy and transparency. She introduces Derrida's "unconditional secret," which approaches secrecy as a structure beyond the logic of revelation, to question "transparency's link with democracy and its cultural place today as a force of good."[31] Both Derrida's and Taussig's formulations of the secret, and their emphasis on complicating the notion of the public secret, are central to my investigation of power in the circulation of secrets.

How would one reserve space for justice in studying the secret and its integral role in the circulation of knowledge? Is justice tied to the secret's revelation? In *A Taste for the Secret*, Derrida addresses this holding space for justice in the secret:

> Between this secret and what is generally called secret, even if the two are heterogeneous, there is an analogy that makes me prefer the secret to the non-secret, the secret to the public expression, exhibition, phenomenality. I have a taste for the secret, it clearly has to do with not-belonging; I have an impulse of fear or terror in the face of a political space, for example, a public space that makes no room for the secret. For me, the demand that everything be paraded in the public square and that there be no internal forum is a glaring sign of the totalitarianization of democracy . . . if a right to the secret is not maintained, we are in a totalitarian space. Belonging—the fact of avowing one's belonging, of putting in common—be it family, nation, tongue—spells the loss of the secret.[32]

Derrida's assertions about the secret's dialectical relationship to transparency concerns a formulation of justice that does not get resolved within the "totalitarianization of democracy." By stating a preference for the secret to the nonsecret because the secret is about "not-belonging," he suggests that democracy and its consensus model require the secret because "if a right to the secret is not maintained, we are in a totalitarian space." Furthermore, maintaining the secret or having a "taste for the secret" may be strategic because, as he points out, if there are no secrets then democracy can itself be totalizing.

The refugee epistemology of history on the run keeps the secret—the "secret war"—open as an important geopolitical event which produced Hmong refugee displacement, but which does not constitute the totalizing structure of their history. Keeping secrets constitutes a way for supposedly liberated subjects to oppose the all-encompassing force of public secrecy. Birchall, in her work on the politics of transparency, has come up with the idea of a "post-secret" to explain that some secrets need to be kept in order to hold democracy accountable or to achieve a greater sense of democracy and justice.[33] Furthermore, Catherine Hundleby proposes "oppositional secrets" in the context of feminist emancipation activism to rethink the impetus toward sharing and transparency in order to resist oppression.[34] She writes, "The unjust secret can teach about the world as it is, whereas the oppositional secret can teach more about the world as it might be."[35] Oppositional secrecy can be an epistemological shift for suppressed and underdeveloped knowledge to emerge in unsettling forms. By placing the Hmong refugee subject at the center of a political history that has been kept out of public knowledge and the historical record, we can understand that some secrets need to be kept and state secrets are not the same as refugee stories.

Through the concept of history on the run, secrecy can be read as an epistemological lens through which to study history and the production of knowledge. The work on secrets in non-Western religions and history already charts a way to think about secrecy as an epistemology. Paul Christopher Johnson's book, *Secrets, Gossip, and Gods: The Transformation of Brazilian Candomblé*, explores the contemporary practice of secrecy in Brazilian Candomblé as a "fluid social boundary, ritually and discursively expressed, informed by historically layered meanings."[36] In particular, the uses of secrets to adjudicate religious meanings, orders, and privileges in the Brazilian Candomblé religion are layered with histories of slavery and resistance as well as discourses about the religion.[37] For Johnson, the purpose is not to investigate the content of secrets, but to examine first how practitioners of Candomblé perceive, classify, and work on the world through the epistemological lens of secrecy, and second how in "secretism," secrets circulate even as, and even because, Candomblé has become a national and public religion.[38] He defines "secretism" as the "the *active milling, polishing, and promotion of the reputation of secrets*," and this meaning is linked to the "circulation of a secret's inaccessibility."[39] Studying secrets, Johnson explains, presents an epistemological double bind: how can one ever know with certainty the true substance and whether one should reveal it publicly? He suggests that the study of secrecy is not "distinct from the quest for knowledge" and there is "little secret content to be exposed as esoteric and public."[40] In opening up the space for pursuing knowledge, Johnson leaves room for justice and power whereby secrets are not only discursive events but also procedures of bodily practice that resist notation.[41] Although Johnson is working in the context of religious practices, his formulation of secretism is useful to consider how Hmong refugees enact embodied practices to keep secrets open, as in my discussion of the refugee grandmother's dragging histories in chapter 5. As such, rethinking secrecy as a structure and epistemological lens can be useful to both those who resist and those who seek to impose power.[42]

The historiographic paradox posed by the hidden and illicit nature of the war and the public knowledge that it was an illegal conflict is at the crux of this exploration of the secret. As Haitian historian Michel-Rolph Trouillot explains, the boundary between history's two meanings—"that which happened" (the historical process) and "that which is said to have happened" (our knowledge of that process)—is fluid.[43] A theory of the historical narrative must acknowledge the overlap between process and narrative because history is a story about power.[44] Within this understanding of the historical narrative, the public knowledge about the secrecy of the war in Laos is not just that it was an illegal conflict. The knowledge that has circulated about this war precisely produces the narrative that it was not supposed to have happened. Thus, Hmong refugee history emerged as a part of the state's illicit history, already structured by secrecy as "an unthinkable history."[45] Extending the analogy of not-supposed-to-have-happened, secrecy contains Hmong refugee history so that it also cannot exist beyond the "secret war."

In linking the Hmong refugee to the structural conditions of the U.S. "secret war" in Laos, this chapter is not a military and social history of the U.S. role in the region. Telling the story of the refugee, then, tells the history of the war's violence through the erasure of knowledge. In this way, the history of Hmong migration must necessarily be linked to the story of the "secret war" and its production of the Hmong refugee through soldiering.[46] This approach does not suggest that Hmong history began with the "secret war," but it establishes the secrecy of the conflict as the evidence of the injustice and violence faced by Hmong and the source of ongoing problems with history and knowledge formation. Following Derrida, I want to keep a space of justice for "the refugee secrecy," so to speak, as an antidote to the Habermasian totalizing public space where all knowledge is assumed to be fully transparent and shared.[47] The refugee matters because the figure of the refugee illuminates the logics of war violence and historical erasure, and furthermore that secrets can be useful for conceptualizing refugee epistemologies.

Analyzing the Hmong case around secrecy as a question about knowledge and history allows for a different articulation of U.S. militarism during the Cold War from national histories. For example, Kim reconceptualizes the Cold War, as I mentioned earlier, as not solely a historical event but also a knowledge production in which the war continues to generate and "teach" new knowledge in making sense of the world.[48] She advances a formulation of the Cold War as a project of U.S. gendered racial formation and empire.[49] Similarly, I situate the "secret war" within Kim's formulation of the Cold War and as part of the war's ongoing circulation of knowledge to understand the records and archives as another front in the global Cold War. Historian Kirsten Weld suggests in her study of Guatemala's secret National Police archives, which documented war crimes during Guatemala's civil war (1960–96), that "the work of containment was not only carried out with guns, helicopters, and development programs: it was also carried out with three-by-five-inch index cards, filing cabinets, and training in records management."[50] More poignantly, keeping secrets in the form of documents and archives disguised U.S. military aggression, undertaken to suppress armed decolonization struggles, as benevolent nation-building. Hence, the war in Laos showcased the U.S. Cold War logic to simultaneously support decolonization globally and to make the world "safe for democracy."[51] The war was secret because the U.S. was intervening in a supposedly neutral country. But I also suggest that the war's militarizing of Hmong as a people who needed saving because they did not fit within statist definitions of national belonging perpetuated the erasure of histories that continue to circulate as Hmong assert the importance of their refugee status as soldiers.

Hmong Soldiering

What was different about this context of secrecy in Laos as opposed to covert military operations in the other decolonizing countries was the not-yet-modern subject as a target of concerted ideas of soldiering, nationalism, and expendability. Soldiering constituted a civilizing tool to "save" Hmong from their lack of a nation or nationalist sentiment, from their purported lack of a written language and history, and from their cultural excesses characterized by tribalism. Such civilizing logic depoliticized Hmong soldiering as mercenary labor at the same time that it demanded political sacrifice and subjection.

Yet, the promise of state- and subjecthood through the sacrifice of soldiering actually manifested in a patronizing gesture of the nation-state to "save" and bring the subject into modernity.[52] Historian Takashi Fujitani explains that the conscription of Koreans and Japanese Americans as soldiers in Japan and the U.S., respectively, during WWII constitutes a positive and productive work of sovereign biopolitical power to "make live" yet reserving the "right to kill." In other words, soldiering for colonial subjects means they "can be killed." This articulation of how the racial Other can be included in the state through soldiering offers insight into the relationships among Hmong, Laos, and the U.S. because it is the promise of inclusion and enhancement of life that marks the act of soldiering. Yet, anxieties about political instability pervade the supposed act of inclusion of the racially differentiated other.[53] It was after defeat in Vietnam that the U.S. felt obliged to "rescue" Hmong as refugees (rather than merely to save them from their primitiveness) due to their large exodus into Thailand. Whereas the U.S. purported to rescue South Vietnamese (and currently some refugees from the Middle East) from a deviant political state to realize freedom, Hmong were saved from not having a political state.[54]

Hmong were fighting and dying not as U.S. subjects/citizens or even as colonial subjects but as not-yet-modern subjects. Their militarization and soldiering constituted that very process of colonization such that war was a colonial modernization project that sought to bring them from primitivity to modernity as subjects who could die for the nation. The coordinated strategy of nation-building for Laos, and encouragement of nationalism for the Hmong not-yet-modern subject, was the particular U.S. militarized liberal version of secrecy that required Hmong lives to replace U.S. lives whereby the Hmong soldiers in the "secret army" served and died in place of U.S. soldiers. An estimated thirty-five thousand Hmong died in battle, while disease and starvation caused the death of almost one-third of Hmong who were displaced from their villages when fighting and bombings destroyed their homes and crops.[55]

Hmong political leaders like Vang Pao and Touby Lyfoung, one of the heads of the Xieng Khouang district, also had their own political imagination through soldiering. They sought alignment with French colonial administrators, the Lao royal family and state officials, and U.S./CIA agents to pursue a version of self-governance. The Hmong political "secret," as one interviewee who was privy to political information at the time explains, was that Vang Pao would ntxeev lub teb chaws (engage in war conflict) and Touby Lyfoung (one of the first members of a minority to be recognized by the king of Laos;

his role as minister to the king earned him the title Phagna in the newly independent nation) would pab txiav txim (maneuver the political waters) if they lost the war. This same informant elaborates that Touby Lyfoung had been offered an opportunity at the time to govern Xieng Khouang, but he refused because his larger goal was to govern Hmong across the borders of Xieng Khouang, Luang Prabang, and Sayaboury provinces, wherever there were high concentrations of Hmong villages, and not be confined to one province. An alliance with the U.S. would provide the weapons to defend their homeland, and, if they helped defeat the Communists, would ensure their claim to live in the region. Hmong refugees reference "the promise" made between the CIA/U.S. and General Vang Pao at the beginning of Hmong involvement in the secret war: if Hmong helped push back the Communists, they would be allowed to live in peace in their homeland. But if they lost the war, the U.S. would help take care of Hmong people in Laos.

General Vang Pao began building his army by relying on his kinship network to recruit young Hmong men. Each Hmong family was required to send at least one male member to the military. Once Hmong became involved in the CIA operation, they not only became soldiers but also had increased access to education. The technologies of war converged with the development of schools in rural Hmong villages and on military bases for Hmong youth like Jesse Fang, one of my informants, who would otherwise not have had the opportunity to access the colonial educational system. Fang recounted going to school during the day and serving in the night watch at the nearby military fort. Indeed, soldiering constituted the process of bringing Hmong into colonial modernity.

Through the lens of Hmong soldiering, the secretness of the "secret war" reflects U.S. democratic ideals of freedom perpetuated by U.S. policies and the CIA. The end of the Second World War engendered the U.S. intelligence network and its approach of secrecy to ensure national security. Congress established the CIA in 1947 through the passage of the National Security Act to centralize intelligence obtained by diverse bureaucracies in order to "craft the best possible analyses and estimates for the president and his advisers."[56] This act, which created not only the CIA but also the National Security Council, the Department of Defense, and other agencies, was in response to legislators' beliefs that the dispersion of intelligence in "scattered military/diplomatic bureaucracies" in the leadup to the Japanese attack on Pearl Harbor resulted in a lack of knowledge about the forces intent on destroying U.S. democracy. In addition, the U.S. sought to gather information on the impending U.S. and Soviet Union competition for nuclear and political power.⁵⁷ But, the political shifts in governance in the decolonizing world also required U.S. efforts to integrate the very function of the CIA as a centralized intelligence organization in the imperialist strategy to institute indirect rule. The deployment of the CIA and its intelligence networks to intervene in global political conflicts for the best interest of the U.S. government has made it difficult to perceive U.S. military interventions as also the practice of hiding information. Classifying foreign intelligence information, therefore, constitutes the practice of the U.S. government to safeguard democracy. State Department and CIA documents, in particular, have been classified to keep sensitive information from the U.S. public and out of the hands of U.S. adversaries. The strategy of promoting a form of U.S. democracy based on freedom in the decolonizing world through the CIA—the relationship between democracy and its ability to keep secrets—constituted one form of liberal militarized empire. Political scientists and CIA historians who have explored the relationship between democracy and the CIA do not deny the state's systematic production of secrets in maintaining its power. Instead, they have shown that tensions between democracy's liberal ideologies and the covert activities perpetuated by the CIA have made the agency the scapegoat for U.S. foreign blunders.⁵⁸

While it is well known that the CIA assisted the overthrows of Iranian premier Mohammed Mossadeq in 1953 and of Guatemalan president Jacobo Arbenz in 1954, was instrumental in the Korean War, and kept close watch on the Soviet Union, information about the CIA's activities to promote other U.S. foreign policy objectives through warfare was kept vague. Indeed, the "secret war" in Laos constituted the longest extended paramilitary campaign undertaken by the CIA, and by extension the U.S. Although U.S. policy makers believed that an independent, stable Laotian state should have been achieved more smoothly because it was a small country with a small political elite, they also viewed Laos as being at the front line of efforts to seal off South Vietnam's borders and to prevent the spread of Communism into Thailand.⁵⁹ Therefore, Laos's sovereignty remained in suspension between being "neutral" in the Cold War struggle yet "available" for covert, direct military actions. U.S. paramilitary action and political manipulation attained heights never achieved before or since in Laos. Unlike the situations in Korea and Vietnam, because of its covert nature, the CIA had the field in Laos all to itself with the support of the military from bases in South Vietnam and neighboring Thailand.⁶⁰

Although the conflict in Laos (and Cambodia) has often been noted as a sideshow to the war in Vietnam—one that was publicly fought for over fifteen years—it reflected many things that made the Vietnam struggle unpopular. For instance, the U.S. Congress did not declare war in Vietnam, Laos, or Cambodia. A widely unpopular war that caused the deaths of 58,220 U.S. troops and at least three million Vietnamese, the Vietnam War constituted what some scholars have termed a "hot" struggle in the global Cold War. The wide-ranging collateral damage of the war caused human, land, and water devastation, along with the mass exodus of Vietnamese refugees. But it was the U.S. defeat in 1975 that marked the Vietnam War as a difficult chapter in U.S. history. Yet despite U.S. historians' and popular assumptions right after the war that the U.S. could not recuperate the controversial and morally questionable actions of the Vietnam War into a good-war narrative as it had been able to do after the Second World War, critical refugee studies scholar Yến Lê Espiritu argues that even the Vietnam War was appropriated to shore up the U.S. liberal empire because of the refugees. She calls this the "'We-Win-Even-When-We-Lose' Syndrome" in which the narrative about the "good refugee" in the U.S. bolsters the image of a benevolent U.S. liberal empire.[61] Yet, what is commonly known as the "Vietnam War" involved more than Vietnam and the Vietnamese people. Critical refugee studies scholar Khatharya Um has explained that the simultaneous conflicts in Laos and Cambodia were considered "critical and marginal" to that war; whereby their singular significance was to further the objectives in Vietnam.[62] In Cambodia, the U.S. launched daily air bombings of the countryside from Thai air bases, which devastated Cambodia's people and landscape and contributed to the rise of Pol Pot and the Khmer Rouge regime in 1975. The Khmer Rouge's goal of ridding Cambodia of Western imperialism resulted in the genocide of more than three million people and the forced displacement of nearly 158,000 Cambodian refugees to the U.S.[63]

The CIA, then, perceived its role in Laos as a model operation. According to CIA historian Thomas Ahern Jr., the "ultimate failure" was "an inadequate criterion by which to judge the quality of the effort devoted to a lost cause." Ahern admits that the CIA's performance was not without flaws, but writes that ultimately "the story of the 'secret war' in Laos reveals an admirable record of flexible, economical management and sound tactical judgment." Indeed, according to Ahern, a more remarkable aspect of that record is the agency's "steady, pragmatic accommodation of cultural sensitivities and of amorphous, competitive command relationships—Laotian, [redacted] and American."[64] The redacted name between "Laotian" and "American" symbolizes the erasure of history with which this book grapples. The agency recuperates the story of the "secret war" and its failure as a success on the levels of CIA management and judgment, culturally sensitive but competitive command of relationships, and the professionally adventurous approach of its personnel.[65] Secrecy, then, is also fundamental to U.S. imperialism's moral and political authority by hiding acts of violence and moral political crises.

The CIA's assessment of its role in the Cold War strategy reveals how the agency and secrecy were an integral aspect of U.S. foreign relations diplomacy, thus its state-making project. Such secrets are often expressed, especially by the CIA and its personnel, as a disconnection between bureaucracy and fieldwork. This sentiment of disconnection between the State Department, Washington, and diplomatic staff on one hand and CIA agents on the other reveals the discrepancies in the goals and actions among the various U.S. government entities involved in Laos. Although the agency would argue that the misalignments between its personnel in the field and bureaucrats in the U.S. contributed to the development of competing ideas and troubles in Laos, together they form integral components of U.S. imperialism based on secrecy. While Laos functioned as the buffer between Communism and democracy, Hmong served as the anchor of diplomacy and militarism, always on hold to be used as an asset when their military service was needed. Together, they inform the larger project of U.S. imperialist intervention in Laos as the nation sought to imagine its postcolonial future. According to the CIA, its "secret" operations sat at the juncture of diplomacy and militarism. The CIA's core beliefs reveal a clear link between secrecy and U.S. imperialism "not only in Southeast Asia but generally in the postcolonial world."[66] In his account of the U.S. role in Laos, *Undercover Armies*, Ahern relates that the agency approaches a "threatened anticommunist government" to "establish its [the government's] benevolent—even paternalistic—concern for the welfare of a predominantly rural population. The military aspect focused on small, mobile units designed to operate in enemy-held territory, challenging Communist control and organizing civilian resistance. The two might be combined, using military resources in rural civic action programs designed to popularize the government and its army."[67] This statement captures the logic used by the CIA and U.S. administration to mobilize the rural population of Laos toward military action in order to popularize the government and its army. The practice of mobilizing militarism "featured a search for a charismatic leader" who could use his resources to "defeat the communists."[68] General Vang Pao and his Hmong army represented this rural military resource to challenge Communist encroachment for the CIA and U.S. in northeastern Laos. Indeed, CIA covert activities aimed to "enlighten" the traditional elite and promote "political modernization" as well as to support military resistance against the threat of Communist takeover.⁶⁹ These two goals combined with U.S. foreign policy making constituted the context of the so-called secret war.

Decolonization and the Cold War in Laos
Pertinent to my concern for secrecy's structuring of historiographical gaps and refugee epistemology is the Cold War overlap between colonial and militarized power. In Laos, the colonial and military overlap resulted in interimperial struggles—in which the French, Japanese, and U.S. empires' liberal strategies converged—that produced the country's status as "neutral yet available." The interimperial struggles constituted the conditions for Hmong political struggles, military service, and refugee displacement. But first, I will briefly discuss how scholarship in the fields of American and Asian American studies focusing on Cold War U.S. politics and culture has situated investigations of war, migration and diaspora, and redress and justice within decolonization's longue durée in the Asia Pacific and Southeast Asian region.⁷⁰ While Cold War studies have linked decolonization and the Cold War, most have taken a teleological approach that views decolonization as the decline of European empire, and in which Cold War struggles compound problems of postcolonial nation-building.⁷¹ I engage with historian Mark P. Bradley's point that the "global discourse and practices of colonialism, race, modernism, and postcolonial state-making at once preceded, were profoundly implicated in, and ultimately transcended the dynamics of the Cold War."⁷² Situating Cold War histories within a global context of transitions of political power highlights the continuities of regime structures that shape war, race, and violence.

Seeing the overlap between decolonization and the Cold War destabilizes teleological notions of decolonization and the postcolonial as progression from colonialism or as completed projects in and of themselves. Rather, they are ongoing processes of negotiation. For example, Elaine Kim and Chungmoo Choi aptly assert that Korea did not have a postcolonial moment due to the multiple layers of Japanese colonialism and its erasure, and U.S. neo-imperial domination in the installation of U.S. military apparatus in South Korea following World War II.⁷³ The Cold War postcolonial interventions reflect what Setsu Shigematsu and Keith Camacho call "militarized currents" in which militarism in the Asia Pacific region is an extension of colonialism.⁷⁴ The interventions extended the colonial civilizing project to justify military violence, comprising the very conditions that shaped the refugee's emergence as a colonial excess. In addition, the suspension of Laos's decolonization demonstrates what Steven Hugh Lee calls the "continuities and distinctiveness about American foreign policy in Asia."[75] Extending historians John Lewis Gaddis and Geir Lundestad's concept of the U.S. as an "informal empire," which sought to foster Indigenous, pro-Western, anti-Communist allies through political advice, economic support, and military aid, Lee explains how the U.S. Cold War strategy combined short-term goals of supporting its allies with the long-term goals to develop "moderate and pro-Western indigenous nationalists."[76] This Cold War development strategy is consistent with U.S. empire's liberal strategies of democratic nation-building. Indeed, the circulation of Cold War policies, which Mimi Thi Nguyen has described as the "workings of liberalism in its imperial form" in the "continuities and innovations between operations of power and violence," emphasizes the negotiation of colonialism into the era of decolonization.[77]

The Cold War view that Laos served as a space for the testing of political struggles between French, Japanese, and U.S. interests precisely illuminates the interimperial links in Laos's place in Cold War geopolitics. Lisa Yoneyama's genealogy of the Cold War postcolonial condition in the Asia Pacific region shows how Cold War studies have overlooked the "transwar continuities" which made "postwar Americanization of racial justice possible."[78] By "transwar continuities," Yoneyama refers to the complicity between the U.S. and Japan prior to and after 1945 to "perceive affinities and convergences of geohistorical elements that have worked together to constitute mid-twentieth-century violence."[79] She explains that ignoring the "transwar continuities" misses the significance of Japanese imperial practices in making the Cold War United States, and by extension, in postcolonial nation-building in Southeast Asia.[80]

In addition, the broadening of colonial tropes about Hmong and Laos transplanted the U.S. settler colonial logic of land dispossession combined with the project of counterinsurgency to disrupt decolonization.[81] If the U.S. Cold War strategy aimed to foster Indigenous proxy governments through the "build-up [of] indigenous military forces and the creation of viable political systems," which is an extension of colonialism, then it must necessarily abort decolonization as a way to civilize the undeveloped Native.[82] While *Indigenous* is used more broadly to refer to nationalists in Asia, Africa, and other former European colonies, and should not be conflated with its reference to first peoples to the land in the settler colonial context, I contend that the particular U.S. fostering of nationalism among ethnic/Indigenous peoples like Hmong, Kha, Brao, and others in parallel with its efforts to strengthen nationalist leaders and their political agendas underscores colonialism and militarism as intertwined, ongoing gendered racial structures.

Indeed, Cold War political ideologies were intricately linked to notions of space in which strategies of containment animated other strategies about expansion. Historians have noted Laos's geopolitical significance for the regional and global intersection of ideologies from the U.S., Vietnam, the Soviet Union, Thailand, Japan, and China.[83] The politics of space in Laos makes visible the decolonizing moment as an overlap of imperialisms such that the colonial geopolitical significance of the region and the wartime—post-WWII and Cold War—"geostrategic calculations" consolidated the region's "position as a looming 'hot' front in the global ideological battleground."[84] According to Albert Lau, Southeast Asia did not exist as a "region" until August 1943, when it appeared in the "wartime military structure set up to spearhead the British-led Allied operations in the newly configured regional theatre."[85] Any preexisting state boundaries prior to WWII, according to Lau, were largely a Western invention of European territorial contestation. The region is strategically located with the lower territories serving as a land and sea barrier between the Indian and Pacific oceans, and could allow for controlling vessel entry. At the same time, the upper territories share a long border with China that made it "possible for China to be encircled and 'contained' from the south."[86] Hence, Laos was significant for French colonialism because the Mekong River would facilitate the European colonial administration's infiltration into China.

The supposed postcolonial period (between 1946 and 1975) of decolonization and nation-building, as historian Simon Creak notes, is crucial for understanding the development of Lao nationalism.[87] It is also important for understanding how U.S. policy toward Laos shaped the country's approach to Southeast Asia during the Cold War.[88] According to historian Seth Jacobs, it was during this critical period that Laos operated as "the testing ground for counterinsurgency and nation-building programs" with particular distinctions such as the "support of unpopular but pro-Western despots, slugging matches between U.S. civilian and military bureaucracies, and ignorance of the needs and problems of the native populations."[89] More specifically, critical omissions from the hegemonic Cold War narrative included the U.S. policies and programs that intercepted the decolonizing process in Laos and Hmong efforts to achieve nationhood. While the resulting "secret war" should be considered a part of the Cold War, analyzing the relationship between Southeast Asia and the U.S. as the region gains importance in the post-WWII era would open up an inquiry of international history to critique the liberal strategies of U.S. imperialism and war at the moment of decolonization.

Laos's Suspended Decolonization

Laos's suspended decolonization was a condition of its perceived "neutral yet available" space and temporally lagging people. In the following pages, I will explore Cold War Laos as a space of interimperial struggles through the early history of a Laos state and colonial territory, the postcolonial transition of power, and the Cold War modernizing approach to development in Laos.

LAOS AND ITS PEOPLE: A COLONIAL PROBLEM

Laos is bordered by China to the north, Vietnam to the east, Cambodia to the southeast, Thailand to the west, and Myanmar/Burma to the northwest. Although modern Laos is landlocked, during its early history as a state under the rule of Fa Ngum (1353–73) Laos achieved extensive territorial authority centered in the capital city of Luang Prabang and extending west toward Chiang Mai (Thailand) and southeast toward the Korat plateau and northern Cambodia.[90] This period, during which Laos was known as the kingdom of Lan Xang ("land of a million elephants"), informed a Laotian sense of national identity for the dominant ethnic Lao group.[91] Lan Xang became one of the more powerful states of mainland Southeast Asia, controlling important trade routes between 1373 and 1406. During its early history, the Lan Xang state was plagued by interventions by its Vietnamese, Burmese, and Thai neighbors.[92] Toward the end of the seventeenth century, disputes about succession fractured Lan Xang into four kingdoms: Luang Prabang, Vientiane, Xieng Khouang, and Champasak in the south, with shifting relations to the Vietnamese court at Hue and the Thai court at Ayutthaya/Bangkok.[93] These different kingdoms made Laos a series of contested territories and, according to Creak, led Southeast Asia scholars to question the existence of a "real" Lao national identity as well as to suggest that French colonialism was the primary influence on the modern nation of Laos.[94] Nonetheless, the feature of overlapping sovereignty in Laos resembled a mandala system of "unstable, center-oriented politics of vague and varying size through which political power was organized."[95] Indeed, the Thai occupation of Luang Prabang and Vientiane among other cities, effectively annexing central Laos at the beginning of French colonial rule in Vietnam (1880–90), facilitated French colonialism in Laos as a form of colonial protection.[96]

Laos was the last territory colonized by the French, after Vietnam and Cambodia. During its colonial rule (1890–1953), France considered the landlocked territory its least important colony and a colonial burden; only one hundred French civil servants were allotted to the country, in comparison to the forty thousand French people in Vietnam to govern the population and exploit the natural resources.[97] Because it was considered a resource-poor colony that did not warrant much colonial development, French colonial administrators invested very little effort in Laos's social, political, and cultural improvement. The French relied on existing political structures to maintain law and order from the administrative capital of Vientiane. While the king of Luang Prabang negotiated to maintain his throne, the Xieng Khouang and Champasak kingdoms were allowed to maintain their social status with very little political power.[98] Few roads or railways were built, and not a single high school was built; those who finished primary school had to continue their education in Vietnam or abroad.[99] French colonial efforts to establish a modern educational system in Laos did not extend beyond the cultivation of a loyal "feudal" elite, and Laos purportedly had the highest illiteracy rate in the region.[100] Only a select few were able to attend school in Vietnam or France. Because Laos seemingly offered few natural resources to exploit, the French imposed heavy taxes to make "Laos pay for itself."[101] There were four ways to raise revenue: a head tax on all males between the ages of eighteen and sixty; taxing the sale of opium, alcohol, and salt; requiring each adult male to perform unpaid corvée labor; and establishing a government monopoly on opium.[102] The head tax was one of the longest-lasting systems (until 1949), and had to be paid in cash. The corvée required each adult male to contribute fifteen to twenty days each year of labor toward clearing jungles, building and repairing roads, serving as porters and messengers, and removing rocks from rivers.[103] Road building served multiple purposes, including facilitating troop movements required for territorial pacification as well as supporting the extraction of raw materials and trade flows.[104] The post-WWII modernization projects were extensions of these earlier colonial practices that aimed to develop Laos's infrastructure, strengthen its anticolonial political movement, and foster nationalism among the ethnic and Indigenous groups.

If Laos presented geopolitical, social, and cultural problems for French colonialism, then the people of Laos contributed even more to its complexity as a quasi-ungovernable territory. The French administration categorized the population according to the landscape in which they lived: the lowlands, the mountain slopes, or the mountain tops. The dominant political and cultural group, the Lao, are called the Lao Lum ("Lao of the lowlands") and belong to the Tai-speaking peoples. The second category is called Lao Theung ("Lao of the mountain slopes") and they dwell in the highlands, belonging to the Mon-Khmer language group. The third category is called Lao Soung ("Lao of the mountain tops") who speak Tibeto-Burman languages and live at elevations above three thousand feet. Hmong and Iu Mien comprise the two major ethnopolitical groups in this category.[105] This categorization scheme organizes the people of Laos in relation to the landscape and close to nature. The system of classifying people with their natural surroundings helped to advance racial ideologies about Laotians as lazy, isolated, and backward. For instance, while French colonial administrators perceived the Indochinese to be a "deficient mankind" and "incomplete," they viewed Lao people in particular as "heedless, lazy and decadent."[106]

The colonial ruler's relationship with the Indigenous and ethnic groups was more contentious, and marked by frequent revolts. The French colonial structure of governing from the administrative capital compounded the problems already experienced by these groups within Laotian society. In other words, Indigenous and ethnic groups experienced the simultaneous and overlapping impact of Laotian governance and French colonialism. For example, these groups had to pay the tax imposed by the French as well as the additional levy demanded by Laotian tax collectors. The Lao Theung groups in southern Laos launched anti-French uprisings between 1901 and 1907. The Tai-speaking groups in northern Laos revolted at various times from 1914 to 1923. A Hmong anti-French rebellion in Xieng Khouang in 1919, led by Pa Chay Lo, called for the establishment of an independent Hmong kingdom.[107] To prevent further acts of resistance, the French established an autonomous Hmong *tasseng* (district) at Nong Het near the Laotian-Vietnamese border to allow Hmong to govern themselves.[108] The Hmong leadership structure at Nong Het, characterized by a back-and-forth struggle between the Lo and Ly clans, would ultimately be divided along ideological lines that reflected the division between the Laotian anticolonial and nationalist movements, with Faydang Lobliayao joining the Lao Issara (Free Lao) and eventually the Pathet Lao under Souphanouvong while Touby Lyfoung led the pro-Western Hmong faction.[109] Touby Lyfoung and his group aided the French recolonization of Laos after WWII and joined the counterinsurgency efforts against the Laotian and North Vietnamese Communists.[110]

Hmong (derogatorily called "Méo"), along with other ethnic groups, were identified as a "colonial problem" that the French viewed as requiring active collaboration of the Lao royal family and Lao social elites because Hmong desired emancipation from the constraints of political and administrative organization.[111] Recognizing Hmong aid to French guerrillas during Japanese occupation, local French military advisor Jean de Raymond suggested to King Sisavang Vong that he diplomatically "welcome the pledge to allow the Meo population to have the privilege, at least, of administrative and judicial relations through the intermediary of notables and functionaries belonging to their own race."[112]

DECOLONIZING LAOS

The overlapping forms of colonial rule by France, and briefly Japan, were informally extended with U.S. involvement so that Laos also did not have a postcolonial moment. Given that the French colonial project in Laos had operated on the logic of the territory as a burden and its people as undeveloped, untamed, backward, and close to nature, the independence and anticolonial struggles reflected Laos's questioned territorial and political status as a small, underdeveloped country that needed protection. In the post–World War II moment, the Japanese proclaimed Laos independent while the French sought to return to resume control.[113] Lao Issara (Free Lao), the Lao anticolonial and nationalist movement led by the three European-educated princes (brothers Phetsarath Rattanavongsa and Souvanna Phouma, and their half brother Souphanouvong) tried to establish a new government at the critical juncture between the end of Japanese occupation and the French colonial return. The Lao Issara and the king of Laos, Sisavang Vong, held competing views on what an independent Laos would look like. While Phetsarath favored unifying Laos with minimal foreign intervention, King Sisavang Vong maintained a preference for French protection because, in his view, "Laos was too small to be independent."[114] On September 7, 1945, Phetsarath was informed that a royal proclamation had continued the French protectorate over the kingdom of Luang Prabang, and he in turn issued a proclamation to unify the kingdom of Luang Prabang with the four southern provinces of Khammouan, Savannakhet, Champasak, and Saravan (Salavang). The U.S., on the other hand, communicated its official position to France that there was no question concerning France's sovereignty over Indochina.[115] On September 15, 1945, Phetsarath declared the unification of the country as the kingdom of Laos under the crown of Luang Prabang. The Lao Issara elected a People's Committee, which on October 12 appointed a provisional government and forced the abdication of King Sisavang Vong.[116] By late 1946, the U.S. position had solidified around lending support to the former colonial powers in their efforts to pacify nationalist movements construed by the U.S. to be Stalinist.[117]

The kingdom of Laos's first popularly elected Constituent Assembly consisted of forty-four delegates chosen on December 15, 1946. These delegates worked on a constitution to declare Laos an independent state within the French Union. This agreement unified the different kingdoms in Laos, and it installed a government headed by Prince Souvannarath, a half brother of Phetsarath. Boun Oum kept his title as Prince of Champasak but renounced his suzerain rights to this former kingdom. He was made inspector general of the kingdom, and the third-ranking personage of Laos after the king and crown prince. The newly installed government created a Royal Lao Army, which would grow to seventeen companies by the end of 1952. On February 7, 1950, the United States and Britain recognized Laos, and the U.S. opened a legation in Vientiane later that year.[118]

The French declaration of July 3, 1953, pledged full independence to Vietnam, Laos, and Cambodia.[119] On October 22, 1953, Laos was granted independence through the Franco-Lao Treaty of Amity and Association.[120] Laos became a member of the United Nations on December 14, 1955, and its government was represented at the Asian-African Conference held in April 1955 in Bandung, Indonesia.[121] The number of global and regional ideologies and interests that intersected in Laos between 1946 and 1975 extended the contested colonial history to give the "impression that the country lacks integrity as a nation."[122] My analysis draws from Creak's important point that there is a gap in the already limited scholarship on Laos regarding this crucial time period of "limited autonomy" for understanding the development of Lao nationalism.[123] "Limited autonomy," as I define it, is an illusion of sovereignty that defined Laos as a problem territory to be neutralized, and categorized Hmong as a subject needing to be saved through military violence. I use it as a key concept to explicate my point that the interimperial struggles of the Cold War in Laos reflected the overlap of political ideologies and the push for autonomy in the region. The international mandates of neutrality at the 1954 and 1962 Geneva Conventions, rather than ushering in peace, instituted imperialist strategies to neutralize territorial sovereignty and co-opt migratory peoples' political desires for state-making. Indeed, the illusion of cultural sovereignty for Hmong enfolded the group within the projects of imperialist expansion and postcolonial nation-building.[124]

The establishment of a unified Laos did not halt the outside interventions that have plagued the country since its early history. The emergence of the Cold War and its triangulation in Southeast Asia interrupted Laos's anticolonial movement. Lau explains that, in Southeast Asia, the two emerging processes of decolonization and the Cold War "conflated in the swirl of competing and interacting post-war forces rapidly emerging in the region, each influencing and being influenced by the other." He further elaborates that "the close identification of the colonial powers with one side of the Cold War, while some nationalists were also Communists, quickly muddied the waters of decolonization and ensured that the processes involved in the dissolution of colonial empires in Southeast Asia became inextricably connected to the political and ideological challenges involved in the pursuit of the global Cold War. Although the Second World War might have made decolonization thinkable, it did not make imperial withdrawal inevitable."[125] In this way, the nature of the Cold War struggle in Laos between the U.S. and the Soviet Union drew upon the anticolonial movements of the Laotian elite (which focused on freeing Laos from foreign intervention) and of the people on the run (who desired political autonomy) to interrupt the decolonization process. In other words, the U.S. involvement in Laos under secrecy presented the illusion of possible sovereignties through militarized colonialism.[126]

U.S. perceptions of the negotiations in Geneva that led up to the 1954 Accords following the French defeat at Dien Bien Phu in Vietnam revealed the conflation of decolonization and the Cold War in Southeast Asia. Upon returning from the opening sessions of the Geneva Conference, U.S. Secretary of State John Foster Dulles claimed that Indochina was a perfect example of the Soviet Communist strategy for colonial and dependent areas, which was laid out by Lenin and Stalin with the goal of taking over much of Asia. He stated that Indochina was vulnerable because the governments of Vietnam, Laos, and Cambodia, although liberated, had not yet received "full political independence" and their peoples were neither adequately organized to fight against Communist-led rebels nor did they feel they had a stake in the struggle. With the realization that Communists could move into all of Southeast Asia, the Eisenhower administration gave particular attention to the region. These U.S. objectives were to strengthen resistance to Communism and to build a broader community of defense in Southeast Asia (extending to the minority groups). As part of its efforts, the U.S. sought to secure agreements for mutual defense; it negotiated treaties with the Philippines, Australia, and New Zealand, among others, to create a regional bulwark against Communist attack and to preserve U.S. interests in Southeast Asia. The U.S., via the Secretary of State, framed its mission as helping the peoples of Asia to secure their liberty: "The United States, as the first colony of modern history to win independence for itself, instinctively shares the aspirations for liberty of all dependent and colonial peoples. We want to help, not hinder, the spread of liberty. We do not seek to perpetuate Western colonialism and we find even more intolerable the new imperialist colonialism of communism."[127] The United States' logic to aid Asian independence from colonialism, Western imperialism, and Communism conflates decolonization with the Cold War struggle. The conflation of the Cold War and decolonization presented opportunities and challenges to nationalists and European powers alike, "hastening decolonization in some territories and prolonging that process in others."[128]

The 1954 Geneva Accords, which ended French colonialism in the Indochinese colonies of Vietnam, Cambodia, and Laos, provided an international legal mandate for neutrality, which accepted Viet Minh control of North Vietnam and asserted neutrality for Laos and Cambodia under a regime to be monitored by an International Control Commission (ICC).[129] While in theory the Geneva Accords prohibited military interventions, in practice the agreement marked the beginning of U.S. presence and militarization of the region. In effect, it was an international legal shroud that allowed the Cold War superpowers to continue administering colonial-like programs in Southeast Asia. The United States, in particular, viewed the "chaotic situation" in Southeast Asia created by the Geneva Conventions as a dangerous context in which Communist forces could gather strength, and feared that a "united, well-led, albeit small Pathet Lao group, supported and directed by North Viet Nam" would be in a position to take control of the country.[130] As a nonsignatory to the Final Declaration of the Conference, the U.S. maintained a presence in Laos under the objective of development, which put it in a position to "observe and to help punish anyone who did not" follow the agreement.[131] In doing so, the U.S. government undertook preemptive actions after the accords' signing to strengthen the Lao government, build unity among the anti-Communist leadership, and heighten the leadership's understanding of the "Communist menace."[132] The U.S. appropriation of the international legal mandate of neutrality to disguise its military activities reveals how the concept of neutrality itself was a convention of secrecy to provide an illusion of decolonization and possible sovereignty. President Eisenhower "insisted that Laos side with the Western camp in the cold war."[133]

The U.S. did not need further prodding when Crown Prince Savang Vatthana probed U.S. diplomats in Paris during the summer of 1954 for reassurances regarding support for Laos in the event of an attack from its Communist neighbors. This request allowed the U.S. to establish a disguised military mission in Vientiane. The Programs Evaluation Office (PEO) was established on December 13, 1955, to provide military aid to Laos.[134] The PEO was set up as a section of the U.S. Operations Mission, which administered the $34 million that the Eisenhower administration provided to modernize the Lao military.[135] The PEO would focus on country development while covertly supporting a U.S. military presence in Laos. It was a thinly veiled Military Assistance and Advisory Group commanding a disguised military aid operation. Initially staffed by retired and reserve U.S. military personnel in civilian mufti, the PEO became a place where active duty military personnel were disguised as civilian employees to "form, train, and support a competent army."[136] The commanding general officer and his staff were effectively removed from the Department of Defense rosters of active service personnel to maintain secrecy and a façade of compliance with the 1954 Geneva Agreement.[137] The PEO mission to develop the country while supporting a covert military operation also involved USAID. Harvey E. Gutman, a USAID representative who served in Laos from 1958 to 1960, estimated that the USAID Laos program at the time had at least a hundred U.S. staff plus a "large number of American and third-country contract teams."[138] The USAID mission had two themes: classic technical assistance and a large category of activities that were funded under "defense support."

The years following Laotian independence were marked by a struggle between different nationalist leaders to define the decolonizing state, which the U.S. viewed as a weak nationalist movement. Three key nationalist leaders and ideologies emerged: neutralists under Prince Souvanna Phouma; the right-wing, prodemocracy and pro-U.S. group under Prince Boun Oum of Champasak; and the left-wing Communist Lao Patriotic Front under Prince Souphanouvong and half-Vietnamese future prime minister Kaysone Phomvihane. Each faction had military control over different regions in Laos. Yet, the Royal Lao Government tried to establish coalition governments that would bridge these three political groups. On May 4, 1958, Laos held elections to formalize the reintegration of the different nationalist parties into a coalition government in a Laotian attempt at sovereignty and self-determination. Despite U.S. hopes that the elections would oust the Communist leadership, Souphanouvong's party and its allies gained the majority of the contested seats in the National Assembly, and the prince himself was elected by the largest margin of victory in every district of the country.[139] Although the elections were largely without incident throughout the country, the results "surprised and disturbed most Western observers" and led many to speculate that they had been rigged by the Communists, who seemed to accomplish at the polls what they had failed to accomplish militarily since 1954.[140] The coalition government allowed Prince Souphanouvong to gain authority over the Phong Saly and Sam Neua provinces while Pathet Lao troops were integrated into the Royal Lao Armed Forces. Neo Lao Hak Xat, the socialist Lao People's Front, also gained representation on a neutralist coalition cabinet under Souvanna Phouma as prime minister.[141] The collapse of this coalition cabinet in July 1958, however, reaffirmed the boundaries of the different factions. It also ushered in U.S. efforts to end neutralism and to support prodemocracy groups. This rivalry between the left, neutral, and right groups would eventually be characterized in the historical record as the Laotian Civil War.

The August 9, 1960, coup d'état led by neutralist Captain Kong Le in Vientiane to rid Laos of external Western influence revealed the ongoing divisions within the Lao nationalist movement. It is important to note that Laotian leaders like Kong Le and Souvanna envisioned a neutral Laos as one that would be free from any external influence, including the West. Yet, the coup exposed how Laotian neutrality was already intertwined with U.S. interests in Vietnam and the global Cold War struggle. These broader contexts exacerbated the divisions of the decolonial movement. After Captain Le retreated to the Plain of Jars, the Soviet Union airlifted military supplies to the forces of the Pathet Lao and of Kong Le, which eventually merged. Meanwhile, the U.S. supplied aircrafts and other military support to pro-U.S. General Phoumi. The U.S. (through the PEO and the Pentagon) also armed Hmong for resistance in the northeast with "2,000 light weapons" to protect their villages from Pathet Lao or neutralist pressure,[142] Hmong aid helped General Phoumi retake Vientiane from the Pathet Lao and Kong Le. U.S. observance of Hmong efforts helped to initiate the biggest "tribal mobilization" that formed the foundation of the CIA's "secret war" in Laos. Although the U.S. aid and development programs were already attempting to influence the ethnic minority populations, it was Kong Le's coup that changed the course of what would become the United States' "secret war" toward the use of a proxy army composed of Hmong and other ethnic minority groups. Laos and Hmong represented colonial and military challenges as a difficult terrain for full U.S. commitment and a not-yet-people for political alliance, respectively, that required neutralization. Chapter 2 will show how the U.S. deployed colonial tropes about Laos and Hmong to justify its intervention, and how the U.S. strategies of neutralization were written in the redacted documents.

2. MISSING THINGS
STATE SECRETS AND U.S. COLD WAR
POLICY TOWARD LAOS

Laos is far away from America, but the world is small . . . [and the] security of all Southeast Asia will be endangered if Laos loses its neutral independence. Its own safety runs with the safety of us all, in real neutrality observed by all. —PRESIDENT JOHN F. KENNEDY, MARCH 23, 1961, PRESS CONFERENCE

On April 17, 1962, a "secret" memorandum on the "Congressional Briefing on Laos" was dispatched to President John F. Kennedy.[1] According to the two-page redacted memorandum (shown in figure 2.1), the briefing had been intended to provide the congressional leadership with updates on developments in Laos to decide on a "mild" suspension of military assistance to Lao General Phoumi. A first glance at the memo shows that the document is heavily redacted, showing that the people, places, and events these missing texts referenced were meant to be kept hidden in making the document available to the public. Further examination of the redactions affirms the obscuring of secrets that required the document to be initially marked as secret. Looking around the redactions at the legible content of the memorandum reveals that Congress and President Kennedy authorized military and economic aid to Laos.[2] Reading redacted documents like this memo together with the limited research and literature written by U.S. personnel about U.S. involvement in Laos and the refugee exodus affirms that the military and civilian aid programs sanctioned by the U.S. and Soviet governments were effectively open secrets.[3] This declassified and redacted memo, which I found among many other similarly marked documents in the records of the Kennedy White House, shows that the practice of designating as "secret" the records of policymakers' open discussions about providing illicit aid to a decolonizing Laos is the hallmark of U.S. state secrecy.

State secrecy was a necessary practice at the time to adhere, at least on paper, to the 1954 Geneva Conventions that declared Laos, Cambodia, and Vietnam independent from France, and which also stipulated that these decolonizing countries were to remain free from foreign military intervention. Yet, the congressional briefing and the drafting of the accompanying memo occurred nearly two months before the July 1962 signing of a second Geneva Convention focused specifically on Laotian neutrality. The necessity for a second Geneva Convention meant that the first international agreement had done little to curb foreign military aid to Laos, or to Vietnam and Cambodia. The congressional briefing did not hide the fact that the U.S. had been supplying economic and military aid to anti-Communist Laotian nationalists as well as indirect aid to Hmong and other ethnic and Indigenous groups through the CIA and USAID since 1955. Viewed in the historical context of a decolonizing Laos and U.S. Cold War policies, the "secret" redacted documents are the blueprints of a U.S. Cold War policy that sought to capitalize on the international mandate of neutrality to militarize Laotian nation-building in order to facilitate imperialist expansions. In the U.S. Cold War imagination, Laos was linked to the United States' broader interests in Southeast Asia. As I explained in chapter 1, the convergence of decolonization and Cold War militarization in Southeast Asia extended colonialism in this region.

If such meetings that are archived through the documents happened and militarized aid was sanctioned by the president and Congress, then the act of marking documents as "secret" operates as a convention of bureaucratic practice—intended not to hide an event, but to suppress the contents of the document from circulation and archiving. The "secret" redacted documents are the paper trails of state secrecy, through which the U.S. normalized its projections of neutrality. In examining these documents, I pose the following question about these paper trails: How does the system of designating information about meetings and U.S. foreign activities as secrets configure the U.S. Cold War neutral policy toward Laos, as well as shape refugee attempts to narrate this history? This chapter examines the declassified documents including maps from President John F. Kennedy's National Security Council Files and Foreign Relations documents from 1961 to 1963, prepared by the John F. Kennedy Presidential Library and Museum, and Thomas L. Ahern's *Undercover Armies: CIA and Surrogate Warfare in Laos, 1961–1973*, published by the CIA. I observe that an essential component of state secrecy is the maintenance of an incomplete archive filled with redacted "secret" papers. "Secret" documents, then, represent common practices of the state and its archive in the production of militarized national epistemologies. This chapter makes two related arguments. First, the state and CIA processing of the documents recording U.S. militarized actions inform the construction of an intelligence bureaucracy in the post-WWII period and the formation of U.S. Cold War policies. The specific U.S. Cold War neutrality policy toward Laos that aimed at building a strong independent country occurred in secret—enabling the U.S. to maintain a presence in Laos without being there—and erased Laos from the Cold War cartography. Second, the U.S. Cold War neutrality policy operated through imagining Laos as an empty, available landscape, and its peoples as a natural defense force because they were an extension of that landscape. State secrets instituted material violence through the war in Laos and continue to institute epistemic violence in the form of ongoing historical erasure of those impacted by war.

Rather than pursuing a recovery project to fill the gaps in the incomplete historical record, this chapter shows that state documents present an epistemological dilemma for knowledge production. Turning the epistemological dilemma of *missing things* into a methodological approach, I look for what the secrets have produced, that is, what the secrets left in their wake. *Missing things* underscores the "secret war" archive—a disparate repertoire of U.S. state documents, stories from humanitarian aid and development personnel, refugee records, and refugee narratives—as a documentary corpus but also as a site where peoples, histories, and places get lost in the mundane processing of papers. In addition, *missing things* analyzes document redactions and erasures as critically engendering refugee narratives that challenge the existing status quo of Cold War knowledge and U.S. national history.

As such, the chapter also examines refugee records to show how refugee processing structures Hmong histories that are missing in the imperial archive. In his excavation of the epistemological and ontological problems of Pakistani bureaucratic documents about city planning, anthropologist Matthew S. Hull argues that scholars need to account for the logics, aesthetics, and norms of bureaucratic texts *and* how these documents engage with people, places, and things to make "(other) bureaucratic objects."[4] While Hull's interest lies in interrogating the paper mediation of relations among people, places, and things, his point that the "regime of paper documents" is a form of governance and that the governance of paper is "central to governing the city" helps elucidate my assertion that the paper trails left behind by U.S. Cold War policymaking show secrets as conventions of document processing.[5] Moreover, Andrew Friedman's study of the formation of the CIA headquarters, a "covert capital" in the northern Virginia suburbs, shows the importance of domestic bureaucracy in U.S. imperial policy.[6] Friedman's argument that the suburban landscape constituted the "home front" where U.S. imperialism became something lived in the everyday, and where empire became "a set of actions" and an "administrative problem," underscores my point that the mundane processing of "secret" documents produces U.S. Cold War neutralization strategy, derived from the international mandated neutral policy toward Laos, as well as the knowledge formation of U.S. militarized liberal empire.[7]

Missing Things in the Archive
In chasing the disparate "secret war" archive, my analysis employs the missing bag with which I opened this book's introduction to anchor a discussion of the archive's production of absences around U.S. imperialism and war. The inscription of Hmong possessions—livelihoods—onto the missing baggage claim form illuminates how things go missing through flight and migration, which in turn reveals the integration of refugee presence in the structures of flight and knowledge formation. The baggage of missing things suggests that we read secret documents for both their *form* and *content*. While the baggage claim form, a paper trail of a Hmong refugee family's migration to the U.S., highlights the mundane processing of a missing bag of personal possessions, it simultaneously emphasizes the burden of said baggage, which represents the excess of "stories that could not be told" and which will be perpetually unaccounted for.[8] Together, these two ideas—the mundane and the excess—reveal the mechanism by which the archive produces the erasure

of historical knowledge, so that there are always missing things, no matter how much we may know about a subject.⁹ In the context of missing things, the emphasis on Hmong soldiers has obscured Laos's decolonization and the U.S. interruption of it, while Hmong remained a colonial baggage that troubled Laotian nation-building as well as U.S. liberal militarized empire.

Following Antoinette Burton, who has unpacked the ways that archives are "constructed, policed, experienced, and manipulated," the missing baggage suggests the unsettled structure and contents of the archive.¹⁰ Indeed, the baggage represents what *is* missing in the archive. Additionally, Joan M. Schwartz and Terry Cook, in their guest editors' introduction to two thematic issues of *Archival Science*, argue that archives are institutions that "wield power over the shape and direction of historical scholarship, collective memory, and national identity." They also assert that archiving is a discipline with its "own sets of theories, methodologies, and practices" through which archivists wield power over the management of records.¹¹ As such, they suggest archives as active sites for the negotiation of social power. Schwartz and Cook's work signals a shift from earlier understandings of archives as passive storehouses, and of archivists as impartial and objective, to a newly critical approach to archival stories and evidence as incomplete, exposing the archive's Truth narrative as subjective and figured in political, social, and economic contexts. Seen in this light, secrets, elisions, and distortions are integral to archives' procedural production of knowledge. Engaging with this shift in archive studies to expose the power of the archive, I explore what it means to dwell in its gaps and erasures and to read "along the archival grain," in the words of postcolonial critic Ann Stoler, who contends that this way of reading elucidates the archive's regularities, logic of recall, densities and distributions, and its "consistencies of misinformation, omission, and mistake."¹² This analysis, which Stoler further distinguishes from a reading "against the grain," makes visible the "power in the production of the archive itself."¹³ Feminist scholar Anjali Arondekar places sexuality at the center of the colonial archive, and argues that the possibility of challenging the archive lies in juxtaposing the archive's "fiction effects" alongside its "truth effects."¹⁴ Crafting a reading alongside the archive illuminates what it does rather than what it is.

This chapter will analyze state and refugee records in both their *form* and *content* to demonstrate how archival documents are fundamental to statecraft. I approach the archival records as a "state-ethnography" where documents and maps comprise the "stories that states tell themselves" about their colonial policies.¹⁵ In the context of excavating documents that were marked

SECRET to hide official policies and practices, such "codes of concealment" as TOP SECRET or CONFIDENTIAL are bureaucratic descriptive inventions that categorize U.S. Cold War policies.[16] Indeed, the de/classified S̶E̶C̶R̶E̶T̶ document exposes redactions as routine in processing historical information for release. I use the intervening slash in de/classification to suggest the ambiguity between the classified and declassified materials, to interrogate the work of redactions to withhold sensitive information, and to indicate that the process of declassification never really completely opens up state secrets. Furthermore, not all documents about Laos have been declassified and made accessible to the public, and not all requests for information were approved. The available documents' declassified status, marked by a secondary crossing out of S̶E̶C̶R̶E̶T̶ and redaction of the content, no longer elucidates the politically charged history of illicit warfare and instead represents the routine exchange of messages between U.S. officials in Washington, D.C., and those in the field in Southeast Asia. S̶E̶C̶R̶E̶T̶ documents mark two things: the conventions of the archive and the U.S. political strategy of neutrality. The baggage of missing things illustrates that we should read S̶E̶C̶R̶E̶T̶ documents as maps that superimpose U.S. military activities with colonizing approaches toward the decolonizing Laotian landscape and people.

As conventions of the archive, the S̶E̶C̶R̶E̶T̶ documents are a part of the problem of knowledge about Laos and about Lao and Hmong refugees, particularly because they perpetuate silences through their lack of information. As such, reading the de/classified materials necessitates an analytical practice to look for the missing things—between the texts, literally in the full spaces left behind by the redactions of text—in order to accentuate their disappearance. Oftentimes, the de/classified records show redactions of words, phrases, sentences, or entire paragraphs to conceal still-sensitive information. Returning to the redacted congressional briefing memo prepared for President Kennedy, I read it as an epistemological map to emphasize the filled spaces—blacked- or blocked-out sentences and paragraph—surrounded by text. The spaces filled with omissions offer their own story of absence. Surrounded by the text left behind, they glare back, beckoning the reader to explore what the remainder of the text might say about this void. In addition, the textual narrative can be viewed as offering a fragmented and incomplete historical account, which is precisely the work of the archive. Together, the redactions and visible texts guide an understanding of the narrative fissures found between the lines, and foreground a conceptual mapping of U.S. Cold War neutralization strategies toward Laos as intervening in its decolonization to create a geopolitically open and politically neutral space for the

Cold War superpowers to measure their ideological and military tolerance toward each other. Such a conceptual mapping in the documents articulates Laos as integral to U.S. imperialist expansion. As testimonies about the past, nonetheless, these documents survive not unscathed, but with parts erased as if the text had been covered over or scraped off. Missing texts as enactments of state secrecy are a function of the archive to normalize history. The erasures in "secret" documents reflect the state's attempts to make sense of its officials' disparate assessments of "what the problems were" in Laos that would require a congressional briefing and reevaluation of U.S. support for key Laotian political figures.[17] The edges of these erasures are markings of knowledge and power that are essential for constructing national memory.[18]

In her investigation of the "intimacies of four continents"—the obscured connections between European liberalism, settler colonialism in the Americas, the transatlantic African slave trade, and the East Indies and China trades—Lisa Lowe names and excavates records about these four continents as an "archive of liberalism" in order to observe how the archive mediates the imperatives of the state to subsume "colonial violence within narratives of modern reason and progress."[19] For Lowe, it is crucial to devise ways of reading across the separate archival repositories to show how "the forgetting of violent encounter is naturalized, both by the archive, and in the subsequent narrative histories."[20] Rather than approach the archive as a fixed site of storage, the records "actively document *and* produce the risks, problems, and uncertainties that were the conditions of imperial rule."[21] Drawing from Lowe's insights regarding the colonial archive, I read the "secret war" archive not for empirical historical information but rather to develop a critique of U.S. liberal empire's expansion in Laos during the Cold War and militarized knowledge production.

Neutralization and the Erasure of Laos in the Cold War Cartography

In a series of CIA maps produced between 1961 and 1963, Laos was emphasized to indicate the country's major role for the U.S. aims in Southeast Asia. Laos shares borders with a number of countries: North Vietnam and China to the north and east; South Vietnam and Cambodia to the east and south; Thailand to the west; and Burma in the northwest (an area commonly known as the Golden Triangle). For the countries to the west, bordering Laos meant bumping up against the dangerous possibilities of Communist insurrection. Laos's dual position as geopolitically surrounded and spatially available

THE WHITE HOUSE
WASHINGTON

~~SECRET~~   April 17, 1962

MEMORANDUM FOR

THE PRESIDENT

<u>Congressional Briefing on Laos</u>

The purpose of this briefing is:
   (a) to bring the Congressional leadership up to date on developments in Laos since their last briefing, and
   (b) to prepare them for a decision to apply a mild form of suspension of military assistance to General Phoumi.

A.   Secretary Rusk, General Lemnitzer and Averell will be able to discuss recent events in Laos from a political and military point of view. You may wish to refer to your conversation with Foreign Minister Thanat, ▓▓▓▓▓▓▓▓▓▓▓▓▓▓▓▓▓▓▓▓▓▓▓▓▓▓▓▓▓▓▓▓ and to your recent conversation with the Lao Ambassador.

~~SECRET~~   - 2 -

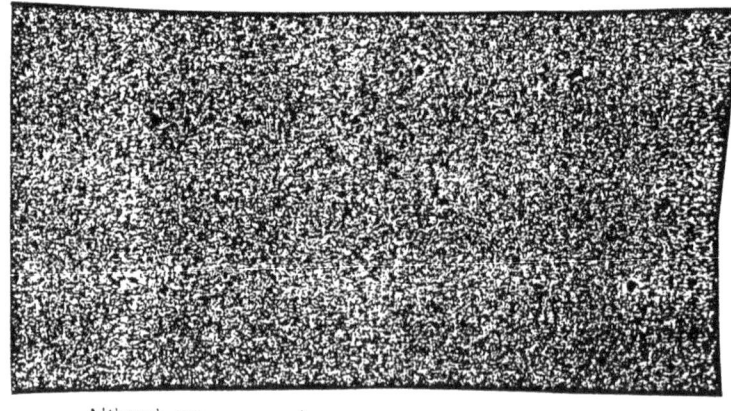

Although

FIGURE 2.1. A memorandum for President John F. Kennedy regarding a congressional briefing on Laos. The two-page memo was heavily redacted when it was made available to the public. Source: President John F. Kennedy's National Security Council Files, Vietnam Center and Archive, Texas Tech University, Lubbock.

made it instrumental for anchoring the rest of Southeast Asia and, at the same time, presented an obstacle for U.S. foreign policy. Historian Martin E. Goldstein and others have meticulously ruled out population, natural resources, and economy as reasons for U.S. interest in Laos, noting that while Laos was not a "barren land," it also did not have an abundance of crucial resources that would warrant U.S. intervention on a massive scale.[22] Indeed, the availability of Laos's timber resources and mineral deposits (including zinc, limestone, copper, lead, gold, salt, tungsten, and phosphates) indicated the presence of important natural resources that would have made it a desirable site of territorial competition or takeover by the U.S. Historians' rejection of the hypothesis that the U.S. interest in Laos was based on its resources reveals that it was not what was in the country but rather what surrounded it that made Laos significant. Laos stood out as a military site, not for its economy or natural resources, but for its territorial ambivalence—neutral yet available—as a decolonizing country.

The CIA maps reveal the U.S. government's creation, from the physical geography of Laos, of a political terrain for assessing global Cold War political struggles. As an example, figure 2.3, titled "Communist Rebel Areas" and dated March 22, 1961, exhibits two different kinds of shading in Communist-controlled northeastern Laos, bordering North Vietnam. A comparison of figures 2.2 and 2.3 shows the progression of Communism westward since December 1960, to the point that it threatened the Laotian royal capital of Luang Prabang and the state government center of Vientiane, and ultimately posed a danger to Thailand. The areas on the maps marked as Communist-controlled not only chart Communist physical and political expansion, but also the U.S. political strategy to neutralize this threat. The corridor of Communist expansion, specifically the north–south route running through Laos, underscores its very landscape as a crucial "geographic frontier" in the struggle for the "free world."[23] The paradox of Laos as a remote yet strategic location, reported in a Kennedy file document called "The Story of Laos: The Problem for a U.S. Foreign Policy," illuminates the central dilemma faced by the United States as it attempted to maintain a presence in the country—a hesitation to build a bastion in a country with inadequate "native resources" and a difficult terrain, set against a reluctance to abandon the U.S. position within the Communist expansion struggle in Southeast Asia. The idea of neutrality, born out of the U.S.'s geopolitical dilemma, would involve the search for a "solution that would keep Laos from being wholly Communist, yet not go so far as to make it a Western ally."[24]

These maps accompanied President Kennedy's press files then, and they now circulate as part of his presidential records at U.S. government repositories and other archival sites such as the Vietnam Center and Archive. They were used in the early 1960s to justify U.S. efforts to "turn Laos into a buffer," rather than using direct intervention, as a strategy to confine the "communists to the mountains of the north while a friendly government controlled the Mekong Valley borders with Thailand and Cambodia."[25] This chapter's epigraph is an excerpt from the March 23, 1961, press conference at which President Kennedy unveiled the CIA map on "Communist Rebel Areas" (see figure 2.4). Kennedy explained that although U.S. Americans considered Laos "far away," its safety was connected to that of U.S. Americans and to the security of the United States. Indeed, Kennedy's use of this series of maps during his press conference to illustrate the spread of Communism across northeastern Laos solidified for a fearful U.S. public the need to intervene in Laos to secure Southeast Asia. Yet, the U.S. interpretation of the 1954

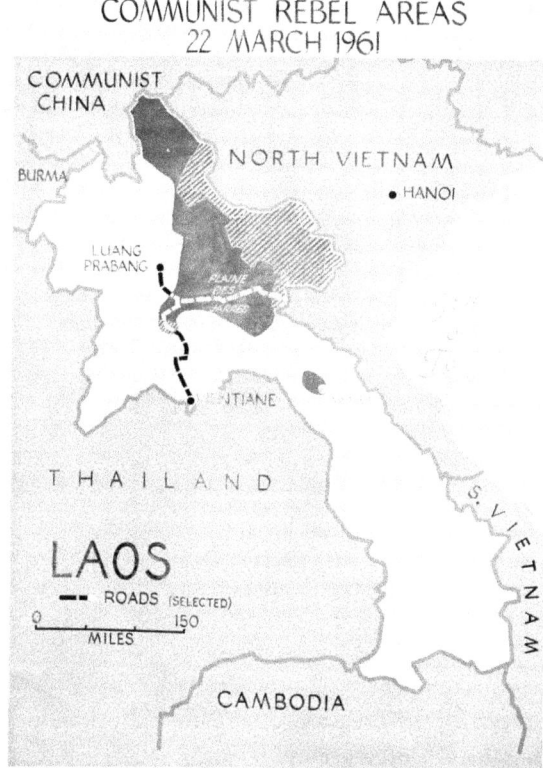

FIGURES 2.2 AND 2.3. These two maps provided by the CIA to President Kennedy showed the Communist expansion areas in December 1960 and March 1961 as evidence of Laos's strategic significance and justification for U.S. military interventions. Source: John F. Kennedy Presidential Library and Museum, Boston.

Geneva Accords' neutrality mandate involved maintaining Laos as a neutral decolonizing territory in which the Communist states and the U.S. could justify intervention but that neither side would fully claim as an ally. The paradoxical designation of Laos as a "neutral yet available" landscape, when its independence emerged at the threshold of neocolonialism, revealed how Laos was simply erased from the global Cold War cartography. Laos has been viewed as a Cold War "pawn" that was crucial yet peripheral to the superpower struggles between the U.S. and the Soviet Union.[26] The maps illustrated that U.S. policymakers were not concerned with eradicating Communism altogether or occupying Laos as a base for military operations, but rather with maintaining the country's status as dependent and in transition. Support for the U.S. neutralization strategies would come in the form of a covert approach to create a secure foothold for accessing the Southeast Asian region. In opposition to this strategy, the Pathet Lao manifesto on U.S. imperialist intervention in Laos characterized the neutral approach

FIGURE 2.4. President Kennedy held a press conference in which he discussed the importance of Laos to the U.S.; see quote in this chapter's epigraph. He presented the two maps, figures 2.2 and 2.3, comparing the increasing Communist expansion into Laos. Source: John F. Kennedy Presidential Library, Boston.

supported by covert activities as the creation of a "new-pattern colony and military base" to further the U.S. policy of military aggression in Southeast Asia.[27]

Policymakers' perceptions of Laos's distinctive landscape as geopolitically important for U.S. interests illustrated the Pathet Lao's claim that Laos had become a "new-pattern colony," though it would not be characterized as a part of what Chalmers Johnson claims as the U.S. "empire of bases," which involved setting up traditional military outposts like those in Okinawa, the Philippines, Guam, or what policymakers imagined for Vietnam to continue colonial occupation.[28] Instead, it seemed Laos would be a location for the United States to take a stand without having an explicit military presence or intent to occupy the country. State Department discussions reveal Laos's relevance through the possibility it offered for the U.S. to affect the surrounding countries. For instance, a "Memorandum of Conversation" detailing a private meeting among State Department officials and several military generals on April 29, 1961, concerning the subject of military action in Laos, clearly shows that the U.S. considered Thailand and South Vietnam the best places to "stand and fight" in Southeast Asia. At most, state officials and military generals conveyed the possibility of holding parts of Laos, mainly the Mekong

Valley area along with the capital of Vientiane, but allowing the "enemy" to have "all of the countryside" and trying to stop both the Pathet Lao and North Vietnamese with U.S. air power. General Geo. H. Decker pointed out that "we cannot win a conventional war in Southeast Asia [because] all the advantage we have in heavy equipment would be lost in the difficult terrain of Laos where we would be at the mercy of the guerrillas." Decker's reference to the "difficult terrain of Laos" highlights the landscape itself as an obstacle for U.S. expansion precisely when that geographic space served as the critical site to begin such a project.[29]

Despite the stated difficulties posed by Laos's landscape, the country was conventionally depicted to showcase how the U.S. could use it to make a stand against Communist expansion. Other maps that illustrated the intricacies of Communist presence in the form of roads and support facilities for combat air operations over Laos and North Vietnam as well as U.S. military authority in the form of airstrips known as Lima Sites, reflected the U.S. conception of Laos as a gateway to the Southeast Asian frontier. Taken together, these cartographies, in their very standardized protocols, are transferable forms of militarized knowledge that obscure stories about Laos's de/colonization.[30] In addition, as evidence for and of U.S. military actions, they give an account of U.S. imperialist intervention in the decolonizing world. This process of masking the U.S. political agenda in Laos through maps and narratives about its landscape reflects similar activities on the home front. Friedman, in his investigation of the connections between the suburban landscape and domestic imperial policymaking, finds that the "seemingly natural privacy of the suburbs lent itself" to secrecy whereby suburban culture and its built environment nurtured the strategies to "cover and deny" imperial relationships.[31] Drawing a parallel with Friedman's analysis of the secrecy that was built into the suburban landscape, I suggest that the Laotian geopolitical cartographies offer a different kind of evidentiary narrative—Laos's unique spatial positioning that is integral to the future of the region. In addition to the "secret" memos and reports' reflection of statecraft, U.S. Cold War maps underscore the power of cartography in nation-building and military operations. Maps are "ideologically loaded" as tools of power to define and control territory from a distance.[32] Like the documents, the maps symbolize "governmental processes of regimentation" where "places, individual homes and complex lives are rendered as mere dots."[33] The maps and texts point to how Laos is missing in the "imperial archive"—official U.S. Cold War government documents—as a site of U.S. imperialism.[34]

This emphasis on Laos's uniquely difficult landscape also nurtured the United States' determination that Laos was not yet a nation-state. Such a move was consistent with U.S. Cold War policy in other areas of the world, and followed the U.S. liberal empire's long-standing precedent of determining which peoples were sufficiently "civilized" to merit intervention into their "freedom" (e.g., assumptions made about Filipinos and Cubans in the Spanish-American War). In a letter on the seriousness of the Laotian situation to Deputy Assistant to the President for National Security Affairs Walt W. Rostow, MIT political science professor Lucian Pye described U.S. problems in subduing Laos in terms of policymakers' failure to recognize that it was "not a nation-state," explaining that Kennedy and his advisers mistakenly applied to Laos policies appropriate in "relations among nation-states." Consequently, Pye stressed that they had at best been made to look foolish and at worst may have permitted a "domestic Laotian controversy to become a genuine international crisis." This logic undermined Laotian sovereignty to rationalize increased covert military aggression in the name of building national unity. Because Laos was not really a state or a nation, Pye explained, Kennedy and others had erred in expecting it "to do things which only a viable, integrated system can do." The failure of previous U.S. aid efforts was evidence that a neutralization policy could not be achieved. The "real problem of Laos," Pye declared, was not U.S. intervention but rather the difficulty it was experiencing in forming a "viable political system." He suggested that this problem required more effort and assistance from the United States to "concentrate on the fundamentals of nation building," in order to develop Laos within the "Western tradition of the nation-state system."[35]

Pye's description of Laos as lacking the fundamentals of a nation-state system rests on the imperialist genealogy of terra nullius to establish territories as empty land that required occupation. The idea of Laos as an empty space utilized U.S. colonial concepts of the "unincorporated" territory, a term from the Insular Cases in early twentieth-century opinions of the U.S. Supreme Court that defined the colonial territories of the United States. The concept of "unincorporated" territory facilitated the ongoing U.S. colonial domination of Puerto Rico as a commonwealth after the U.S. invasion in 1898. As the concept was applied to Cold War Southeast Asia, Laos was not a nation-state because it occupied an ambiguous historical position between an underdeveloped French colony and an unprotected territory where the Cold War superpowers vied for political influence. Pye and other modernization theorists, by asserting that Laos lacked the nation-state tradition, suggested the need to develop Laos and its people. This produced the material consequences of U.S. diplomatic maneuvers among the Laotian elite, covert military operations, and aid projects that undermined the decolonizing nation's sovereignty and instituted militarized, colonial violence.

Furthermore, Laos was perceived as lacking a traditional nation-state system because it purportedly could not govern its people—including the various ethnic and Indigenous groups that were understood to be available for colonial domination and rescue. At the same time as the efforts by modernization theorists like Rostow and Pye to guide the White House toward undermining Laos's sovereignty, historian K. T. Young sent a report to President Kennedy entitled "A New Look at Laos" that presented a "radically" new approach to Laos.[36] While dated a month prior to Pye's letter to Rostow, Young's report aligned with the political science professor's assessment of Laos's nation-state problem. Young pinpointed the absence of a nation-state political framework in Laos as an internal problem of social organization and political governance. He offered an eight-point program to change the situation, which would involve the implementation of a Village Promotion Program to promote national unity. The report's compelling assessment of the crux of the Lao problem found that the issue was neither military nor diplomatic but rather a matter of "internal social and political re-assembly [requiring] some putty around the 'plate glass' and some fasteners in this 'foam-rubber frontier.'"[37] Young's description of Laos as a "foam-rubber frontier" echoed Kennedy's "New Frontier" of world power and industrial development in Southeast Asia. Tracing the historical development of a *national* myth, historian Richard Slotkin articulates the "New Frontier" as a symbol to "summon the nation as a whole to undertake a heroic engagement in the 'long twilight struggle' against Communism" along with social and economic injustices.[38] In turn, the Kennedy administration projected this vision onto Laos and imagined its unincorporated peoples as instrumental to this "New Frontier." Projections of the "New Frontier" enfolded Laos and the rest of Southeast Asia into the genealogy of imperialist cartography. Yet, integral to the specific character of Laos as a "foam-rubber frontier" was what the U.S. imagined as two related issues: the divisions among the Lao leadership and the lack of nationalism among Laos's numerous Indigenous and ethnic groups.

The U.S. policy of neutrality toward Laos, by which the imperial power sought to influence the decolonizing nation's development toward a Western tradition yet not fully invest in its development, located the Laotian crisis within a larger Cold War framework as a site to test Soviet reactions to U.S. maneuvers.[39] Historian Kenneth L. Hill explains that Laos was a test case "to determine whether the cold war protagonists could accept solutions that were less than completely satisfactory in relation to areas or problems where they had only marginal interests" in order to avoid superpower confrontations.[40] This strategy, according to Pye, examined "hypotheses about Soviet behavior," including the assumption by President Kennedy and his advisers that the Russian leaders' rapport with the Pathet Lao would influence control over Pathet Lao strategy and military actions.[41] Laos's independence as a small and "militarily dwarfed" nation provided the rationale for its use as a U.S. "laboratory," not necessarily for controlling Communism, but for thwarting the socialist superpower. By extension, CIA historian Thomas Ahern explains that the U.S. neutrality stance "preserves a Laotian buffer state" while avoiding the "intention to challenge Beijing's territorial integrity."[42]

Yet, while Kennedy's advisors asserted Laos's importance as part of a broader Cold War strategy to test Soviet influence but not challenge Chinese geopolitics (since doing so would produce an even greater geopolitical dilemma for the U.S.), policymakers and military leaders still had to deal with the immediate and imminent threat of Communism in Southeast Asia. They viewed a key problem in the Laos situation as "North Vietnam's failure to withdraw any significant forces from Laos, while U.S.-supported military programs there sought to resist Hanoi's encroachments."[43] More specifically, these policymakers and military leaders questioned whether South Vietnam and Thailand could be held if Laos were lost. In the same April 29, 1961, "Memorandum of Conversation" mentioned earlier, Deputy Assistant Secretary John Steeves is recorded as reminding those present that the U.S. had declared it would not give up Laos because "if this problem is unsolvable then the problem of Viet-Nam would be unsolvable." He further implored the other participants that "if we decided that this was untenable then we were writing the first chapter in the defeat of Southeast Asia." Admiral Arleigh Burke emphasized that each time ground is given up it is harder to stand the next time: "If we give up Laos, we would have to put U.S. forces into Viet-Nam and Thailand. We would have to throw enough in to win. . . . [We should] make clear that we were not going to be pushed out of Southeast Asia. We were fighting for the rest of Asia." If the larger goal was to gain access to or create successful foreign policies in Asia, then it was symbolically important to take a stand in Laos. The small country figured as a launching pad for U.S. imperialist expansion since the U.S. was unwilling to put forth the "greater effort" required to hold the bordering countries without Laos as the critical anchor and buffer. Specifically, Thailand would have to be defended from the "other bank"—the Thai side—of the Mekong River rather than from the Laotian side.[44] Yet, the U.S. could not fully invest in a military campaign to launch a conventional war in Laos. The U.S. neutral policy to take a stand in Laos without being there was intended to keep the country marginal in the Cold War struggle, which was consistent with the U.S. aim of moving into Southeast Asia without bringing Laos to center stage in the region—and, by extension, in all of Asia.

Despite Kennedy's stated commitment to maintaining a neutral Laos, he concluded that the Laos problem "was not susceptible to a military solution."[45] Historian Seth Jacobs noted Kennedy's challenges with the Forces armées du royaume (FAR) or Royal Lao Armed Forces (RLA), for which the United States paid 100 percent of the military budget: "RLA troops showed little stomach for combat, regularly retreating in the face of Pathet Lao thrusts," compounding the "logistical challenges posed by a mountainous land lacking sea access, railroads, airstrips, and all-weather roads."[46] By mid-1962, Kennedy remarked to his advisers that the U.S. would fight in Vietnam if it had to fight for Southeast Asia.[47] Thus, the U.S. commitment to increase troops in Vietnam was inextricably linked to the inability to figure out a clear military or diplomatic solution for Laos. Yet, the U.S. maintained its policy of neutralization to "preserve a noncommunist Laos while leaving the ground combat to indigenous forces" even as it publicly shifted its focus to Vietnam.[48] Continued U.S. involvement in Laos included covert political, military, and economic activities to foster nationalism among the Indigenous and ethnic minority peoples. Laos's ambiguous geopolitical position, perceived as a problem in and of itself due to the convergence of the Cold War and Vietnam War policies and military practices, presented a dilemma for U.S. militarized Cold War knowledge, the archive, and "secret" war-making.

By the time of this debate about maintaining a presence in Laos without committing military forces, the CIA had established "guerrilla bases" that covered most exits from the Plain of Jars and had trained a small Hmong force as "the main barrier to communist encroachment from the northeast."[49] The U.S. reluctance to operate a conventional war led military strategists to envision an operation with "no Americans on the ground" and the CIA playing a "purely supportive role."[50] The U.S. Cold War perception about Laos's *not yet* nation-state status and the United States' neutrality policy that aimed to "save" Laos from domination by the Pathet Lao, Hanoi's supposed surrogate, allowed the U.S. to simultaneously contend with the Soviet Union–armed paramilitary units among Laos's *not yet* peoples. Hmong recruits were employed as U.S. "surrogates" to defend their territory in the mountains of northeastern Laos and to divert substantial North Vietnamese forces from

South Vietnam.[51] By the late 1960s, historians realized that Laos was an unfortunate test case in Cold War diplomacy.[52] The U.S. policymakers and CIA paper trails on neutrality, rather than hiding secrets, are actually where state secrets were inscribed, and then erased.

Hmong as Colonial Baggage: Solution and Threat to
U.S. Cold War Policy

While Laos was erased from the Cold War cartography as not yet a nation-state, Hmong appeared in the U.S.-generated militarized cartography that simultaneously explained and normalized the need for arming Hmong in defense of that very territory. Yet, the explanations themselves showcased a tension between the possibility of a Hmong defense force to affirm Laotian national unity *and* the very threat that arming Hmong could pose for nation-building. The tensions arose from colonial tropes that depicted Hmong as "close to the land" and able to traverse its physical terrain but also as irrational subjects lacking a national sensibility. So, while Laos is missing in the imperial archive, Hmong refugees are missing as the colonial baggage of a militarized U.S. liberal empire that instituted neocolonialism toward Laos and militarized colonialism toward Hmong, as well as Laotian anticolonial nation-building that sought to subsume Hmong as national subjects.

Consistent with the militarized knowledge produced about Laos as an empty space, the CIA-generated military cartography consolidated the image of Hmong as a natural part of the landscape. The two maps reproduced below from Ahern's CIA history of the U.S. "secret war" (figures 2.5 and 2.6) exemplify the way in which Laos's ethnic groups were mapped as integral to the terrain, supporting the idea that they could serve as a natural buffering force against the Communist threat. The maps present a "patchwork" of territories, a term used to describe the country's various minority groups, which plot the people onto the land. A CIA map (figure 2.5) showing population distribution illustrates this spatial imagining of peoples from Laos onto the terrain in which ethnic Lao occupy the land along the Mekong River bordering Thailand to the royal capital of Luang Prabang, considered "the best land." The groups "dispossessed" of political rights inhabit the "higher, and poorer, land." This latter category of peoples, therefore, exist as "hill tribes"—a natural feature of the landscape.[53] Indeed, this military categorization of people was consistent with how ethnohistorical knowledge organized the social and political hierarchy of Laos and its peoples around its topographical

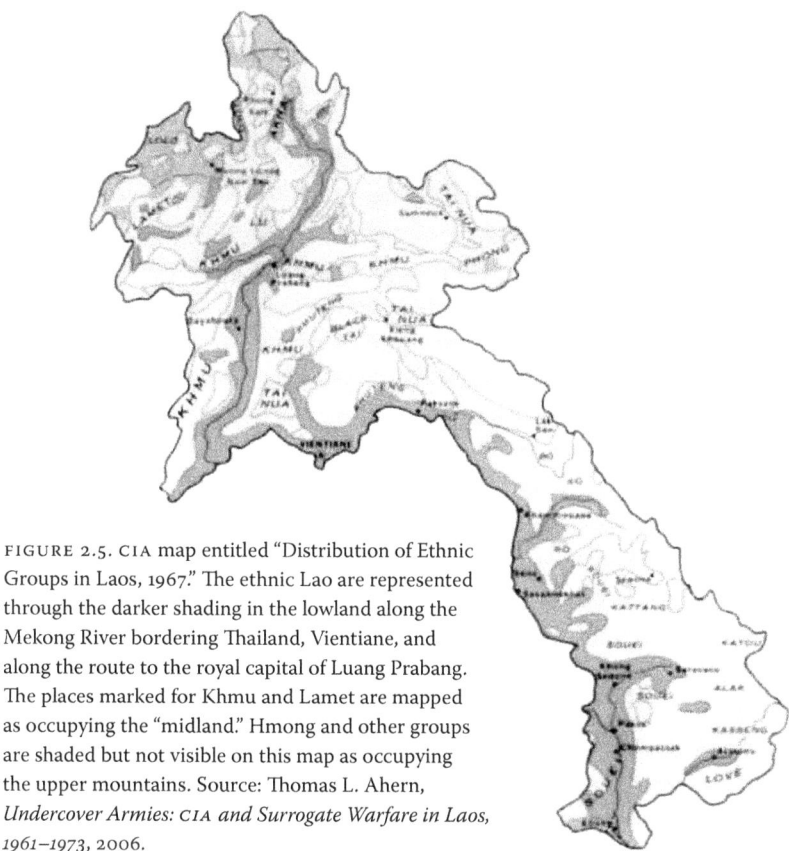

FIGURE 2.5. CIA map entitled "Distribution of Ethnic Groups in Laos, 1967." The ethnic Lao are represented through the darker shading in the lowland along the Mekong River bordering Thailand, Vientiane, and along the route to the royal capital of Luang Prabang. The places marked for Khmu and Lamet are mapped as occupying the "midland." Hmong and other groups are shaded but not visible on this map as occupying the upper mountains. Source: Thomas L. Ahern, *Undercover Armies: CIA and Surrogate Warfare in Laos, 1961–1973*, 2006.

elevations—lowland ethnic Lao, highland minorities, and mountaintop "hill tribe" groups. Parceled into different military regions, Laos's various ethnic and Indigenous groups were predisposed as a strategic defense force for that region's topography. Although Hmong lived in different parts of northern Laos, from Nong Het near North Vietnam to Sayaboury bordering Thailand, their concentration in Xieng Khouang Province, around the Plain of Jars, made them ideal for combat in that difficult terrain. Hence, the military cartography of Xieng Khouang and the Plain of Jars, which comprise the RLA's Military Region II (MR II), explained the arming of Hmong to defend their homes, families, and livelihoods against Communist threats. U.S. unaccountability was built into Hmong soldiers' participation in the military program as a "resistance movement." The U.S. calculations of whether to stand and fight in Laos were very much tied to the way that the U.S. imagined the Laotian political and geographical landscape, onto which Hmong and other ethnic groups were mapped.

The map of "Distribution of Ethnic Groups" across Laos aligned with the views of modernization theorists like Pye, Rostow, and Young (all of whom served as Kennedy administration policymakers and advisors) that Laos was a questionable sovereign state with little governance over its various minority groups. According to the map, Laos's *not yet* nation-state status was a product of more than just its difficult terrain and weak nationalist/anti-Communist leaders, but was inextricably linked to Laos's inability to govern the peoples who lived far from the central government of Vientiane.[54] A report on the "Chronology of Events in Laos" from the Kennedy Files noted that

> a gulf has always existed between the central government in Vientiane and the people in the countryside, and those who have governed Laos have never established effective authority or won the respect of all the various peoples who make up the Lao nation. *The non-Communist political factions have never achieved unity or cohesion and have tended to view one another with as much suspicion as they do the Communist left.* As a result, no strong, effective non-Communist leadership has emerged since Laos achieved independence. The Communist Pathet Lao, supported by North Viet-Nam, Communist China, and the U.S.S.R., have taken advantage of these fundamental weaknesses in the political and social fabric of Laos bringing the country into a state of chaos and near civil war.[55]

The charge that Laos "never achieved [political] unity or cohesion" justified U.S. efforts to build coercive diplomatic and covert military campaigns with the goal of undermining the North Vietnamese Communist regime. The concerted U.S. Cold War cartography and policymaking already envisioned Hmong as a people who were displaced from a central Lao governance structure and scattered across the Laotian territory. Since the decolonizing government of Laos had not been able to assert authority over the peoples living within its territorial boundaries, the above excerpt suggests, those very groups were susceptible to Communist influence just as much as they could be coerced into the Lao neutralist regime and U.S. Cold War policies. Even if they could be recruited to join a U.S./CIA "secret army" to undermine the Communist regime, that goal could be thwarted by the peoples themselves. Hmong were considered colonial baggage for Laos and the U.S.; this was both a problem and an asset because Hmong could be the natural defenders of Laos, yet they were not Lao national subjects who could have a national sensibility, and, therefore, were ungovernable.

Since Hmong presented a colonial burden as a malleable people that could potentially be attached to any of the political ideologies and parties involved in Laos, the Hmong problem was chief among the list of items that the U.S. wished to discuss with Prince Souvanna Phouma during the anticolonial and neutralist prime minister's visit to the U.S. in July 1962, soon after the July 23 signing of the 1962 Geneva Accords. For instance, Souphanouvong considered Hmong to be armed bandits while the right wing viewed them as a "minority tribe" that needed help. Hmong loyalty to Souvanna and the king was also an important asset to the new neutral government.[56] In this context, Hmong were considered a necessary colonial asset that could be rescued and managed as soldiers to bolster the developing postcolonial nation-state and to strengthen U.S. neutrality policies. The logic of saving a people through military recruitment also buttressed the U.S. Cold War policy of nation-building. The U.S. policy toward Laos was in this sense an anomaly compared to its broader Cold War agenda of supporting dictatorial governments, because the imperialist state sought to build a strong Hmong force that would be loyal to the Lao government but a dependent ally of the United States. For example, a State Department Memorandum of Conversation regarding the meeting with Souvanna reveals that he suggested bolstering his government by bringing Hmong to the lowlands for compulsory military service where they could be educated and introduced to "modern urban life." In his view, exposure to life in the fertile lowlands and proximity to the central government could foster a sense of national belonging. U.S. policymakers, however, urged him to keep Hmong in the highlands and to publicly support Hmong efforts to fight Communism because the CIA had already trained and armed a Hmong RLA commander, Vang Pao, and his recruits.[57]

Keeping Hmong in the highlands made sense from a military standpoint because they lived in the provinces bordering North Vietnam, which were prime locales for encounters with North Vietnamese and Pathet Lao soldiers in ground combat. Juxtaposing a map of the ethnic groups (figure 2.5) with another CIA map of the Ground War, 1961–75, which depicts MR II (figure 2.6), makes clear that the heavy fighting on the ground occurred in areas of Xieng Khouang Province with a concentrated Hmong population.

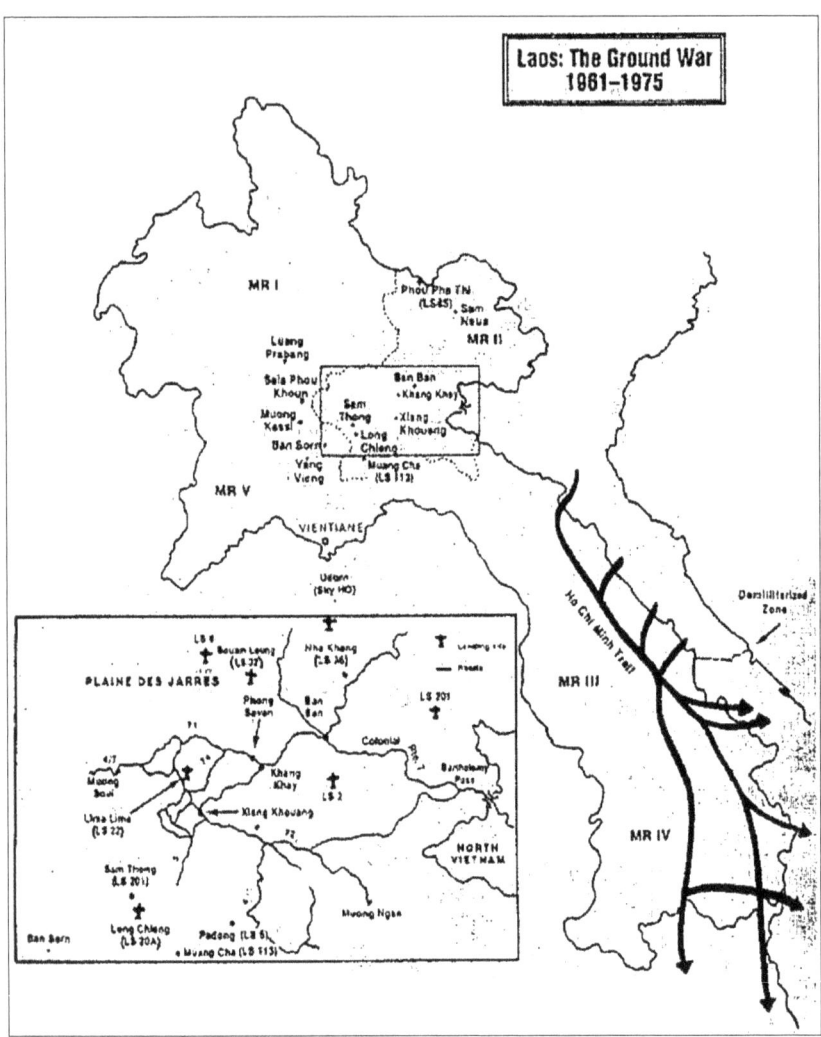

FIGURE 2.6. A CIA image of Laos illustrating the different military regions (MRs) with an enlargement of MR II where the ground war involving the "secret army" under General Vang Pao's command operated. Several important landmarks for the ground war and key features in Hmong refugee stories are indicated in the enlargement, including Long Cheng (the "secret" military base), Sam Thong, Pa Dong, and the Plain of Jars. Source: Thomas L. Ahern, *Undercover Armies: CIA and Surrogate Warfare in Laos, 1961–1973*, 2006.

The enlargement shown in figure 2.6 outlines the area where Hmong forces operated through the geographic markers of Pa Dong, Long Cheng, and Sam Thong. Pa Dong was the site of the first meeting between Vang Pao, CIA paramilitary agent Stu Methven, and case officer Bill Lair, who was the chief architect of the "secret army," as well as responsible for training the first three hundred Hmong volunteers in January 1961.[58] Long Cheng served as the "secret" military base for General Vang Pao and his Hmong army while Sam Thong functioned as a humanitarian base for refugees and wounded soldiers. While reporters could visit Sam Thong to document the U.S. humanitarian aid provided by USAID to those internally displaced by or wounded in the fighting, the media did not have access to Long Cheng and its military operations.

Crucial to Laos's geopolitical position as a buffer for the U.S. to "prevent the communists from penetrating Southeast Asia" was its colonial infrastructure and minority groups that would fortify the country's ability to inhibit or concede to Communist assault.[59] Within MR II, the famous Plain of Jars plateau in Xieng Khouang Province was a strategic location offering a tactical advantage in military operations. Although not shown in the CIA map, two roads constructed during the period of French colonization (Routes 6 and 7) lead directly from North Vietnam to the Plain of Jars. These two roads were important for Communist infiltration into Laos as well as for operations by U.S.-backed forces and the CIA seeking to intercept Communist soldiers and supplies. Hmong who called MR II home and whose villages and farms (their main source of livelihood) were located near these two routes between Xieng Khouang Province (including the city of Xieng Khouang) and Houaphan Province (including the city of Sam Neua) presented the best option for the CIA, which sought to rally Hmong to defend their homeland in the service of the U.S. policies of containment and nation-building. In fact, most Hmong soldiers were trained and fought battles along these routes.

As an example, the Hmong village of Pa Dong, where the CIA trained the first three hundred Hmong volunteers, was located about eight miles south of the Plain of Jars.[60] In *Undercover Armies*, Ahern paints Pa Dong as a part of the natural landscape to illustrate how it exemplifies the captivation and "eerie attraction" of Laos's geography for U.S. personnel and policymakers: "Ban Pa Dong, 4,500 feet above sea level, epitomized the eerie attraction that Laos—especially upcountry Laos—held for nearly all the Americans who worked there. With neighboring peaks hidden behind towers of cumulus clouds, the village stood in crystalline air on a ridgeline that sloped, first gradually and then precipitously, until it disappeared in the stratus clouds that concealed the valley below. The dying swish of the helicopter's main rotor only emphasized the stillness of a perfectly calm day."[61] This portrayal of a Hmong village high in the mountains and disappearing into the clouds conveyed the U.S. imagination with operating a counterinsurgency program to thwart the Communist regime right "under the enemy's nose."[62] The romanticized depiction of Laos's difficult yet picturesque terrain suggests that the CIA's ability to successfully maneuver and use the landscape for a covert war would mean the U.S. could conquer this "new frontier" to emerge as a Cold War superpower. Indeed, the recruitment of Hmong as soldiers in northeastern Laos exposed the overlap of U.S. Cold War cartography of the CIA's ground war onto French colonial cartography.[63] Laos was a means to an end, to stop Communist takeover and maintain U.S. military bases in South Vietnam and Thailand.

In addition to overlapping with the French colonial development of Laos, the U.S. Cold War cartography deployed as an asset colonial tropes about Hmong closeness to nature and the idea of a people inextricably connected to the very landscape they called home. According to Ahern, after Lair received approval from Ambassador Winthrop G. Brown and Washington for his proposal to train and arm at least three hundred Hmong volunteers, he needed to transport Vang Pao and a U.S. operative (whose name has been redacted from the record) to the village of Pa Dong because they were being slowed by the bulky WWII-vintage radio and generator they were carrying. Lair decided to copilot a helicopter with Air America pilot Clarence "Chuck" Abadie to carry Vang Pao and the unnamed individual along with a few of the "_____ [redacted] communicators" to Pa Dong. The helicopter would be forced to make two trips because it was impossible to climb to the elevation of Pa Dong with all the passengers on board. Abadie, Lair, and the unnamed individual took off on the first trip without Vang Pao and the "communicators," but even with the reduced load the helicopter was unable to clear the last ridgeline on the way to the village. Ahern recounted that the helicopter brushed the treetops, stalled, "drop[ped] onto the reverse slope," and "careened down the hill" while still upright.[64] Miraculously, Lair and the unnamed U.S. American escaped unscathed, dragging an unconscious Abadie from the wreckage that was on the verge of exploding. Even more fortunate for the three U.S. Americans, and consistent with their perceptions of the landscape, was the Hmong man who came to their aid. Ahern writes: "Serendipity appeared in the person of a Hmong tribesman, who jogged up the slope in the tireless gait of mountain people, running on the leathery feet and splayed toes of a man who had never worn shoes."⁶⁵ This description of a Hmong man coming to the rescue of Lair and his pilot in a "tireless gait" with "leathery feet and splayed toes" likens Hmong to the natural landscape as a "mountain people." Hmong physical features are figured as extensions of the landscape.

U.S. experiences with the landscape and encounters with Hmong left a lasting impression on how the U.S. Cold War policy could remain neutral by building a "secret army" of local people to protect their homes and villages as a way to contain the Communist threat from North Vietnam. In other words, the U.S. geopolitical dilemma regarding Laos and its roles in Southeast Asia could be addressed by recruiting Hmong as a clandestine force. Once the U.S. committed air power to South Vietnam in 1964 and ground troops in 1965, Hmong became even more important as a military asset against the Pathet Lao and Viet Minh. In comparison to the Viet Cong who were depicted as highly mobile and able to "bedevil Saigon's road-bound heavy infantry," Ahern described Hmong soldiers as "irregulars [who] flitted over mountain trails or moved by air to occupy key high ground and to harass Hanoi's tanks and artillery." The tactical advantage in Laos purportedly followed the monsoon; the North Vietnamese Army advanced during the dry season, usually early November to late May, and gave ground to Hmong operations when the rains washed out the "primitive road system."⁶⁶ These depictions presented Hmong as capable of controlling the primitivized landscape, strategically positioned as a clandestine force to divert Communist expansion.

While the CIA and U.S. policymakers saw Hmong tactical advantage as an extension of their inherent connection to the landscape, Hmong viewed their advantage as a knowledge of the land and their commitment to protect that land as home and a source of livelihood. Protecting their homeland was a political agenda, as scholars and Hmong leaders have noted, born out of a Hmong desire for sovereignty in the forms of nationhood and territory. Historian Mai Na Lee has argued that the Hmong political agenda since the French colonial period aimed for territorial sovereignty: a Hmong kingdom. The quest for a Hmong state, according to Lee, influenced how different Hmong leaders sought legitimation from various state and colonial powers to negotiate the terms of Hmong sovereignty.⁶⁷ Hmong leaders, therefore, saw the decolonization of Laos as an opportunity to seek some form of sovereignty—an effort which, Lee notes, has shifted toward settling for autonomy.⁶⁸ The historical political differences among Hmong leaders consolidated during the "secret war" period in two polarizing figures: Vang

Pao, a military general who led the Hmong alliance with the right-wing anticolonial Lao nationalists and the United States, and Lo Faydang, a leftist leader who led a Communist Hmong faction in alliance with the Pathet Lao and North Vietnam.

Yet, the political alignments between Hmong leaders like General Vang Pao and Lo Faydang and Lao anticolonial nationalists like Phouma and Souphanouvong during the U.S. war years were not always smooth when understood within the longer anticolonial struggles of people like Hmong against state and imperial power. In the post-WWII years, as Laos struggled to gain independence and establish state sovereignty, its various Indigenous and ethnic groups challenged the governance of the emerging independent state as well as the vestiges of French colonial rule. Efforts by Hmong, Kha, and Brao to establish autonomy within Laos collided at the muddy intersection of decolonization movements and Cold War geopolitics. The various decolonizing states of Southeast Asia, especially Laos and Vietnam, played on these ongoing anticolonial movements by dangling the possibility of autonomy to the Indigenous and ethnic groups within their territories in order to fold these groups' political agendas into the governments' decolonization efforts. As such, these groups played significant political roles in the Communist strategy of a "people's war." Historian Geoffrey Gunn explains that even the Viet Minh pursued alliances with minorities by introducing a minorities policy proposing "cultural autonomy in principle" and stipulating "equality between peoples of Vietnamese, representation in the National Assembly, [and] respect for minority languages and scripts."[69] Without the support of the Kha and certain Hmong leaders, Gunn suggests, the Communist Pathet Lao would not have been able to claim a popular base because Prince Souphanouvong, the leftist, anticolonial Lao nationalist supported by Hanoi, attracted few Lao to his movement before 1954.[70] Pathet Lao influence among the Kha and Hmong shaped the military conduct of the conflict and determined organizational strategy in hill bases and liberated zones.[71]

On the U.S. Cold War policy front, Hmong contact with U.S. personnel as a potential force emerged through their role in the French colonial regime. Vang Pao was on the U.S. radar well before CIA paramilitary agent Methven and case officer Lair met with him on January 10, 1961, to begin exploring "the Hmong tribe's potential for irregular warfare" as a right-wing resistance force against the neutralist Kong Le and Communist Pathet Lao.[72] The CIA had contacted Vang in 1955, when he was a major commander of the RLA in Xieng Khouang Province, and the highest-ranking Hmong in the army. He had fought with the French against the Japanese occupation of Laos during

WWII at the age of thirteen, and later with the French Expeditionary Force against the Viet Minh in 1953 and 1954. Vang Pao's military and cultural credentials made him an important asset for a covert military operation that would enable access to Hmong forces but also ensure that they did not revolt against the Lao government. His rapport with the Hmong population made him, as the CIA described, the ideal "man we've been looking for."[73] As Ahern recounts it in *Undercover Armies*, Lair's first question to Vang Pao at the January 10, 1961, meeting was, "With the communists and neutralists installed on the Plain of Jars, what exactly did the Hmong people want to do?" Vang Pao responded that Hmong had two alternatives, either flee to the west or stay and fight, and he indicated that "he and his people wanted to stay."[74] In the context of the immediate danger of conflict between the Communist regime and the U.S. imperialist regime that had already brought violence, disruptions to livelihood, and destruction of vegetation and farms, the choice to stay and fight seemed less like a choice than colonial coercion. Two weeks after Lair's first meeting with Vang Pao, the U.S. armed "the first 300 Hmong volunteers" in Padong in January 1961 with "three C-46 cargo planes cross[ing] the Mekong into Laos carrying weapons and equipment."[75]

The recruitment and equipping of Hmong soldiers under the command of Vang Pao was a part of the U.S. "hill tribe" program, which was followed by similar efforts in Vietnam, when the CIA observed that North Vietnamese were moving supplies south through the Laotian panhandle.[76] Members of the Kha, who lived in the Bolovens Plateau in the southernmost part of the panhandle, were also incorporated into the program. The U.S. State Department meeting with Souvanna in July 1962 revealed the two governments' similar colonial agendas to incorporate Hmong into the nation through military service—civilizing through soldiering. Yet, the U.S. focus on Laos's ungovernable peoples as a problem reveals that its Cold War policy to build a U.S.-leaning democratic postcolonial Laos state meant keeping them as wards of the "new" state *and* as U.S. colonial subjects.

Yet, even Ahern notes Vang Pao's wariness of this "unofficial" alliance with the U.S. because it might repeat the Hmong colonial experience with France. He linked French and U.S. military projects in Laos by confronting Methven about the possibility that the U.S. Americans would eventually abandon their Hmong allies as the French had done in 1954, asking: "Would the United States stay the course, if it began helping the Hmong, or did he risk having aid cut off and his people left to the mercy of the North Vietnamese?" To this, Methven vaguely assured him that "any American commitment would be honored as long as it was needed."[77] This ominous beginning foreshadowed

U.S. abandonment of Hmong after its defeat in Vietnam in 1975, when an "American commitment" was no longer "needed."

These questions from Vang Pao, and the fact that the CIA/U.S. was supporting a people it considered not-yet-modern, revealed an uneasy alliance. While Hmong may have been adept at guerrilla fighting with their abilities to navigate the terrain, "an American presence in Hmong country" was required to enforce effective training and advising.[78] Indeed, U.S. Major General Richard Secord benevolently characterized Hmong as "Iron Age Guerrillas"—the "Little Guys" or "Meo irregulars"—who possessed innate fighting skills but lacked the discipline that would afford them status as a conventional force.[79] Recounting the initial training of Hmong volunteers at Pa Dong, Ahern described them as "Iron Age tribesmen" who were the "best natural riflemen that Lair _____ [redacted] had ever seen" because they knew how to clean and maintain their rifles and carbines within minutes.[80] Ahern believed that their ability to learn quickly made Hmong "natural" fighters because they only needed a few hours at the improvised firing range before moving on to combat organization and tactics.[81] However, Hmong skills with firearms were mitigated by their lack of "fire discipline," with the result that they exhausted their ammunition supply in their first encounter with advancing Pathet Lao forces two weeks after the first weapons were dropped.[82] While arming Hmong was intended to be a temporary "surrogate for a surrogate" to prevent "the enemy" from consolidating its control while the United States and the Royal Lao Government developed the Royal Lao Army into a regular fighting force,[83] the primitive, clandestine army would be the backbone of the Cold War armed conflict in Laos as well as the CIA's largest covert operation.

On Refugees and the Record

This chapter has excavated the *missing things* in U.S./CIA "secret" but redacted documents to examine how state secrecy as a convention of the United States' militarized liberal empire's paper regime structured Cold War neutralization policies toward Laos. I conclude my analysis of paper trails by turning to look at their production and meaning for the refugees displaced from this conflict, who were already missing in the imperial archive. In analyzing refugee records, I show that if the classified document that served as a mechanism of statecraft was hardly a secret, then the resettlement application constituted a mundane apparatus that benignly listed Hmong applicants' previous militarized occupations. It is my hope that the epistemological dilemma of the imperial record—missing things—and my reformulation of this dilemma into a methodological approach can be applicable to an analysis of the refugee record.

The 1973 Paris Peace Accords and the North Vietnamese victory in 1975 marked the official end to the fifteen-year "secret war" in Laos. The U.S. could no longer provide material support to anti-Communist Hmong forces. As Communists marched toward Long Cheng, General Vang Pao's "secret" military base, the few CIA advisors who had not yet left the region conspired to force the general to leave the base, and to effectively abandon the army he had amassed over the years. While the general was airlifted to Thailand, hundreds of thousands of Hmong—soldiers who abandoned their posts to find their families; students, farmers, and fractured families who had lost too many members to the war—escaped on foot toward the Thai border if they could or sought refuge in the jungle.[84] While this official end to the Vietnam War and the "secret war" inaugurated the largest exodus of refugees outside of Europe, these refugees' complex histories as U.S. soldier-subjects were subsumed by their status as subjects in need of humanitarian rescue. For Hmong refugees, in particular, their roles in an illicit war and the classified status of U.S. state and CIA records pertaining to the conflict marked them as illegible to be considered as U.S. allies who could qualify for resettlement through the State Department's refugee task force.

The increasing number of Hmong refugees who appeared on the Thai side of the Mekong River posed an unexpected problem for the personnel of the State Department's refugee task force, who had only been charged with processing Vietnamese refugees. Former State Department personnel Lionel Rosenblatt has publicly stated that he directed the refugee task force toward Hmong refugees arriving in Thailand, a group that was unknown to the task force, to fill the remaining eleven thousand spots that had been targeted toward Vietnamese refugees.[85] The unexpected demand for processing of Hmong refugees, I suggest, had the unintended effect of exposing Hmong soldiering and U.S. covert war. To be sure, the seemingly benign process of resettlement for the initial eleven thousand Hmong refugees and those who came after constituted state management of the refugee into a proper immigrant subject. Inquiries such as "What was your occupation?" comprised procedural refugee processing. Yet, Hmong refugees' long responses show up in the written record merely as lists of occupations such as military, soldier, student, farmer, and embroiderer. Like the missing baggage's simultaneous embodiment of the mundane and excessive, these occupational categories make up the un/familiar things that are out of place and time within a standard application. This documentation of Hmong refugees' professional backgrounds was based on volunteer resettlement agents' imagination of Hmong as potential immigrants who would contribute to, rather than burden, the U.S. But Hmong training and skills in the context of U.S. militarism represented an encumbrance not so much because these occupations were seen as obsolete in the U.S. but because they served as reminders of the nation-state's production of violence and displacement.

The refugee records I examined are resettlement case files held at the University of Minnesota's Immigration History and Research Center. The archive's restrictions against duplication of the refugee resettlement collection, however, demanded a different approach to sifting through Hmong refugees' case files. Because I could not record any identifying information about the applicants, I documented their occupations and skills, work histories, and education. The inventory I compiled became an unofficial list of military enrollments that serves as evidence of America's "secret army." The word "soldier" appears most frequently on this list, often paired with "student" and "farmer." Each new line in the list shown below (chart 2.1) represents a different family and their application, which recorded either the occupation of the head of the household or the occupations of both the husband and wife. Seeing "military" and "soldier" written into the record about Hmong refugees strangely neutralizes U.S. militarism as a benign part of Hmong life in Laos; yet it symbolizes a haunting in the archive's structure.

This list projects a mishmash of occupations ranging from the militarily skilled professions of military intelligence and medic/pharmacist to agriculturally skilled rice farmer. Hmong women's occupations are primarily listed as farming, domestic work, embroidery, seamstress, and sometimes student. But the different pairings show how Hmong soldiers were both students and farmers, either before or after their military duties. They foreground the residual reminders of lives lived in war, and the embodied violence of the "blind right eye" note accompanying one man's military occupation.

Unlike the classified documents, these applications are neither hidden nor erased. But the applications represent state management of refugee resettlement and Hmong histories through their fragmentary mapping of Hmong lives onto compartmentalized ways of knowing on the page. They contain the "Hmong secrets" in the imperial archive—that information which exceeds the private and familial, and yet cannot be assimilated into the state's documents. In chart 2.1, each line traces a family story, detailing generations of soldiers and students living under different imperialist regimes. For example,

CHART 2.1. Occupation and Skills (VOLAG Bio)

Farmer, embroidery, seamstress for three female adults (2 daughters) in the family
    Gardening
Hand-sewing, seamstress
Basket maker
Student
Farmer
Soldier, farmer
Teacher (general), Rice farmer ("no special skills" listed on the same form under other information and interviewer's comments)
Domestic help
Embroidery, farmer
Military ("blind right eye" listed under Health for this individual)
Student, farmer
Military, farmer
Embroidery, farmer
Student, military
Farmer, student
Embroiderer, farmer
Student/Machine sewing
Military/farmer
Medic, pharmacist
Seamstress
Army, mapping, intelligence—typing (Eng & Lao)
Farmer, embroidery
Fabrcatng: Jewlr [sic]

NOTE: Hmong refugees' indication of their occupation and skills in their resettlement applications as a representation of Hmong enrollments in the "secret army." VOLAG is the abbreviation for Voluntary Agency.
SOURCE: Author duplication of individual family case files, Immigration History and Research Center at the University of Minnesota. Recorded by Ma Vang on March 3, 2010.

many of the fathers of Hmong men who joined the fighting at age sixteen for the U.S. worked as porters for the French during the 1930s and early 1940s or were soldiers for the occupying French army after WWII. Some soldiers were not particularly eager to fight on the front lines but felt an obligation to help the Hmong leader, General Vang Pao, "because the country was at war."[86] Hmong students returned from their studies to join the fighting or continued studying to become teachers of Lao history, geography, and

English. Often, families were forced to move from village to village to escape the war's violence while their husbands and sons fought in the war. Several young Hmong women trained as nurses to care for wounded soldiers, which taught them skills beyond farming and embroidery, but all lived an existence shaped by leaving. The methods of recording education and work history on the applications allow glimpses of these stories.

Read together, education and work history provide more context for the general list above by offering dates that situate active military duty during the war. The dates reveal that these individuals fought in the later years of the war, but details about their training in "combat tactics" for two and a half months and their seven years of education allude to the conditions confronting Hmong during the war (see chart 2.2). Perhaps most striking are the dates and ranks listed under "Work history" that specify their status as 1st Lieutenant or Sergeant. A note about a wounded right knee but "NOW NO problems" illuminates the irony of the wound as proof of military service, yet something that does not disqualify the applicant for resettlement. In other words, these descriptions reveal the suppressed violence of war in making the refugee, which illuminates another way in which secrecy is applied in the production of refugees. Moreover, specialized training and skills explained in the following list bring to the fore Hmong participation in activities beyond the role of soldier, challenging the cartography of the Hmong guerrilla fighter. Yet, the soldier has become the most salient symbol of Hmong racial difference, and a claim for Hmong legal entry into the U.S. as refugees.

Re-creating lists of Hmong occupations from refugee resettlement applications powerfully remaps the complexities of Hmong lives in Laos beyond the categories of student, farmer, teacher, soldier, seamstress, medic, and domestic worker. Reading these lists offers a Hmong presence, in contrast to the mapping of war and violence from the U.S. imperial perspective in which Hmong are primarily represented as "natural" barriers to the Communist enemy. This remapping insists on rendering a Hmong presence in the spaces where things are missing. Their presence in the refugee records challenges the U.S. Cold War spatialization of Hmong as natural "fasteners" for the nation and foregrounds a "continuous, ongoing storytelling" that rejects the historical coverup inherent in the valorization of an "unofficial" Hmong–U.S. alliance.[87] Native feminist scholar Mishuana Goeman contends that re-creating spatial communities that have been defined by colonial notions of spatial belonging involves promoting forms of "spatiality and sovereignty found in tribal memories and stories."[88] Looking at the fragmented lists above, I imagine a different documentation that rearranges and gathers together the

CHART 2.2. Refugee Education and Work History

Education:
"Trained in Laos in combat tactics total 2.5 months"
    (listed under Special training, diplomas, certificates)
Hmong (illiterate); Lao (fair) speaking only
Studying sewing at camp sewing center
Reads and writes English, good listening comprehension
Public health training in camp hospital
7 years education

Work history:
Housewife
1970–72: Taxi-Driver
1972–75: Soldier, second lieutenant
1970–1975: military—Highest Rank: LT., was a platoon leader of 19 or 20 persons, wounded in right knee (superficially), NOW NO problems. Also kept company accounts & records for a year
HW/Farmer
1972–1975: soldier, Rank: 1st/Lieutenant
Housewife
Sewing in camp
Military 71–75
1969–1975 Soldier, Rank: 1st/sgt.
Farmer
S.G.U. Soldier (1969–75)

NOTE: Author compilation of Hmong refugees' education and work history in their resettlement applications to represent how military involvement appears in refugee records.
SOURCE: Author duplication of individual family case files, Immigration History and Research Center at the University of Minnesota.

incomplete narratives. Strung together, the occupations remap Hmong assertions of presence in space and time, rather than absence from the archive and identification as not-yet-subjects. Indeed, the mundane activities of filling out an application or attending a family gathering are already loaded with these stories that could not be told elsewhere.

In a scene in the backyard of a family gathering from the documentary *Among B-Boys*, a film about Hmong American youth and hip-hop culture, an uncle pulls out his wallet to show a card identifying him as a Hmong veteran of the CIA and U.S. "secret war" in Laos. He raises his hand to identify himself to the camera, filmmaker, and audience, declaring in Hmong: "CIA, Hmong. Hmong, CIA."[89] Flashing the card from his wallet, the uncle further states that "we have CIA cards" to prove our claims. This scene from a film on Hmong American break-dancers in California's Central Valley brings into sharp relief this ongoing storytelling. Hmong Americans with whom I watched the film identified the uncle as their father, grandfather, or uncle who always tells his story about the war to whoever will listen. Their reactions suggest a familiarity that they and I share with the stories that we were not supposed to forget. Such moments captured on film and interpellated by Hmong American viewers serve as a reminder that statements like this uncle's are often unwritten and mundane because they surface among things that are familiar. Yet, the statement demands that the listener pay attention to these fleeting notes that are always in danger of being erased.

In addition to the way that Hmong storytelling undermines the imperial mapping that displaces Hmong from history, the uncle's CIA ID card is a counter-use of the documents that sought to interpellate and define him as "refugee" and "loyal soldier."[90] This counter-use of the document is not the same as counterevidence, and it should be understood as part of the storytelling where Hmong participate in knowledge circulation about the war. The document is more than an evidential form of knowledge. The CIA ID card was produced by a veterans' organization, Lao Veterans, Inc., to identify Hmong veterans for services and benefits such as those described in the Hmong Veterans' Naturalization Act, which I discuss in the next chapter. This veterans' organization drew upon the emphasis on the textual record as "proper" identification to promote Hmong veterans' visibility and subjectivity as participants and collaborators in the war. The veteran ID card appropriates conventional recording to generate a list of army recruits that does not exist in the state or military records. Yet, the reliance by veterans' organizations and the veterans themselves on positive knowledge to mark their presence in history risks erasing those identities that cannot be demonstrated by an ID or state-issued document, or even the legal legibility of these ID cards. Storytelling continues to hold importance for communicating historical experiences that cannot be captured in the imperial archive, and is in fact still used by these same veterans even as they hold their ID cards.

Similarly, as a record of the joint military violence and humanitarian aid efforts that mark the "secret war," Hmong who provided aid supplies carry their own identification cards issued by the U.S. Embassy in Laos. Dan Moua, a former U.S. Embassy employee, explained that he tracked the movement of supplies such as food, tarps, medical equipment, and other items during the war, noting that these supplies were sent directly from the U.S. Embassy (and the ambassador) to the front lines of battle. Moua also discussed how soldiers are often valorized for their active participation in the war and suggested that all civilian workers such as USAID employees, policemen, teachers, nurses, etc., should receive the same commendations.[91] The ID cards carried by Hmong veterans and embassy workers reveal a different story, one in which the figures of the soldier and refugee are intertwined, and which presents militarization as a form of humanitarianism. Moua stressed that his ID card does not expire—"indefinite" is indicated as the date of expiration—and that he could return to Laos to temporarily work for the embassy. Bringing together the CIA ID with the USAID/U.S. Embassy ID underscores the "unofficial" Hmong-U.S. alliance. It also reveals how these documents, carried by the veteran and aid worker, are housed not in the archive, but on the body so that they constitute the archive of secrets and its embeddedness in the Hmong refugee.

Hmong refugees' use of documents to assert their different roles and responsibilities during the war opens up a tracing of the "secret war" paper trails by returning to the refugee records with which I opened the introduction, to explore how the archiving of refugees remaps U.S. logics of Laotian emptiness and Hmong displacement to foreground a Hmong presence. This active presence points to alternative sites outside of the archive where different forms of documentation and Hmong refugee histories might emerge.

3. THE REFUGEE SOLDIER

A CRITIQUE OF RECOGNITION AND
CITIZENSHIP IN THE HMONG VETERANS'
NATURALIZATION ACT OF 1997

U.S. refugee and citizenship discourses conventionally signify the rescue and inclusion of displaced subjects into the nation-state without a critical engagement with the historical contexts constitutive of their conditions.[1] While these unresolved pasts are erased or recuperated to reaffirm U.S. moral and political benevolence for rescuing the stateless other, they also have the potential to unsettle the rescue and inclusion narrative and, in turn, expose the contradictory work of U.S. empire in debates about state recognition. The emergence of Hmong in a complex configuration as rescued yet unassimilated refugees, "natural" soldiers/warriors, and recently terrorists (see chapter 4), along with the convoluted U.S. response, demands an interrogation that centers the U.S. "secret war" in Laos. This chapter picks up from where chapter 2 left off to examine how the U.S. law tries to elide Hmong refugees as an imperial dilemma by resolving them into U.S. citizens. As such, the law also produces a particular representation of the refugee figure who deserves citizenship, which reveals secrecy in militarism and rescue. This chapter examines the site of state recognition and citizenship as a limited arena in which to address the "secrets" of war, violence, and displacement. Furthermore, it underscores how recognition productively exposes the contradictions of empire. Thus, this chapter asks: How does the U.S. government deal with keeping the war "secret" in the national record and memory while addressing the integral role of Hmong in it? How does citizenship discourse as the promise of political inclusion construct Hmong racial difference? The Hmong Veterans' Naturalization Act of 1997 as a supposed "moment of inclusion" or of "eligibility to citizenship" illuminates the refugee soldier figure who emerged as an ally through U.S. global interventions but was displaced as a refugee precisely because of their military service for the United States. I argue that the state employs the refugee soldier figure, the purported "new friend" of freedom and democracy, as a worthy subject of state recognition and citizenship, but this figure critiques U.S. empire and the nation-state as contradictory in producing violence as rescue.

Through an analysis of the unique case about the Hmong veterans' legislation, I show how state recognition draws on two central narratives of alliance and racial primitivity to reinforce the project of rescue and inclusion. For instance, shifting formulations of Hmong as willing soldiers, as "incidental" refugees, and as "primitive" stateless people throughout the congressional hearing foregrounds the misrecognitions and construction of racial difference constitutive of recognition.[2] Citizenship discourse, more than a form of legal inclusion, ideologically recuperates the "secret war" into a usable past in order to justify the war's benevolence as a civilizing project (recuperates the "secret war" and Hmong into a special category for recognition). I formulate the refugee soldier figure, then, as an expression of the humanitarian (rescue and civilize) and militaristic work of empire but also as a critique of these imperialistic designs. This figure and its racial difference disrupt the narratives of rescue and assimilation central to refugee and citizenship discourses through their collisions with each other. Although specific as a formulation of the Hmong-U.S. relationship, my discussion of the figure points to the broader global processes of racialization, citizenship, and "secret" wars.[3]

This chapter is organized into three sections. First, I chart the "global historical" emergence of the refugee soldier figure as a problem of history and the law through a discussion of the context of war and the legislation's attempts to keep the refugee and soldier separate. Second, building on critical analysis of the "politics of recognition," I show how the debate about citizenship as an "equal exchange" for Hmong refugees'/veterans' "sacrifices" reproduces the structure of inequality and violence, and how alliance thus highlights the refugee soldier's ambiguity. Finally, this essay demonstrates how citizenship signifies the possession of nationhood, yet the refugee soldier's condition of statelessness haunts and troubles this resolution. I conclude the chapter with Hmong veterans' unaddressed claims about the military duties they performed, one of which was the rescue of U.S. pilots, for which they constructed a memorial. Thus, I contend that the offer of citizenship, in this case, is about the United States and its recuperation of a political relationship with the "new friend"—signifying the incorporation of a not-yet-modern people into modernity and nationhood—rather than being entirely about the "right to have rights." I read the statements in the congressional hearing "against the grain," paying close attention to the gaps and fissures of the record, to illustrate how Hmong's indefinable status haunts this offer of citizenship as a resolution of the war.

The Refugee Soldier Figure: The Contradictions of Empire, Recognition, and Citizenship

In examining the Hmong veterans' legislation, my analysis complicates the un-redressability of the "secrets" or problems of U.S. empire and history in underscoring the limits of recognition to atone for the past and, in turn, the myth of citizenship as a marker of assimilation into the nation-state. This chapter challenges the idea that citizenship necessarily resolves the refugee's condition of statelessness, deconstructing the legislative efforts to recognize the soldier and rescue the refugee, a crucial combination to "embolden the perpetuation of U.S. militarism."[4] But, my analysis elucidates that the refugee and soldier together do not have a place in the law or national memory. In doing so, I pay critical attention to the "global/historical" context of the U.S. war abroad that produced the Hmong refugee soldier as a subject of U.S. freedom and democracy.

The refugee soldier figure emerged from the paradox of the U.S. "secret" involvement in Laos—the recruitment of Hmong as "guerrilla" soldiers and their abandonment as refugees.[5] This strategic coupling of the refugee and soldier figures exposes the U.S.'s rescue aims as it waged a "secret war" with Hmong labor against the North Vietnamese Army and Pathet Lao. The refugee soldier figure is an impossible subject where both the refugee and soldier are subjects of different discourses that do not converge. My point is that when the two do converge, this figure can begin to unravel the foundational assumptions about the "secret war," U.S. citizenship, militarism and humanitarianism, the production of truth, and history. The conjoining of military and humanitarian projects, then, produced an extralegal figure whose troubling moral political status undermines the legitimacy through which a nation-state engages in war.[6] The following discussion will show this extralegal condition because the refugee soldier cannot be a subject of either military archive/law or refugee archive/law. Hence, the mid-1990s congressional hearing's preoccupation with questions about "documentation" and "verification" of military service, in order to keep the categories soldier and refugee separate, reveals the state's dual goals to foreclose unwanted legacies of a war—one that was not supposed to exist—and to establish itself as benevolent through its rescue.

The refugee soldier figure as a category of analysis, then, highlights the global/historical emergence of Hmong racial subjects that conjoins the national and transnational as crucial to understanding how subjects emerge always already through violence and in relation to each other. It constitutes a strategic pairing of the hyperfeminized and hypermasculinized constructions of the refugee who lives "at home" and the soldier who fought abroad. The category links conventional ideas about the "liberator"/"rescuer" as soldier figure with the "victim"/"rescued" as refugee figure to underscore the nexus of violence abroad and "violent belongings" at home within the U.S. imperialist and nation-building logic. This relationship embodies, borrowing from Amy Kaplan, the nexus of how empire takes place both abroad and at home—exerting its power at the junction between the domestic and foreign.[7] At the same time, the figure disrupts the distance of time and space, reconfiguring temporality to enmesh what is considered "then" into "now," and "there" into "here." It provides a crucial understanding of the U.S. state's ideologically convoluted work to incorporate and reject the refugee soldier figure as constitutive of but subversive to its construction. Employing this figure as a category of analysis illuminates how empire works generally to resignify U.S. militarism as a freedom project, violence as rescue, and how the simultaneity of violence as rescue enables my analytic. Furthermore, the figure contributes to a more nuanced conceptualization of the refugee as a figure or an idea that advances a critique of the nation-state as a site of violence rather than a place of refuge.[8] The refugee soldier shapes the refugee as a threat to liberal democracy and to national memory.

While the war's conditions produced this figure, the Hmong Veterans' Naturalization Act of 1997 as redress signifies a reemergence of its dilemma.[9] The legislation proposed to "expedite the naturalization of aliens who served with special guerrilla units in Laos," intending to acknowledge those who served with the United States through English-language and U.S. history exam exemptions in the naturalization test.[10] Additionally, the legislation intended to assist Hmong and Laotian veterans of the "secret war," along with their spouses and widows, through the naturalization process owing to their difficulty in "becoming Americans" or attaining U.S. citizenship. As declared by several congressional members, this legislation would enable Hmong to express their allegiance to the United States and reunite with families overseas as well as ease their "assimilation" into the nation.[11] As its title indicates, the bill attempts to link the Hmong "alien" with the U.S. "noncitizen alien," assimilating the international soldier into that of the national figure. In other words, the bill's valorization of the soldier figure consisted of the reworking of the refugee figure as an immigrant figure, which erases the latter by severing it from the former, and leaves unexamined the context of production of the refugee.[12] To confer citizenship to alien or noncitizen soldiers who served the nation,[13] the legislation centralizes yet sidesteps the questions of language and history as markers of eligibility.[14] The bill proposed to bypass the naturalization policies already in place, which allow individuals over fifty-five years of age with at least fifteen years of residence, or over fifty years of age with at least twenty years of residence, to naturalize without the English-language requirement. Hence the crucial questions within the debate were the following: Why should the U.S. government give special consideration to Hmong and Laotian veterans through this legislation, especially when it might open the door for other groups to make similar claims? And how would the state reconcile the dilemma of recognizing some refugees as soldiers in order for its agencies to determine eligibility in the bill's implementation, when there is no state record of a "secret army" or its enrollments? Drawing from critiques of the "politics of recognition"—that the recognition-based models of liberal pluralism with state agencies constitute failed projects because they reiterate colonial relationships and mark racial difference—I consider how citizenship reproduces the unequal Hmong–U.S. relationship (as a "debt" owed) that the naturalization legislation seeks to address.[15]

Legal Historical Dilemma: The Law as an Active Archive

My examination of the naturalization bill's subcommittee hearing seeks to contextualize the above questions and illustrate how the refugee soldier figure as a legal historical dilemma in its excess of the law and archive critiques the logic of state recognition. In his discussion of the legal subjectivity of the "gay Pakistani immigrant" within the neoliberal restructuring of state power and the family, Chandan Reddy suggests that the law is an "active archive" or a mode of record-keeping that documents the "confrontation of social groups with the universality of 'community' and the 'state'" to produce social differences. The law subjugates "historical and social differences" as a precondition of the emergence in the national record.[16] If what emerges in the national record is already mediated and shaped by relations of power, then the refugee soldier is the limit of the archive who remains uncategorizable, undefinable, and outside of national boundaries. The archive of the law becomes a site in which the issues of government secrecy and the U.S. illicit role in Laos are brought forth but disavowed in order to represent Hmong as deserving subjects of U.S. citizenship. As a consequence of historical absence, the Hmong refugee is put on stage for examination to negotiate the terms of citizenship in relation to the past.

The question of "proof" interrogates not only Hmong refugees'/soldiers' "Hmongness" but also their veteran status. It would be difficult for the United States Immigration and Citizenship Service (USICS), formerly Immigration and Naturalization Service, to prove veteran status because the soldiers who fought in "guerrilla units" relocated to the United States as "refugees." Therefore, the question of proof renders the refugee as a ghostly figure, only hinted at through its "incidental" categorization and the legislation's "technical" concerns, but always already haunting configurations of the soldier figure. U.S. Representative Bruce Vento (D-Minn.) vehemently contends that despite the problems with numbers and identification, proof is embodied in the "war wounds" of the veterans: "We have to have proof of the fact that they're Hmong . . . so they lifted up their shirts and showed me the war wounds."[17] Wounds etched in the same body of the soldier and refugee, however, mark its authenticity and paradoxical production—the recruitment as soldiers and displacement as refugees. Representative Vento's gesture toward the body as evidence to resolve the gap in the archive suggests the body as an alternative site for information rather than a place of embodied difference. Elaine Scarry, formulating the relationship between the body and nation-state, asserts, "What is remembered in the body is well remembered." In times of war, she further contends, what is first visible is the "literalness with which the nation inscribes itself in the body; or the literalness with which the human body opens itself and allows 'the nation' to be registered there in the wound."[18] Although Scarry mainly refers to the relationship between the nation and its citizen-soldier, this formulation can be extrapolated to rethink the assertion that "proof" of war lies in the "wounds" on the bodies of Hmong veterans. If what is "remembered in the body [about the 'secret war'] is well remembered," then the wound, in fact, registers the nation's role in Laos. Thus, the Hmong soldier's scarred flesh embodies not only the U.S. cause in Laos and Southeast Asia but, more importantly, the inscription of violence and trauma engendered by the U.S. nation. The "record of war survives in the body" of the refugee soldier as the unknowable costs of war—the "people who were hurt there," the people who inflicted the hurt, and the people who still hurt here in the United States.[19]

The congressional hearing's recasting of the war wounds into an alternative form of information highlights the problems in the textual transmission of knowledge, which elides the wounds' implication in U.S. military violence and the messiness of experiences of violence between soldier and refugee. Textual knowledge formation assumes that the soldier's identification can be determined through documents in the national archive. Archival memory's transmission of knowledge through the "fixed" mediums of texts, documents, maps, letters, videos, and so forth, "sustains power" and "exceeds the live" because it "works across distance, over time and space."[20] The fixity of text and writing "over time and space" makes them reliable and verifiable. An exchange between representatives Lamar Smith (R-Tex.) and Vento, however, reveals the record's inability to capture the tensions between the refugee and soldier figures. They assert,

> MR. SMITH: How is it that we can determine who fought and who would, therefore, be due some special consideration by Congress?
>
> MR. VENTO: Mr. Chairman, on page 3, I indicate the matter of proof that would be necessary, in other words, the review of refugee processing documents given; a high commissioner on refugees has the information with regards to camps; *they've kept some records*.[21]

Representative Smith's question highlights the importance of determining "who fought" and should be "due some [congressional] consideration." In this inquiry, the phrase "who fought" appears to reference the soldier—the person (who) engaged in war/military service (fought). Representative Vento's response directs the enquirer to the "refugee processing documents" and the records kept by the "high commissioner on refugees," suggesting that the person "who fought" in the war is documented there. This begs the question: To whom does the "who" in "who fought" refer—the soldier or the refugee? Although the "who" appears to indicate the soldier, the "secret" conditions of the war's production also suggest the refugee question. Conventional knowledge situates the soldier figure as consenting to engage in war for the nation-state; whereas the refugee figure represents the unconsenting victim of war. In other words, the difference between the soldier and the refugee figures lies within their roles as liberator and liberated. The exchange cited above, however, shows an ambiguous relationship between the two, positing the refugee soldier at the border between consent and coercion. In doing so, it renders the archive on refugees an incoherent project of refugee regulation.[22] It is where the soldier figure bumps up against the refugee figure.

The refugee soldier figure as a problem of the archive illuminates its (im)possibility to become the law's subject, exposing the fallibility of the refugee archive to validate guerrilla service. Louis D. Crocetti Jr., associate commissioner for examinations for USICS, explains the law's inability to adequately determine soldier status because it must rely on the confirmation as a refugee:

> In essence, a naturalization applicant under this provision of law would simply have to *present documents claiming to have served* in a special guerrilla unit. Current statutory requirements for other *former or active duty military require certification of service* by the Department of Defense, [and so] *short of military records, the only confirmation for the Service would be if the applicant was admitted to the United States as a refugee* from Southeast Asia, and would have been old enough to perform military service during the Vietnam conflict. It is the experience of the Service in implementing programs which rely on affidavits such as the Immigration Reform and Control Act of 1986 that fraud may be prevalent.[23]

Crocetti asserts that the verification process for naturalizing under military service provisions requires attainment of "certification of service by the Department of Defense." This presumes that the Department of Defense kept enrollment records of its "secret army" and considers "guerrilla units" a part of its military force. Crocetti, however, contends that "short of military records, the only confirmation for the Service would be if the applicant was admitted to the United States as a refugee," implying that only the refugee record can offer insight into this issue. But because the "refugee files are [deemed] dubious at best as means of verification," the USICS would not be able to rely on "any of that data" as evidence of military service. Representative Smith's vehement questions—"Is there any way to determine how many Hmong actually fought? Is there any way to determine or verify a person's participation?"—underscore the law and state's inability to address this tension between the refugee and soldier, and its inability to confront the history of secrecy.[24] The absence from military records and a reliance on the unreliable refugee archive, again, reveal the site of war as the production of racialization of Hmong as extralegal subjects. The refugee record also illuminates the missing figure of the Hmong woman who would also have been admitted as a refugee, whose eligibility for citizenship is only through their gendered domestic labor as the spouses and widows of the veterans. Each figure, refugee and soldier, haunts the other as an unresolved and incomplete configuration; and both unsettle the discourse of citizenship through their displaced position.

The refugee soldier as a category of analysis foregrounds the changing and troubling status of the refugee figure. It reveals the omission of critical discussions about the "secret war" and the United States' illicit role in constructing and managing not only U.S. secrets but, more importantly, secrets concerning Hmong soldiers' status as part of the "secret army," the atrocities Hmong encountered, their refugee status due to the act of soldiering, and the U.S. abandonment after the war. These absent accounts about Hmong refugees/soldiers prompt Colonel Wangyee Vang, former soldier and president of Lao Veterans, Inc., to insist on Hmong as "political refugees" rather than "economic migrants" in order to force a deeper examination of the war and underscore U.S. responsibility when congressional members attempted a quick resolution. His statement illustrates the nexus between the soldier abroad and the refugee at home: "The Hmong soldiers did not come to America as economic migrants; they came to America as political refugees because they were veterans of the U.S. Special Guerrilla Units and other special units in the United States' Secret Army in Laos. The United States has a special obligation to them."[25]

The refugee soldier highlights the refugee as a troubling moral political figure who inhabits a condition of statelessness—the precarious spaces between the technicality (legal definition) and reality (lived experience) of being "enemy aliens."[26] Employing the former figure interrogates citizenship's claim to resolve the refugee's supposed temporary condition of statelessness precisely because the permanence of stateless status unhinges the national order.[27] Furthermore, statelessness haunts the refugee and citizen because it suggests the condition of rightlessness.[28]

"Their Contribution Plus Our Role": Hmong as an Ally
The refugee soldier analytic highlights the anxieties of Hmong political status as an ally to the United States and the limitations of contractual citizenship—a relationship based on an "equal" exchange. Hence, I show how "eligibility to citizenship" recuperates Hmong status as willing soldiers as well as makes apparent the conditions of difference in the political relationship between Hmong and the United States. Repeated characterizations of Hmong veterans as "wartime allies," "former allies," and "valuable allies" to the United States' cause, fighting "alongside Americans when many Americans were unwilling to do that," construct a singular narrative about Hmong refugees/veterans.[29] This U.S.-centric perspective leaves unexamined the desires, stakes, and tensions imbued in Hmong's guerrilla service. I argue that it is precisely the naming of the Hmong veterans as the "new friend"—one racialized as always already behind—that allows the United States to justify its involvement in Laos and recuperate Hmong veterans as deserving of U.S. citizenship. Denise Ferreira da Silva explains that the "new friend" is indistinguishable from the enemy because it lacks self-determination and the ability for self-regulation and self-development.[30] This "new friend of freedom"—a "subject in becoming"—requires military intervention to help it sustain and develop self-determination.[31] Da Silva's rendering of U.S. empire's dilemma helps to imbue the figure with a critique of U.S. militarism's rendering of certain bodies as crucial yet expendable subjects of empire. This "new-friend" logic renders the violence of war as necessary and just, because it simultaneously functions as a rescue of the racial other, who can never be self-determined. It enables the nation-state's representatives to project the Hmong-U.S. relationship as part of the U.S. global project of identifying its allies to dismantle Communism or the "evildoers" in order to achieve world leadership. Representative Vento's statement illustrates this move to incorporate Hmong into its global project: "Although it wasn't apparent then, the Hmong contribution and actions had a major impact on achieving today's global order and the preeminent role of self-determination around the globe."[32] This alliance not only affects the national context of belonging for Hmong veterans thirty years after the war, but also enacts onto the global stage the United States' primary role in defining self-

determination: a belonging contingent on a willingness to sacrifice.[33] Alliance helps to define U.S. hegemony.

The coupling of friendship with sacrifice naturalizes willingness with guerrilla service. Representative Vento declares that it was the ally's willingness to fight that saved U.S. soldiers' lives and upheld its military power: "It's these extreme sacrifices made by the United States and the role that we played there, the Hmong in the jungles and highlands, whether in uniform or whether in peasant clothing; thousands of soldiers, of course, U.S. soldiers and airmen lives were spared in this conflict because of the contributions made."[34]

The "sacrifices" and "contributions" of Hmong veterans, then, are the replacements of their lives for those of U.S. soldiers. U.S. Representative Patrick J. Kennedy (D-R.I.) affirms the relationship between the act of death for the nation and its prerogative to "make live,"[35] now through citizenship, in the following statement: "The Lao and Hmong Veterans have fought and died in the name of American democracy—now it is our turn to honor and repay them for their service to our great nation."[36] The willingness to die "deserves" "payment" because it establishes the sovereign and contributes to its power to determine who lives or dies. Their deaths in the "name of American democracy" represent a sacred sacrifice that must be honored. Yet another statement from U.S. Representative Scott L. Klug (D-Wisc.) reiterates this narrative of honor and recognition: "The Hmong sacrificed for our country during the Vietnam War and they deserve our respect and gratitude."[37] Deploying the narrative of sacrifice to make sense of the dead and still-living as the "new friend" of freedom and democracy forecloses the multiple and fragmented memories into a single story about dying for the nation. The U.S. state's naming of the alien soldier as one who can be sacrificed and, if he lives, become a potential citizen, in order for the United States to simultaneously recognize sacrifice but deny its involvement in the production of the refugee, elides the refugee as a threat to citizenship and the nation-state.[38] The Hmong soldier, then, reflects and foregrounds broader global strategies of power that mark certain bodies as expendable because they exist outside the law.

Citizenship as recognition and payment for the soldier's sacrifice reflects its contractual status. Social contract theory focuses on the idea of man's relinquishment of his rights in order to enter into government, thus making the distinction between the state of nature and state of law. This idea of citizenship centralizes the subject based on voluntary will of the individual.[39] In these accounts, only the rational being can become a subject because only they can enter into a social contract to be protected by the law. In the case of Hmong, the narrative of deserving U.S. citizenship in exchange for one's life might represent a delayed and perverted version of the social contract theory, but citizenship constitutes a myth because it inheres only in those deemed capable of material, social, and intellectual independence—subjects who voluntarily enter into the contract.[40] U.S. Representative Sonny Bono's (R-Calif.) statement attests to the fairness of social contracts, but contrarily demonstrates who is in a position to give and give up life: "If giving them a pittance for dying for us or getting blown up for us or getting killed for us is out of the question, it is not fair in exchange. I think humanity survives on exchange; if you buy something, you get something; if you ask somebody to do something for you, you pay them; if you ask people to die for them, and they say, 'What for?' 'Just do it.'—I don't think that's a good exchange."[41] He declares that the United States should make a "fair exchange" with Hmong; U.S. citizenship for "getting blown up for us or getting killed for us," suggesting that citizenship, emergence as legal/political subject, constitutes the ultimate form of payment for human sacrifice. Representative Bono's assertion of the reciprocity of "humanity" signifies that exchange constitutes the nurturing of life for risking death in which "you ask people to die" and "you pay them." The exchange of membership to a nation-state for one's life is, in fact, not a payment of honor but rather a reward for the "other," which reconfigures the United States as a patron to rescue Hmong refugees not only from their status of noncitizen soldier but also from their condition of statelessness.

The sacrifice narrative's potency, in its conjoining of one's willingness to fight for the U.S. cause with citizenship status, nonetheless enables a transnational inquiry of the boundaries of citizenship. Citizenship as an exchange for death and as a marker of a prior political relationship further constructs Hmong as already "Americans." Thus, it necessitates the claim that Hmong veterans were fait accompli U.S. citizens fighting "for the United States" in Laos. Commissioner Susan Haigh, Ramsey County, Minnesota, in her support of the bill, declares that conferring citizenship would represent an "official" government acknowledgment of Hmong veterans, who were already "American patriots" forged in a transnational context. She states, "It [the act] will be a clear statement by our Government and by all of us that we acknowledge the Hmong as true American patriots; that we are honored to count them as our fellow citizens."[42] Commissioner Haigh's characterization of Hmong as "American patriots" bestows the labels *American* and *patriot* to those who fought for the United States elsewhere. The transnational permeates the national production of historical knowledge in claims that the

United States has a responsibility to incorporate Hmong veterans into its national polity as a result of their recruitment and services overseas. Legal national inclusion represents the "welcome home" of already-citizens who gave their lives to the state. Representative Vento asserts that Hmong "were tested by risking their lives. Now it is time for Congress and the President to recognize that test of sacrifice and to give the Hmong the honor, dignity, and recognition they deserve by accepting them as our fellow citizens. Only then will we finally be able to say that the Hmong are home in America."[43]

The assertion that Hmong soldiers were already transformed into an image of "true Americans" through "risking their lives for the values and beliefs that we revere as Americans and saving American lives," however, becomes a symbolic gesture because the naturalization legislation would not offer them veterans' status or benefits.[44] For example, the congressional discussion simultaneously establishes an unnecessary bestowal of veterans' benefits to Hmong veterans because legal citizenship constitutes the final gesture: "So I think that one more gesture here—this doesn't deal incidentally with veteran's benefits. . . . Nor would the legislation give Hmong people who served in the Special Guerrilla Forces veteran's status or make them eligible for veteran's [sic] benefits."[45] These stipulations against veterans' status and benefits simultaneously foreclose and illuminate the refugee soldier as the limit figure to this welcoming narrative. U.S. responsibility stops with the conferral of juridical inclusion to "integrate" Hmong refugees/veterans and make it easier for their U.S.-born children to adjust to U.S. life.[46] Furthermore, the bill facilitates the naturalization process with a waiver of the English test, but it does not connote an immediate citizenship. Citizenship, then, becomes a symbolic gesture to formally include Hmong veterans in order to resolve the paradox of the United States' reliance on alien soldiers to fight its cause, yet proclaiming that they were already U.S. citizens through their "sacrifice" or death for the nation.

The recognition of Hmong veterans for their "contributions" reproduces the violence of U.S. militarism through its recuperation of the nation-state as moral and benevolent for addressing the soldiers' sacrifices. Citizenship constitutes a reward for the veterans that privileges the United States and its preeminent role as a moral leader who fulfills its commitments and promises, rather than contending with the war and the Hmong role. Instead, the United States' lack of commitment is constructed as "only" its inability to "rescue" Hmong soldiers, its allies, having abandoned them to political persecution after the war and delayed in acknowledging their efforts.[47] The National Asian Pacific American Legal Consortium's statement to Congress highlights the U.S. betrayal in not "fulfilling" its promise of citizenship: "Many of them [Hmong veterans] believed they would gain American citizenship. Now, many soldiers and their families feel betrayed and forgotten."[48] The terms *betrayal* and *forgotten* illuminate how the nation is forged on forgetting the "deeds of violence that have taken place."[49] One Congress member proclaimed a U.S. moral responsibility to aid those who "need our help," because abandoning them is not what a "global leader" does: "The Hmong people need our help. It is wrong to abandon these men and women who served as valuable allies to us during the Southeastern Asian conflict."[50] Indeed, the bill doubly benefits Hmong and the United States: "This legislation not only benefits the Hmong who served, but also America as a whole through the deserved recognition and justice granted to our allies. It is time to recognize and reward their contribution by passing the Hmong Veterans' Naturalization Act."[51] These statements deploy a narrative of political alliance, one based on difference, to conceal and justify the U.S. illicit role in Laos through its delayed recognition of Hmong sacrifices.

"Special Category of Native-Language-Having-No-Written-Form": Hmong as (Illiterate) Stateless

While the previous discussion illustrates how the refugee soldier as the "new friend" unhinges the construction of an equal political alliance for naturalization, this section further demonstrates that this differentiated citizenship relies upon the coupling of alliance with (il)literacy. I show how the pairing of alliance and (il)literacy marks Hmong's status as "primitive" and stateless—not-yet-modern—and always already in excess of the nation-state and modernity, as well as how this excess opens up a critical engagement with the war and the concept of citizenship. The lack of language/English skills thus constructs a "special category" of "native-language-having-no-written-form," highlighting the unique case of Hmong as the refugee soldier and the "new friend" who requires help under the law. This "special category" of "individuals who are prevented from learning English by the unique circumstance of their native language having no written form"[52] signifies "Hmongness" as simultaneously an eligibility and limitation to the law, pointing to the difficult issue of the bill and marking Hmong racial (temporal) difference. The lack of language in its "written form" does not suggest an insufficient skill that can be learned, but rather an irreducible difference of the racialized subject who is considered to be out(side) time. Such a characterization suggests that the lack in language is precisely the lack of history. Diana Taylor's challenge of the centrality of the "writing = memory/knowledge equation" in Western epistemology, and the sustaining of power through archival memory, are important to my analysis here.[53] As she argues, "the very 'lives they [Indigenous and marginalized groups] lived' fade into 'absence' when writing alone functions as archival evidence, as proof of presence."[54] Her insistence on an engagement with "embodied knowledge" to look toward the repertoire of memory rather than archival memory as the transmission of cultural memory/knowledge clarifies my point that the memory of war survives in the body. Hence the congressional discussion's privileging of language as having a history through the categorization of Hmong language as lacking a written form enables the United States to relegate Hmong as outside the linear trajectory of history. Illiteracy connotes a lack of not only language but also history and nationhood, which are embodied in the concept of differentiated citizenship because "their command of the English language is insufficient to successfully complete the naturalization process."[55] This concept signifies a right to nationalism that those deemed stateless do not have.[56] The concept of lack is integral to the project of secrecy's rescue narrative, deployed to justify one's worthiness as an object of rescue. Affirmations of the bill's good intentions and Hmong veterans' "sacrifices" and "contributions" then simultaneously foreground Hmong lack of "self-development and self-determination."[57]

The predicament of the Hmong-language-having-no-written-form relies on two competing narratives: the recent development of a written language and the wartime disruption of learning. Representative Vento asserts, "This [waiving the English language test and residency requirement] is necessary because learning English has been the greatest obstacle for the Hmong patriots, as written characters for the Hmong language have only been introduced recently, and whatever chances most Hmong who served may have had to learn a written language were greatly disrupted by the time spent fighting alongside U.S. forces."[58]

This statement marks their linguistic insufficiency as a difference inherent in their "primitive" culture because the "written characters . . . have only been introduced recently." Yet, it also explains that learning was disrupted by fighting in the war, which further emphasizes illiteracy as a cost of war and constitutive of statecraft rather than an inherent inability.[59] The English language—symbolic of modernity and civilization—represents the code of entry for Hmong and other racialized groups. However, the sympathetic rhetoric toward Hmong—that they cannot help not knowing English—pervades throughout benevolent utterings such as "the English language

[is] a significant barrier for the Hmong who are a distinct ethnic group who lived in the isolated mountain regions of Vietnam and Laos."[60] Their isolation and primitivism in the "mountain regions" cannot be blamed, and it is the "responsibility" of the United States to "civilize" and "assimilate" this group through citizenship. In this context, Hmong are "rewritten" into U.S. history based on their marked difference. Commissioner Haigh points to the daunting barrier: "The vast majority of the Hmong generation who grew up fighting in this war for America never became literate in their own language, let alone in the English language, and the illiteracy is a daunting barrier for the many older Hmong who want to become citizens."[61] This assertion suggests the infancy of the Hmong written language as others have explained as a sign of premodernity. It exposes again another cost of war—the youth of Hmong soldiers whose generation "grew up fighting in [the] war for America." The National Asian Pacific American Legal Consortium, although sympathetic, reiterates these two key factors in the "high illiteracy" refrain: "First, Hmong was not a written language until about 40 years ago, leaving many within the community who were never taught to read or write in their own language. Second, the war interrupted formal education, further contributing to the high illiteracy rate."[62] The signifiers of culture and violence for the case of Hmong-language-having-no-written-form present the language question as an indicator of Hmong's "new-friend" status, as undeveloped and outside modernity.

It was the war, however, that compounded the abject living conditions and the problems with learning. Colonel Wangyee Vang's submitted statement underscores the conditions produced by the war: "The intense and protracted clandestine war in Laos and the exodus of the Hmong and Lao veterans into squalid refugee camps, or internment in reeducation camps, did not permit the veterans the opportunity to go to school.... [T]he fact that a written Hmong language was not used in much of Laos until late in its history have compounded the problems of literacy for the Hmong and taking the U.S. citizenship test in English."[63]

More importantly, descriptions of the conflict as an "intense and protracted clandestine war" and its aftermath of "squalid refugee camps," or "internment in reeducation camps," contextualize the inability to learn language as a consequence of the abject conditions of war and expose the contingency of modern subjectivity based on the possession of language and writing. The late development of a written Hmong language refers to the Romanized Popular Alphabet system of writing developed by Bertrais, Barney, and Smalley. Language and writing, then, continue to signify civilizing projects to bring the "primitive" or "native" whose "integration ... has been hampered by vast differences of culture and level of development" into history.[64] These fleeting moments of possibility for critical engagement with the war are contained within the repetition of the statement that "Hmong don't have language" and are not allowed to be a part of the congressional debate because they only appear in the published congressional record as submitted statements. Hence it is precisely the politics of recognition and inclusion that produced problems of linguistic insufficiency.

Instead, the construction of illiteracy as a cultural pathology conceals yet cannot betray U.S. violence. This pathology casts Hmong culture as a hindrance and disability to possessing language and history—rendered a medicalized cultural disorder—in order to conceal the trauma involved in imposing the English language on Hmong in the first place. The use of medicalized language in the congressional hearing replicates the prevailing discourses about refugees as "pathetic," "depressed," and having multiple psychological issues, most prominently posttraumatic stress disorder. The consortium continues with an assertion of psychological and physical disabilities, citing that "many [Hmong veterans] also came in with mental and physical disabilities acquired as a result of the war, making it extremely difficult for them to learn a new language."[65] Finally, the debilitating effects of a recent acquisition of written language prevent Hmong from learning any language, including their own: "While the Hmong have their own language, their language has no written form until recently. This makes the English language requirement as it relates to possessing the ability to read and write ordinary words in English particularly prohibitive."[66] Despite the existence of a written Hmong language now, the war's damaging impact is so severe that they are still struggling to learn their own language, which makes writing "ordinary words in English particularly prohibitive" or difficult. This dominant construction about Hmong having neither written language nor skills contradicts the fact that Hmong soldiers performed the crucial role of military intelligence gathering, among other responsibilities, for the CIA during the war. The Hmong "irreducible (moral and mental) difference"[67]—through the repetitions about Hmong-native-language-having-no-written-form and the disruption of Hmong veterans' learning owing to the war—marks the Hmong refugee soldier as the "new friend" who is crucial yet incapable and requires help or "special consideration" under the law, rather than the "true friend of freedom." This characterization of the Hmong soldier as a "subject-in-becoming" exposes the illusion held by U.S. congressional members and the state about Hmong soldiers who "fought and died alongside Americans" as equal allies.[68] The language/English lack racially marks the "new friend" as a primitive who, rather than attaining citizenship as *payment*, is *bestowed* citizenship as a *reward*.

This irreducible racial (cultural) difference presents an anxiety for the U.S. state because it challenges the institution of U.S. citizenship and race-neutral policies. The refugee soldier as a simultaneously eligible and limited figure threatens the meaning of citizenship and state sovereignty, which naturalizes birth and nation,[69] and the very fabric of the institution that grants that ideal. The "domestic" issues of belonging are explicitly highlighted in Center for Immigration Studies' Mark Krikorian's reminder of the national principle of "racially and ethnically neutral immigration policy" that prohibits special considerations: "National origins quotas were rightly eliminated from the immigration law in 1965. The principle of a racially and ethnically neutral immigration policy in the national interest, however, cannot be upheld if the immigration law is shaped by the special pleading of the myriad ethnic groups that make up our population."[70] This argument suggests a colorblind policy implying that formal equality in immigration policies leads to equality in practice. At stake is the concern that allowing for these special considerations would enable the principles of U.S. citizenship to be shaped by "myriad ethnic groups" rather than the state. And yet the state preserves the power to decide on exceptions to suspend such principle and law; for example, President Trump's Muslim ban in January 2017 and "zero-tolerance policy" in April 2018 to separate families seeking asylum at the U.S.-Mexico border. Immigration law is, in fact, shaped by the "differential inclusion" of different racialized groups and works precisely on the basis of inequality in practice.[71] "Special considerations" and "differential inclusion," thus, can work to exclude groups based on racial difference.

Furthermore, Krikorian calls the Hmong veterans' bill an "affirmative action citizenship," through which others—he mentions Mexicans—are made to wait and follow the naturalization process while Hmong veterans seek special consideration: "What's more, the inequity of such legislation could inflame ethnic grievances and conflict. Mexicans, after all, are the largest national origin group seeking naturalization, and they are expected to meet all the normal requirements, while other groups, perhaps viewed as more sympathetic by some, would be admitted without meeting many requirements—affirmative action citizenship, if you will."[72]

Here, Krikorian refers to U.S. racial politics' articulation of the possibility of "ethnic grievances and conflict." A comparison with Mexican immigrants underscores the distinct differences and similarities between these two groups in terms of immigration and relationship to the United States. However, I am most interested in this particular linking of Mexican immigrants and Hmong veterans' relationships to citizenship and the nation for what it reveals about the strategies of power. The argument to withhold citizenship concerns the context in which Mexican immigrants, constituting the largest group seeking naturalization, must meet all the requirements while Hmong veterans, representing a small number, have access to "affirmative action citizenship." "Affirmative" and "sympathetic" actions enacted by the state produce a convergence between military work abroad in the Hmong soldier figure and a transformation of the Hmong refugee at home into the U.S. "immigrant," both racialized and coupled with illiteracy. Thus, the issue here is not about fairness and equality in the practice of the law for Hmong refugees/veterans and Mexican immigrants, but rather concerns how the unequal practice of policy is precisely at the forefront of nation- and citizenship-making. I contend that the particular context of the "secret war," its absence from popular and academic discourse, and its lingering secrets illuminate an understanding of the work of nation-building to extend "life" to those who can die for the nation precisely because they lack language as a necessary marker of modernity.[73] This opens up the discussion about the flexibility of U.S. citizenship in its implementation—it can be rewarded and revoked.[74] Citizenship remains an ambiguous category of the nation-state and vulnerable to "special interest" ploys that would "cheapen" and "debase" the "meaning of Americanism" that requires congressional vigilance in order to "safeguard" its "integrity."[75]

On the Loyal Ally

I conclude this chapter by highlighting the four components of my argument and gesturing toward the possibilities of the refugee soldier figure. First, I examined the law, the Hmong Veterans' Naturalization Act of 1997, through the congressional record as a site for the emergence and negotiation of the tensions regarding a Hmong place within U.S. history and their presence in the nation-state. Second, I examined the figure of the refugee as posing that very threat to the law's role in instituting recognition and resolution, precisely because its mobile, unfixed condition refuses documentation. Third, the chapter illustrates the ambiguity and (im)possibility of citizenship in relation to questions of the refugee and territoriality. The legislation's coupling of alliance with lack of literacy signifies the anxieties of granting citizenship to the refugee soldier, the "new friend" whose statelessness suggests a haunting presence of U.S. imperialism. And finally, this chapter foregrounds the elision of Hmong/refugee/war from the historical record through the soldier figure, though inevitably betrayed by the presence of surviving Hmong veterans, which exposes the record's inability to capture this shifting status. The law as a record shifts and refashions the meanings of citizenship.

The Hmong Veterans' Naturalization Act of 1997 and its passage in 2000 constitute but a moment or episode in the domestic and global events more than forty years after the "secret war." I analyze state recognition as a productive but incomplete site to explore questions of empire, citizenship, "secret" wars, and racial difference. Other events within the last decade and a half (after the legislation)—the events of 9/11, normalized trade relations between Laos and the United States in 2004, Hmong American community activism, the Real ID Act's passage as a provision of the USA Patriot Act, Hmong's emergence as terrorists through the "materials support" bar,[76] and the arrest on June 4, 2007, of General Vang Pao[77]—foreground the urgency to contend with the war and the refugee soldier figure produced from it. First- and second-generation Hmong Americans' continued insistence on remembering the lingering "secrets" through cultural activities attempt to make the past live in its incomplete and fragmented forms. Nonetheless, tracing this figure through the refugee's mobile, unfixed status illuminates questions concerning Hmong, citizenship, terrorism, and the nation-state. The refugee soldier figure as a new category of analysis constitutes an important lens to understand the global implications of the U.S. wars in Southeast Asia.

The legislation was but one domain in the politics of recognition. Hmong veterans along with their Lao counterparts also insisted on other forms of public recognition through the construction of several veterans' memorials at Arlington National Cemetery, in Sheboygan, Wisconsin, Fresno, California, and St. Paul, Minnesota. At Arlington, the Lao Veterans of America pushed for a recognition plaque to honor their service. Dedicated to "The U.S. Secret Army in the Kingdom of Laos 1961–1973," the plaque reads: "In memory of the Hmong and Lao combat veterans and their American advisors who served freedom's cause in Southeast Asia. Their patriotic valor and loyalty in the defense of liberty and democracy will never be forgotten."[78] The plaque marks the secrets and affirms Hmong and Lao veterans' loyalty, suggesting that the soldiers deserve to be buried in this national site. But like the legislation, the plaque's marking of the secrets of U.S. war is haunted by the nation-state's inability to bury those dead soldiers at Arlington. After years of advocacy from Hmong and Lao veterans, however, the Hmong Veterans' Service Recognition Act was enacted on March 23, 2018, as part of the Consolidated Appropriations Act of 2018. Introduced by Democratic Representative Jim Costa, whose district includes Fresno and Merced where a concentrated population of Hmong refugees/Americans live, and cosponsored by Democratic representative Raul Ruiz and Republican representatives Don Young and Paul Cook, the legislation would provide "appropriate honor to these aging veterans, these soldiers, who fought for their own independence and freedom and aligned themselves with the United States in the 1960s and early 1970s."[79] The burial legislation would only offer benefits to some veterans, those who pass after the bill's enactment, and as with the citizenship legislation, to valorize the soldier.

Of the various forms of recognition, the veterans' memorial in Fresno, California, poignantly communicates the sacrifices of life of the soldiers to which the citizenship legislation alluded. In December 2005, the Lao Hmong American War Memorial was dedicated to remember and honor Hmong veterans who were recruited and trained to fight in the "secret war." The memorial was conceived and constructed with the support of then Fresno Mayor Alan Autry as something he would do for the Hmong community in Fresno for securing the Hmong vote in his mayoral campaign. Hmong community organizations held him to that promise and came up with the concept of a memorial, forming a planning committee to fundraise for and design the sixteen-foot bronze statue and marble base, which took five years to complete (2000–2005) (figure 3.1). Although the memorial is not new in its commemorative work of remembering and forgetting, it is different as a device to locate the gaps in our knowledge about the past. As such, the war memorial attempts to bridge a material and symbolic gap of violence by figuring the historical context of Hmong service to the U.S.—rescuing downed U.S. pilots either dead or alive—in order to contextualize the Hmong sacrifices for the nation-state. The memorial's embodiment of a Hmong claim to history and violent belonging upholds the benevolence of U.S. democracy at the same time that it indicts the government for producing so many Hmong casualties. This generated public history was necessary to understand how the U.S. role in Laos relied on the sacrifice of their lives, and to make sense of the claims for recognition in this chapter and the following one.

The visual imagery captured in the statue memorializes Hmong soldiers as "freedom fighters" and rescuers. Indeed, the Hmong claim that they were "freedom fighters" rests on the soldiers' roles as rescuers of U.S. pilots. In his words, General Vang Pao describes the three main missions of his Hmong army in operating the "secret war": "first, to stop the flow of the North Vietnamese troops through the Ho Chi Minh Trail into Laos on their way to attack

FIGURE 3.1. Completed in 2005 to commemorate the Hmong and Lao veterans who fought for the U.S. and sacrificed their lives to rescue U.S. pilots. Photo by author, September 8, 2009.

South Vietnam, second, to rescue any American pilots during the Vietnam War, and third, to protect the Americans that navigated the B-52s and the jets to bomb North Vietnam."[80] For the cause of freedom and democracy, they protected Laos and Hmong by protecting U.S. interests and soldiers. In interviews with five veterans and community leaders involved in creating the memorial, I asked about the significance of the three soldiers figured in the statue. All five interviewees explained that the three figures convey one of the duties of Hmong soldiers: to rescue U.S. pilots who were shot down in their bombing and intelligence missions. One of the interviewees, Yer Vang, former soldier and secretary for Lao Veterans, Inc., explains the memorial's significance in the following way:

> The design . . . tells the story of when the Americans came to work in Laos and the pilots were shot down. If one pilot was shot down, there would be seven, eight, nine, ten of our soldiers to go rescue, using their lives to replace in order to get the American. It doesn't matter how many of our soldiers got killed; as long as the American is rescued then

114 Chapter Three

that is the biggest honor (*txiaj ntsim*) and heaviest price. So that you have more than ten lives to replace one person, this is the price that they owe us.... That's why we decided to make this [the memorial] ... that we are all human beings and yet we give up more than ten people to replace/save one person.[81]

Yer's poignant statement reveals how the rescue of U.S. pilots engendered the heavy casualty of Hmong soldiers in a ratio of ten-to-one. The missions to rescue downed pilots, saving those still alive or retrieving the dead, was to make sure that the U.S. American bodies did not remain in enemy territory, which involved ten Hmong soldiers to rescue one U.S. life. This duty to rescue the life or bodily remains of the U.S. American regardless of the number of Hmong lives lost remains a central paradox and unresolved cost of the war because this uneven bargain is an irreplaceable loss endured by Hmong.

For Hmong veterans/refugees like Yer, the visual imagery captured in the statue memorializes their "freedom fighter" status as rescuers (of U.S. pilots), and comprises their claims to belonging in the U.S. It fills in the gap of knowledge about a war that was not publicly fought or contested and where the preservation of U.S. American life was a duty. The memorial symbolizes how Hmong are concretely here in the U.S. because they sacrificed their blood for the land so that U.S. Americans could live and Hmong could have a better life. This assertion of Hmong refugees'/veterans' contributions establishes a U.S. debt owed to them. The U.S. government should be indebted to this grateful Hmong refugee for defending freedom, a debt that it cannot escape from.[82] As the following chapter will show, the tensions in the politics of recognition whereby Hmong veterans/refugees insist on its incomplete project and their belonging as U.S. citizens become apparent through the arrest of General Vang Pao on charges of terrorism, signaling the breakdown of the precarious refugee soldier figure.

4. THE TERRORIST ALLY
THE CASE AGAINST GENERAL VANG PAO

On June 4, 2007, U.S. federal agents arrested General Vang Pao, the former U.S. ally extraordinaire during the "secret war" in Laos and all-around Hmong leader, on a warrant issued by U.S. federal courts. Federal agents also arrested nine other Hmong community leaders (a tenth defendant was arrested later in the month) and a white former lieutenant in the U.S. National Guard. The warrant alleged the group intended to purchase $9.8 million in illegal weapons as part of a plot to overthrow the government of Laos.[1] An undercover agent for the Bureau of Alcohol, Tobacco, Firearms and Explosives (ATF) filed an affidavit alleging the group "was on the *verge* of launching a *sophisticated* plan to overthrow Laos' communist regime," and noting that General Vang and others had issued orders "to destroy these government facilities and make them look like the results of the attack upon the World Trade Center."[2] An eighteen-page blueprint of the plot titled "Operation Popcorn" (Political Opposition Party's Coup Operation to Rescue the Nation) outlined "exactly how Laos could be transformed into an *American-style democracy* with free elections, freedom of speech, a new constitution and judiciary, and a congress including Hmong and other ethnic minorities."[3] The weapons were allegedly going to be smuggled through Thailand to launch the coup,[4] in an echo of U.S. operations during the war in Laos in which U.S. planes flew from the Udorn air base in Thailand to bomb northeastern Laos and North Vietnam. With the unveiling of these plans, the group faced charges of violating the United States Neutrality Act, which prohibits U.S. Americans from planning or acting on U.S. soil to overthrow a foreign government with which the country is at peace.[5] The charge of violating the Neutrality Act reveals the relationship between secrecy and betrayal in liberal empire, and (for those who remember) the U.S. violation of neutrality for Laos, Cambodia, and Vietnam.

The legal case against General Vang Pao and his associates illuminates an urgent political question that has surfaced in the contemporary global concern about asylum seekers from majority-Muslim countries: Can refugees also be terrorists? Arguably, a legal approach to the case would demonstrate the general's arrest as a breakdown in the politics of recognition of the refugee soldier discussed in chapter 3, and that indeed Hmong refugees have become terrorists in the post-9/11 context of reinvigorated militarism and liberal strategies of empire. My analysis of narratives about the case shows how the provocative question of whether refugees can become terrorists points to the larger context of U.S. liberal imperial relations around the world, which relies on tenuous alliances that can be broken. I develop a layered argument to suggest the refugee's coconstitutive formation with the ally and the terrorist to challenge the idea that citizenship or expulsion necessarily resolves the refugee's condition of statelessness or atones for historical violence. The refugee is an "an/archive," recording the repetition of violence, yet the violence is always subject to erasure and remains elusive.[6]

By examining the media coverage of the case against General Vang Pao and his alleged accomplices, as well as Hmong refugee/American mobilizations, I have formulated the concept of the terrorist ally with which to specify the position of the refugee in this particular moment of terrorist threat. I make two related arguments about the emergence of the terrorist ally as a gendered racial figure of U.S. liberal empire and how it offers a critique of historical erasure. First, I argue that this conjoining of the ally and the terrorist underscores the seemingly untimely convergence of the Cold War ally with the post-9/11 Al Qaeda terrorist, and is consistent with the U.S. liberal empire's strategies to reframe and rename the formerly allied soldier, who is also an indebted and grateful refugee, as a terrorist. The untimeliness of the terrorist ally draws out how history on the run articulates histories that do not stand still to unravel the secrecy of state governance's recasting of the refugee more than forty years after the end of the wars in Southeast Asia. While the terrorist ally exposes state governance, Hmong refugees'/Americans' expressions of loyalty to former soldiers and the U.S. institute a silencing of other refugee perspectives. I conceptualize the terrorist ally both as an "assemblage" that is not entirely resistant and alternative but underscores "contingency and complicity with dominant forms,"[7] and as a refugee "compositional subject" whose political claims are already embedded within existing antiterrorism and refugee discourses.[8] While this chapter highlights the convergence of U.S. liberal imperial strategies, I also take the opportunity opened up by General Vang Pao's case in the contemporary environment of reinvigorated militarism and Islamophobia to illuminate how the liberal imperial strategies of keeping secrets produced the refugee and reframed this figure as a terrorist.

While the terrorist ally as a threat signals a breakdown in the precarious refugee soldier arrangement I discussed in chapter 3, it simultaneously shows how this faithful yet unreliable former ally can also be a "terrorist." The terrorist ally, then, represents a fissure in historicity's progress, revealing how the U.S. empire's "liberal ways of war" institute what Mimi Thi Nguyen calls the "gift of freedom" and the debt that follows.[9] I further argue that the figure of the terrorist ally highlights the multiple perspectives surrounding the case, and discuss how they represent postwar rearticulations of history to open up questions about the relationship between Hmong and the United States. Although they were not always outwardly critical of the United States as an imperialist and racist state, Hmong refugees'/Americans' mobilizations around this case, amid the secrets and silences, articulate the past in relation to the present. Paying attention to Hmong community politics and mobilizations means pursuing what feminist scholar Jasbir Puar asserts as a "historicizing biopolitics of the now." She explains that rather than viewing the past-present-future triad as three discrete temporalities, it is possible to understand their convergence as reflecting a record of "the future that is already here."[10] Taking into account a future that is already here necessitates an investigation of how the narratives and political positionings surrounding this case were complicated by race, gender, and generation.

Framing the "Loyal Ally" Refugee

The arrests of General Vang Pao and his associates sent shock waves through the Hmong community in the United States and globally, across the international Hmong diaspora and in Laos, raising fears about what the U.S. government's next move would be. If a government that General Vang Pao was closely allied with and loyal to could arrest him, then every Hmong person was vulnerable to accusations of criminal activity, and thus incarceration. Older Hmong refugees/Americans were stunned, "not so much at the accusations but at the American prosecutors for turning their backs on a war hero" who was continuing to defend democracy and freedom in Laos—the project they had fought for during the war.[11] News of the arrests spread quickly through mainstream and ethnic press coverage, Hmong radio stations, and social networks. Because the general had become a father figure for many Hmong in the U.S., the impact of the arrests surpassed even the high-profile 2004 case in which Chai Soua Vang was charged with killing six white hunters and wounding two others in northern Wisconsin.[12] Hmong communities across the country quickly organized public demonstrations, the largest of which was concentrated around the state capitol in Sacramento, California, and the nearby courthouse where the defendants would appear for their arraignment.

Although Hmong Americans expressed a range of support for and dissent against General Vang Pao, support of the general as a "freedom fighter" through the mass demonstrations in cities with large Hmong populations became the basis for opposition to the case. Protest rallies in Sacramento drew up to eight thousand people at their peak.[13] The depiction of "Hmong terrorism" in the charges against the group[14] and the vocal response by Hmong communities brought to public attention how the long history of U.S. involvement in Southeast Asia during the Cold War—and especially the role of Hmong in the war in Laos—has remained unresolved and collided with the "new" liberal imperial strategies of the global war on terror. The figure of the refugee turned terrorist or terrorist ally can illuminate the liberal imperial strategies as reliant on unilateral force to name the terrorist and map an "axis of evil" as well as institute mass killing. In contrast to Cold War strategies intended to contain the enemy threat and liberate (modernize) the unfree and uncivilized, the global abolishment of terror seeks to target and destroy any threat. Yet, traces of the old liberal agenda remain in the projects of liberating oppressed brown (Muslim) women and modernizing autocratic regimes.[15]

U.S. press coverage of the case depicted the alleged plans as a real-world spy novel and likened the plot to Hollywood films such as *Rambo*, while portraying the defendants, and the Hmong community along with them, as trapped in the past.[16] Indeed, this tragic rendition of the case as focusing on a people who cannot get out of the past bolsters how the U.S. liberal discourse of freedom and democracy configures the indebted and grateful Hmong refugee as a loyal ally. Indeed, this rendering has created a highly unsettling compromise of what I have called the refugee soldier in the previous chapter to comprehend the Hmong-U.S. relationship and to assert Hmong claims to legal and social belonging.

To be sure, the fact that Hmong leaders were arrested illustrated the continuation of U.S. projects of secrecy. In a *Sacramento Bee* report, the authors cite the argument by lead prosecutor Robert Twiss that General Vang Pao is the "most dangerous of the defendants" and therefore should not be released on $1.5 million bail: "Vang has the power with one phone call to put into operation a coup against the Laotian government or even order a contract on the life of the undercover federal agent whose work led to the charges against the men."[17] This statement depicts General Vang Pao as inherently inclined to perpetuate violence and war because he was still capable of carrying out an alleged coup. By extension, the general's influence on significant sectors of Hmong refugee/American communities means that they constitute would-be "freedom fighters" who could continue the failed plans, and are supposedly embodied by the thousands of Hmong protesters. Another *Sacramento Bee* article's account of the rallies describes the Hmong protesters as "warriors" awakened by the general's arrest: "Unlike his musket-lugging Hmong guerrilla fighters, Monday's warriors were armed with American flags, protest signs and their lungs."[18] This portrayal shows the Americanization of Hmong who are no longer killing—assumed to be done over there—but peacefully protesting here in America. Yet the killing that was done over there has been so embedded in the Hmong soldier category that it inflects this image of protest as a demonstration of Hmong as perpetual warriors who are "symbolically armed" to fight alongside General Vang. Even this image of protesting Hmong embodies both their Americanization and racial backwardness as a people "culturally disposed toward killing and aggression."[19] Therefore, a bail bond totaling $7.5 million for eight of the eleven defendants reflected the seriousness of the charges and the danger this group was alleged to pose to the security of both the U.S. and Laos.[20] The dual representation of General Vang Pao as "freedom fighter" and terrorist—a pathologized refugee and dangerous threat—conjoins his refugee soldier status with the terrorist ally who is capable of drawing together past and present U.S. military strategies.

On September 18, 2009, after more than two years of pressure from Hmong communities and allies, all charges against General Vang Pao were dropped. This unexpected move by United States attorney Lawrence Brown came as a surprise after Judge Frank Damrell initially denied the defense's motion to dismiss the case on May 11, 2009. Even the explanation offered by the U.S. Attorney's Office for its decision to drop the charges was perplexing, stating that continued prosecution was no longer warranted based on the totality of the evidence in the case. To add to the confusion, the other ten defendants remained under indictment.[21] However, less than a week after Vang Pao's death from pneumonia with cardiac complications on January 6, 2011, all charges against the remaining defendants were dropped on January 11, 2011, bringing to a close a case that had put the Hmong community on edge and cast doubt on their status as loyal U.S. Americans.

To unpack the case's central dilemma of the refugee ally who can also become a terrorist, my analysis follows the news coverage and public demonstrations through comments in online articles and in action on the streets. This tracing of media and public discourses involves an ethnography of the media to get at the cultural framing of the concepts of "terrorist" and "ally." My analysis of media and public discourse aims to make visible the relationships between various competing narratives about Hmong as allies, refugees, and terrorists that may seem disparate. Indeed, as feminist ethnographer Lila Abu-Lughod explains, the location of ethnographic work on media allows for balancing social criticism and policy critiques.[22] I approach my examination of online comments as a study of the actions of people who may not have otherwise been heard rather than as a study of media itself.[23] In this way, Hmong activities—including writing news articles and online comments, and participating in and posting videos of the rallies—show the assemblage of the terrorist ally. While the case's hypervisibility in the media opened up some recounting of General Vang Pao's past crimes of war that contradict the hero narrative about him, the overarching story of him as a savior reveals how the U.S. state and Hmong refugees/Americans know what not to tell so that refugee histories remain on the run.

Foregrounding the mobilization around the case seeks to illuminate the "compositional" claims about Hmong belonging in the U.S. Laura Kang explains that engaging in "compositional struggles" necessitates attention to what is said along with questions of why and how this articulation differs from previous "knowledge-claims and representational endeavors" precisely because this is an "embedded production."[24] It is a historical analysis that relies upon new media including online comment forums to engage with a more ephemeral refugee archive than that provided by state records and the law. In addition to focusing on mainstream news outlets such as the *Los Angeles Times* and *New York Times*, I specifically explore online comments from articles and editorials published in *Hmong Today*, a Minnesota ethnic newspaper, which is published both in print and online. Although the newspaper publishes some articles in Hmong, most of the news stories are written in English. *Hmong Today*'s editor, Wameng Moua, wrote several editorial pieces concerning the arrests and the state of Hmong leadership, especially from the perspective of 1.5-generation and second-generation Hmong Americans, which sparked the online comments I analyze here. These online forums are "less mediated" and more spontaneous and can reveal the tensions and contradictions that might not be visible in the original piece or through other ethnographic sites. At a time when family and community allegiances were important for displaying unity and strength, the online "comment function" constituted a useful tool for 1.5-generation and second-generation Hmong Americans to critique U.S. imperialism and the general. With the option of posting anonymously or pseudonymously (which all of the respondents chose to use) commenters had greater liberty to respond to each other and the author. Nonetheless, online comments are mediated by their attachment to the "already existing knowledge and discourse" in which they are embedded, including the larger narrative of Hmong relationships with the U.S. in Laos and the war on terror.[25] Many of the comments provide perceptive linkages between the "secret war" and the U.S. war in Iraq, and narrate a history that drags the past into the present. This process of dragging suggests the overlap of histories across space and time—the Cold War onto the war on terror—to redress the war's injustices.[26]

Terrorist Ally: Refugee as An/archive

Historical erasure legally and ideologically frames the refugee ally as a terrorist. Describing the attempts to transcribe the atomic bomb experience onto human skin whereby the body is where many of the atomic marks were recorded, film scholar Akira Mizuta Lippit coins the phrase *act of anarchiving* to encapsulate how writing on the body functions as a ritual repetition of the original violence.[27] The "anarchive" or "antiarchive," Lippit explains, is a secret archive of the visible at the moment of its appearance.[28] Here, the terrorist ally embodies the repetition and overlap of U.S. empire's liberal strategies of war and violence. This figure's potential to enact violence is rooted in the fact that violence has been acted upon them. I borrow the idea of the anarchive to explore how the framing of the refugee as a terrorist ally records the repetition of violence as it overlaps with the Hmong refugee's efforts to reassert history and knowledge.

The terrorist ally, as a conjoining of the former ally with new configurations of the terrorist, signifies the refugee's potential threat of disloyalty and the exposure of the U.S. liberal empire's unending forms of violence. In addition, this figure represents the precarious position of Hmong as U.S. citizen-subjects who can be expelled yet still indict the nation-state's perpetuation of violence. While chapter 2 looks for the trace of the missing things, this chapter shows how histories arrive in wreckage once they are revealed, destroyed and parceled out for Hmong refugees/Americans to decipher. The untimely seizure of memory as it "flashes up at a moment of danger," Walter Benjamin's well-known phrase, enables Hmong refugees/Americans to "articulate the past historically" by dragging the past into the present.[29] Because Hmong histories have not been distinctly recorded but are embedded in and move along several nodes of recollecting, this method of recalling the past is distinct from other forms of critical remembering predicated on an archive of subjugated memories. The terrorist ally is a refugee threat and an archival juxtaposition to drag up U.S. liberal empire's disparate histories and to challenge the claims that its wars are over, as well as to contend that the war was not a secret for Hmong refugees. The terrorist ally as an analytic to examine the compositional configuration of the refugee illuminates the repetition of historical violence and drag/pushback against that repetition. The charge of terrorism rerecords historical violence while at the same time opening and dragging up Hmong assertions of history and secrets. In chapter 5, I will elaborate on drag as a feminist refugee praxis, borrowed from literary critic Elizabeth Freeman's articulation of drag as embodiment of history into time binds, of remembering loss through embodiment.

In their excavation of how sexuality is central to the creation of a certain knowledge of terrorism, Jasbir K. Puar and Amit S. Rai argue that the construct of the terrorist relies on a knowledge of sexual perversity such as failed heterosexuality, Western notions of the psyche, and a certain queer monstrosity.[30] Using Foucault's concept of monstrosity to articulate the "terrorist-monster" discourse in the present war on terrorism, they maintain that the "terrorist has become a monster to be quarantined and an individual to be corrected."[31] Their formulation of the "terrorist-monster-fag" figure sheds light on the assumed abnormal psyche of the refugee as one who pines for a long-gone past and plans a coup in a forgotten and neutralized government and space. In her conceptualization of the assemblage of the Muslim terrorist figure, Puar explains that "the invocation of the terrorist as a queer, nonnational, perversely racialized other has become part of the normative script of the U.S. war on terror."[32] She explains that in the cases of Osama bin Laden and Saddam Hussein, images in popular culture portrayed both figures as "monstrous by association with sexual and bodily perversity," associations which encompassed homosexuality and failed monogamy or an Orientalist version of polygamy.[33] Indeed, she argues that the Orientalist invocation of the terrorist is a discursive tactic that foregrounds the collusion between homosexuality and U.S. exceptionalism, yet, one that includes U.S. national gay and queer subjects at the negation of racial and sexual others.[34] The discursive deployment of the terrorist as a racial and sexual other relies on the imagined geography of the "Orient" as a historically devalued, perverse place. In the terrorist ally configuration that emerged through the charges against General Vang Pao and his alleged accomplices, the historically imagined empty land of Laos, in which Hmong are positioned as natural inhabitants of the landscape, operates as the target of terrorist violence and a specter of U.S. militarized empire. Furthermore, the particular construction of Hmong as historically nongeographic and ahistorical worked to reinforce the perversity of the terrorist ally. Such historical emplacements of terra nullius onto Laos and displacements of Hmong from history and geography makes his purported virility aberrant because the terrorist ally relies on expired tactics and outdated weapons.

While the concept of the terrorist ally reflects the nonnormative, queer formation of the Muslim terrorist figure, it also emphasizes the specter of Cold War historiography that emerges as a refugee ally trying to rescue their people. The terrorist ally is a configuration of excessive and perverse Hmong patriarchy. Hmong protests against the charge of terrorism overwhelmingly deployed a patriarchal discourse about General Vang Pao as a father figure who led Hmong refugees to the U.S. Yet, the legal charges and public discourse enact a paternalistic view—Hmong are excessively and perversely patriarchal and violent while the U.S. is optimally patriarchal and appropriately violent—of the general and the other defendants, depicting them as threats paradoxically both because of their relationship with the U.S. and for their inherent disposition to violence. As such, the portrayal of terrorism as a spectacle of violence opens up gendered formations about Hmong and regarding Hmong claims to a precarious history and presence in the United States, which are not always critical of the U.S. and must also be closely examined.

Constructions of gender, specifically that of deviant Hmong masculinity, are an important component of the terrorist ally. We, as the U.S. public, have seen two "popular" eruptions into contemporary U.S. culture and politics that have radically decontextualized the longer histories of migrations and war. One is the narrative represented in the Hollywood film *Gran Torino*, which I take up in the next chapter, where white male tutelage and Cold War atonement are predicated on flattening the differences between North Koreans and Hmong allies. The plot centers on the reform and redemption of a Korean War veteran, Walt Kowalski, played by Clint Eastwood, who also directed the film. Walt is haunted by his memories of killing young Korean soldiers in the war and by his discontent with the invasion of troublemaking immigrants in his suburban Detroit neighborhood. The film recuperates the forgotten Korean War veteran into a heroic U.S. figure, depicting a double foreclosure of U.S. imperialism in Southeast/Asia by conflating North Korean soldiers with Hmong youth. This juxtaposition relies on paternalism and emphasis of Hmong cultural difference to enhance Walt's symbolic representation of the U.S. and his reform. It also portrays a Hmong masculinity in which young men can only be legible as gangbangers and effeminate teenagers to be either eradicated or saved by white masculinity. The second popular eruption is the well-publicized story of Chai Vang, the Hmong hunter who was convicted for killing six white hunters in Wisconsin. Here, Hmong masculinity is already violent; Hmong men are inherently disposed to killing, a form of violence that has been attributed to their role in the war. These instances portray the violence as a problem of general Asian backwardness and a specific premodern condition of Hmong as a people who do not have a geographic homeland. I suggest that these gendered representations of a Hmong disposition to violence depict a deviant Hmong masculinity that is rooted in the ontology of the former ally's illogical virility. While General Vang Pao as a former ally enacts violence in the name of rescuing his people, he is simultaneously subjugated to U.S. heteropatriarchal logic and violence.

The terrorist ally's gendered form rests upon the twinned configurations of Hmong deviant masculinity that exists within a patriarchal structure as subject to U.S. paternalistic management, and a virile masculinist subject who provides protection. Iris Marion Young, in her analysis of the "logic of masculinist protection" of the U.S. security state after the attacks on 9/11, explains how this logic is associated with "the position of male head of household as a protector of the family, and, by extension, with masculine leaders and risk takers as protectors of a population."[35] The patriarchal logic subjects citizens to state power and allegiance, since they are not supposed to do anything that undermines the power of the sovereign. Young observes that this logic relies on a version of masculinity associated with ideas of chivalry, in which "the gallantly masculine man is loving and self-sacrificing, especially in relation to women. The role of this courageous, responsible, and virtuous man is that of a protector."[36] Those subjected to this logic must defer to the protector because in the face of threat there cannot be divided wills.[37] General Vang represents both the protector and the one needing protection because his heroism is a product of the U.S. project of militarism and rescue. For instance, in the case of terrorism and Hmong protests, General Vang embodies the feminized subject of the state because he has been caught and must subject himself to the power of the sovereign as both a terrorist and citizen-subject.

Yet, this logic is also fitting to analyze the declarations of the general's heroism from Hmong public demonstrators. In so doing, the feminized subjectivities of Hmong protesters look up to him with "gratitude for his manliness and admiration for his willingness to face the dangers of the world."[38] Although Young specifically examines the relationship between a state and its citizens in times of threat, especially President George W. Bush's use of the "logic of masculinist protection," her arguments provide a useful framework for understanding how Hmong attempt to interpret the general's actions as those of a masculine protector in order to argue for his innocence. This logic suggests that General Vang is not inherently evil because his alleged plans were meant to protect and save his people. There should be no question as to his stance because a hero whose objective is to save people does not seek to kill, and his acts of killing are justifiable. Statements about how he is merely carrying out Bush's plans in the alleged plot attribute this "logic of masculinist protection" onto the configuration of him as a hero.

The case against General Vang Pao reveals the "compositional" subject formation of the Hmong refugee figure as a loyal U.S. American, a terrorist, a helpless refugee, and a U.S. citizen. It also underscores the "compositional struggles" through which Hmong contend with the media's representation of their concerns as a nostalgic reliving of the past.[39] The refugee compositional subject opens up critical analysis of the physical rallies and virtual protests as "critical re-memberings of identity and its possible composition" that challenge Hmong racialization within the contexts of U.S. imperialism and multiculturalism.[40]

The Terrorist Ally Is Consistent with U.S. Policies
The terrorist ally demonstrates coherence with liberal empire and the state through parallels between U.S./CIA activities in the Middle East and in Laos, and between the general and other former U.S. allies who have faced similar charges. Passing references to Laos in U.S. press coverage of the government's activities in the Middle East after 9/11 and of CIA operations in Afghanistan generated significant interest among Hmong news organizations. On December 16, 2001, *Hmong Times* reprinted an article from the Associated Press, "CIA's Paramilitary Force a Cross between Spies and Soldiers," under its Community section.[41] The article revealed that the CIA had sent spies into Afghanistan and the surrounding countries after an officer was killed in Afghanistan. These personnel were tasked with supplying weapons, training rebels fighting the Taliban, and gathering information, and were authorized to interrogate prisoners and defectors. Their presence in countries suspected of being sources of terrorists before the arrival of military forces reflected the covert nature of their work. Specifically, officers from the CIA's Special Activities Division "are called upon when the president wants covertly to advance U.S. foreign policy, influencing government without any signs of U.S. action." The article briefly traced a genealogy of the paramilitary force, which has been used in Central America, Angola, and Afghanistan, stating that this force ran Air America, the "CIA's covert effort in Laos." Although the article contained only one brief reference to Laos, it was worthy of being reprinted in a Hmong American newspaper. It is important to note that this reprinting suggests an analysis of the parallels between U.S. covert military strategies in Laos and the Middle East, especially its placement in the Community section rather than under Nation or International News. This implicit analysis of U.S. foreign policy through the covert activities of the CIA aligned with Hmong reporters' investigations into U.S. policies in Laos after the arrests of General Vang Pao and his associates.

The issue of Hmong terrorism raised by the General Vang Pao case revisits the Vietnam War as a difficult chapter in U.S. history, especially the U.S. role in Laos. Because this past has not been dealt with publicly, the spectacle of the arrests and protests emerged as an exceptional moment in the U.S. treatment of Hmong refugees/Americans. Even contemporary relations between Laos and the U.S. are still mired in the context of archival secrecy that defined the war. In April 2011, the news organization McClatchy published a report and released several U.S. classified cables it obtained from WikiLeaks regarding the arrests in 2007. Michael Doyle, the report's author, suggested that the memos "shed light on the complicated relationship between the United States and Laos, a global odd couple with a war-torn past and many domestic offspring."[42] This report and the cables showed how General Vang Pao's arrest facilitated state relations between the two countries in areas of their relationship where the U.S. had previously experienced difficulty.[43] One of the cables reveals how the arrests produced "unusually friendly overtures from the Lao government." U.S. officials suspected that those Laotian officials, including Ministry of Foreign Affairs spokesman Yong Chanthalangsy, who favor closer cooperation with the U.S. viewed the arrests as "a good time to press ahead with initiatives that they previously saw as non-starters." Hence, the thwarted plot seemed to have beneficial implications for U.S.-Laos relations, and for the global war on terrorism. Carol A. Stabile and Carrie Rentschler write that "U.S. concerns about the 'security' of other states, and the interventions that have followed from these concerns, have proved to be synonymous with U.S. economic interests in the eyes of much of the world," which highlights the U.S. concern for Laos's national security precisely due to negotiating economic agreements with the nation-state.[44] The favorable response from certain Lao officials shows how these countries are changing their policies as well to become more closely allied with the U.S. But, Doyle's description of these two countries as a "global odd couple" signifies their historical and contemporary differences and unlikely relationship, which continues to revolve around the dilemma of historical secrecy.

The "global odd couple" is odd in the context of the Vietnam War rhetoric deployed by the assembled defense and prosecution teams to articulate history as something that exists in the past. As such, comparisons that might connect U.S. imperialist expansion during the Cold War with current policies in the global war on terrorism instead posit the alleged coup plot as a remnant of history rather than contention with that past in the present. Yet, the fact that the Laos-U.S. coupling is perceived to be odd suggests the incongruence over the understanding of the Cold War between Southeast Asian refugees and nonrefugee Americans.[45] As an example, U.S. secret strategies to intervene in Laotian decolonization and to save Hmong from their not-yet condition may seem odd because U.S. Americans perceive their government as benevolent. The perceived historical oddity rationalizes Hmong alleged terrorist acts as a product of the tragic psyche of the racialized refugee exile, and pathologizes Vang Pao and the other defendants as attempting to carry out the same covert military tactics in order to continue a war that has ended for the U.S. Furthermore, the insinuations about Laos and the U.S. as a "couple" suggests the persistence of the "ally," where Laos as a state ally is subordinate but also complicit with U.S. state antiterrorism policies. Hmong protesters remind us that the U.S. treatment of Hmong as terrorist is consistent with its past and current policies. Their compositional struggles constitute the "ideological suppositions and methodological tactics" that make their claims productive in articulating Hmong presence and making visible the ongoing practices of U.S. imperialism.[46]

Attempts to dispute the government's case often depicted the general as an aging and ailing leader from a different historical period and a forgotten region, an image that did not seem compatible with the terrorist zealots frequently represented in the media. A *Los Angeles Times* article published three days after the arrests characterizes the case as the latest example of "anti-Communist warriors," part of a familiar story about historical nostalgia among other Southeast Asian refugee leaders. Anti-Communism is rendered as a refugee problem, and described in terms of refugee communities' inability to move on while "most Americans have relegated [the war] to history books."[47] The reporter, Ashley Powers, explains that Southern California has been the breeding ground for many "foiled plots" by refugee leaders who continue to wage battles over their homelands:

> When federal agents took an elderly Hmong man who relies on heart medication and a cane into custody this week, Vang Pao became the latest anti-Communist leader in Southern California's suburbs to be accused of trying to rekindle a long-ago war. In recent years, the region has contributed a number of chapters to the annals of conspiracies that read like spy novels—a reflection that for some people in immigrant enclaves such as Orange County's Little Saigon and Long Beach's Little Phnom Penh, the Vietnam War never ended. Amid the foiled plots and bombs that sputtered are a cadre of Hmong, Cambodian and Vietnamese "freedom fighters" waging battles that most Americans have relegated to history books.[48]

This account of anti-Communist politics and activities makes the Vietnam War an event that has "never ended" for these "warriors."[49] Thus, the charges criminalize these refugee men for rekindling a closed chapter in U.S. history and characterize them as trying to relive that past. This portrayal attempts to narrate a linear story about what must safely remain in the past rather than examining how these moments actually blast open the past into the present. These negotiations of not only when the war ends but also what it was about and for whom the stakes matter most continually dissolve a metahistory about the Vietnam War as contained in one country, about Vietnamese people, and from which the U.S. can claim some measure of victory for successfully rescuing the refugees. The arrests trouble the historical narrative that has relegated the war to the "history books." My point here concerns the question of who can conjure up the past, on what terms, and for what purpose. For the refugee leaders, the same rules of unofficial alliances built on militarism and rescue still apply because the U.S. continues to use them to subvert nation-states' sovereignties in the global war on terrorism.

Nonetheless, the federal government's arrest of the general, which was insidiously named "Operation Tarnished Eagle," was unexpected but not exceptional in this post-9/11 moment of "reinvigorated militarism." *New York Times* reporter Tim Weiner makes the link between the Cold War and the current war on terror in an article almost a year after the arrests, titled "Gen. Vang Pao's Last War," in which he highlights the prosecutors' naming of General Vang as a "Laotian bin Laden": "Now the war on terror has engulfed Vang Pao in his land of exile, California. . . . His prosecutors painted him as a Laotian bin Laden. . . . Few former friends of American foreign interests have fallen further from favor in Washington's eyes . . . the old general's defenders contend that the case against him is the consequence of a misguided post-9/11 zeal."[50] The prosecutors interweave the narrative of a Vietnam War exile with the contemporary story about the search for Osama bin Laden to produce this composite of "Laotian bin Laden." General Vang and bin Laden are conjoined as "tarnished [former American] eagles" (reminiscent of Operation Tarnished Eagle) who have "fallen" from "favor in Washington's eyes" because they were once useful "new friends" but now pose national security and global threats.

In the comparison between the general and other former U.S. allies, some Hmong Americans' online comments charge that U.S. imperialism operates by relying on local leaders globally as a means to buffer its expansionist project. It is well known that Osama bin Laden was formerly a U.S. ally during Russia's war in Afghanistan, trained and armed by the CIA to defeat the United States' geopolitical enemy. In light of the transformation from ally to terrorist that is embodied by bin Laden and General Vang, some Hmong Americans believed that the U.S. government created the case against Vang Pao to provide material evidence for the continuing global war on terror.[51] Indeed, the general's trajectory as a sacrificial former U.S.-backed ally is similar to that of others, like Saddam Hussein and Manuel Noriega; Vang Pao, however, serves as a surrogate for the real U.S. target, Osama bin Laden, who was not killed until 2011. General Vang's case most closely resembled that of Noriega, the Panamanian military officer and politician, trained in and supported by the U.S. but later removed from power in a U.S. invasion. Noriega's fate—convicted of drug crimes and imprisoned by the U.S. government—served as an example of what could become of the general.

The Hmong terrorist ally is similar to yet different from the figures of bin Laden, Hussein, and other terrorist constructions. The Hmong terrorist ally is similar to Puar and Rai's formulation of queer monstrosity in that Hmong queerness emerges from the imagined geography in which Hmong are associated with the terra nullius of Laos, marked as backward by statelessness and illiteracy. Relatedly, Kong Pha explains that Hmong nonheteronormative practices of polygamy and having large families have been cited as evidence of Hmong racial backwardness, and I suggest comprised sites of regulating Hmong sexuality in refugee processing. He reclaims the nonheteronormative formation of families as constitutive of Hmong queerness.[52] Furthermore, the Hmong community's not-yet-modern status queers the purported virility of the terrorist ally who yearns for a feminized yet unfulfilled homeland. General Vang Pao's crime lies in the untimely act that no longer holds potency because he relies on expired tactics and outdated weapons. In addition to being monstrous, inhuman, or excessively freedom loving or pathologically patriarchal, violent, and loyal, the Hmong refugee is also distinguished for their "backwardness" in not having modern, heteronormative families, or through an inability to understand how modern statehood functions. Hmong "backwardness" marks Hmong refugees as terrorists in that they operate on the basis of social, religious, and political ethics that are incongruent with those of the rescuing state. Hence, their crime is not that they desire a free but impossible homeland; instead, it is that their "backwardness" prevents them from understanding that only the U.S. government is allowed to name the enemy.

Therefore, General Vang Pao's alleged actions, rather than being an irrational desperation of a forgotten ally, are in fact aligned with U.S. liberal policies. In arguing for the defendants' innocence during arraignment and bail hearings, lawyers for the group did not try to deny the charges but instead offered explanations for the alleged actions, which they linked to the unofficial Hmong-U.S. alliance during the war. Given the Hmong history of working with the CIA, the lawyers argued, "the defendants believed they had the government's unofficial blessing."[53] The defense lawyer for Lo Cha Thao declared in court that the undercover agent and others gave the alleged conspirators the impression they were connected to high levels of the U.S. government. The idea of purchasing missiles was actually suggested by the federal agent. Jon Keker, Vang Pao's attorney, contended that the defendants thought the alleged coup would gain support from the CIA and that their actions were only meant to help the Hmong in Laos who are still facing persecution for supporting the U.S. during the war.[54] This encouragement demonstrates how the government or at least some of its representatives aligned with and helped carry out the "terrorist plot." But according to the "unofficial blessing" claim, Hmong contentions with history deploy the expired rules of covert military violence to achieve political ends. Here again, the refugee is a terrorist ally who is a danger to sovereignty because he has never had sovereignty to begin with.

Following this line of argument, the charges against Vang Pao constitute legal entrapment not only of the alleged coup plotters but of the Hmong diasporic community. *Hmong Today* contributor Chong Jones explains that the Neutrality Act was first breached by the U.S. government and the CIA "by providing and furnishing money for a military expedition in the sovereign nation of Laos." Bringing together the U.S. actions in Laos, the dilemma of the general's leadership, and the Bush administration's failures, Jones declares: "Most U.S. citizens don't even know where Laos is let alone what happened there forty years ago. The recent U.S. policy shift in terror activities by the Bush administration once again will *commit another betrayal of its former ally*. Ironically, the charges filed against Vang Pao are the same criminal *acts exercised by the U.S. that started this atrocity. Vang Pao is the product of U.S. policies*. Now U.S. policies will condemn him for his alleged actions."[55] This statement's juxtaposition of Hmong and U.S. illicit activities shows the dragging of histories across time and space because Hmong history on the run continues to unfold how refugees narrate their political subjectivity. It captures the multiply layered narratives articulated in online comments and protest rallies about the arrests and simultaneously highlights four key points: first, it foregrounds the plight of those still in Laos who face the aftermath of the "secret war"; second, it highlights parallels between alleged Hmong actions and the U.S. preemptive war in Iraq; third, it contests and reassigns the terrorist label; and finally, it foregrounds Hmong experiences as racialized subjects in the U.S. Jones suggests that what the U.S. public might have thought of as its government's "shadowy" legacy of secret warfare in Laos actually represents a common practice. Specifically, Jones contends that the crimes the Hmong defendants are alleged to have undertaken are the same "criminal acts exercised by the U.S. government." Thus, the charges of terrorism against the general and the Hmong community necessarily indict the U.S. for perpetuating what it criminalizes as racialized terror in the post–Cold War context as well as its Cold War crimes. The point here is that the

U.S. is responsible for its illicit policies and for the general's arrest, exposing the U.S. as a site of violence rather than a place of refuge for the refugee.

Jones's statement, along with the rest of the article, also captures the heteronormative rationalizing of Hmong-U.S. relations and General Vang Pao's alleged terrorist actions to save his fellow Hmong people. Jones's observation that General Vang was arrested for trying to carry out "the same criminal acts exercised" by the U.S. attempts to align these two instances and understand histories as linked. For example, Jones calls the U.S.-Hmong relationship a marriage—a characterization that mirrors the "global odd couple" perception—that was consummated when the U.S. government began supplying Vang Pao and Hmong soldiers with weapons and money. This marriage ended in divorce in 1975 with U.S. abandonment, when only two planes evacuated a "handful" of the forty thousand Hmong civilians waiting on the Long Cheng tarmac.[56] Hence, Jones foregrounds how the case is ironic because "the union between the U.S. and Vang Pao has finally come full circle."[57] This heteronormative reading of the Hmong-U.S. relationship as a marriage, with General Vang and Hmong as the submissive partner supplied with weapons and money, reinscribes normalcy to this unequal and illicit alliance. This dragging up of the past also involves a masculinized military couching of history to show the terrorist ally's protection of Hmong as on par with the actions of other powerful historical figures. Yet, Jones's taking up of the "global odd couple" descriptor does not negate the point about how U.S. violations could potentially disrupt imperialist power.

Jones's tracking of the case through U.S. policies illuminates how policy making in the contemporary context still drags up the conditions of an unfinished war, specifically through the Bush administration's successful negotiation of normal trade relations with Laos in 2004 and provisions in the USA Patriot Act passed in 2006. Their article exposes the legacy of U.S. violations and secrecy in its relationships with Hmong and Laos, and also underscores the plight of those Hmong soldiers and civilians who could not escape and are still in hiding in Laos. They await the general's return to either continue the fight or to rescue them. According to fact-finding missions by international human rights agencies and Hmong refugees/Americans, this group endures the Laotian government's violence whereby Laotian troops "hunt" them "like animals" to exterminate the resistance.[58] Jones reflects on the connection between General Vang Pao's arrest and their struggles in which the Hmong leader feels obligated to "help the helpless" because the U.S. had not lived up to its promises. The alleged coup, therefore, is a necessary act of violence to draw attention to this situation and to help his former soldiers and fellow Hmong people. Hence, the irony is that it is only when the colonized resort to violence through self-inflicted wounds that the imperial violence against them gets recorded in the imperial archive.[59] Hmong protested the Bush administration's move toward normalized relations with Laos, citing these human rights abuses as cause for the U.S. to refrain from political and economic relations. Hmong refugees/Americans in the U.S. protesting the case reference the unrescued former Hmong soldiers and their families who are on the run in Laos as justification for General Vang's alleged actions.

Protests against General Vang Pao's arrest reveal that the refugee and its missing baggage of war does not fit the loyal ally construct. The Hmong refugee figure emerges as a lagging presence of U.S. empire's project of militarism and rescue. For instance, Hmong claim that the war is not yet over because the U.S. has not completed its task of rescuing a contingent of Hmong soldiers and their descendants. Their declarations of allegiance allow Hmong refugees/Americans to criticize the U.S. for moving on to the "War on Terror" when the "Vietnam War" is not yet over. Anonymous respondents assert that: "THE WAR IN VIETNAM IS NOT OVER YET, SO I HAVE NO IDEA WHY THE US JUST GOT UP AND LEFT WHEN THEY KNEW, THEY KNEW THAT MY PEOPLE WERE STILL IN THE JUNGLES OF LIFE SUFFERING AND BEING MURDERED [sic]."[60] This specific claim that the "war in Vietnam is not over yet" reflects the continuation of U.S. undeclared wars, exposing the undeclared beginnings and ends to any war since the Vietnam War. The charge that the "US just got up and left" when so many Hmong are still in the jungles names the multiple times that the U.S. left its former ally. First, it references U.S. abandonment in 1973 (the war officially ended for U.S. Americans but not for Hmong) when the government withdrew aid and pulled out of Laos, leaving Hmong refugees/soldiers to fend for themselves in the wake of Communist takeover. Second, the U.S. "got up and left" again in continuing to ignore the plight of those who could not escape to Thailand's refugee camps and still had to endure violence in Laos. The arrest of General Vang Pao and others is a third leaving that compounds the previous U.S. abandonments because it has recoded these Hmong leaders as terrorists instead of U.S. allies. Unrescued refugees who are the missing baggage that needs to be claimed signify unfinished wars, highlighting the global war on terrorism as a continuation of the wars fought in Southeast Asia. Yet, the general has also been criticized for actually leaving Hmong refugees in Laos in a state of limbo in order to further his project of continuing the war to oust the Communist government because they serve as evidence of Communism's abject treatment.[61]

General Vang not only represents a terrorist ally for the state but also for a vast majority of Hmong, mainly for alleged war crimes and money swindling from Hmong refugees to support an exile movement to take back Laos, the very crime he was charged with in 2007. Hmong American readers of *Hmong Today* anonymously refer to the general as a "con-artist" who deceived hundreds of Hmong parents and grandparents by collecting "donations" to support a false cause. His arrest, then, exposed the underside of Hmong refugee community politics, where he, as a "VERY GOOD con-artist," deserves "any and all jail time that he gets."[62] To be sure, even though the prevailing narrative valorizes him, he represents competing meanings for the Hmong diasporic community.

Hmong American Mobilization

Given the limited history about General Vang Pao as a success of the CIA's covert operations, the image of this ally who had saved U.S. soldiers' lives did not quite match up with the threat of the terrorist. Hmong protesters recuperated this gap to express reverence for General Vang as their leader and hero, proclaim faithfulness to democracy, and denounce the U.S. government. The protests show how General Vang, the most visible refugee soldier, constitutes a central figure for Hmong political mobilization, identity formation, and history-making in the United States. Hmong refugees/Americans who contest his configuration as a terrorist generate a public discourse about him as a heroic father figure. The terrorist ally's deviant masculinity, both subjugated to U.S. rescue and an agent for rescuing Hmong refugees, becomes more apparent through Hmong glorification of General Vang as a hero who delivered them from war. Taken together, Hmong refugees/Americans who voice support for General Vang may attempt to question history's omissions but also end up correcting the historical record about their role in protecting freedom.

Hundreds of protesters also organized in other cities away from the epicenter of the Sacramento jail and courthouse, such as St. Paul/Minneapolis, Detroit, and Madison, where large concentrations of Hmong live. Participants in these rallies dressed in coordinated clothing consisting of white tops and black bottoms. This coordination lent visual impact to the events, which showcased dramatic scenes of Hmong, young and old, women and men, mostly those who had never participated in such public "dissent," making sure their voices were heard. This uniformity in color-coding of protesters' dress signifies a Hmong peaceful resistance as obedient citizens of the state to correct a government mistake in arresting their leaders.⁶³ The uniform color-coding alternatively represents the rallies as performing the march of the general's Hmong army, which the prosecutors alleged as the threat posed by General Vang. Carrying mostly homemade signs with messages like "FREE GENERAL VANG PAO," "Gen. Vang Pao Is a Symbol of Peace, Freedom + Democracy," and "Gen. Vang Pao Is Leader of the People," Hmong protesters spent days after the arrests and during the hearings rallying for justice and the immediate release of General Vang. He quickly became the most prominent figure in the protests, inspiring chants of "FREEDOM!" Although they deployed the liberal empire's trope of freedom, the chants were also a call to free Hmong history under arrest. In those early days of mobilization, Laotian and Vietnamese refugee leaders also rallied with the South Vietnamese flag waving in the crowd, revealing how this moment represented an opportunity for collective remembering among Southeast Asian refugees about their pasts that are not yet over. A *Sacramento Bee* article reports that the demonstrations portrayed a mix of feelings, from patriotism for the United States and indignation about abuses toward Hmong people in Laos, to loyalty to longtime Hmong leader General Vang Pao. The article describes a little girl who marched carrying a poster of General Vang that stretched from her neck to her knees, epitomizing how the refugee soldier's claim to belonging pervaded all segments of the Hmong community.⁶⁴

General Vang Pao's arrest made it possible for Hmong to come together and mobilize. Xang Vang, one of the general's closest advisors, maintained that throughout thirty years of community involvement "he has never seen the Hmong people so united for anything before, seeing those who have criticized General Vang Pao now fighting at his side."⁶⁵ The strong showing of support is encouraging for potential Hmong unity. Although this may be attributed to the high turnout at the protest rallies to a singular glorification of the general, it also highlights a shift in Hmong community politics ushered in by his arrest. The belief that he brought Hmong people together at a time when belief in him and in returning to Laos had been waning represents an important perspective about his alleged actions and the ensuing public demonstrations. The second generation, in particular, made up a significant proportion of protesters, inspiring faith among the elders that a generation of Hmong who had previously shown little interest in Hmong history might remember and continue to work for rights, justice, and visibility.

Images of Hmong demonstrators kneeling with hands clasped in a worshipful position along with statements declaring the general's generosity and "gift" of rescue circulated in the mainstream and ethnic press coverage of the

FIGURE 4.1. A demonstration held in Sacramento, CA, on May 12, 2009, to contest the charges of terrorism by the U.S. government against General Vang Pao and his associates. Source: Moua Moua (photographer).

events. This defense of General Vang Pao's innocence (past and present) represents an effort to secure a Hmong present and future by crediting him with bringing Hmong refugees to the U.S. One anonymous reader contended that "whatever GVP [General Vang Pao] did in the past is wrong but he brought us here and protesting for him is the only gift we can ever paid back to him [sic]."[66] This statement ties Hmong history and belonging to the general. It reminds Hmong refugees/Americans that "he brought us here" and that the protests in support of him are a "gift" or offering to express our gratitude to him (shown in figure 4.1). Hence, Hmong legal and social belonging cannot be divorced from the masculinized figure of the general. One Hmong woman, Kay Yang, exclaimed to a *Los Angeles Times* reporter two days after the arrest, "I don't care what they say, I'm on his side."[67] Hmong women also deployed the masculinist discourse and were strongly represented in the protest rallies. Their presence and voices added to General Vang's heroic image as both military and community leader. Otherwise, Hmong women's perceived roles as displaced victims would render their claims illegible for demanding justice for government misconduct. The declarations of allegiance to General Vang certainly anchored the beginnings of mobilizing around the case.

To glorify the general for leading Hmong to the U.S. is necessarily to justify the war and its means. Some Hmong take up the issue of justifying the war and the general's alleged actions in the charges. One individual writes: "think if the secret war never happened. the communist will still make its way into laos and then we still have to fight. now no gun power from the U.S. we will soon be eliminated [*sic*]."[68] Such claims recuperate the war and violence as necessary for Hmong liberation from their conditions because alliance with the U.S. equipped Hmong with the means to defend their way of life. This respondent's assertion that Hmong would have had to fight Communism on their own in the face of certain elimination highlights a belief among some Hmong refugees, including those I formally interviewed, that the Hmong position without a country made them vulnerable to Communist oppression if they had not allied with the United States. General Vang's military leadership gave Hmong life in asking them to die for the cause of freedom. Even with the arrests and terrorist charge, Hmong veterans conveyed pride in their service to the U.S.[69] The tone of these multiple and multisited demonstrations fits into the image of Hmong as loyal, freedom-loving refugees. The appeals to the U.S. government for the general's release and mercy toward those refugees still in Laos align with Phoung Nguyen's description of Vietnamese refugees demonstrating in favor of U.S. government intervention in the "boat people crisis" as falling "neatly into two visible but unequal categories: the helpless refugee and the anti-communist crusader."[70] In contesting the terrorist allegations, Hmong protesters espouse and embody both the helpless refugee and the "freedom fighter." This liberation narrative imbues the Hmong refugee figure with history and belonging, which negated the violence of the war.

Others expand on crediting General Vang Pao with liberation by explaining that he symbolized a Hmong emergence into modernity. Wameng Xiong of Hmong American AD HOC, an organization created to track the case and organize the protest rallies, recuperates his legacy in a biblical metaphor as "leading us to this country": "We . . . remember General Vang Pao for bringing our Hmong people out of Laos, fighting in the war to help the American government against the Communists, to remember his legacy of leading us to this country. It makes me think about myself and people of my generation. If we didn't have the General then I would still be a farmer boy working on the land (farming), maybe I wouldn't even be alive. We are grateful (*txaj ntswg*) for General Vang Pao."[71] This assertion that Xiong would "still be a farmer" in Laos or not even be alive without the general's leadership in bringing Hmong to the U.S., and progress, proclaims a certain benevolence in the Hmong leader's close relationship with the U.S. government and his foresight to evacuate from Laos. As someone who has been instrumental in organizing efforts to seek justice for the general and the other Hmong defendants, Xiong links his education and leadership to the liberatory image of General Vang. Xiong further reveres the general as a father figure who had "taught us to live a good life in America so that we support and love each other."[72] These statements bolster a version of the U.S. refugee rescue and liberation discourse that makes the U.S. the site of refuge for Hmong refugees/veterans and elides the state's production of war and their historical displacements.[73] They also make the war inseparable from General Vang Pao's leadership, a coupling that constituted the turning point for Hmong liberation from premodernity (farming) to modernity (Xiong as leader of a Hmong American justice organization). Xiong's assertion complicates the U.S. project of secrecy by suggesting the war was beneficial to Hmong, because allying with the U.S. eventually facilitated Hmong resettlement in the U.S. Therefore, Xiong's question of, "What's the point to go to trial? The general is a hero," suggests that General Vang's status as a heroic father figure should prove his innocence and make going to trial a pointless legal action.[74]

Although General Vang's heroism emerged from his wartime leadership, Wameng Moua explains that it also came from a deep love for his people. The *Hmong Today* editor wrote an opinion piece on June 18, 2007, exploring the question of what the general meant for his parents' generation and what his arrest might mean for the second generation. Moua asserted that the elder generation perceived the general as a "George Washington or a Martin Luther King" because "he delivered a higher standard of living and a taste of the promised land" through his bravery and heroism. Our parents "honored the man as though he just opened the sky and handed civilization to the Hmong people." Moua went on to reflect that he had not seen the general's "love" until the Hmong leader's arrest because it "sometimes takes sacrifice for a leader to speak loudest." This kind of sacrifice makes his heroic image endure beyond the first generation, compelling Moua to proclaim: "He is my hero. He is the Hmong hero. His legacy is forever intact."[75] Such claims reinforce masculinity in the general as "my hero" whose legacy will stay intact, despite the arrests, because he has made an ultimate sacrifice for his people in order to lead them to a better life. As a collective "Hmong hero," General Vang helps bridge the gap between the first and second generations, to strengthen a sense of Hmong identity that is tied to the legacy of a man who will stop at nothing to deliver his people from persecution. It is important to note that these expressions of loyalty institute a silencing of other Hmong refugee perspectives.

Furthermore, the assertions about General Vang Pao as the "son of Laos" and key U.S. ally ties Hmong loyalty to the nation-state.[76] Such assertions about democracy reveal Hmong loyalty as a product of the nation-state and its policies. Hmong faithfulness is expressed to the U.S. government, yet it is also deployed to attain justice and equality. Keith Camacho explains in his study on Chamorro commemoration that loyalty may have been initially used as a form of control by U.S. and Japanese colonial governments to create the "loyal Chamorro subject," but it also became a "mechanism for indigenous adaptation and survival, rather than being perceived as outright subjugation." He further elucidates these mechanisms as petitions for U.S. or Japanese recognition in which some Chamorros viewed loyalty as a means of achieving equality and a "shared sense of 'nationality' with their respective colonial powers."[77] Drawing from Camacho's discussion of loyalty, I contend that Hmong-expressed faithfulness to U.S. democracy and freedom represents a condition of the war. In addition, the idea of freedom also gets strategically taken up by Hmong refugees/Americans to continue to make claims about the unfinished business of the war's ends. Thus, their claims about General Vang draw together the transnational, global context of war, violence, and nation-state domestic and international policies in order to open up the conditions of possibility for a retelling of histories on the run. This case shows how the state looms in the spaces of indistinction between the ally and terrorist, and yet how slippage between both categories signifies an ontological rupture for the nation-state.

While all the mobilizations deployed the liberal multicultural rhetoric of justice and equality that reaffirm the U.S. state and democracy in order for the Hmong participants to be legible as dissenting subjects, they also worked to recast the U.S. Vietnam War story. This ultimate concern for justice is featured in the activists' positioning as U.S. citizens. During an October 15, 2010, protest rally, Dr. Nhia Lue Vang, one of the rally speakers, drew on the contemporary conditions of Hmong who are now enfranchised with U.S. citizenship to make certain demands of its government as "good citizens" and U.S. taxpayers. Rather than the injustice of being charged with terrorism, Hmong face injustice through the federal government's misconduct and misuse of their tax money by continuing to prosecute the case, Vang argued.

Dr. Vang, along with the protesters, also formulated a broader analysis of Hmong efforts during the war. In doing so, he narrated Hmong efforts which

The Terrorist Ally 141

saved American lives in the following way, and I quote him here: "We have been involved in the great task that supported South Vietnam where the U.S. Army was and we had to block the troops that brought supply from the North.... We stopped so much troops and supplies; that's why the American casualty was little, only fifty-eight thousand. Otherwise, it could have been 300,000 American troops who lost their lives in Vietnam [*sic*]."[78] This recounting of U.S. soldiers' bodies that could have been lost in South Vietnam remembers the Vietnam War as part of a great Hmong task to stop the flow of troops and supplies to the south through the Ho Chi Minh Trail. Instead of the ten Hmong who died for every U.S. pilot saved that the Fresno war memorial symbolizes (see chapter 3), Dr. Vang's claim places the Hmong refugee soldier's duties within the larger context of the Vietnam War and in relation to U.S. troops in South Vietnam. The conflict in Laos sustained the life of U.S. militarism by saving its citizen-soldiers, and ultimately cushioning the U.S. defeat. His retelling of this story on the stage of a Hmong American movement draws Hmong narrations about history up against U.S. Vietnam War history, and underscores how a "secret" war that the U.S. lost suppressed Hmong refugee histories.

Conclusion

Since the U.S. war against terror began, the country has resettled 784,000 refugees. This number includes two thousand Syrian refugees since the war in Syria began in 2011. Although there has been no history of terrorist attacks perpetrated by refugees, and refugees must face more than two years of screening before they can set foot on U.S. soil, refugees are now widely seen as presenting a danger to U.S. national security, as seen in the heated rhetoric that greeted the Obama administration's 2015 proposal to resettle more than ten thousand Syrian refugees. Republican governors, making up more than half of the nation's governors at the time, along with right-leaning immigration groups, urged the Obama administration not to pursue its proposal to resettle refugees, and vowed to refuse to accept refugees into their states.[79] These groups feared terrorist infiltration among the refugees, especially after news reports suggested that one of the men who carried out coordinated terror attacks in Paris in November 2015 might have gained entry as a refugee. Those who opposed the resettlement of Syrian refugees highlighted the cases of a few refugees radicalized while living in the U.S., including two Somali refugees from Minnesota and the Boston Marathon bombers who were granted asylum as children.[80]

Refugees and immigrants became even more vilified as posing terrorist threats after the 2016 U.S. presidential elections and the January 27, 2017 executive order banning the citizens of seven Muslim countries from entering the U.S.[81] Instead of the more benevolent narrative about the "good" refugee as deserving of rescue, the current discourse shores up U.S. exceptionalism, promotes distrust toward refugees, and advocates the tightening of national borders.

The concept of the terrorist ally, which this chapter has unpacked, captures all the anxieties about refugees in the contemporary moment. This figure reveals that such gendered, sexualized, colonial, racial anxieties reflect the tenuous U.S. alliances around the world, then and now. Thus, the terrorist ally also juxtaposes histories of the Cold War and the war on terror to function as an an/archive for the repetition of violence. By closely considering the U.S. government's arrest of General Vang Pao in 2007 and Hmong American protests against the charge of terrorism, I have argued that the refugee's threat as a terrorist is already structured by U.S. policies. As such, the "good" and "bad" refugees are part of the same imperialist project. This configuration of the refugee as both docile and threatening, I contend, represents the dichotomy at the core of the shifting racial meaning of the refugee's relationship to the nation-state as a fugitive figure. Being a refugee from the U.S. "secret war" already marks one as a potential terrorist to the nation-state paradigm because one already exists outside of it. Furthermore, Hmong American mobilizations against the legal and ideological framing of the terrorist assert that the alleged terrorist acts were produced by imperialist logics and are in alignment with current state policies. At the same time, they seek to establish a different story about the "secret war" that focuses on the number of U.S. lives saved, in order to remake history. The next chapter will build on the dragging method as a feminist approach to show how the figure of the Hmong refugee grandmother drags up stories on the run for refuge in each other.

5. THE REFUGEE GRANDMOTHER

SILENCE AS PRESENCE IN
THE LATEHOMECOMER AND *GRAN TORINO*

In Kao Kalia Yang's book *The Latehomecomer: A Hmong Family Memoir*, her grandmother is a source of knowledge who represents how stories about a life on the run are told. Grandma's split earlobe, for example, marks her flight and escape from a tiger in the jungle that prevented her from wearing jewelry for the rest of her life. Yang recounts that "Grandma wore the mark of that flight in the absence of decoration. . . . My grandma had outrun a tiger to live in this country. I wondered if a person could run forever" (210).[1] The "absence of decoration" on the ear makes poignant the negating story of escape, but it also functions as a reminder of the presence in running. Her stories embody a liveness that "encircle" the children such that the act of encircling provides a protectiveness and maternalness around the refugee.[2] Grandma symbolizes the concept of knowing how one lived in the urgency of lives lost in the absence of state-recorded markers. When thousands of Hmong men, women, and children have been lost to a war with no name and remain unaccounted for, those who survived its devastation hold tight to the possibility of marking their presence, no matter how fleeting it may seem. She functions as the trace of the fallen pieces of a life in war, always trying to fit their broken edges together and create points of holding on. Her stories comprise traces of the past to produce a possibility for witnessing, for which Yang writes: "In front of the window with her feet in my lap, she told me the stories of her life in Laos. It was a life that I didn't know but held close, imagined I saw, wanted to cherish" (231). This scene of storytelling is a part of the familial and intergenerational relations that reinvigorate Hmong Americans' engagements with the past and are consistent with early Asian American literary criticism. They emphasize a desire to hold close and cherish a life and to imagine connections to the past and future.

This chapter examines the ways in which these markers and remnants of lives lived not only are there to speak but also can be seen to be "on the run" in the sense that memories simultaneously are illuminated by and escape the remains. Yang's poignant reflection on her grandmother's life suggests that the missing baggage explored in the introduction signifies not just what goes missing in the archive, but the very material and symbolic items and stories that get left behind or are carried with refugees that exist in a refugee archive. Remnants such as the luggage as well as the stories that accompany these objects of exile make up the "fugitive knowledge" of histories that run.[3] To illuminate the remnants and stories as material possessions and see them "on the run," this chapter turns to refugee narratives in film and literature. Rather than recuperate the knowledge that escaped the traditional archive, I argue that even the stories that emerge in the cultural texts elude being the very remains of exile, and yet they render material Hmong historical presence as a process of becoming legible through the refugee grandmother. I name this process where the silences serve as the presence of a refugee archive dragging histories in which it captures the elusive materiality of narratives that run and orients their coming to legibility as what Mark Rifkin calls "being-in-time," rather than "becoming past" or moving toward a liberal future in the settler colonial and imperial timescapes.[4] Dragging histories, then, negotiates the silences as presence. The intentional crafting of these memories in Yang's *The Latehomecomer* and the Hollywood film *Gran Torino* drags to the fore the things that do not fit but can surface beyond U.S. national culture. In relation to the refugee soldier turned terrorist ally who is formulated through state secrecy as knowledge, the grandmother drags history by stringing memories everywhere, embedded in and embodied by people.

Through an examination of *The Latehomecomer* and *Gran Torino*, the chapter shows how Hmong women's simultaneous storytelling and silences render material the concept of history on the run at the same time that the materiality remains ephemeral. By challenging the distinctions between history and memory, the chapter foregrounds women as a crucial analytic of history on the run that works to disrupt how the Hmong refugee has been rendered knowable as a valorized soldier. It also challenges the popular understanding of the Hmong refugee woman as a non-English-speaking subject who is unable to attain citizenship. My aim is neither to naturalize women's narratives within the domain of the family nor to posit women as the natural producers of or receptacles for memory. Rather, I examine the way that silence in the archive and the silencing of Hmong histories is a gendered process, which obscures the familial narratives that suture Hmong histories about war, leaving, and the remaking of shattered lives. Similar to the way that my analysis in chapter 2 dwells in the gaps and fissures of the archive of secrets, my reading of the memoir and film contends with the silence that the secrets have discursively produced, particularly through English and the language of militarism. My analysis begins with Yang's grandmother to center the grandmother figure as one who drags history to underscore the silences and unspeakability of militarized violence. The grandmother guides the process of coming into orality and writing, one whose memories are embodied yet also provide texture for Hmong in historical time as unsettled and "becoming." This analysis of the grandmother opens up a reading of *Gran Torino* that shifts the overarching plot of the motion picture from one about the redemption of white masculinity toward that of Hmong histories on the run/that are always arriving.

Dragging Histories and Articulating Silences

Through the grandmother figure, I consider how what is said becomes the privileged form of articulating history and the silences emerge as the unsaid or unarticulated history. She symbolizes the way that silences can be articulated through a refugee archive of ephemeral, embodied knowledge formation. It is her storytelling in the Hmong language, not English, that represents a repertoire of memories which are interspersed everywhere and embedded in family narratives; they are not really lost, they just went missing or were secreted. Thus, the missing suitcase that was detached from the Hmong family upon their arrival in the U.S. exists within the repertoire of delayed retellings of memories. The grandmother figure represents the refugee archive that anchors Hmong-produced histories and knowledge and exposes the power strategies of secreting knowledge. Silence is both oppressive and productive in articulating Hmong histories in the politics and practices of Hmong refugee/American remembering.

In her analysis of silence in the work of Asian American women writers, King-Kok Cheung argues that silences can also be articulate.[5] Cheung explains that these writers "question the authority of language (especially language that passes for history) and speak to the resources as well as the hazards of silence."[6] My analysis takes up this critique of language to interrogate how silence suppresses history yet also becomes productive for formulating Hmong belonging. Although the secrets and silences of Hmong families and communities structure how history is narrated and what kinds of stories become legible, I interrogate systemic forms of silencing and how Hmong women, who cannot have a place in the secret military history, interrupt them. However, speaking creates a double bind for Hmong women because its legibility requires English skills as well as the availability and ability of language itself to grasp speech's meaning. And yet, Hmong women's speaking requires being heard through the narrative of soldiering espoused by Hmong men who make up the majority of community leaders, if they are heard at all.

Although silence is most associated with the absence of speech, it represents more than speech by establishing being in place and time. That silences can be articulate, then, suggests that they can also be present. Silence as articulation and presence is a narrative act and an embodied practice performed by the grandmother to pass on the stories of her diasporic life and to tie the family together. It is a refugee "orientation" where stories can have their own trajectories beyond being enfolded into the military and soldiering narratives.[7] Literature has become increasingly important as a tool for Hmong Americans to reconsider the impact of war and Hmong refugee experiences in the absence of historical records. Even so, Hmong American writers encounter the question of "how to begin" writing when their experiences are unrecognizable to U.S. readers who know little or nothing of Hmong histories. Two Hmong American anthologies, *Bamboo among the Oaks* (2002) and the more recent *How Do I Begin?: A Hmong American Literary Anthology* (2011) explore the political and epistemological dilemma of what I once characterized as "a nonrecognized Hmong writing system and a history of running."[8] I argued that Hmong "history on the run" produced a "Hmong deterritorialized subjectivity" which is simultaneously linked to the "persistence of the refugee's condition of homelessness in exile." In my view, it is the refugee's act of running that "renders Hmong American literature mobile, in a state of writing on the run."⁹ *The Latehomecomer*, in particular, contends with the tensions of the systemic silencing and footnoting of Hmong histories within the record and public discourse through the themes of war, migration, history, gender, identity, and belonging. Yang's struggles with silence demonstrate Hmong knowledge's difficult relationship to language and writing. However, it is her grandmother's act of dragging histories—recounting Hmong oral stories in spite of the silence and enacting silences—that anchors Yang's coming into literacy. Literary scholar Aline Lo clarifies that Yang "encourages her audience that a group can write their way into belonging and that it is not only the individual immigrant body that can be flexible, but also the national body."¹⁰ She suggests that *The Latehomecomer* offers a displacement narrative that upholds self-identification on family continuity and finding refuge in writing rather than the nation-state.¹¹

The narrative in *The Latehomecomer* focuses on Yang's family's experiences of multiple migrations, beginning with their escape from Communist persecution to the jungles of Laos after the U.S. departure in 1975, to life in Thailand's refugee camps, and then to present-day Minnesota. The family includes seven brothers with their wives and children, but centers on their matriarch, Yang's grandmother. Although the memoir recounts her family's experiences, it interweaves her parents' stories with her own recollections through the grandmother's narrative, establishing her grandmother as the anchor for home, history, life, place, and family. The narrative is filled with wonder and admiration for the grandmother's life as a young Hmong woman in Laos, her struggles as a young widow caring for seven sons, the terrifying escape from Laos to Thailand, the uncertainty and instability of life in the U.S., and her return journey to Laos and to reunite with the ancestors (in China) at the end of her life. Grandma is a shaman and a herbalist, a "woman of girth and substance" who helped deliver Yang in the refugee camp. She is an independent woman who stood alone at the beginning of her life as an orphan and at end of her life as a widow. Yang describes her grandmother as a woman who has experienced leaving too many times but who "would travel far for those she loved, on a journey that must have been scary, unpredictable, and lonely" (157). She is a woman, as Yang explains in a reading of the memoir, who only spoke Hmong and for "all of her life . . . signed her name with a shaky X."¹² Grandmother "did not try to be American"; she remained a perpetual refugee who problematized the notions of home and belonging. Although Yang's grandmother is a Hmong-speaking and English language–challenged elder Hmong woman, she is a source of historical and cultural knowledge around which the world of the family, and especially of Yang herself, revolved.

Indeed, Yang negotiates her becoming a writer through her grandmother such that silence generates becoming and presence. What does intergenerational silence look like and how does the grandmother enable its articulation as presence? Written as an ode to her grandmother from Yang's perspective as a 1.5-generation Hmong American who was born in the Ban Vinai refugee camp, Yang asserts an urgency for Hmong children to help their parents and grandparents remember their existence in America, so the elders can leave a trace of their unwritten lives when they must return back to the clouds. The notion of clouds comes from a story that many Hmong parents and grandparents tell children of her generation, of babies who live in the sky and "can see the course of human lives." As Yang relates, "the people who we would become we had inside of us from the beginning, and the people whose worlds we share, whose memories we hold strong inside of us, we have always known" (xiv). This short story about how "we have chosen our lives" is the narrative entry point that enables Yang to reckon with the path of her life as it intertwines with the lives of her family members, especially Grandma. Yang explains that she wanted the book to speak to the "moment of fleeing and fighting, the moment in between, the moment that a life like mine come from [sic]."[13] As such, it became a story of a young writer from the East Side of St. Paul "trying to garner a voice in a world where she'd gone silent."[14] She reveals that she was silent for most of her young adult life because she saw how the world did not want to hear her mother and father speak, and only began speaking out after the publication of her book.[15] Yang writes that "a silence grew inside of me because I couldn't say that it was sometimes sad to be Hmong, even in America," showing that the gratefulness Hmong refugees were supposed to feel could not explain the sadness of watching the adults struggle to remake their lives (151). Yang interprets her silence in the context of the silencing of Hmong history in which the "Hmong inside the little girl fell into silence." The narrative contends with the tensions that result from systemic silencing of history and her family's experiences, through which she saw how the "world only knew skin-deep the reaches of Hmong" in their footnoting in the history of a world where Vietnam was only Vietnamese, Laos belonged only to the Laotians, and the war was only U.S. American (4).

Yang's silence also serves as a metaphor for the incommunicability of a Hmong past. Historical secrets generate a discursive silence about who Hmong are, so that what becomes legible must fit into a tragic discourse of fighting for the United States. Yang's silence during her youth and her later "rustiness" at speech symbolize what it means for Hmong—whose existence has been marked by experiences of violence and displacement, and by struggles for survival—to be silent in the absence of historical records. This silence is not rooted in the inability to speak but rather is reflective of the incomprehensibility of Hmong speech and the unrecognizability of a Hmong voice. She relates that, at school, speaking English was harder than "knowing the letters that made the words"; the difficulty lay in the language's incomprehensibility of Hmong meaning so that the simple explanation for her silence emerged as "I had no voice in English" (147). Yang's unexplainable silence, and that of her parents, as well as the impatience of her teachers, were central to her school years. She explained to her parents that, "I had no voice in English. I said sometimes when I wanted to talk, I couldn't find my voice, and then when I did—the person, a kid or a teacher—would already be gone" (147).

There are many silences, as Foucault maintains, and they are among the strategies that underlie and permeate discourses.[16] In *The Latehomecomer*, they accompany the singular narrative about Hmong as soldiers who were paid to fight for the U.S. so that their deaths and the human legacies of war become Hmong burdens to bear. Jenny Edkins's notion of unspeakability illuminates the broader implications of Yang's silence as a failure of language through a crisis in the social order so that "what we can say no longer makes sense; what we want to say, we can't . . . [because] there are no words for it."[17] Silences, therefore, constitute Yang's answers to her teacher's questions "without words" and the rust that had formed over those words when forced into speech (166–67).

Yang's struggles to understand the conditions of a Hmong life accentuate the presence of her grandmother, who softens the harshness of loss and absence, cushioning her granddaughter's "entry into the world with her strong hands" (252). In this way, the refugee grandmother who has experienced the violences of war and displacement is one who also guides a knowing of that reality. Yang's silence gave way to writing in order to leave a trace of the lives and deaths that, like her grandmother's, had gone unwritten, and as a way to invite Hmong Americans to seek refuge in each other. Grandma's stories, in their orality, are dangerous to modern state epistemologies because they constitute a form of embodied knowledge that guided Yang's writing and enabled her to work through the barrier of her silence.

Yang writes about her grandmother carrying bags as she moves between her sons' homes. The bags' and grandmother's movements reflect the memories of war and her distrust of being confined to space, yet an insistence that her children and grandchildren know the places of her life. Grandma's constant movement and dragging along her belongings show how she managed to stay mobile in order to pass on histories and knowledge in spite of the confines of her status as a Hmong-speaking refugee woman. Even when she repeated often the stories she liked, Yang "knew that Grandma had those that she didn't tell often at all" about loss and having to grow up too fast (220). Instead, she "carried everything with her, unable to trust the safety of place" (215), looking to "tie things together" (216) and trying to "fit the jagged edges together, no matter how crudely, so that her life was never completely empty" (225). Yang describes growing more attentive to her grandma, spending her college Christmas vacation and summer breaks with her by the window with "Grandma's wide feet in my lap." Grandma's life in the U.S. was a series of visits to each of her sons' homes. Yang writes:

> I was home, and Grandma had come to share our moldy house, to spend time with us. She slept on the used queen-sized bed in the little bedroom without a closet, her assortment of bags stacked against one wall. In one bag was a coffee machine—a gift from one of her grandchildren. In another there was a Polaroid camera, another gift. The remaining bags were an odd assortment: a heavy one with flower patterns the color of blood, a gray one that used to be black and had zippers around the sides that could make it big or small, and still more bags from her children and grandchildren, as well as the occasional suitcase she bought for herself. She carried everything with her, unable to trust the safety of place. (215)

The assortment of bags that Yang's grandmother carried as she traveled from one son's house to the next may seem like an untidy and fleeting way of living where nothing is permanent. The bags carry everyday items like a coffee machine and a Polaroid camera, things given to her by her grandchildren so that the world her grandchildren live in is fastened together and linked to the image of their grandma moving around the homes of her seven sons. Even the suitcase, although the main signifier of travel, only makes an occasional appearance among the bags. The baggage of missing things the Hmong family lost en route to the U.S. is transmuted into multiple bags that track Grandma's movement.

She must carry everything in order to tie her stories to her and her children. Not only does Grandma carry the bags, she also uses those plastic bags to create ropes. Yang writes that in the last years of her life,

> She would spend hours before the window twisting the plastic strips [cut from plastic shopping bags] into ropes, carefully massaging the lengths of cut plastic into the exposed, unwrinkled skin of her leg. Wearing her thick reading glasses, she spent her days making bags and bags of twisted plastic ropes. She said that there were always uses for ropes in life, things to tie together. My father said that Grandma had never been a lazy woman and didn't know how to keep her hands still. We all watched as she made work for herself. (216)

Although making bags full of rope made from bags is a practical way for Grandma, who is no longer seen as productive in the market economy of the U.S., to create work for herself, the ropes themselves are intended to tie things together so they can be carried along. Grandma's act of dragging her belongings between each of her sons' homes articulates an alternative definition of historical memory in which her stories and acts of stringing family and things together draw up Hmong memories to blast their history out of its silence. Foucault offers in *The Archaeology of Knowledge* an approach to history or a way of speaking about history that is focused on the processes of discourse rather than the event or "official" knowledge about it. He explains that one must interrogate the "groupings that history suggests" or "unities" of history to "break them up," to see "whether they can be legitimately reformed."[18] For Foucault, in historical analysis one must take the precaution to disconnect the unquestioned continuities of discourse that are premised on the themes of a "secret origin" and an "already-said" that is "never-said" running beneath the articulated but which it covers and silences.[19] Instead, he argues that "discourse must not be referred to as the distant presence of the origin, but treated as and when it occurs."[20] Following his method for critical analysis to pay attention to the articulated silences in discourse, I suggest that Grandma's stories are Hmong refugee histories that permeate the larger historical narrative about the war's secrecy.[21] In this context, Grandma's distrust of place and attempts to fit jagged edges together are "irruptions" of the "manifest discourse" that depict her as silent to mark her foreignness. The figure of the refugee grandmother creates "different points of holding on" to make possible a transformative reception of histories that are elusive of an "origin" (225).

Grandma's acts of drawing together the family's experiences tie historical narratives to human movement rather than to the geopolitics of the nation-state. Her movement makes history mobile. Literary scholar Elizabeth Freeman's discussion of "temporal drag" in *Time Binds* provides an important analytical perspective for understanding Grandma's acts of dragging refugee histories. She explains that "drag" as a form of gender performativity is associated with "retrogression, delay, and the pull of the past on the present."[22] Reading artist Sharon Hayes's performances "of collisions between bodies past and present" to conceptualize "temporal drag" and open up the specters of feminism, Freeman suggests that "drag" can be "central to theorizing the mobility of gender identification and the visible excess that calls the gender binary into question."[23] In doing so, "drag" as an excess can be a "signifier of 'history' rather than of 'woman' or 'man.'"[24] Drag is the "act of plastering the body with outdated rather than just cross-gendered accessories."[25] Such a resurrection of drag can exceed gender confines and begin to talk back to history. Freeman's notion of drag helps situate my observations of Grandma's acts of dragging histories in unfixing reality and history as not fixed, but rather manufactured through a sustained set of acts by both the state and the Hmong refugee grandmother. Indeed, Grandma's act of massaging the cut plastic strips "into the exposed, unwrinkled skin of her leg" is not a display of the ballroom drag performance, but a "plastering" of her body with nonbiodegradable material. The children and grandchildren's witnessing of how plastic can be made useful through contact with flesh shows the possibilities of history's malleability and ongoing relevance. Dragging histories signifies the move to theorize a feminist, nonheteropatriarchal articulation of histories of migration that are without an origin and so must continually be repeated.

This alternative formation of historical narratives through the act of dragging means centering Hmong women's knowledge over and against the representation of a singular, monolithic Hmong woman, who is silent or silenced because she only speaks Hmong. Dragging histories also decenters the "universal" and Western scientific discourse as the sole source of knowledge, and critiques systems of imperialism, race, and patriarchy that have sought to speak for and act on behalf of Hmong and racialized immigrant women. The process of dragging histories maintains and transmits Hmong refugee/American histories through the practices and interactions between Hmong women. The orality and embodied knowledge of Yang's grandmother's stories, while guiding Yang's engagement with writing, also illustrates the mediated passing of stories and handing off of baggage, from grandmother to granddaughter.

Dragging histories is not a recovery process, but rather a tracing of unsettled Hmong refugee lives that are tied to running from place to place as well as a yearning for return home. It means remembering the loss as loss that cannot be recovered and hence compelling the loss to be told.

The possibility of return happens in death because the soul must pass through those same places of violence and refuge. As much as they function as reminders of loss, the stories that recount Grandma's life allow her to revisit the important places of her life in order to guide her back at the end of her life: "When Grandma was alive, she had said that we should listen to her stories so that one day, when the time came, we would know the places of her life. I now realized why" (253). Grandma's storytelling is a strategy to negotiate the anxieties about dying in the U.S. without her grandchildren knowing how she lived. The stakes are too high not to conjure up "sympathy for the dead" to offer glimpses into the markers that make Grandma's loss so poignant.[26] The Qhuab Ke (guiding the way) ritual in a Hmong funeral leads the spirit of the dead in a backward fashion through all the places it lived to the place of its birth in order to find the placenta, buried in the ground of the house after birth, and make its way back to loved ones who have passed before. The children are supposed to know these different places of Grandma's life so that they can help her properly retrace her path. During Grandma's funeral service, Yang describes how the man (a Qhuab Ke ritual master) who would teach Grandma's ntsuj plig the way back placed copies of her Social Security card and alien resident identification card into her right hand and started chanting, telling her that she had died in Minnesota and the journey back would be a long one (253). She would need these documents that had defined her as legal alien but illegible citizen-subject on such a journey, which ironically authenticates her life.

Yet, finding the way back means reencountering the devastation and displacement of the war, which made the journey home a precarious process. Yang writes that in the part of the journey where Grandma had been instructed to cross the Mekong River back to Laos,

> the guide apologized at this point for no longer being able to take Grandma directly to each place where they had been during the five years in the jungle. He explained that after all, it had been a war, and they had been running for their lives, and their homes had been only made of banana leaves, stacked on top of small tree limbs. There would be no markers left. There was no way anyone could remember the many places they had hidden, one mountain cave or the next. He only wanted her to do her best. (255)

The guide's reminders of what these places of leaving and escaping were like in the time of the war and its aftermath foregrounds the erasure of those years in the jungle, where there are no markers of the lives lived there. Grandma would have to try her best to muddle through the unmarked places of her life and escape. This journey indeed exemplifies the Hmong refugee escape where there cannot be traces of their flight not only because it was a "secret" war but also because of the way that secrecy necessitated an erasure of Hmong lives and deaths. Yet, Grandma's journey reminds her children and grandchildren that history is fugitive but also filled with directional markers so they are never really lost even when they are silenced.

Refuge in Each Other: Hmong Refugee Temporality
I extend the reading of silence with the political and ethical stakes of Yang's grandmother's dragging history to examine the larger implications of the memoir as a commentary on Hmong temporality of collective memory-making and becoming. Dragging histories makes up the collective practice and process of becoming-subject and being-in-time imbued through the grandmother carrying her things. Furthermore, the idea comprises the everyday interactions between Hmong grandmother and granddaughter, a maneuvering that happens within and beyond the text. Yang's memoir, therefore, hovers at the intersection of what Hmong Americans know and what Hmong grandmothers can teach as they insist on our listening. Its narrative builds upon the trajectory of a voice lost and found, pieced together through the love of a grandmother. The memoir's expounding of how memories are reproduced over time attaches these memories to Hmong Americans for the purposes of holding on, of not forgetting, and of seeking refuge in each other. Thus, the memoir foregrounds refuge as a process in becoming rather than a site of resolution where things are over and done with. Here, history and memory work together as "social practices with a politics" to organize knowledge and community.[27]

As it contends with the subplotting of Hmong lives and unwritten deaths, *The Latehomecomer* emphasizes the ephemeral status of histories that run as the witnesses grow old, precisely because it would seem "as if they had never lived" (214).[28] By telling "our lives in America" as "our story," the memoir looks toward a future of collective remembering yet to come. Yet, Hmong stories are dangerous because they surface, not entangled with the redemption of heroic white masculinity as in *Gran Torino*, but ephemerally through the attachments of Hmong stories onto each other when records fail. Yang reminds us that the hope and dreams of her generation are rooted in the conviction that "we are here together because we belong together."[29] The memoir as a "people-making narrative" suggests a distinctive Hmong temporality in which the story is both a collective telling and in the process of becoming.³⁰

As such, *The Latehomecomer* constitutes a crafting of collective memories rather than communicating individual recollections. For Yang, a memoir is a collection of memories that are more than one's own. It is a story about a life and many other lives shaped by a history that was kept secret, but which can belong to all of us and which we can find in each other. Conventionally, the genre of memoir privileges the individual story in recounting the trials and triumphs of one's life. The form of memoir writing itself connotes the very production of memories in its recounting of how things were. Although memoir, like documentary film, is fraught with questions about objectivity and truth, it is Yang's play with memory's constructedness that highlights the presence of silence. Yang's use of the genre foregrounds how memories are forged, in this case, from multiple stories. Her family memoir is a memory-work of creating a narrative from stories rather than a work of memory that takes the stories as offering Truth in and of themselves because it involves the very production and mediation of Hmong histories and memories about war, leaving, and homemaking/belonging. In an interview and discussion of her work, Yang explained the possibility of writing the book as a memoir:

> The book begins in 1975 when the last Air America planes leave the country with a declaration of genocide against the Hmong, only the Hmong didn't know it. And I wasn't born yet but it is a memoir. And memoirs are not only the memories we hold but they are the memories passed on to us and they exist within a bigger world of memory. So that's where it begins, lots of research, lots of going back to the stories that were told to me not because I was writing a book but because everybody wanted to explain why my life was the way it was. Why Thanksgiving was Meals on Wheels and why Christmas was Toys for Tots. And so I've heard all these stories and it would be inaccurate of me to allow the story to begin the day I was born.³¹

This statement suggests that the production of history through stories passed on to the generation born after the war explains the shape of her life, living a second-classed version of the American Dream. She maintains that "memoirs are not only the memories we hold [because] they exist within a bigger world of memory," and delineates how memories are not just one's own but are threaded through others' recollections. Lo explains that refugee narratives that are also autobiographical, such as Yang's, must necessarily retell one's family's escape in truthful as well as compelling ways which involve fanciful reimaginings of flight. Such "fanciful flights," Lo argues, allow the author to reclaim the flight narrative from one about victimhood to a "complex and nuanced understanding of refugees."[32] Yang's parents' love story during their families' life on the run in the jungles in the years immediately following the Communist takeover, in particular, demonstrates the embellishment of young love in the time of escape. Thus, Hmong narratives emerge in fragmented and intertextual fashion because they are embedded everywhere. The postponed arrival of these stories in everyday moments troubles state secrecy. The routine practices of a grandmother's storytelling, therefore, powerfully convey how memories already circulate, communicated as narratives of a life lived on the edge of belonging in a crisis of U.S. rescue. Connecting the "secret war" with this notion of memoir takes war violence beyond individual life. This is a memoir that recollects that which was not meant to be remembered, like the "secret war" because it was a secret, or things that happened before one can remember. Yang's retelling while filling in some historical gaps also "forges an entirely new and embellished version based on her imagination."[33]

What makes the memory-making in Yang's memoir powerful is how the stories carry and become the remnants of histories that run. Latehomecoming symbolizes the gendered racial formation of history whereby Hmong are disposed as late in emerging into modernity because their nonrecognized writing and history of running have relegated them to the "waiting room of history."[34] Such memories are what McGranahan calls "arrested histories," delayed in the present but yet to come.[35] Yang's embellishment of the past allows for Hmong latehomecoming memories to be articulated, and to threaten the dominant Vietnam War discourse. For instance, Yang explains that the first time literary agents in New York rejected her book, they reasoned that the "Vietnam [War] was a horrible chapter in our history [and] people didn't want to revisit that chapter."[36] Her work unsettles the benevolence and permanence of refuge within the nation-state because the memoir does what memory scholars Shoshana Felman and Dori Laub explain that art can do: it "inscribes (artistically bears witness to) what we do not yet know of our lived historical relation to events of our times."[37] Hence, Yang's book bears witness to a past that the U.S. has not yet dealt with, and whose histories are "latehomecoming." These histories are late in arriving and lag in time because they have been deferred through Hmong displacement outside of nation and history. Latehomecoming memories are nonetheless present in their fugitivity and nonarrival.

Yang's memories become impressions of the remembrances her parents carry and pass on to their children to help them remember. Stories about the past, rather than producing complete images of how it really was, are crafted from memories made on the run to create enduring impressions of fleeting moments that shape knowledge in the present. Yang gives an account of her mother's efforts to hide the pictures of her family at the Mekong River's edge in such a way that she would remember to recover them in the frantic rush to escape Laos:

> With her fingers she dug into the moist ground of a bamboo patch. In the shallow hole, she placed all the pictures of her brothers, her mother, herself. She felt the bamboo trunk with her hands in the dark. If she ever touched that bamboo again, she told herself, forming the words on her lips, she would remember. One day, she would tell her brothers and her mother that she still had the photos of them from before the war. She would tell them that she would never forget them because the way they were was burned into her heart. (37)

The act of forming the memory as she hid the pictures suggests the elusive history on the run. Yang's mother's memory is formed around embodied knowledge, the tactility of the moist ground and the bamboo trunk, with hands in the dark and a promise to remember. These symbols evoke the place where the photos were buried and serve as a reminder that the images were "burned into her heart." Remembering is elusive in its very promise of forgetting. Yet even when Yang's mother promises herself that she will not forget, forgetting exactly where she buried the pictures and knowing that she will not be able to recover them constitute how she remembers.

Yang's father also enacts memory-making on the run when, in the aftermath of the war, he runs out of his village into the jungle to escape the Communist searches for and persecutions of Hmong who sided with the United States. Her father had never visited the grave of his father, who died when Yang's father was young. He knew of the place from what his brothers told him with "their fingers pointing to a mountain that looked like an uneven green box rising out of the ground." Yang recounts this moment of memory production when the family ran out of their village: "My father, with a chicken tucked underneath his shirt, his thick black hair sticking straight up from his head, kept looking back at the mountain where his father's body was buried. He says that if he closes his eyes, he can see the imprint of the mountain on his lids. He'll always know the way back" (12). The image of the mountain imprinted on his eyelids offers an assurance of a rooted knowledge

The Refugee Grandmother 159

of where or what this way back entails. The impression of place is embodied yet ephemeral, and it requires continual reinforcement. This does not mean that her father does not know the way back, but rather that the strategy of imprinting operates as an imagination of the way. These imprints of an imagined place are intended by Hmong parents to help Hmong Americans to not forget and somehow "know the way back."

Such impressions can fade, blend together, and make blurry what, how, or why we wanted to remember things. They reveal how memories emerge mediated, and we need help to remember them. Despite her father's insistence that "he'll always remember the way back," he must reproduce his memories for Yang to help him remember. Even though these reprints are layered against something else, and, in this case, a different mountain, his memories are never really lost so long as Yang remembers that her father's father was buried on a mountain like that one. Yang recalls her father's impression of the mountain where his father was buried:

> I had never been on a real mountain. I had only heard of it all my life. And I knew that my grandfather had died a long time ago, when my father was just a baby. I thought it was a good thing, that even if we are only babies when our fathers die, we always remember the places where they are buried. Some day we could find our way back if we wanted to, to say thank you, and to say hello, and maybe to tell them: this is my daughter and she has never met you and she did not know where you were buried but I am showing her now so she will help me remember. (96)

This crafting of memory to help each other remember serves as Yang's literary technique to narrate her family story, yet it is one that many other Hmong families use to remember the journey and those who have been buried along the way in unmarked or absent graves. Hmong American literary representations often include mountains and hills to reclaim such sites as places of belonging.[38] It is a story that is attached to many other stories and cannot be foreclosed. The memoir's use of overlapping remembering is symbolized in how memories correspond with places, movement, and gendered racial identity.[39]

Embodied Knowledge

The remnants and stories do not just represent memories, they carry knowledge which is linked to places not mapped as official sites of the nation-state. This fugitive knowledge which resists institutionalization and escapes the traditional archive emerges as embodied—the social bonds between feet and land.[40] As a people who move, Hmong traverse the different nation-states of Laos, Thailand, and the U.S., carrying stories that help them navigate the colonial and state-based boundaries that silence and fix Hmong histories and epistemologies.[41] These stories underscore a vexed sense of refuge that is already enfolded in the violence perpetrated by state entities. As such, Laos represents the yearning for homeland: "they [the parents and Grandma] carried a yearning for the land on the other side of the river—the foundations of centuries of myth, of legend, the soil of so many Hmong dreams" (40). Laos was also "a land that they loved . . . the land holding the grave of their father" (41). Yet, it was the location of a war that caused Hmong families' displacement. While the muddy earth of Laos allowed the family to stay together during their escape by following each other's footprints, it also abused their bare feet during months of running that made their raw feet bleed.

In Thailand's refugee camps, Yang learned that it was a place whose ground did not love everyone. Yang remembers Ban Vinai Refugee Camp as a place where she and her grandmother shared fond memories because they were surrounded by people who loved them (67). For Yang, the camp represented "warm laps . . . [and] the beat of many different hearts against my ear, the rhythm of life" (59). However, it was a place that didn't love Dawb, her older sister, who survived polio with a weakened leg:

> "I love the ground," I would say.
> "Why?" Dawb wanted to know.
> "Because it loves me."
> "It doesn't love me."
> The ground didn't love Dawb. She could not walk straight, since her legs were not equal in strength. Everywhere she went, she limped her way there. Whenever there was a wall close to where she stood, she placed a small, dirty hand on it for support. (67)

Yang's parents were also immobilized by their inability to help themselves and their child: "Every time they saw her struggling after the other cousins on some adventure, they looked down at their feet, helpless but unwilling to stand still; they shuffled in place. I saw this and I knew that the ground did not love everyone" (67). Place can be carried along in memory as feet that stand still and as unloving earth.

The refugee camp also represented a place of confinement for refugees who experienced daily trauma and physical violence. A man Yang respected "would speak of memories he carried of this place I called home," of boys, women, and girls who faced brutality and sexual violence when they snuck out of the camp to forage for food to supplement the insufficient rations provided by the United Nations. The encounters with Thai men on such trips meant rape for the women and girls: "Little girls and tired women, walking out of the groves of trees, blood seeping in between legs, some crawling along the ground. Threads torn, skin broken, eyes wild and empty. Hmong men were beaten. Hmong blood seeped into the Thai earth, drops and streams to be washed by the monsoon rains that fell each year" (63). At the same time that Hmong refugees found temporary refuge from being on the run, the camps' humanitarian violence immobilized their connections to alternative ways of being.

Yang explains that her family lived in the housing built after World War II for returning soldiers and their families when they first arrived in the United States. It was low-income housing yet built to last, and the housing "waited for us, soldiers from a different war, not returning to families but to remnants of them" (131). Hmong families are themselves remnants, their arrival belying the missing members who were either resettled in other U.S. cities or lost to the violence of war and flight. While the low-income housing had been intended to help returning U.S. soldiers, it becomes a marker of Hmong refugees' poverty and of their ill-fitting history on the run, and keeps the Hmong residents on the periphery of U.S. history. In fact, Hmong families are effectively the latehomecoming remnants from a "secret war," "returning" to occupy a place in history not made for them.

Yang's representation of grandmother's feet embedding dirt from the different nation-states where she has lived, in particular, carries that knowledge of what happened in those places. She writes: "Grandma's feet were wide and tan, the skin was leathery. The nails of her toes were long and thick, tinged with brown. The soles of her feet showed the cracks of many years of walking in flip-flops or without shoes. The ridged lines were filled with dirt from years before: dirt from California, dirt from Thailand, dirt from Laos. The earth had seeped so deeply into her feet that no matter how hard we scrubbed, it would not come out" (216). Grandma's earth-tinged and ridgelined feet give texture to the knowledge that cannot easily be captured.

After an ambush by North Vietnamese and Pathet Lao soldiers that scattered the fleeing family, Yang narrates, those who regrouped decided to separate: the women and children would surrender while the five remaining men continued searching for the missing family members, after which they would return to rescue those who had surrendered so they could all escape to Thailand. The surrendering group was led by grandmother because "an old woman would not be a threat" (21). As the men accompanied the women and children to the "ridge of a hill," the bare-footed group "followed each other's footprints" in the wet and slippery ground (22). As grandma led the group slowly toward the enemy camp because "their bare feet were raw from running," "her wide feet clung to the ground" (23, 22). While the children and women's feet bled from running, Grandma's wide feet symbolize her strength to anchor and keep the family safe. In the enemy camp, Grandma refused to let anyone drink the water that had been contaminated by chemical attacks on the village. Yang describes how in that situation and many others, Grandma "was strong for her daughters-in-law and her grandchildren. She kept them safe" (27).

When the men in the family returned to help the women and children escape from the enemy camp, instead of following each other's footprints as they had done before, "the group walked backwards, with sticks in their hands, covering up each step as they treaded higher and higher toward safety" (32). And again, after making the frightening Mekong River crossing, the family walked along the bank of the river on the Thai side, "their feet making soft prints on the wet earth" (40). Yet when the family walked into the United Nations compound to register as refugees, Yang's "father's feet stilled" at the impending prison of the refugee camp with its wire fences and guards (44). The stillness of the feet that had been running symbolizes the immobility of the refugee camp. The movement of feet, their relationship to the earth, and their physical condition all illustrate how the memoir captures the refugee's flight as attached to the earth rather than unrooted leaving. This method of remembering emerges within the contradictions of the promise of recognizable state territory as refuge, specifically the challenges of life in the U.S.

The Refugee Grandmother in Gran Torino

Considering how Yang's grandmother drags history opens up a feminist reading of the film *Gran Torino* (2008) through the film's Hmong-speaking grandmother character and actor. The film depicts the reform and redemption of Korean War veteran Walt Kowalski (Clint Eastwood), who is haunted by his killing of young Korean soldiers in the war and by his discontent with the invasion of troublemaking immigrants in his suburban Detroit neighborhood. Walt is a blue-collar widower who worked in the Ford factory for fifty years, putting the steering column in cars like his prized 1972 Gran Torino. The Gran Torino symbolizes a rite of passage—toward either proper white masculinity through inheritance or a deviant racialized masculinity of inner-city gang life that signifies improper ownership through attempts to steal the car. Walt embodies the Gran Torino because he worked in the factory where it was made and he is as much of an antique as it is.[42] Walt and his car both symbolize the glory and decline of Detroit as a postindustrial city of crumbling neighborhoods that no longer works the way it used to, in contrast to the newly arrived Hmong families who are trying to remake their lives around him.[43] This juxtaposition relies on paternalism and Hmong cultural difference to enhance Walt's symbolic role as a stand-in for the U.S. and for his redemption, a framing where the grandmother cannot be imagined. The film, unlike the memoir, is not a story that revolves around the refugee grandmother, but my reading centers her role and how it disrupts the central plot and character.

Most discussions about the film *Gran Torino* have centered on whiteness and masculinity, ideals possessed by Walt and lacking in the young Hmong men portrayed in the film. Plagued with a terminal illness and by his memories of war, Walt finds redemption for his actions in war, especially in his killing of young Korean soldiers, through "saving" his teenage Hmong neighbors, siblings Sue Lor (Ahney Her) and Thao Vang Lor (Bee Vang), from the local Hmong gangs in order to find their own peace in the world. Specifically, Thao is the key to Walt's reform. As an elderly white man and veteran who is equipped with the tools to navigate life in the U.S., Walt represents the source of canonical U.S. knowledge. He sets out to "man up" and "save" his young Hmong neighbor who possesses neither the necessary life skills nor heteronormative masculinity needed to succeed in the United States and in urban Detroit. The treatment of Hmong women is more complicated, because they function either as representations of incapable Hmong communities or as exoticized subjects, one-dimensional tropes that are often repeated in the portrayal of Asian American women in mainstream media. Thus, it is precisely Sue and the sexual violence against her that emboldens Walt to sacrifice himself in order to save both Hmong teenagers.[44] In doing so, the film recuperates the forgotten Korean War veteran into a heroic U.S. figure, depicting a double foreclosure of U.S. imperialism in Southeast and East Asia by conflating North Korean soldiers with the Hmong youth.

The film's combination of popular representations of Asian Americans, a "forgotten" Korean War history, and traditional notions of white masculinity creates an uneasy structure for a Hmong narrative. Juxtaposing Asian American stereotypes with heroic white masculinity enables the plot's redemptive work of Americanization and (white) masculinization for

Hmong American youth. In doing so, it reveals the patriarchal framing of Hmong and Asian American women as a hypersexualized threat (Sue as the "dragon lady" or the helpless innocent requiring a white male savior) and men as effeminate (Thao as emasculated).[45] More poignantly, this frame infantilizes the Hmong siblings as children who need saving from their debilitating community and culture where there are no Hmong adult men to protect their interests and guide them. Exploring how the film's depictions of Hmong characters are "closely aligned with stereotypical representations of Asian Americans" alone or through the lens of masculinity, then, cannot fully address the gendered racial framework of white masculinity as salvation for nonwhite peoples.[46] Formal and informal academic conversations about the film have been important in rethinking the multiple connections in Asian American historiography that are inextricably linked to U.S. imperialism in Asia through the framework of Hmong refugees/Americans. The Midwest is not without its own tangled Asian American history; Detroit was the site of groundbreaking Asian American struggles for civil rights and justice following the 1982 murder of Vincent Chin by two laid-off white autoworkers. Chin's brutal murder galvanized a generation of Asian Americans to fight for justice (legal and political), at a time when the Asian American movement had entered a period of consolidation and professionalization. At the same time, the media stereotyping of Asian Americans as the "model minority," which began in the 1960s, intensified with the rise of Japanese economy and U.S.-Japan auto industry competition in the 1980s.[47] The ongoing meaning of Chin's case continues to impact and raise political consciousness among Asian Americans today, particularly a recent consideration of Chin's narrative in Tony Lam's documentary *Vincent Who?* (2009). It is an Asian American story that is remembered and passed on by activists to inspire new generations of activists. It continues to circulate as part of Asian American historical and cultural memory. Hence, *Gran Torino* occupies a space in this circuit of Asian American history, memory, activism, and popular representation and opens up a discussion about Hmong Americans in relation to Asian American racial formation as a global configuration that is fraught with secrets.

In the film, Hmong refugees are a foreign threat to Walt's neighborhood, and, by extension, their presence drains local and federal resources. Thao and Sue's grandmother as a Hmong-speaking matriarch represents the helplessness and inscrutability of Hmong families. Three generations of Hmong women—Sue, her mother, and her grandmother—make up the matriarchal Lor household, which Walt believes is at the root of Thao's emasculation.

They are unable to protect themselves from other nonwhite threats—most immediately the Hmong, Latino, and Black gangs threatening the neighborhood. The mirrored depictions of Sue and Grandma, in which the granddaughter embodies a younger, "spunky" version of her grandmother, constructs Hmong femininity in opposition to Hmong and U.S. masculinity, one needing saving. But as the following discussion will show, it is the subplot of Walt's encounters with Sue and Thao's grandmother, and her assertions of the historical encounter between Hmong and the U.S., that exposes Walt's benevolence as a veiled form of U.S. (symbolic and material) violence. Like Yang's grandmother, this grandmother is a source of knowledge and the anchor for the family. Likewise, Chee Thao who plays the grandmother drags history to disrupt the film's plot, to imagine feminist Hmong histories that center movement, place, and gender.

While *Gran Torino* casts Walt as a benefactor to Thao and Sue, it is the encounters between Walt and Grandma that illuminate the contact between the U.S. and Hmong as a gendered racial project predicated on saving or civilizing Hmong from their supposed "primitive" status as a people without a geographic homeland who were represented in CIA maps and documents as a part of the landscape. These encounters that are portrayed in the looks that Grandma throws at Walt, her admonishment of her children and Walt for his presence in their house, and her perch on the porch where she can keep an eye on Walt make up the subtext and unsubtitled moments of the film. It is telling that Grandma's unsubtitled dialogue seems to convey insignificant utterings and gibberish so that non-Hmong audiences have no context within which to understand her antagonism toward Walt but as illegible soundtrack thickening the plot.[48]

The overlapping histories of war shape Walt and Grandma's interactions and their adversarial yet mutually constituted depictions. Indeed, Walt and Grandma's exchanges portray antagonism but do not offer a social context from which the resentment derives. Grandma's relationship with Walt troubles the film's redemption of white masculinity and foregrounds the possibility of engaging with war memories that do not "fit the script" and demand our dwelling in the past when and where they emerge outside the official discourse.[49] Cedric Lee, the Hmong cultural consultant for the film who was involved in the casting of Hmong extras in Detroit and who acted as Hmong language interpreter on set and provided postproduction translation for subtitles, confirmed that there were no Hmong lines in the script—half of the Hmong dialogue was scripted in English and fed through interpreters, while the other half came directly from the Hmong actors.[50] He explained further that the Hmong actors improvised many of the "emotional scenes" because "there was no real direction." Within the context and confines of the storyline and Hmong participation in the making of *Gran Torino*, the Hmong actors negotiated "how to tell our story and our side." Lee gives insight into Thao's unscripted and unsubtitled lines as telling our story by explaining that "she was speaking how she felt and wanted to let the world know."[51] Her exacting yet unsubtitled statements, which combine the film's scripted dialogue with the Hmong actors' understanding of their roles, drags up the past as untranslatable tensions. The untranslatability of her dialogue reflects the U.S. public's inability to address the "secret war," and, by extension, the "forgotten war."

Here, we can read *Gran Torino*'s portrayal of Hmong characters beyond their negation as illegible foreigners propelling the development of Eastwood's character to focus on what Hmong American audiences were excited about—the fact that it was about Hmong people, and that Hmong actors and characters were making "Hollywood history" by beginning a Hmong foray into popular culture.[52] The film is not a Hmong American production per se, but it is a rare example of Hmong representation in U.S. popular media. Like U.S. media representations of other racialized groups, the film elicited a mixture of concerns, particularly about its references to Hmong culture and gangs. My analysis is less interested in detailing the film's cultural misrepresentations than in examining the roles of its Hmong cast and crew in producing a cultural product that they and other Hmong Americans might have a stake in. In this way, I consider *Gran Torino* a significant moment in Hmong American cultural production, due to the contributions of the Hmong actors and production assistants. Anthropologist Louisa Schein and Hmong American activist Va-Megn Thoj suggest that the work and experiences of Hmong actors and production assistants require viewers to see *Gran Torino* as part of a Hmong craft imbued with the complexities and contradictions of refugee memory and contemporary Hmong American community formation.[53] Indeed, this perspective reveals how the Hmong actors work to denaturalize and subvert the trope of a definitive Hmong character, showing it to be "contingent and always in production."[54] The legacy of *Gran Torino* will remain a complicated matter for Hmong Americans, because according to Ly Chong Thong Jalao "all the previous tensions and repressed histories have not been worked through on an equal footing by all parties involved."[55] Indeed, the portrayals of Sue and Grandma highlight some of the tensions and repressed histories between Hmong and the U.S. and suggest a critique of Walt's heroic white masculinity.

While many film reviewers/critics claim that *Gran Torino* embodies Eastwood's long career as an actor and director and that it was a good way for him to go out, Chee Thao, who played the grandmother, also made connections between her own life and that of her character in the film. This link between the actors and their characters reflects the intertextuality within the film's narrative about different histories and colliding memories, opening an analysis of the film in the context of Hmong American historiography. As the following discussion will show, Thao expands the concerns about redemption and belonging that are tied to white masculinity beyond their fixedness and says they are about her story, reflecting her life of loss, migration, and contradictions in the U.S. The way that Thao uses the character of Grandma to drag up her experiences and to invoke Hmong wartime history underscores the centrality of race, gender, and movement to understand the text beyond its confining masculinist narrative.

In a panel at the University of Minnesota a few months after the release of *Gran Torino*, entitled "Hmong Speak Out on *Gran Torino*: A Discussion with the Hmong Actors," Thao was asked to talk about the role she played and to explain some of the lines that were in Hmong because she had improvised parts of them. She expressed frustration at the unsubtitled statements because she had hoped to communicate the context for the film's references to the war in the lines she performed. With a single sheet of paper of the notes she had prepared, she stood among the panelists with microphone in hand and said:

> I am going to talk about my life and coming to this country [the U.S.] before I talk about the movie. In 1975, our country [*teb chaws*] fell [*tawg*]. That's when the Americans came to lie to us, right? So we lost our country and so they [U.S. Americans] had to accept us to live [*yug peb*] in this country. [She hesitates and stutters as she says this next part] My husband and I became Chao Fa [those who fled to the jungles], that's why we got lost. [More hesitation as she looks at her notes] In 1987, I came to Thailand but I immediately came to the U.S., I didn't stay in Thailand because I wanted to come to the U.S. and we were soldiers so they expedited us through. So we came to this country and I got to be in this movie, it's like the story of [came from or is a reflection of] my life [*zoo li los ntawm kuv lub neej xwb nav*].[56]

Thao enacted a telling that invited listening, and portrayed a practice of narration, dragging histories, that she has done repeatedly, especially through the opener when she said, "I am going to talk about my life." Thao's presentation performed her embodiment of Grandma and the story of loss of country and family members. Here, Thao's abbreviated story of war, violence, loss, and displacement provided a political/historical context for her unsubtitled lines. But more poignantly, she claimed that the conditions of war that resulted in the Hmong loss of their "country" shaped how she wanted to portray her character, Grandma, because it was also a story that reflected her own. Thao's testimony-like presentation of her story to connect with *Gran Torino*'s narrative simultaneously asserted her suitability as an actor for the role and offered a narrative parallel to Walt's story. Her character's interactions with Walt invoke a historical connection between Hmong and the U.S. that would otherwise go unnoticed. Therefore, the specters of Hmong historical memory are wrapped up in Walt's redemption and the resolution of U.S. historical and contemporary dilemmas. Thao's statement reveals how the everyday dilemmas about history, redemption, and neighborhood violence are connected to the surfacing of memories.

Mediating Memories, Negotiating Legibility

The character of Sue, though not a particularly nuanced depiction of a Hmong woman, is developed through complex and multilayered symbolism. The film first introduces Sue as Thao's older sister who forces her younger sibling to perform women's chores such as washing dishes and gardening. She is initially portrayed as his protector against the Hmong gang's efforts to initiate him as a member. Her friendship with Walt, after he puts a stop to the gang's scuffle with Thao on the front lawn, hints at the racialized and sexualized encounters between Asia and the West/U.S. in which Asian women represent the exoticized East to be penetrated by white men from the West. She mediates Walt's entry into the Hmong community, where their interactions enhance his image of heroic white masculinity. At the same time, she thrusts upon Walt the material realities of Hmong experiences in the U.S. stemming from the war. In these instances, Sue intersects her grandmother's memories with Walt's haunting memories of the Korean War. It is here that I find the character of Sue most productive, because she connects Grandma's memories to their lives in Detroit, disrupting the film's centralization of Walt's attempts to unpack his war memories.

Sue's combination of innocent teenager and knowledgeable historian begins to unnerve Walt and destabilize the film's narrative. An exchange between Sue and Walt on the topic of where Hmong are located and why they are in the U.S. parallels Grandma's (largely unsubtitled) insistence on

America's betrayal and remembering of Hmong lives lost in the war. After Walt comes upon Sue's encounter with three "dangerous" Black youth, he rescues her from their clutches and on the ride home asks:

> WALT: Where the hell is Humong, I mean Hmong, anyway?
>
> SUE: No, Hmong isn't a place. It's a people.

"Where is Hmong anyway?" is a simple question repeated in multiple encounters, in film and everyday life, signifying a curiosity to locate Hmong geographically and historically. It is a question about place as a geographic marker, a historiographical indicator (where in history do they belong?), and, more poignantly, an allusion to place as a site of refuge.

The question haunts *Gran Torino*'s narrative because it conjures up the refugee figure to disrupt the film's themes of redemption, white heteronormative masculinity, and the white man as the "savior" of the foreign other. More than a geographic question, Walt's query illuminates the dilemma of the Hmong refugee figure and the issue of refuge in the U.S. Therefore, Walt's further inquiries of "How did you end up in my neighborhood then? Why didn't you stay there?" cannot be answered without implicating the U.S. wars in Southeast Asia. Sue reminds Walt and the viewer that Hmong helped the U.S. and their undesired presence in this Midwestern neighborhood is intricately connected to U.S. actions in Southeast Asia:

> SUE: It's a Vietnam thing. We fought on your side. And when the Americans quit, the Communists started killing all the Hmong. So we came over here.
>
> WALT: Yeah. Well, I don't know how you ended up in the Midwest. There's snow on the ground six months out of the year. Why does a jungle people want to be in the great frozen tundra?
>
> SUE: Hill people. We were hill people. Not a jungle people. Booga-booga-booga . . . Blame the Lutherans, they brought us over here.

Sue's shorthand explanation of Hmong presence in the U.S. underscores the plight of Hmong refugees/Americans and gestures toward the overlapping of Korean War and Vietnam/"secret war" narratives that recurs throughout the film. These overlapping stories produce unintended meanings about haunting war memories, such as the implied parallelism between Walt's guilt about his role in the Korean War and the U.S.'s guilt concerning its illicit activities in Laos. This turn in the film resignifies the story of redemption as an incomplete refugee rescue narrative whereby the U.S. refugee resettlement policies have failed to provide Hmong and other Southeast Asian refugees with adequate services, let alone acknowledge the U.S. role in producing the refugees' displacement. At the same time, the Hmong presence in his neighborhood makes the Korean War veteran uneasy because it elicits unwanted reminders of his actions and the U.S.'s own "forgotten" role in Korea. When Father Janovich, the Catholic priest who works with Hmong refugees in the neighborhood and who coaxes Walt to confession, reassures Walt of the distinction between war and peace in which confessing one's sins leaves behind the burdens of war, Walt insists that war is chaotic, unplanned, and unprincipled so that the things that haunt him are "what he isn't ordered to do." This assertion of Walt's apparent unpeacefulness symbolizes the histories that haunt the U.S. about its wars in Southeast Asia because it was not supposed to be there. Walt's inner struggles, which make him appear grumpy to his family and neighbors, are the result of the collision of these messy histories and his knowledge that the conditions of war are burdensome and are difficult to unload in the absence of adequate language to convey them. Instead, he growls at his children, who cannot understand him, and at the Hmong neighbors whose presence conjures up too much. In his inarticulate discontent, Walt represents not only the disgruntled Korean War veteran but a nation trying to grapple with its past. The story of redemption then is turned on its head so that it is the U.S., rather than Walt, that is redeemed as that place of refuge where Sue and Thao can find peace. They need and deserve saving from the inner-city life of strife and delinquency to be transformed into proper U.S. American subjects. Sue and Walt's exchanges attach the story of Hmong fighting on the U.S. side onto the overarching dilemma of Walt's guilt about Korea, which shows how state and historical secrecy is entangled with other war memories and becomes public knowledge. This entanglement symbolizes the im/possibilities of knowledge about the war.

Sue's exclamation of "booga-booga-booga," complete with hand gestures, after correcting Walt that Hmong are "hill" not "jungle" people, neutralizes this potentially disruptive account of how Hmong fought on the side of the U.S. and were forced to flee Communist persecution after U.S. abandonment. At the same time, "booga booga" is a common racist taunt directed at African Americans, and its use by Sue displaces the "jungle" people onto this group. Sue's use of the refrain elides the history of African Americans in Detroit because they are represented in the film as thugs from whom Walt must rescue Sue. Although she may be in danger of sexual violence, Sue also takes up the racist language in the discomforting end that aligns her with anti-Blackness. The gesture infantilizes her as a racialized, gendered youngster from the very hill or jungle that she protests, and it discredits her as a racist by aligning her with Walt's casual racism. Sue is a sympathetic character in part because she can assimilate into white racism, even more naturally than her brother.[57] At issue here is the concern that any knowledge claims about Hmong history emerge mediated, postponing an understanding of U.S. war and imperialism, slavery and anti-Black racism, and the history of Black auto workers that was central to Detroit's industrialization.[58] The use of a racist gesture delays further surfacing of war memories even as Sue's challenges here about U.S. abandonment link Grandma's dispersed but overlaid accounts of this history throughout the film.

Dragging Histories in the Unsubtitled Dialogue
Thao's story and Hmong historical memories emerged, then, through the everyday encounters between Grandma/Thao and Walt/Eastwood. Thus, Walt and Grandma's mutual antagonism and eventual "friendship" forged through moments of improvised acting/dialogue in the unplanned narrative can be reread as illuminating a convoluted Hmong-U.S. relationship. Grandma serves as Walt's nemesis, one who can out-spit him, and she also keeps a watchful eye on the neighborhood, especially on Walt. In a scene where they are sizing each other up, she mutters in Hmong (subtitled): "Why does that old white man stay here? All the Americans have moved out of this neighborhood. Why haven't you left? Let's see him run away like a rooster?" Walt knows that she "hates his ass" and she expresses this every time he is around, but always in Hmong. The film suggests that Walt and Grandma, who both keep watch over neighborhood goings-on from their porches, have shared enemies in the Hmong gang members. However, they serve as foils for each other. Walt conflates Hmong with Koreans; Grandma's reasons for disliking Walt provide historical context for a Hmong story in the film that counters and complicates the baggage Walt carries as a Korean War veteran. Walt and Grandma's relationship, therefore, symbolizes a supposed postcolonial paradigm of contact, interaction, contamination, and self-acknowledgment in which the narrative framing of Walt, Thao, Sue, and Grandma function as, according to Francesca Tognetti, "a mirror and as an enemy line."[59] However, such a teleological trajectory is fictionalized as a savior narrative in which Walt discovers himself through interactions with his Hmong neighbors in order to save them. Grandma's appearances throughout the film, rather than resolved as self-discovery, are instances of disruption in the main plot. Viewing the film through these nodes of dis/order attaches her story to that of Walt's.

At the same time that Walt dislikes the changing look of his neighborhood, Grandma questions his presence in the neighborhood and in her house because she fears it will bring trouble to the family. Grandma's wariness about Walt's seemingly benevolent presence around the family materializes in the climax of the movie with the drive-by shooting and Sue's rape. The attack on the family is a consequence of Walt's intervention with the Hmong gang. After seeing Thao hurt, Grandma proclaims in this last line, pointing at Walt (untranslated): "I was afraid that the white American man had killed my son." When Sue arrives home bruised and beaten with blood streaming down her legs, Grandma exclaims accusatorily (untranslated): "I told you all not to allow the white American man to come to our house. I am not happy with him. What is he going to say about this?" Grandma's protests against Walt as mentor and a father figure to Thao and Sue are attempts to avoid what she had witnessed during and after the war: the broken promises of democracy and an American Dream. Her implication of Walt's white masculinist benevolence in the shooting and Sue's rape explains her aversion to his presence and denies him redemption because his meddling has brought violence upon her family.

Yet Walt's "sacrifice" to "save" Sue and Thao from the Hmong gang by letting the gang members shoot him in front of witnesses recuperates his actions as justifiably benevolent. Before the penultimate scene, after he has locked Thao in the basement for his own safety, Walt walks his dog Daisy over to Grandma who sits in her usual rocking chair on the porch, keeping an eye out for him and the neighborhood. Again, her dialogue here is unsubtitled as he approaches with Daisy, intending to leave her with Grandma. Here, Grandma states that "these Americans lie to Hmong that they'll take our husbands and sons to go to war and will compensate us. That is a lie . . . Lied to us so that we no longer have a home and land to live in . . . You must take care of us (*yug peb*; 'make us live')," while Walt says: "I need you to watch my dog. Yeah, I love you too." Walt's intentions to confront the Hmong gang and "save" Thao and Sue to give them peace, and to find peace for himself through an act of self-sacrifice to atone for his actions during the Korean War, converges with Grandma's assertion that he and the U.S. must be accountable for the illicit war and violence that resulted in the deaths of thousands of Hmong men (and women) and for Hmong displacement. Grandma's account of these "unwritten deaths" is attached to Walt's simultaneous act of disavowal as he busily secures Daisy's leash to her chair. Their overlapping dialogue, the act of speaking to each other, yet addressing different concerns, makes Walt's Christlike death "bittersweet": sweet in the salvation and bitter in its foreclosure and misunderstanding of the past.

These scenes of Grandma's and Walt's overlapping statements suggest that an unacknowledged Hmong perspective is already present within the overarching narrative of *Gran Torino* as well as within U.S. history about its wars in Southeast Asia. Indeed, this Hmong perspective "may not have a single accessible language of its own," as trauma studies and literary scholar Cathy Caruth explains, but the film opens the possibility for Hmong historical memories "within an address to those who speak another language, and who view the story . . . from the perspective of another past."[60] Therefore, in tracing Walt's prejudice and assertion of white masculinity in relation to Grandma's subtle and unsubtitled memories, *Gran Torino*'s ending and his death symbolize the debt the U.S. owes Hmong in order to "make them live" and help them survive as recompense for carrying U.S. pilots to safety. The Gran Torino symbolizes the values of masculinity, independence, innovation, and benevolent imperialism, held by Walt and by the U.S., as well as the historical centrality of working-class and middle-class populations that shaped Walt and his Detroit neighborhood. Walt's death at the hands of a Hmong gang—a symptom of failed U.S. social policies—recuperates the past so that Sue and Thao are supposedly enabled to lead assimilated U.S. lives. We see this in the final scene as Thao inherits the prized Gran Torino, which Walt denied to his own children, in a symbolic embrace of Hmong Americans as part of the multicultural U.S. family.

My point here is that Grandma's very unscripted and unsubtitled dialogue is entangled with the central plot about Walt's redemption. While Walt relives his nightmare of Korea, Grandma vehemently reminds him, and Thao hopes to tell the audience, that there is another war with its own veterans whose roles remain unacknowledged and are always at risk of not being remembered. The translation of language and meaning reveals the mediated emergence of memories that must always surface attached to a more legible narrative to a white U.S. American audience, that of the Korean War veteran. Though useful for understanding how trauma can be inaccessible, Caruth's privileging of voice as a mode of speaking that "transmits the difference of its voice" reveals the limits of a psychoanalytic perspective.[61] I suggest, following postcolonial feminist critiques, that the structure within which the content is made known—both the voice and its meaning—demand attention in *Gran Torino*.[62] The other can only speak and be incorporated into the dominant narrative in the context of white male savior (as in Sue's telling about the "secret war") while challenges to the savior narrative emerge as illegible speech and are erased.

Grandma's unsubtitled statements and performance highlight the dragging process for articulating Hmong American histories. Grandma's lines, although translated in postproduction by Lee, are unsubtitled in the final cut and, therefore, rendered untranslatable because they cannot fit within the premise of the Eurocentric and masculinist narrative. The historical context they underscore weighs too heavily for a story about U.S. redemption and white masculinity/benevolence to carry and be able to explain. Thus, the lines remain unsubtitled to depict flattened Hmong characters and to reinforce ideas about Hmong backwardness and inscrutable foreignness. Nonetheless, Thao's account of her performance provides a context from which memories can surface beyond the film's narrative into the public discourse about it. Thao recounts her purposeful performance of her lines as a way to make sure that U.S. audiences know about their government's perpetuation of violence globally:

> They told me to say that Americans asked us to go to war and they will take care of the women and children, if our husbands and sons died in war. So I said it like that. But, our husbands and sons did die in the war yet they [U.S. Americans] didn't take care of us. I wanted them [director or interpreter] to translate it like that in the movie. Only Hmong people know, Americans don't know so I wanted Americans to know that their leaders lied to Hmong people. So that the story [of *Gran Torino*] will slightly [*nyiam qhuav yog*] be a story about us right now.[63]

Although she was directed to testify to how Hmong husbands and sons fought and died in the war, Thao refuses this narrative's characterizing of Hmong as willing soldiers and allies for the U.S. Thus, she draws together what she was told to say with what she wanted to convey by qualifying her line with "these Americans lie to Hmong" in order to communicate what Hmong people know—that U.S. Americans must also acknowledge their government's policies and practices that produce violence and death. Thao's insistence on the film's audience learning of the context and conditions of U.S. betrayal makes legible the lines of the Hmong actors so that they do not constitute the unintelligible mumbles marking Hmong foreignness but rather, as she says, narrate a story that might slightly resemble "us right now."

Grandma's lines also illustrate a violent Hmong-U.S. relationship that eludes legibility because these tensions do not make sense within the narrative about Walt and/as the United States. *Gran Torino* makes "enough" sense without Grandma's assertions. Lee describes this final scene between Grandma and Walt as coming from Grandma/Thao: "We're just like, just yell at him. You don't like him, yell at him. A lot of that stuff she just threw out." Thao later asked Lee why these particular lines were not subtitled precisely because her intention was for the audience to know what she was saying. Lee did not have an answer for her then but explained in my interview with him that, from a filmmaker's perspective, the absence of subtitles functions to make sense of the story:

> Obviously he [Eastwood] did a whole movie with subtitles with the Japanese film [*Letters from Iwo Jima*]. But if it doesn't have to be subtitled, then it shouldn't. If the story makes sense without you knowing what they said then what's the point of subtitling it? So there's a lot of things that weren't subtitled and that was one of them and the grandma asked me: why didn't they subtitle it? I guess she wanted that to be out there and I didn't have an answer for her because I didn't make that decision.[64]

Here, *Gran Torino* makes sense without Grandma's assertions. The stories of the Korean War, liberal individualism, white heteropatriarchy, and Americanization/assimilation make in/accessible a historical witnessing of Hmong memories. Yet Lee's point clarifies that subtitles are unnecessary here, whereas they might have been integral in *Letters from Iwo Jima* (2006), the film Eastwood previously directed, because the content of the dialogue only comprises part of the performance to convey a Hmong narrative. The other components of the performance include Thao's anger, watchful looks, questions, and her matching position on the porch in relation to Walt. Curiously, rather than rescripting the memories as part of the narrative, the decision to leave them as unsubtitled presents a crisis in the film that compels a closer listening to expose how even the narrative in the scripted text actually enacts a form of silencing, such as the film's portrayal of Sue's telling that gets assimilated into Walt's racism. Such a listening also accentuates assertions about the war and the figure of the speaking Hmong woman.

The unsubtitled dialogue in most of Grandma and Walt's encounters is not so much about mis/untranslation, but rather the way that her dialogue does not fit with the film's plot when brought into English and written language. So, this move in the film's production is an act of silencing the story about Hmong Americans. Yang's experience with the harshness of English, recounted in *The Latehomecomer*, elucidates both grandmas' dilemmas with English/language because she writes about her grandmother's lack of English knowledge and the difficulty of rendering her/Hmong experiences in language. Subtitles are insufficient for communicating silenced histories. The unsubtitled dialogue signifies the breakdown of English and official texts to communicate the crisis in the social order or state power. Yet, reading the unsubtitled Hmong dialogue in *Gran Torino* provides the space for constructing and foregrounding Hmong American histories beyond the script and text to make possible the awareness of missing knowledge—a possibility of witnessing the secreting of knowledge—through embodied action and cultural agency. As such, Grandma's performance in these scenes is significant because it carries meaning for the Hmong American actors and film crew who witnessed it, and for a Hmong American audience who eventually saw it on screen.[65] Because the lines were unwritten, they illuminate the political crisis of uncontained histories of the role Hmong played in a war that was not supposed to exist. Once again, in *Gran Torino*, the Hmong characters are made to participate in a narrative that does not reflect their experiences and whose terms they did not create. But the actors are determined to give their characters a different telling, to imbue the narrative with a story that is meaningful to the past in the present. The space or scene of indistinct chatter in film signifies the moment of dragging up the crisis and violence that threaten to expose the plot and its secrets. Hence, the climax of the film in which the family encounters the violence of a drive-by shooting and Sue's rape underscores the dilemma of Hmong American narratives when brought to the fore. It is always in such unscripted and unwritten scenes where things are not planned that memories and secrets surface.[66] An awareness of missing knowledge gets dragged up through embodied performance to disrupt racial masculinist and heteropatriarchal discourses. Thus, Grandma's voice and address demand a listening that one "cannot fully know but to which [one] nonetheless bears witness."[67] The space of "mute repetition" serves as a site of that very act of witnessing because Grandma's assertions have entered into popular discourse within the circuit of overlapping narratives threaded along nodes of histories that can never really be kept hidden.[68] Such engagements reveal the limitations of Hollywood's attempts to contend with a complicated Hmong history and serve as a "challenge for the Hmong to tell their own story, on their own terms."[69]

Conclusion

In this chapter, I have used everyday encounters and dilemmas, represented primarily through two grandmothers, as a way to conceptualize dragging histories as a feminist refugee practice that seeks to attach otherwise disparate histories to each other. Through an analysis of the memories that surfaced in *Gran Torino* and *The Latehomecomer*, I argue that Hmong women disrupt and work through the silencing of Hmong histories to unsettle the masculinist narratives of loyalty and refuge and assert Hmong presence in becoming. These memories are strung through the stories of two grandmothers, who function as sources of knowledge both of the things that have happened and of those yet to come (157). My reading insists that the grandmas who "only speak Hmong" are not silenced, and that through their speech, secrets constructed during a war are embedded everywhere in our stories and lived lives. These two texts question how we come to know that something is secret, revealing that the process by which secrets emerge in popular discourse can be tied to state and public narratives. In this discussion, secrets' reinscription revolves around white masculinity and refugee rescue. Thus, the telling of refugee histories aims to find a way back and to envision a future in which Hmong histories and refuge are attached to each other through embodiment. As Yang writes: "We, seekers of refuge, will find it: if not in the world, then in each other" (274). Where other people might look to a place in the world to belong, Hmong could find refuge and belonging in each other, and could create "many different places of holding on" (225). Storytelling and performance are strategies not to betray the past but to "encircle" it. Encircling allows for the remnants of war to remain "on the run" and unsettling. They create historical attachments that suggest how refuge is already uneasy in place but which can be carried and sought in each other. It is the mobility to seek refuge rather than the finding of a permanent place that insists upon our not forgetting.

EPILOGUE

GEOGRAPHIC STORIES FOR
REFUGEE RETURN

Geographic stories is a phrase from Katherine McKittrick.[1] I conclude *History on the Run* by continuing the discussion of the geographic implications of refugee storytelling that I began in the introduction. Both the Hmong refugee epistemology of history on the run and my own methodologies of looking for missing things and the refugee archive, after all, are filled with directional markers that give life to refugee worlds along with the unmarked and unnamed places from which Hmong refugees originate. More specifically, I ask how Hmong American writers and artists engage with redactions and missing things without recovering their absence. I turn to Hmong American poetry to show how refugee narratives locate refugee stories and lives in place—locales that are often unmarked by the nation-state. Native feminist Mishuana Goeman's poignant question, "What happens when the poet takes over the cartographer's tools?," opens up readings of Hmong American poetry to map how the missing things are tied to refugee places.[2] I propose the concept of refugee (re)mapping to read these artistic expressions, and I argue that Hmong American poetry imagines refugee migration and the possibilities of refugee return across space and time. Against the problematics of displacement—the liberal rescue narrative that positions displaced peoples as not belonging anywhere and unable to return—refugee (re)mapping aims to locate refugee stories and lives in place. Geographic narratives and presence are embedded in history on the run such that the fugitive histories do not just run unhinged, so to speak, but are anchored in the possibility of returning to the ancestors and becoming "ancestral knowledge."[3] The return in the Hmong cosmological view requires retracing the places one has lived, therefore, (re)mapping Hmong presence in space and time through the convergence of stories that carry place. Thinking return approaches the plig as an ontology that carries Hmong knowledge and opens up histories on the run as not just distinctive to the refugee but a framework for understanding marginalized historiographies rooted in the repertoire of community and ancestral knowledge to redefine history and geography.[4] While Hmong refugees may not be able to physically return to Laos as homeland, their pligs can return in death to Laos and the ancestral homeland of China. Return through death constitutes a "political claim to Hmong sovereignty and a Hmong kingdom" such that death undoes Hmong displacement.[5]

Refugee (re)mapping highlights the intersections of gender, place, and knowledge. I formulate this concept by, first, borrowing the idea of "(re)mapping" from Goeman who describes it as "the labor Native authors and the communities they write within and about undertake, in the simultaneously metaphoric and material capacities of map making, to generate new possibilities."[6] Building on Goeman's idea, I engage with Hmong American poetry as a writing device to (re)map refugee migration through Hmong refugees' return. Second, critical refugee studies has reconsidered mapping to locate refugee stories and acts of resistance—for example, my work with the Critical Refugee Studies Collective on the Story Maps project to gather refugee stories and map them on a digital mapping platform, which is inspired by Goeman's theorizing and her Mapping Indigenous LA project, to unmap the apolitical humanitarian data and discourse on refugees. The collective asks: How can we map refugee communities and resilience across different geopolitical boundaries? How can we map refugee presence without relying on the very humanitarian data that present them as objects of rescue? In addition, feminist refugee geographer Alison Mountz has come up with the idea of feminist countertopographies to map the spaces in between nation-states (detention centers, the sea, etc.) occupied by those in geographic limbo to rethink maps as transgressive and disruptive rather than as affirmations of the status quo. I am interested not in traditional, colonial forms of cartography, but rather in what Goeman proposes as decolonial cartography that includes conceptual and narrative mapping against liberal militarized regimes.

As I discussed in chapter 2, U.S. maps of the spread of Communism in Laos showed locations of Communist activity as places of impending conflict. Hmong who lived in the region were seldom represented. Conflict zones were the very sites that produced refugee displacement, and U.S. strategies to contain Communism were simultaneously represented by confining Hmong to the region of the "secret war," Military Region II on the maps. While Communism was the overarching target of U.S. covert activity, Hmong were also a target as expendable U.S. proxy soldiers who could also be civilized. Today, the involvement of humanitarian agencies in the ongoing refugee crises in the Middle East, Africa, and Southeast Asia (less so in Central America because refugee migrations from this region have been cloaked under the debate on unauthorized immigration) has given rise to a number of websites that map the regional and global flows of refugees. The majority of this online cartography is data driven, usually based on data provided by the United Nations High Commissioner for Refugees. The resulting maps show refugee migration from colonial peripheries to imperial centers such as Europe and North America. These maps perpetuate ideas about refugee populations as masses that emerge, unconnected to the actions of militarized imperialist regimes, to threaten the security of benevolent nation-states. This narrative is visually reinforced by depictions of refugees as "living traces" of violence, yet dehumanized as distant and anonymous masses.[7]

Refugee (re)mapping is a method of gathering refugee stories, not as a progression from escape to rescue, but along the elusive nodes of forced migration. It enacts a feminist refugee epistemology of "cartography as epistemic mapping" to chart refugee reference points for survival and return.[8] The method fashions a version of feminist refugee geography by which refugees and their children born in exile imagine the nonplaces of mountains, hills, slopes, and rivers as reference points to reclaim histories and places necessary for survival and return. In doing so, it provides a reading of refugee stories out of order, in a nonlinear fashion. Refugee (re)mapping makes present Hmong refugee epistemologies for the future in relation to the past. Hmong refugees/Americans have deployed the available configurations of the refugee soldier (chapter 3) and the terrorist ally (chapter 4) to disrupt liberal empire's innocence, yet these narratives also worked to discipline, pathologize, primitivize, and criminalize Hmong. The concept, then, makes absent present U.S. liberal militarized empire and national histories to radically transform geographies as bodies as reference points of refugee life/survival and knowledge. I use refugee (re)mapping to examine the poetry of Hmong American poet Mai Der Vang, which addresses refugee exile, (non)belonging, and desires for home and return through the motifs of body, land, and the spirit. Vang's book of poetry, *Afterland*, draws on the refugee archive to make present the absented, missing things that were redacted during war or lost through flight by inviting Hmong sacred energies to return—to be grounded and reembodied.

My discussion in this conclusion to the book offers a preliminary analysis of *Afterland* to underscore how the "afterlives" of forced displacement challenge the linear rescue narrative that the refugee condition ends "after" resettlement or in death. The concept of "afterland," rather, suggests the "endings that are not over" for the exiled refugee in the afterlife of postwar existence. "Afterland" also conjures the afterlife, not as a utopian haven but as an opportunity for refugee return through the spirit when the body meets the land in burial. As a concept, "afterland" imagines a radical (re)mapping of what it means to (and the possibilities of) return when one cannot do so, and what it means to belong to a place when nonbelonging is foundational to refugee ontology. *Afterland*'s (re)mapping of social space allows refugee resilience, survival, and return through sacred energies and spiritual reembodiment. As such, *Afterland* invokes Hmong sacred energies to frame refugee experiences of flight, the (im)possibility of a Hmong origin, the breakdown of resettlement, and the return; these concepts form the structure of the book.

Vang draws on the Hmong cosmological belief that the *ntsuj plig* (spirit) can be embodied and one must call upon it to be with the body in flight and trauma. In relation to my discussion of the refugee grandmothers' dragging histories in chapter 5, I suggest that to call upon the spirit, beyond the Hmong ritual practice of soul-calling, is a process that does not distinguish between different moments of trauma because the act of calling the spirit strings together traumatic events beyond the immediate one. To call the spirit is about embodiment in which "spiritual work [is] a type of body praxis, as a form of embodiment."[9] In this way, *Afterland* is a reflective and imaginative soul-calling that invites the sacred—which has been lost in the process of forced flight and trauma—into the lives of Hmong refugees/Americans. A set of Vang's poems in *Afterland* deals with soul-calling or spirit meal offering to call for the ntsuj plig's return to and recognition of home. As such, *Afterland* can itself proffer a *hlua khi tes*, a blessing string used in soul-calling ceremonies to secure health and luck, to tie Hmong Americans together through concerns about history, survival, and return to the future past.

Vang's poems deploy the spirit as a way to frame Hmong refugee history and experiences. In the poem "Transmigration," the refugee calls upon and gathers their spirit to leave along with their material possessions: "Spirit, when I flee this jungle, you must too."[10] This direct address to the spirit reminds it to journey with the body as a guide and acknowledges its presence and importance as a companion. The refugee anticipates the things they will encounter, such as "half-decayed" bodies and crossing the Mekong River, and instructs the spirit to not "run off" at the smell of flesh nor "wander to chase an old mate" but to stay close.[11] The refugee continues to remind the spirit:

Spirit, we are in this with each other. . . .
[. . .]
When I make the crossing, you must not be taken no matter what the current gives.
[. . .]
[Y]ou must follow me to the roads and waiting pastures of America.
[. . .]
I am refugee. You are too. Cry, but do not weep.[12]

Here, the spirit also made the jungle journey, water crossing, and plane migration to the United States with the refugee. Thinking through transnational feminisms in late capitalism and neocolonialism, transnational feminist M. Jacqui Alexander's work in *Pedagogies of Crossing* intervenes in the multiple spaces of knowledge production to make visible the forces that structure contemporary conditions. In this work, she suggests wrestling with the spiritual dimensions of experience, even her own writing process, to contend with the Sacred subjectivity that cannot be archived. Drawing the metaphor of "crossings" from the "enforced Atlantic crossing," she writes about the Middle Passage that "not only humans made the Crossing . . . Grief traveled as well."[13] In this way, "Sacred energies made the Crossing," housed in the memories of the forced migrants, indicating that forced migrations carry cosmological systems.[14] Vang's poem acknowledges the spirit's "crossing" in forced migration so that it can, as Alexander claims, "instruct us on the perilous boundary-keeping between the Sacred and secular, between dispossession and possession, between materialism and materiality."[15]

If the refugee spirit also made the "crossing," how can this Sacred energy that continues to be hidden—one of the missing things—be made present without recuperating it as found? Vang's particular ritualistic approach to poetry, which employs the rhythmic chants of Hmong ritual ballads, produces geographic narratives necessary for the survival and return of Hmong refugees. The "ritual poem" offers the possibility of engaging with the spiritual dimensions of the Hmong refugee experience through what Goeman calls "narrative mapping" to open up "the process by which marginal peoples are appropriated as emblems of the liberal tradition of inclusion as a form of progress."[16] The poem that gives its title to the collection and serves as an epilogue is a cartography of the Hmong funerary ballad (Qhuab Ke) to show the spirit the path of return to reunite with the ancestors. The funerary ballad ensures that the spirit does not wander or stray on its return journey after the death of the body. Composed of five parts, the poem narrates the return journey of the dead back through the different places they have lived. But the poem begins at the end of the journey in part I where the refugee spirit must dig for its "finest blouse," the placenta, in the home of birth to don the "birth shirt" to meet the great aunt spirit who "swaddles me with voice of tourmaline."[17] Part II depicts the guiding oratory of the ritual chanter whose "Voice as chain / As zephyr / As sandalwood / As psychopomp" guides the spirit in the journey through the "violet night" of "the rotten lemon grove" and "above chestnut plains" in part III.[18] Part IV reveals the language map of the spirit guiding the refugee return through the places the refugee has lived.

> To meet the end is to go back
> Through every dwelling,
>
> return my footfalls
> to yesterday's land.
>
> Fresno, California.
>
> Merced, California.
>
> Lansing, Michigan.
>
> St. Paul, Minnesota.
>
> Ban Vinai refugee camp, Thailand.
>
> Long Cheng, Laos.

Sayaboury, Laos.

I go to funerals to meet the ancients.
I go to funerals
To keep.[19]

In the poem, the refugee spirit is positioned to "go back" and "return my footfalls." Land and place are positioned as "yesterday's" because the refugee spirit has left them, yet still belongs to them and must return to them. The oratory ritual return joins the literary going-back to produce a "language map" that makes visible the pattern of migration. Rather than disparate locations across state boundaries and oceans, these are places that connect the refugee survival to their spirit's return. What may seem like many miles in geographic terms can be traveled in breaths—hence, "ritual poem" conveys embodied geography. As Goeman explains in her analysis of Leslie Marmon Silko's *Almanac of the Dead*, the novel "provides a critique of a faltering present in stories that (re)map narratives of the past."[20] In particular, Goeman's reading of Silko's "act of mapping" in the "Five Hundred Year Map" accompanying the novel helps me think through the story mapping in Vang's poem. Goeman writes that Silko's legend offers tools to decode the map, and the map showcases tribal memory and not territoriality, and mapmaking is always in contestation.[21] Vang's poem is a reproduction of Hmong refugee social space through the rhythm of the funerary ballad.

Part V reveals a legend or the tools of embodied geography as well as the position of travel. This last part of the poem shows how to return by indexing geography through the body's position and movement (drifting) as well as its integral functions (breathing).

Drift now as the creature
Not meant to land,

Wings in reverse against wind.
How to index my geography,

Map two miles from inhale to breath.
To recycle the chronology of a clock,

Borrow the ladder
From a shaman's dream:

Once, I lived in the valley.
Then I moved to the tent of ghosts.

Next came partitions of ice.
Metallic roads.

Once, I was born in a bowl.[22]

"From inhale to breath" is the poetic (ritualistic and literary) cadence of Hmong space and time. Vang's ritual poem neither elegizes the refugee death as the end of migration, nor burial in California's Central Valley near the foothills of the Sierra Nevada—among sequoias rather than bamboo—as a disconnection from homeland. Instead, it opens up possibilities for finding home in the land, for imagining geographies in the unmappable parts of the landscape. Mai See Thao explains in her work on Hmong Americans exploring diabetic healing by returning to Laos, to position their bodies in that land and place among loved ones left behind, that "the only possible return to Laos is through death."[23] In "Your Mountain Lies Down with You," Vang writes:

But you come as a refugee, an exile, a body seeking mountains
meaning the same in translation.

Here they are.

Place your palms on the grasslands. Feel the foothills rise
with gray pine and blue oak.[24]

In this reading, the body is mountain is land/earth. For the living, ritual serves an important purpose, "I go to funerals to meet the ancients," in which they witness the process of becoming an ancestor as well as the ancestors who are waiting to meet the newly deceased. Attending funerals is a way not just to keep the ritual practice but to retain the knowledge embedded in those rituals. The "ritual poem" opens the space for spiritual time to reveal how things can happen at the "very same instant in time"—the beginning can start at the end, and a map can be deciphered in written words.

I offer this brief reading of Vang's poems in *Afterland* to demonstrate how second-generation Hmong American writers/poets re-present the stories that elders tell them, what they did not experience, and how unsaid things get transmitted. At the heart of literary and artistic expressions about Hmong refugee experiences and the "secret war" is the question: What does one do with the redactions and missing things? Even more, Vang's insightful poems illustrate the crucial questions of what to do with Hmong refugee stories: How do you take care of stories once they have been told? How does taking care of stories also show care for refugees?

How is care a kind of justice for secrets? My reading of *Afterland* suggests that charting refugee return by taking care of the spirit—soul-calling of the ntsuj plig from the site of trauma or guiding it back to reunite with the ancestors—constitutes an important way to care for Hmong refugees and their stories. Acknowledging the spiritual dimension of Hmong refugee forced migrations frames the refugee as never really lost but always capable of returning to those who call upon the refugee's spirit and remind it to dwell in the present.

NOTES

INTRODUCTION

1 The Refugee Studies Center (RSC) holds many reports and studies of refugee resettlement in the U.S. as a part of its service to refugees. The resettlement files belong to the International Institute of Minnesota, an organization that helped resettle Hmong families in the 1980s and early 1990s in the state, and are stored at the Immigration History Research Center at the University of Minnesota. The International Institute of Minnesota collection includes the individual case files of Hmong families who have resettled through the agency. These files record each Hmong family's application for resettlement along with a range of documents from legal records to casual notes: application forms, letters, sponsorship affidavits, agency memorandums, student progress evaluations for English as a Second Language (ESL) classes, and rent receipts among other miscellaneous items.
2 The International Institute of Minnesota collection placed permanent restrictions on duplication of these private family records to protect the families' identities. This permanent restriction is based on the fact that these files contain sensitive personal information about Hmong families and their descendants still living in Minnesota and other states.
3 I use "community" to refer to the church and charity communities that sponsored Southeast Asian families. But there are other entities that could be burdened such as cities.
4 I use "Hmong" instead of "the Hmong" throughout this book in an effort to de-objectify the group.
5 Personal communication with Yang Cheng Vang, June 17, 2020.
6 Mai See Thao, "Bittersweet Migrations: Type II Diabetes and Healing in the Hmong Diaspora" (PhD diss., University of Minnesota, 2018), 92.
7 M. Thao, "Bittersweet Migrations," 93.
8 M. Thao, "Bittersweet Migrations," 93.
9 I am referring generally to the soul-calling practice, but there are specific versions of the ceremony depending on the situation. Some common soul-calling ceremonies include

calling the soul of a newborn, someone who is ill, one who has experienced a traumatic event such as an accident (vehicle, falling down in the presence of a deceased person [at funerals], etc.) and may or may not be visibly ill, an encounter with another spirit, and a celebration (birthday, blessing, etc.). My discussion of ntsuj plig in this paragraph and the rest of the book only scratches the surface of the complexities of the Hmong cosmological system and animist beliefs. I use *spirit* and *soul* interchangeably as landing terms to describe the Hmong concept of ntsuj plig depending on the context because neither term encapsulates the multiplicity of ntsuj plig (communication with Palee Moua, June 17, 2020). I follow Mai See Thao's naming of ntsuj plig as spirit wherever possible because it connotes a multiplicity of spirits who are hosted by a person's body yet "may act on their own accord based on their desires and wants" as if it is "independent of the individual who witnesses their plig's return" to Laos (communication with M. Thao, June 15, 2020). Yet, the practice of *hu* (call) plig has been used in research and popular texts, in medical settings, and colloquially as soul-calling. Although I use *soul-calling* (as a recognizable idea) to refer to hu plig, soul as a concept about the essence of one's morality, affect, artistic expression, or individuality may not capture the multiplicity and mobility of ntsuj plig in the same way that spirit does. My point here is that translation is part of the problem because it typically forces the fitting of Hmong concepts into English and Judeo-Christian epistemologies. My consultations with Palee Moua, Mai See Thao, Ya Yang, and Yang Vang show the complexity of understanding ntsuj plig and inform my intention to center this concept on its own terms (using spirit and soul situationally) instead of providing any easy translations. For further reading on Hmong cultural practices, see Chai Charles Moua, *Roars of Traditional Leaders: Mong (Miao) American Cultural Practices in a Conventional Society* (Lanham, MD: University Press of America, 2012).

10 "Our Secret Army," narr. Mike Wallace, prod. Barry Lando, *60 Minutes*, CBS, 1975, television; available online at Sheena Kalies, "Hmong Our Secret Army CBS 60 Minutes," August 13, 2015, YouTube video, 16:15, https://www.youtube.com/watch?v=L4U2P7tsOAQ.

11 Former State Department employee Lionel Rosenblatt spoke about arguing for Hmong refugees to be included in the Task Force for Indochinese Refugees at the event "The History behind the Hmong Refugee Exodus," Hmongstory 40 Project, August 22, 2015, Fresno City College. In addition, General Vang Pao's CIA handler (case officer) Jerry Daniels testified and pushed the State Department to resettle Hmong refugees.

12 For an in-depth history about the Hmong pilots who were trained and flew T28 planes, see Chia Youyee Vang, *Fly until You Die: An Oral History of Hmong Pilots in the Vietnam War* (New York: Oxford University Press, 2019).

13 The most famous Hmong pilot was Lue Lee. The veterans I interviewed were lieutenants, colonels, and foot soldiers, and served in the military court.

14 Some of my interviewees were students, U.S. embassy employees, medics, and police officers.

15 Laura Hyun Yi Kang, *Compositional Subjects: Enfiguring Asian/American Women* (Durham, NC: Duke University Press, 2004), 2. Laura Kang's figuration of the Asian/American woman as a compositional subject of overlapping identity and disciplinarity helps to comprehend the Hmong refugee who is a former soldier ("good"), turned

terrorist ("bad"), and the claims to history. Pivoting the refugee around a compositional framing is not in opposition to the refugee as a paradigm; instead, it provides more specificity to the Hmong refugee.

16 Much of the scholarship produced about Hmong refugees perpetuates this frame of recounting Hmong refugee histories as linked to the war without critically interrogating this history. These monographs on Hmong refugees' experiences introduce the "secret war" as background for Hmong migration to the U.S., without analyzing how that history continues to inform their integration into U.S. society and how they might narrate their stories. See Nancy Donnelly, *Changing Lives of Refugee Hmong Women* (Seattle: University of Washington Press, 1997); Lillian Faderman, *I Begin My Life All Over: The Hmong and the American Immigrant Experience* (Boston: Beacon Press, 1998); Anne Fadiman, *The Spirit Catches You and You Fall Down: A Hmong Child, Her American Doctors, and the Collision of Two Cultures* (New York: Farrar, Straus and Giroux, 1997); and Wendy Walker-Moffat, *The Other Side of the Asian American Success Story* (San Francisco: Jossey-Bass, 1995).

17 I thank Mimi Thi Nguyen for helping with this articulation of the concept (personal correspondence, February 2019). On "fugitive knowledge," see Gesa Mackenthun and Andreas Beer, eds., *Fugitive Knowledge: The Loss and Preservation of Knowledge in Cultural Contact Zones* (Münster: Waxmann Verlag, 2015). "Fugitive knowledge" emphasizes the "loss of knowledge" during colonial and imperial encounters, whereby it gets relegated to the margins, "languishing in a state of dismissal" (7, 10). For Gesa Mackenthun and Andreas Beer, "fugitive knowledge is not gone but absent, meaning that it is still somewhere," and their edited volume demonstrates "how knowledge becomes transient, evanescent, and ephemeral in cultural contact zones" (7). Citing Sebastian Jobs's concept of "uncertain knowledge," they explain that fugitive knowledge resembles more rumor, gossip, denunciation, etc., which are asymmetrical and selective preservations of knowledge. These could be "unofficial, often orally transmitted, and potentially subversive knowledge" that proliferates in situations of war, conflict, or systemic social inequality (Mackenthun and Beer, *Fugitive Knowledge*, 10; paraphrasing the work of Julius Scott, Marcus Rediker, and Peter Linebaugh). While what Mackenthun and Beer discuss is knowledge that may have been written, just excluded by not being in print or circulation, and could be recuperated, their suggestion that fugitive knowledge requires paying attention to the margins of a site's spectacle gets at the point of history on the run as refugee ways of knowing in the spectacle of war, secrecy, and loss (12). History on the run is not recuperative but remains elusive.

18 Ann Laura Stoler, *Along the Archival Grain: Epistemic Anxieties and Colonial Common Sense* (Princeton, NJ: Princeton University Press, 2010), 3.

19 Carol McGranahan, *Arrested Histories: Tibet, the CIA, and Memories of a Forgotten War* (Durham, NC: Duke University Press, 2010), 22.

20 Simeon Man, *Soldiering through Empire: Race and the Making of the Decolonizing Pacific* (Berkeley: University of California Press, 2018), 4. I use "U.S. liberal militarized empire" to refer to how U.S. emergence in the post–World War II period constituted an overlap between colonialism and militarism to incorporate the decolonizing nations into its version of democracy (Man describes this as liberating the countries to "make

them function within the global economy" [8]) and to liberate the people as subjects of freedom (Mimi Thi Nguyen, *The Gift of Freedom: War, Debt, and Other Refugee Passages* [Durham, NC: Duke University Press, 2012]). See also Lisa Yoneyama for discussions of U.S. empire as a militarized liberatory project that extended colonialism (*Cold War Ruins: Transpacific Critique of American Justice and Japanese War Crimes* [Durham, NC: Duke University Press, 2016]).

21 Man, *Soldiering through Empire*, 10, 5.
22 I thank the anonymous reviewer for helping elaborate on the particularities of the "secret war" archive.
23 Roderick Ferguson's definition of epistemology as "an economy of information privileged and information excluded" and giving rise to particular subject formations helps me articulate the historical erasures about the war as epistemic violence. Roderick Ferguson, *Aberrations in Black: Toward a Queer of Color Critique* (Minneapolis: University of Minnesota Press, 2004), ix.
24 I use the terms *material* and *materiality* throughout the book, especially in chapter 5, not to connote the concrete or "real" in the Marxist context, but rather in the transnational feminist idea of possession, knowledge in this case, in all its forms.
25 Historian Mai Na Lee cautions the writing of Hmong into history primarily through the emphasis on General Vang Pao, the "secret war," and Hmong refugees. See *Dreams of the Hmong Kingdom: The Quest for Legitimation in French Indochina, 1850–1960* (Madison: University of Wisconsin Press, 2015), 17.
26 The field-defining texts include Yến Lê Espiritu, *Body Counts: The Vietnam War and Militarized Refuge(es)* (Berkeley: University of California Press, 2014); M. Nguyen, *Gift of Freedom*; Viet Thanh Nguyen, *Nothing Ever Dies: Vietnam and the Memory of War* (Cambridge, MA: Harvard University Press, 2016); Eric Tang, *Unsettled: Cambodian Refugees in the New York Hyperghetto* (Philadelphia: Temple University Press, 2015); Khatharya Um, *From the Land of Shadows: War, Revolution, and the Making of the Cambodian Diaspora* (New York: New York University Press, 2015). Also see the Critical Refugee Studies Collective at https://www.criticalrefugeestudies.com.
27 See Giorgio Agamben, "Beyond Human Rights," *Open* 15 (2008): 90–95; and Y. Espiritu, *Body Counts*, 10.
28 Y. Espiritu, *Body Counts*, 11.
29 See M. Nguyen, *Gift of Freedom*; and Tang, *Unsettled*, respectively, on the refugee as a critique of liberalism.
30 M. Thao, "Bittersweet Migrations," 5; and Sucheng Chan, ed., *Hmong Means Free: Life in Laos and America* (Philadelphia: Temple University Press, 1994).
31 M. Thao, "Bittersweet Migrations," 5.
32 Martin Stuart-Fox, *A History of Laos* (Cambridge: Cambridge University Press, 1997); quoted in M. Thao, "Bittersweet Migrations," 5.
33 M. Lee, *Dreams of the Hmong Kingdom*, 25.
34 Ma Vang, "Writing on the Run: Hmong American Literary Formations and the Deterritorialized Subject," in "Refugee Cultures: Forty Years after the Vietnam War," special issue, MELUS: *Multi-Ethnic Literature of the United States* 41, no. 3 (2016): 90, https://doi.org/10.1093/melus/mlw031.

35 M. Lee, *Dreams of the Hmong Kingdom*, 63.
36 Vwj Zoov Tsheej nrog Yaj Ntxoov Yias thiab Txiv Plig Nyiaj Pov, *Haiv Hmoob Li Xwm* (Quezon City, Philippines: Association Patrimoine Cultural Hmong, 1997). Although I translate this title to The Hmong History because it provides Hmong history in China, *xwm* as a concept for *teej tug* (which means ideas, traditions, histories, and things of Hmong origin) does not directly translate to history. For an extended discussion of Hmong historical chronology constructed from Chinese records, see M. Lee, *Dreams of the Hmong Kingdom*, esp. chapter 1, "Hmong Alliance and Rebellion within the State (1850–1900)."
37 Although the term *refugee* was coined a century later in the 1951 Refugee Convention, I use it here to describe early Hmong forced migration to Southeast Asia to challenge the ethnohistorical accounts that Hmong were nomads and to disrupt the convention's legal definition and historical limitation of the term. This does not negate the fact that Hmong refer to themselves as a "people without a country," which has exceeded the time frame, before and after, of their legal refugee status.
38 Danilo Geiger, "Some Thoughts on 'Indigeneity' in the Context of Migration and Conflicts at Contemporary Asian Frontiers," in *The Concept of Indigenous Peoples in Asia: A Resource Book*, ed. Christian Erni (Copenhagen: IWGIA and AIPP, 2008), 189–90.
39 For a discussion on settler colonialism as a logic of elimination, see Patrick Wolfe, "Settler Colonialism and the Elimination of the Native," *Journal of Genocide Research* 8, no. 4 (2006): 387–409. Maile Arvin, Eve Tuck, and Angela Morrill, theorizing Native feminisms, assert that settler colonialism is a structure. See "Decolonizing Feminism: Challenging Connections between Settler Colonialism and Heteropatriarchy," *Feminist Formations* 25, no. 1 (2013): 8–34. In this context, I will use ethnic and Indigenous together as separate categories throughout this book because in the settler colonial context, Indigenous peoples have a nation-nation relationship with the state and are not the same as ethnic or racial groups. But, as Ian G. Baird and others have noted, Indigeneity is difficult to separate in the Southeast/Asian context, so using them together connotes their indistinguishability in Southeast Asia. See Ian G. Baird, "Colonialism, Indigeneity and the Brao," in *The Concept of Indigenous Peoples in Asia: A Resource Book*, ed. Christian Erni (Copenhagen: IWGIA and AIPP, 2008), 201–21.
40 Baird, "Colonialism, Indigeneity and the Brao," 203.
41 Baird, "Colonialism, Indigeneity and the Brao," 205.
42 Baird, "Colonialism, Indigeneity and the Brao," 204.
43 Palee Moua, quoted in Sheng Xiong, "Hmong Mental Health Narrative," July 2, 2019, unpublished community organizing document.
44 M. Thao, "Bittersweet Migrations," 3.
45 See Ma Vang, "Rechronicling Histories: Toward a Hmong Feminist Perspective," in *Claiming Place: On the Agency of Hmong Women*, ed. Chia Youyee Vang, Faith Nibbs, and Ma Vang (Minneapolis: University of Minnesota Press, 2016), 28–55.
46 Katherine McKittrick, *Demonic Grounds: Black Women and the Cartographies of Struggle* (Minneapolis: University of Minnesota Press, 2006), 40.
47 Yer J. Thao, "Culture and Knowledge of the Sacred Instrument Qeej in the Mong-American Community," *Asian Folklore Studies* 65, no. 2 (2006): 252. "[H]Mong have had a long history of migration far from their homeland."

48 M. Lee, *Dreams of the Hmong Kingdom*, xix.
49 M. Jacqui Alexander, *Pedagogies of Crossing: Meditations on Feminism, Sexual Politics, Memory, and the Sacred* (Durham, NC: Duke University Press, 2006), 294.
50 McKittrick, *Demonic Grounds*, 33.
51 Jack Halberstam, "The Wild Beyond: With and for the Undercommons," introduction to *The Undercommons: Fugitive Planning and Black Study*, by Stefano Harney and Fred Moten (New York: Minor Compositions, 2013), 11.
52 Harney and Moten, *The Undercommons*, 28. Aylwyn Walsh borrows from Harney and Moten's thinking about fugitivity as an approach to suggest "fugitive knowledge" in performance theater, which involves shifting the "modes and means of documentation," the archive, from focus groups to a "practitioner's reflexive diary." Aylwyn Walsh, "Fugitive Knowledge: Performance Pedagogies, Legibility and the Undercommons," *Applied Theatre Research* 6, no. 2 (2018): 132.
53 Hmong unsettled history mirrors what Eric Tang describes as a process of being "unsettled" for Cambodian refugees in an "unending state of arrival at liberalism" and in the U.S. Tang, *Unsettled*, 14.
54 Jennifer Hyndman, "Introduction: The Feminist Politics of Refugee Migration," *Gender, Place and Culture* 17, no. 4 (2010): 453–54. In this special issue on the feminist politics of forced migration, feminist refugee geographers deploy a feminist analysis of mobility and displacement. In the special issue's introduction, Hyndman establishes the importance of feminist frameworks to trace power relations that shape gendered displacement.
55 Jennifer Hyndman, "The Geopolitics of Migration and Mobility," *Geopolitics* 17 (2012): 249. Also see Doreen Massey, "Power-Geometry and a Progressive Sense of Place," in *Mapping the Futures: Local Cultures, Global Change*, ed. J. Bird, B. Curtis, T. Putnam, G. Robertson, and L. Tickner (New York: Routledge, 1993): 59–69.
56 Hyndman, "Geopolitics of Migration and Mobility," 249.
57 I borrow this phrasing from McKittrick's *Demonic Grounds* where she explains that "Black matters are spatial matters" to suggest the inseparability between space and Black women's subjugation and struggles for liberation (xii). I draw from McKittrick's conceptualizing to allow me to say that Hmong refugee histories are inseparable from their migration patterns and geopolitical concerns.
58 McKittrick, *Demonic Grounds*, xii.
59 McKittrick, *Demonic Grounds*, x.
60 McKittrick, *Demonic Grounds*, xii. Also see Stephanie M. H. Camp, introduction and "A Geography of Containment: The Bondage of Space of Time," in *Closer to Freedom: Enslaved Women and Everyday Resistance in the Plantation South* (Chapel Hill: University of North Carolina Press, 2004), 1–11, 12–34.
61 Mishuana Goeman, *Mark My Words: Native Women Mapping Our Nations* (Minneapolis: University of Minnesota Press, 2013), 4, 6–7.
62 Goeman, *Mark My Words*, 5–6.
63 Goeman, *Mark My Words*, 6, 9–10. The patterns of migration move on and off home bases enacted by her Seneca family and community as they move from "city to city to rural areas, from place to place" for work and survival, reflecting the experiences of Native people who inhabit both urban places and reservations.

64 In theorizing Okinawa's Cold War liminal status as "liberated yet occupied," Lisa Yoneyama explains through a reading of the novel *The Cocktail Party* that the Okinawan protagonist and the Chinese refugee figure share a similar unease of belonging, of "in-between-ness, liminality and survival." These two figures have "no recourse to law" and "no standing in local politics" in Cold War Okinawa. Not only are these figures stateless, they live in a state with a suspended sovereignty. For Hmong refugees, their not-yet-modern status signifies this political predicament of not having a political state and yet living in the suspended, not yet nation-state of Laos. See Lisa Yoneyama, *Cold War Ruins: Transpacific Critique of American Justice and Japanese War Crimes* (Durham, NC: Duke University Press, 2016), 78.

65 Dipesh Chakrabarty, *Provincializing Europe: Postcolonial Thought and Historical Difference* (Princeton, NJ: Princeton University Press, 2000).

66 Sai Kua Thao, interviewed by author, August 2010.

67 I borrow the concept of orientation from Mark Rifkin, *Beyond Settler Time: Temporal Sovereignty and Indigenous Self-Determination* (Durham, NC: Duke University Press, 2017).

68 Bliss Cua Lim, *Translating Time: Cinema, the Fantastic, and Temporal Critique* (Durham, NC: Duke University Press, 2009), 10.

69 M. Nguyen, *Gift of Freedom*, 17.

70 M. Nguyen, *Gift of Freedom*, 16; italics in original.

71 Lim, *Translating Time*, 26, 12, 2.

72 Lim, *Translating Time*, 26, 12.

73 Rifkin, *Beyond Settler Time*, 2.

74 Rifkin, *Beyond Settler Time*, viii.

75 Rifkin, *Beyond Settler Time*, 4.

76 Christian Culas and Jean Michaud, "A Contribution to the Study of Hmong (Miao) Migrations and History," *Bijdragen tot de Taal-, Land- en Volkenkunde* 153, no. 2 (1997): 223. They establish that for centuries, numerous groups (small societies) have crisscrossed the Southeast Asian Massif—a geographic region of highland plains and mountains inhabiting the northern parts of Burma, Thailand, Laos, and Vietnam, and Southwest China—fleeing from aggressors or seeking better opportunities, and they currently live all over these remote mountain ranges (211).

77 Alfred McCoy has published several volumes that argued that opium was the chief commodity at the center of the "secret war." He asserted that General Vang Pao was an opium dealer and the CIA used its planes to facilitate the movement of opium. In this way, the "secret war" was itself a cover for an extensive CIA involvement to aid a supposed Hmong trade and to enrich the coffers of General Vang in particular. I reference one of McCoy's works to gesture toward this existing literature. See *The Politics of Heroin in Southeast Asia* (New York: Harper and Row, 1972). Alfred McCoy along with Culas and Michaud explain that Hmong, Lolo, and Yao were the chief opium producers in southern China, pressured by Chinese leaders to grow poppies and produce raw opium for sale to compete with European and U.S. trade taking over the Chinese market. See Culas and Michaud, "Contribution to the Study of Hmong (Miao) Migrations and History," 218–19. It is important to note that the Hmong refugee/American

community writ large, and specifically the veterans and refugees, reject this claim that their involvement in the "secret war" was primarily to facilitate the opium trade.

78 Even unsettled is the colonial archiving of the designation for "Hmong" in relation to the group's self-naming. While Hmong were related to Miao—Imperial China's designation which connoted a primitive people to be exterminated/eliminated—the Lao, Thai, and Vietnamese governments used the derogatory term *Maew/Méo*, meaning cat, to distinguish Hmong once they moved to these territories in the mid-nineteenth century. French colonialism and U.S. militarized imperialism took up this designation in their encounters with Hmong. Therefore, Hmong showed up as "Méo" in CIA and other U.S. government militarized and diplomatic archival documents during the war period. As such, the state's militarized knowledge formation views Hmong as a people who have not only been "set outside of human law" but prior to it. The emergence of "Hmong" in the record was produced by state epistemologies of refugee processing as much as it was a project of scholarly knowledge production. Lionel Rosenblatt, a former U.S. State Department employee who helped resettle Hmong refugees, explained during a series of public panels and interviews to commemorate the fortieth anniversary of the end of the wars in Southeast Asia for Hmong refugees that the Hmong refugee resettlement process was the defining moment to change the "Méo" to Hmong designation in the record. The refugee task force personnel interviewed Hmong leaders who unequivocally asserted their people's name as Hmong, and wanted it denoted in their resettlement records. In another context toward the end of the "secret war," Dr. Yang Dao, the French-educated first Hmong to earn a doctorate, published a book in which he made the political claim to define Hmong to mean a free people. See Dao Yang and Jeanne L. Blake, *Hmong at the Turning Point* (Minneapolis: Woodbridge, 1993). This meaning was taken up by Sucheng Chan in the title of her book, *Hmong Means Free*. This book comprises Hmong stories based on Chan's Hmong students' writings and their interviews with family about life in Laos and what it means to be Hmong in the U.S. These important moments marked the presence of Hmong in the academic archive.

79 François Marie Savina, *Histoire des Miao* (Paris: Société des missions-étrangères, 1924).

80 While Jean Michaud calls the French Catholic missionaries "incidental ethnographers," it is clear that Catholic missionaries and ethnography were intertwined with the imperialist project in Southeast Asia. See Jean Michaud, *"Incidental" Ethnographers: French Catholic Missions on the Tonkin-Yunnan Frontier, 1880–1930* (Leiden: Brill, 2007); and Patrick J. N. Tuck, *French Catholic Missionaries and the Politics of Imperialism in Vietnam, 1857–1914: A Documentary Survey* (Liverpool: Liverpool University Press, 1987).

81 Fr. Yves Bertrais, "About Us," Hmong RPA website, accessed March 15, 2018, http://www.hmongrpa.org/aboutus.html.

82 Philippe Chanson, "Father Yves Bertrais, An Essential Figure in the History of Hmong Christianity," *Exchange* 22, no. 1 (1993): vii–17, https://doi.org/10.1163/157254393X00092. He also published a series of Hmong language/studies books, and because he worked with Hmong refugees after the war (in particular, the Hmong refugees who resettled in French Guiana), he accumulated a sizable collection of diaries, handbooks, photographs, maps, letters, etc. Center for Southeast Asian Studies, "The Father Yves Bertrais

Collection," Hmong Studies Consortium website, accessed September 15, 2017, https://hmongstudies.wisc.edu/wp-content/uploads/sites/420/2019/02/Bertrais-Collection-Boxes-Guide-Chong.pdf. This collection is on permanent loan from the Oblates of Mary Immaculate at the University of Wisconsin-Madison.

83   See Ian G. Baird, "Indigeneity in Asia: An Emerging but Contested Concept," *Asian Ethnicity* 17, no. 4 (2016): 501–5; Neal B. Keating, "Kuy Alterities: The Struggle to Conceptualize and Claim Indigenous Land Rights in Neoliberal Cambodia," in "Indigeneity and Natural Resources in Cambodia," special issue, *Asia Pacific Viewpoint* 54, no. 3 (2013): 309–22; and Tanya Murray Li, "Indigeneity, Capitalism, and the Management of Dispossession," *Current Anthropology* 51, no. 3 (2010): 385–414.

84   James C. Scott, *The Art of Not Being Governed: An Anarchist History of Upland Southeast Asia* (New Haven, CT: Yale University Press, 2010).

85   James C. Scott, "Hill and Valley in Southeast Asia . . . or Why the State Is the Enemy of People Who Move Around . . . or . . . Why Civilizations Can't Climb Hills," in *The Concept of Indigenous Peoples in Asia: A Resource Book*, ed. Christian Erni (Copenhagen: IWGIA and AIPP, 2008), 166. Relatedly, Jens Dahl characterizes the process of state-making after colonial independence in Asia and Africa as the production of marginalized peoples who "lived in mountainous areas remote from the centers of the new states and other inhabited regions considered marginal to the mainstream economy of the new states, such as desert and semi-desert regions." See Jens Dahl, *The Indigenous Peoples and Marginalized Spaces at the United Nations* (New York: Palgrave Macmillan, 2012), 14.

86   I borrow from Bruce Granville Miller's work in *Invisible Indigenes: The Politics of Nonrecognition* (Lincoln: University of Nebraska Press, 2003) to refer to nonrecognized peoples as groups who claim distinct historical and cultural linkages to Indigenous peoples, yet are not legally recognized by the nation-state to claim such rights.

87   M. Lee, *Dreams of the Hmong Kingdom*, 49.

88   Giorgio Agamben, *Homo Sacer: Sovereign Power and Bare Life*, trans. Daniel Heller-Roazen, ed. Werner Hamacher and David E. Wellbery (Stanford, CA: Stanford University Press, 1998), 134.

89   See Giorgio Agamben, "We Refugees," trans. Michel Rocke, *Symposium* 49, no. 2 (1995): 114–19 (paragraph 1), available online at European Graduate School, accessed March 15, 2012, http://www.egs.edu/faculty/agamben/agamben-we-refugees.html; and Hannah Arendt, "We Refugees," in *The Jew as Pariah*, ed. Ron H. Feldman (New York: Grove Press, [1943] 1978), 55–66.

90   In comparing the two conventions, Paul Weis observes their distinctions of more favorable and less favorable treatment of refugees and stateless persons, respectively (259). The convention stipulated three standards of treatment for stateless persons: treatment accorded to nationals of the contracting state, the treatment accorded to nationals of the country of habitual residence, and treatment as favorable as possible, and not less favorable than to aliens in the same circumstances (247–48). See Paul Weis, "The Convention Relating to the Status of Stateless Persons," *International and Comparative Law Quarterly* 10, no. 2 (1961): 255–64.

91   Jane Perry Clark Carey, "Some Aspects of Statelessness since World War I," *American Political Science Review* 40, no. 1 (1946): 113.

92 Hannah Arendt, "The Decline of the Nation-State and the End of the Rights of Man," in *The Origins of Totalitarianism* (New York: Harcourt, Brace, and World, 1951), 163.

93 Arendt, "Decline of the Nation-State," 159. Arendt contends that the intersection between stateless and displaced persons is a precarious one because the dilemma of statelessness gets ignored through the creation of legal distinctions, de facto and de jure categories.

94 Hannah Arendt, "Statelessness" (lecture, April 22, 1955), 3; available online at Hannah Arendt Papers at the Library of Congress, Speeches and Writings File, 1923–1975, accessed March 15, 2012, https://memory.loc.gov/cgi-bin/ampage?collId=mharendt_pub&fileName=05/052290/052290page.db&recNum=2&tempFile=./temp/~ammem_4O3c&filecode=mharendt&prev_filecode=mharendt&itemnum=2&ndocs=2.

95 Arendt, "Statelessness," 2.

96 David Theo Goldberg suggests that the nation-state's conception as inevitable and permanent narrates statelessness as "irrational" and stateless groups as having neither face nor identity and constituting a threat to the state. See David Theo Goldberg, *The Racial State* (Malden, MA: Blackwell, 2002), 40.

97 Linda Kerber, borrowing from Arendt, historicizes statelessness within a U.S. context and conceptualizes it as a changing practice, not just for refugees but also for those who are denaturalized through various factors including race, gender, economic status, and so forth. Rather than trace defined ethnic groups who have been made stateless, Kerber examines the conditions under which groups become vulnerable to statelessness and inhabit the ambiguous spaces between "the domestic and the foreign, between the national and the international, between sovereignty and subjugation" (735). While statelessness has been most usefully understood as a status or condition, Kerber additionally considers it as a practice that is produced as the citizen's other through (the lack of) documentation, court decisions, border and prison guards (745), along the lines of state security, race and ethnicity, ideal workers, and gender (744). Kerber's analysis, however, is hopeful for an expansive concept of citizenship that does not leave room to account for how a denaturalized status destabilizes the nation-state. See Linda Kerber, "Toward a History of Statelessness in America," *American Quarterly* 57, no. 3 (2005): 727–49. The question about the particular process of Hmong racial formation as a people produced outside of history through the state's erasure of historical knowledge remains difficult to explicate within a stateless framework. I hesitate to definitively name what I am describing here as Hmong statelessness because the term still centers the nation-state. Thus, configuring Hmong along with other groups as state*less* negates them as subjects who lack history and nation, which has justified the very projects of U.S. militarism and rescue to incorporate them.

98 Diana Taylor, *The Archive and the Repertoire: Performing Cultural Memory in the Americas* (Durham, NC: Duke University Press, 2003), 19.

99 Jacques Derrida, *Archive Fever: A Freudian Impression* (Chicago: University of Chicago Press, 1996), 2–3.

100 Derrida, *Archive Fever*, 4. For further discussion of the archive's active work, see Ann Laura Stoler's explanation that colonial archives are "generative substances, as documents with itineraries of their own" (*Along the Archival Grain*, 1).

101 Taylor, *Archive and the Repertoire*, 19.
102 Taylor, *Archive and the Repertoire*, 20.
103 Taylor, *Archive and the Repertoire*, 20–21, 3, 2.
104 McGranahan, *Arrested Histories*, 25, 24.
105 Lisa Yoneyama, *Hiroshima Traces: Time, Space, and the Dialectics of Memory* (Berkeley: University of California Press, 1999), 27.
106 Yoneyama, *Hiroshima Traces*, 27.
107 Yoneyama, *Hiroshima Traces*, 5.
108 Yoneyama, *Hiroshima Traces*, 147. I also include in this discussion of the politics of knowledge Lisa Lowe's formulation of the "intimacies of four continents" as an analytical category to illuminate the transatlantic histories of colonialism, labor, race, gender, and sexuality to trace a genealogy about Asian American pasts. Rather than recuperating what has been lost, Lowe urges "a productive attention to the scene of loss." See Lisa Lowe, "The Intimacies of Four Continents," in *Haunted by Empire: Geographies of Intimacy in North American History*, ed. Ann Laura Stoler (Durham, NC: Duke University Press, 2006), 208.
109 Saidiya Hartman, "Venus in Two Acts," *Small Axe* 12, no. 2 (2008): 11.
110 Hartman, "Venus in Two Acts," 13.
111 Panivong Norindr, "On Photography, History, and Affect: Re-Narrating the Political Life of a Laotian Subject," *Historical Reflections* 34, no. 1 (2008): 90.
112 I thank the anonymous reviewer for suggesting "counterintuitive figures" to organize the different registers of secrecy and refugee epistemologies throughout this book.
113 Laura Kang, in *Compositional Subjects*, proposes this original methodology to trace the figuring of Asian American women in the U.S. and transnational contexts.

CHAPTER 1

1 Thomas P. Conroy, "Highland Lao Refugees: Repatriation and Resettlement Preferences in Ban Vinai Camp, Thailand" (report, Bridgette Marshall Collection, Southeast Asian Archive Special Collections, Langson Library, University of California, Irvine), 13.
2 Interviews with Xaiv Kuam Thoj, Nyiaj Kuam Vaj, Soua L. Lo, Jesse Fang, Youa Yang, Col. Wangyee Vang, and Yer Vang.
3 Ironically, the small amount of literature that is available about Hmong involvement in the "secret war" exceeds that devoted to the Lao or any other groups from Laos. Consistent with my argument about the deployment of colonial tropes, I attribute the relative abundance of literature on Hmong to the fascination evident in anthropological inquiries and the memoirs of U.S. personnel with the Hmong ability to quickly learn Western combat tactics and weapons operation despite their premodern state. As an example, see Roger Warner, *Shooting at the Moon: The Story of America's Clandestine War in Laos* (South Royalton, VT: Steerforth Press, 1998).
4 See John P. Hittinger, "The Soldier and the Citizen: Lessons from Plato and Aristotle," International Society for Military Ethics website, accessed January 10, 2020, http://isme.tamu.edu/JSCOPE95/Hittinger95.html; and Christian G. Samito, *Becoming American under Fire: Irish Americans, African Americans, and the Politics of Citizenship during the Civil War Era* (Ithaca, NY: Cornell University Press, 2009).

5 For a discussion of rural development in Asia through private philanthropies, see Nick Cullather, *The Hungry World: America's Cold War Battle against Poverty in Asia* (Cambridge, MA: Harvard University Press, 2013). To link Salvadoran refugees with U.S. policies, see Stephen Macekura, "'For Fear of Persecution': Displaced Salvadorans and U.S. Refuge Policy in the 1980s," *Journal of Policy History* 23, no. 3 (2011): 357–80, https://doi.org/10.1017/S0898030611000145. For discussion on Central American refugees and their acts of resistance and solidarity to form "mobile communities" in border crossing to escape state violence, see Molly Todd, *Beyond Displacement: Campesinos, Refugees, and Collective Action in the Salvadoran Civil War* (Madison: University of Wisconsin Press, 2011).

6 Chalmers Johnson, *The Sorrows of Empire: Militarism, Secrecy, and the End of the Republic* (New York: Metropolitan Books, 2005); and John D. Kelly and Martha Kaplan, "Nation and Decolonization: Toward a New Anthropology of Nationalism," *Anthropological Theory* 1, no. 4 (2001): 419–37.

7 Simeon Man, *Soldiering through Empire: Race and the Making of the Decolonizing Pacific* (Berkeley: University of California Press, 2018), 11.

8 Iyko Day, *Alien Capital: Asian Racialization and the Logic of Settler Colonial Capitalism* (Durham, NC: Duke University Press, 2016), 17–18.

9 Day, *Alien Capital*, 18.

10 Lisa Yoneyama emphasized the idea of "interimperial" to characterize the decolonizing struggles in Laos in personal correspondence in April 2017. Additionally, Augusto Espiritu uses "inter-imperial" to gesture toward the cooperation, competition, and conflict between empires along with subaltern attempts at maneuvering agency. See Augusto Espiritu, "Inter-Imperial Relations, the Pacific, and Asian American History," *Pacific Historical Review* 83, no. 2 (2014): 238–54. I also follow the Asian American and American studies critique of the Cold War as a longue durée, a decades-long, multisited conflict that extended from World War II as well as overlapped with decolonization struggles and neocolonial efforts.

11 Kelly and Kaplan, "Nation and Decolonization," 427.

12 On supply drops, see William M. Leary, "CIA Air Operations in Laos, 1955–1974: Supporting the 'Secret War,'" Central Intelligence Agency Library, accessed June 15, 2017, https://www.cia.gov/library/center-for-the-study-of-intelligence/csi-publications/csi-studies/studies/winter99-00/art7.html.

13 Timothy N. Castle, *At War in the Shadow of Vietnam: U.S. Military Aid to the Royal Lao Government, 1955–1975* (New York: Columbia University Press, 1993), 2.

14 See Chia Vang, *Fly until You Die: An Oral History of Hmong Pilots in the Vietnam War* (New York: Oxford University Press, 2019). According to the website Legacies of War, "from 1964 to 1973, the U.S. dropped more than two million tons of ordnance on Laos during 580,000 bombing missions—equal to a planeload of bombs every eight minutes, 24 hours a day, for nine years—making Laos the most heavily bombed country per capita in history." Legacies of War, "Secret War in Laos," Legacies of War website, accessed September 15, 2017, http://legaciesofwar.org/about-laos/secret-war-laos/.

15 Castle, *At War in the Shadows of Vietnam*, 66.

16 For example, once the CIA realized that better helicopters and better-trained pilots than CIA pilots would be crucial to Air America's operations in Laos, Air America vice president for operations Robert E. Rousselot hired four experienced U.S. Marine Corps helicopter pilots who obtained their discharges in Okinawa to fly the UH-34s (transferred from the Marine Corps). See Leary, "CIA Air Operations in Laos."

17 Roger Warner explains in *Shooting at the Moon* that "the T-28s were rigged with three-sided frames on the fuselage into which metal insignia plates could be slid: the Lao insignia on one side, the Thai insignia on the other, or no insignia at all" (132).

18 John Prados, *Presidents' Secret Wars: CIA and Pentagon Covert Operations from World War II through the Persian Gulf* (Chicago: Ivan R. Dee, 1986), 279. Also see Ralph McGehee, "Bombing Laos," Hartford Web Publishing website, published October 9, 1995, accessed March 12, 2015, http://www.hartford-hwp.com/archives/54/057.html.

19 See Yến Lê Espiritu, "Rethinking 'Collateral Damage' in the Vietnam War: The Other Others in the Circuits of U.S. Empire," in "(Re)Collecting the Vietnam War," special issue, *Asian American Literary Review* 6, no. 2 (2015): 122, 133–39; Sarah Kenyon Lischer, "Collateral Damage: Humanitarian Assistance as a Cause for Conflict," *International Security* 28, no. 1 (2003): 79–109; and Cathy Schlund-Vials, "Collateral + Damage," special issue, *Asian American Literary Review* 6, no. 2 (2015): 122.

20 Kou Yang, "The Deadly, Horrible Mess We Made Still Plagues Indochina," *Modesto Bee*, March 5, 2015, http://www.modbee.com/opinion/opn-columns-blogs/community-columns/article17237951.html.

21 See Cindy I-Fen Cheng, *Citizens of Asian America: Democracy and Race during the Cold War* (New York: New York University Press, 2013); Kandice Chuh and Karen Shimakawa, *Orientations: Mapping Studies in the Asian Diaspora* (Durham, NC: Duke University Press, 2001); Jodi Kim, *Ends of Empire: Asian American Critique and the Cold War* (Minneapolis: University of Minnesota Press, 2010); Christina Klein, *Cold War Orientalism: Asia in the Middlebrow Imagination, 1945–1961* (Berkeley: University of California Press, 2003); and Lisa Yoneyama, *Cold War Ruins: Transpacific Critique of American Justice and Japanese War Crimes* (Durham, NC: Duke University Press, 2016).

22 Kim, *Ends of Empire*, 16. Kim's excavation of the Cold War as an "epistemology and production of knowledge" because it "exceeds and outlives its historical eventness" helps me pinpoint the "secret war" as a historical event and knowledge production project.

23 See Jacques Derrida, *Geneses, Genealogies, Genres, and Genius: The Secrets of the Archive*, trans. Beverley Bie Brahic (New York: Columbia University Press, 2003); Jacques Derrida, *The Gift of Death*, 2nd ed., trans. David Wills (Chicago: University of Chicago Press, 1995); Jacques Derrida, *Literature in Secret*, trans. David Wills (Chicago: University of Chicago Press, 2008); and Jacques Derrida and Maurizio Ferraris, *A Taste for the Secret*, trans. Giacomo Donis, ed. Giacomo Donis and David Webb (Malden, MA: Polity Press, 2001).

24 Derrida, *Geneses, Genealogies*, 33.

25 Derrida, *Geneses, Genealogies*, 20.

26 Michael Taussig, *Defacement: Public Secrecy and the Labor of the Negative* (Stanford, CA: Stanford University Press, 1999), 5.

27 Taussig, *Defacement*, 7, 2.

28 Taussig, *Defacement*, 6.
29 Elias Canetti, *Crowds and Power* (New York: Farrar, Straus and Giroux, 1984), 290; and Taussig, *Defacement*, 7.
30 Jodi Dean, "Publicity's Secret," *Political Theory* 29, no. 5 (2001): 624–50.
31 Clare Birchall, "There's Been Too Much Secrecy in This City: The False Choice between Secrecy and Transparency in US Politics," *Cultural Politics* 7, no. 1 (2011): 134, https://doi.org/10.2752/175174311X12861940861905. Also see Birchall's "The Politics of Opacity and Openness: An Introduction to 'Transparency,'" *Theory, Culture and Society* 0 (2011): 1–19, https://doi.org/10.1177/0263276411427744.
32 Derrida and Ferraris, *A Taste for the Secret*, 59.
33 Birchall, "There's Been Too Much Secrecy in This City."
34 Catherine Hundleby, "The Epistemological Evaluation of Oppositional Secrets," *Hypatia* 20, no. 4 (2005): 49, 51.
35 Hundleby, "Epistemological Evaluation of Oppositional Secrets," 55.
36 Paul Christopher Johnson, *Secrets, Gossip, and Gods: The Transformation of Brazilian Candomblé* (New York: Oxford University Press, 2002), 5.
37 For Johnson, the layered means of secrecy are the "secrecy of African hermeneutics carried by slaves to the shores of Brazil; the secrecy as resistance to the slave colony and kingdom; the secrecy of hidden affiliations with the newly formed Afro-Brazilian religion under the First Republic; the gradual replacement of secrets by secretism, the discourse of 'depth' and 'foundation' after Brazilian Candomblé became known as 'national' under the Second Republic; and, finally, the layering of these uses of secrets and secretism to adjudicate religious meanings, orders, and privileges in contemporary practice." P. Johnson, *Secrets, Gossip, and Gods*, 5.
38 P. Johnson, *Secrets, Gossip, and Gods*, 7.
39 P. Johnson, *Secrets, Gossip, and Gods*, 3; italics in original.
40 P. Johnson, *Secrets, Gossip, and Gods*, 8. The use of secrets has appeared in reclaiming Indigenous, local, and non-Western epistemologies. See Robert Allen Warrior, *Tribal Secrets: Recovering American Indian Intellectual Traditions* (Minneapolis: University of Minnesota Press, 1995).
41 P. Johnson, *Secrets, Gossip, and Gods*, 5.
42 P. Johnson, *Secrets, Gossip, and Gods*, 4–5. Johnson suggests that "secrecy can be as useful to those who would resist authority as to those who seek to impose it" (4–5).
43 Michel-Rolph Trouillot, *Silencing the Past: Power and the Production of History* (Boston: Beacon Press, 1995), 2, 3. Kirsten Weld further takes up an investigation of history's two meanings in her excavation of the National Police archives in Guatemala City as a way to tell the story of state repression in Guatemala and postconflict reengagements with that history. See Kirsten Weld, *Paper Cadavers: The Archives of Dictatorship in Guatemala* (Durham, NC: Duke University Press, 2014).
44 Trouillot, *Silencing the Past*, 23, 5.
45 Trouillot, *Silencing the Past*, 70-107.
46 At the same time, this story analyzes the Laotian postcolonial struggle and the U.S. perception of its landscape as empty and open for military occupation in so far as it helps to illuminate the Hmong refugee narrative.

47 Lisa Yoneyama helped clarify this point in personal correspondence in April 2017.
48 Kim, *Ends of Empire*, 8.
49 Kim, *Ends of Empire*, 9.
50 Weld, *Paper Cadavers*, 15.
51 Barry Rubin, *Secrets of State: The State Department and the Struggle over U.S. Foreign Policy* (New York: Oxford University Press, 1985), 5.
52 According to Sucheng Chan, the U.S. promised to take care of Hmong if they fought for the U.S. See Sucheng Chan, *Hmong Means Free: Life in Laos and America* (Philadelphia: Temple University Press, 1994).
53 Takashi Fujitani, "Right to Kill, Right to Make Live: Koreans as Japanese and Japanese as Americans during WWII," *Representations* 99 (2007): 18, 19, 34.
54 There is also the case of Iraqis recruited as translators for the U.S. invasion in Iraq who are now pursuing refugee status due to persecution.
55 Keith Quincy, *Harvesting Pa Chay's Wheat: The Hmong and America's Secret War in Laos* (Spokane: Eastern Washington University Press, 2000), 5.
56 David M. Barret, *The CIA and Congress: The Untold Story from Truman to Kennedy* (Lawrence: University Press of Kansas, 2005), 9. The CIA's timeline of its intelligence history shows U.S. information gathering prior to the attacks at Pearl Harbor when President Roosevelt appointed World War I veteran William J. Donovan as "Coordinator of Information" in July 1941. See CIA, "About CIA: Timeline," Central Intelligence Agency website, last updated April 26, 2016, https://www.cia.gov/about-cia/cia-museum/experience-the-collection/text-version/timeline.html.
57 Barret, *CIA and Congress*, 9. Also see Rhodri Jeffreys-Jones, *The CIA and American Democracy* (New Haven, CT: Yale University Press, 1989). For a discussion of the politics of secrecy in U.S. security policies, see Edward A. Shils, *The Torment of Secrecy: The Background and Consequences of American Security Policies* (Glencoe, IL: Free Press, 1956).
58 See Barret, *CIA and Congress*; Jeffreys-Jones, *CIA and American Democracy*; and Thomas L. Ahern Jr., *Undercover Armies: CIA and Surrogate Warfare in Laos, 1961–1973* (Washington, D.C.: Center for the Study of Intelligence, 2006); available online at NSA, "The CIA's Vietnam Histories," National Security Archive website, accessed October 1, 2010, https://nsarchive2.gwu.edu//NSAEBB/NSAEBB284/6-UNDERCOVER_ARMIES.pdf.
59 Prados, *Presidents' Secret Wars*, 262.
60 Prados, *Presidents' Secret Wars*, 261–62.
61 Yến Lê Espiritu, "The 'We-Win-Even-When-We-Lose' Syndrome: U.S. Press Coverage of the Twenty-Fifth Anniversary of the 'Fall of Saigon,'" *American Quarterly* 58, no. 2 (2006): 329–52.
62 Khatharya Um, "The 'Vietnam War': What's in a Name?," in "Thirty Years AfterWARd: Vietnamese Americans and U.S. Empire," special issue, *Amerasia* 31, no. 2 (2005): 152. Um observes that the Vietnam War is popularly imagined as "being *in*, *about* and *for* Vietnam," locating its dilemma politically and geographically in a specific country. Given its highly contested place in U.S. history as the "war with the difficult memory," popular understanding about "Vietnam" has yet to contend with the histories and human

legacies of Laos and Cambodia. Um enhances our critiques about the Vietnam War by foregrounding how the conflict unfolded differently in Laos with Hmong collaboration.

63 See Aiwha Ong, *Buddha Is Hiding: Refugees, Citizenship, the New America* (Berkeley: University of California Press, 2003); Eric Tang, *Unsettled: Cambodian Refugees in the New York Hyperghetto* (Philadelphia: Temple University Press, 2015); and Khatharya Um, *From the Land of Shadows: War, Revolution, and the Making of the Cambodian Diaspora* (New York: New York University Press, 2015).

64 Ahern, *Undercover Armies*, xvii. Furthermore, Ahern assessed the program as "important only to those who were there" because it became for the CIA participants "the adventure of their professional lives" (xvii). This point about the ultimate experience of the CIA elides the experiences of those who were drawn into the war not for professional adventure but for their survival.

65 The supposed success of the "secret war" was something that the CIA and U.S. government could not achieve in Cuba in the failed Bay of Pigs Invasion, which was an embarrassment for both the agency and the Kennedy administration.

66 Ahern, *Undercover Armies*, 5.

67 Ahern, *Undercover Armies*, 5.

68 Ahern, *Undercover Armies*, 5.

69 Ahern, *Undercover Armies*, 1.

70 Lisa Yoneyama offers a succinct discussion of decolonization's longue durée in *Cold War Ruins*. Also see Melani McAlister, *Epic Encounters: Culture, Media, and the U.S. Interests in the Middle East since 1945* (Berkeley: University of California Press, 2001). Albert Lau makes a similar claim about the overlap between decolonization and the Cold War in his work on Southeast Asia in the Cold War. See his introduction to *Southeast Asia and the Cold War*, ed. Albert Lau (Abingdon, UK: Routledge, 2012), 1–12.

71 See Leslie James and Elisabeth Leake, eds., *Decolonization and the Cold War: Negotiating Independence* (London: Bloomsbury, 2015).

72 Mark P. Bradley, *Imagining Vietnam and America: The Making of Postcolonial Vietnam* (Chapel Hill: University of North Carolina Press, 2000), 8.

73 Elaine Kim and Chungmoo Choi, eds., *Dangerous Women: Gender and Korean Nationalism* (New York: Routledge, 1997), 3.

74 Setsu Shigematsu and Keith Camacho, introduction to *Militarized Currents: Toward a Decolonized Future in Asia and the Pacific*, ed. Setsu Shigematsu and Keith Camacho (Minneapolis: University of Minnesota Press, 2010), xv–xlviii.

75 Steven Hugh Lee, *Outposts of Empire: Korea, Vietnam and the Origins of the Cold War in Asia, 1949–1954* (Montreal: McGill-Queen's University Press, 1995), 4.

76 S. Lee, *Outposts of Empire*, 5, 6.

77 Mimi Thi Nguyen, *The Gift of Freedom: War, Debt, and Other Refugee Passages* (Durham, NC: Duke University Press, 2012), 6. Also see McAlister, *Epic Encounters*.

78 Yoneyama, *Cold War Ruins*, 19.

79 Yoneyama, *Cold War Ruins*, 49, 50. She explains that it was the U.S. and Japanese competition over the discourse of racial and colonial justice, in particular, that constituted the Cold War Americanization of racial justice (19).

80 Yoneyama, *Cold War Ruins*, 20.

81 See Patrick Wolfe for a discussion of settler colonialism: "Settler Colonialism and the Elimination of the Native," *Journal of Genocide Research* 8, no. 4 (2006): 387–409. Also, Roxanne Dunbar-Ortiz has argued that counterinsurgencies began with the settler colonial project and were extended to other parts of the world, in *An Indigenous Peoples' History of the United States* (Boston: Beacon Press, 2014).
82 S. Lee, *Outposts of Empire*, 5, 6.
83 See Arnold R. Isaacs, Gordon Hardy, MacAlister Brown, et al., *Pawns of War: Cambodia and Laos* (Boston: Boston Publishing, 1987); Joshua Kurlantzick, *A Great Place to Have a War: America in Laos and the Birth of a Military CIA* (New York: Simon and Schuster, 2017); and Martin Stuart-Fox, *A History of Laos* (Cambridge: Cambridge University Press, 1997).
84 Lau, introduction, 5.
85 Lau, introduction, 5.
86 Lau, introduction, 5.
87 Simon Creak, *Embodied Nation: Sport, Masculinity, and the Making of Modern Laos* (Honolulu: University of Hawaii Press, 2015), 5.
88 Seth Jacobs, *The Universe Unraveling: American Foreign Policy in Cold War Laos*, The United States in the World (Ithaca, NY: Cornell University Press, 2012), 3.
89 Jacobs, *Universe Unraveling*, 3.
90 Geoffrey C. Gunn, *Political Struggles in Laos, 1930–1954: Vietnamese Communist Power and the Lao Struggle for National Independence* (Bangkok: Editions Duang Kamol, 1988), 24.
91 Chan, *Hmong Means Free*, 2.
92 Gunn, *Political Struggles in Laos*, 25–27.
93 Chan, *Hmong Means Free*, 3; and Creak, *Embodied Nation*, 4.
94 Creak, *Embodied Nation*, 3.
95 Creak, *Embodied Nation*, 4.
96 Gunn, *Political Struggles in Laos*, 27. French explorer-administrator August Pavie, installed as the first vice consul to the king of Laos in 1887, orchestrated French colonial rule in Laos.
97 Chan, *Hmong Means Free*, 6.
98 Chan, *Hmong Means Free*, 6.
99 Chan, *Hmong Means Free*, 7.
100 Gunn, *Political Struggles in Laos*, 33.
101 Gunn, *Political Struggles in Laos*, 7.
102 Gunn, *Political Struggles in Laos*, 7. Opium was a major income source for the French colonial regime, and Hmong were the primary opium producers. Hence the noted connection between Hmong and opium as a cash crop began during French colonialism and extended to the period of U.S. intervention.
103 Gunn, *Political Struggles in Laos*, 7.
104 Gunn, *Political Struggles in Laos*, 34.
105 Chan, *Hmong Means Free*, 3.
106 Creak, *Embodied Nation*, 18.
107 Chan, *Hmong Means Free*, 8.

108 Chan, *Hmong Means Free*, 8.
109 Through a gender analysis, Mai Na Lee asserts that this leadership structure was influenced by women and by marriage alliances. See her chapter, "The Women of 'Dragon Capital': Marriage Alliances and the Rise of Vang Pao," in *Claiming Place: On the Agency of Hmong Women*, ed. Chia Youyee Vang, Faith Nibbs, and Ma Vang (Minneapolis: University of Minnesota Press, 2016), 87–116.
110 Chan, *Hmong Means Free*, 10.
111 Gunn, *Political Struggles in Laos*, 226, 227.
112 Quoted in Gunn, *Political Struggles in Laos*, 226.
113 The Japanese declaration of Laotian independence is another missing interimperial link, which ended the latency of Laos's sovereignty but manifested as postcolonial independence in 1944 even briefly due to Japanese imperial policy.
114 Andrea Matles Savada, ed., "Events in 1945," in *Laos: A Country Study* (Washington, DC: GPO for the Library of Congress, 1994); available online at Library of Congress Country Studies website, accessed March 12, 2015, http://countrystudies.us/laos/13.htm.
115 Savada, ed., "Events in 1945."
116 Ellen Joy Hammer, *The Struggle for Indochina, 1940–1955* (Stanford, CA: Stanford University Press, 1967), 134, 135.
117 Gunn, *Political Struggles in Laos*, 180.
118 Andrea Matles Savada, ed., "The Kingdom of Laos," in *Laos: A Country Study* (Washington, DC: GPO for the Library of Congress, 1994); available online at Library of Congress Country Studies website, accessed March 12, 2015, http://countrystudies.us/laos/17.htm.
119 John Foster Dulles, "Indochina—Midway in the Geneva Conference: Address by the Secretary of State, May 7, 1954," website of The Avalon Project: Documents in Law, History and Diplomacy (Yale Law School), accessed March 13, 2015, http://avalon.law.yale.edu/20th_century/inch022.asp.
120 Andrea Matles Savada, ed., "The Pathet Lao," in *Laos: A Country Study* (Washington, DC: GPO for the Library of Congress, 1994); available online at Library of Congress Country Studies website, accessed March 12, 2015, http://countrystudies.us/laos/18.htm.
121 Andrea Matles Savada, ed., "Initial Difficulties," in *Laos: A Country Study* (Washington, DC: GPO for the Library of Congress, 1994); available online at Library of Congress Country Studies website, accessed March 12, 2015, http://countrystudies.us/laos/20.htm.
122 Creak, *Embodied Nation*, 5.
123 Creak, *Embodied Nation*, 5.
124 Here, I use the idea of sovereignty in terms of nationhood, traditional practices and governance, and epistemologies. I draw from the Indigenous scholarship on sovereignty and nationhood. See Glen Coulthard, *Red Skin, White Masks: Rejecting the Colonial Politics of Recognition* (Minneapolis: University of Minnesota Press, 2014); Mishuana Goeman, *Mark My Words: Native Women Mapping Our Nations* (Minneapolis: University of Minnesota Press, 2013); and Audra Simpson, *Mohawk Interruptus: Political Life across the Borders of Settler States* (Durham, NC: Duke University Press, 2014).
125 Lau, introduction, 3–4.
126 Lisa Yoneyama, in *Cold War Ruins*, explains that in Okinawa, the illusion of sovereignty happened not under secrecy but with an explicit idea of Japan's residual sovereignty.

127 Dulles, "Indochina."
128 Lau, introduction, 4.
129 Ahern, *Undercover Armies*, 3.
130 *The Story of Laos: The Problem for a U.S. Foreign Policy*, John F. Kennedy National Security Files on Asia and the Pacific: 1961–1963, Vietnam Center and Archive, Texas Tech University, n.d.
131 Ahern, *Undercover Armies*, 3.
132 *Story of Laos*.
133 Prados, *Presidents' Secret Wars*, 262.
134 Savada, "Initial Difficulties."
135 Billy Webb, *Secret War* (Bloomington, IN: Xlibris, 2010), 42.
136 Webb, *Secret War*, 43.
137 Savada, "Initial Difficulties."
138 Harvey E. Gutman, interviewed by Stuart Van Dyke in August 1997, in *Laos Country Reader*, accessed April 2016, http://www.adst.org/Readers/Laos.pdf.
139 Prados, *Presidents' Secret Wars*, 262. The elections were an upset for U.S. interests and conservative groups such as the pro-American Committee for the Defense of National Interests.
140 Robert Gilkey, "Laos: Politics, Elections and Foreign Aid," *Far Eastern Survey* 27, no. 6 (1958): 91.
141 Prados, *Presidents' Secret Wars*, 262.
142 Ahern, *Undercover Armies*, 27. Because the Military Assistance Program lacked the flexibility to "exploit the Hmong potential," the U.S. Mission in Vientiane took it upon itself to ask the Pentagon for WWII-vintage B-26 aircraft to execute photographic missions over Laos and North Vietnam (28).

CHAPTER 2

Epigraph: President John F. Kennedy, press conference remarks, March 23, 1961. President John F. Kennedy's National Security Council Files and Foreign Relations documents from 1961–63 prepared by the John F. Kennedy Presidential Library and Museum and held at the Vietnam Center and Archive, Texas Tech University. Also see John F. Kennedy Presidential Library and Museum website, accessed January 10, 2020, https://www.jfklibrary.org/asset-viewer/archives/JFKWHA/1961/JFKWHA-020/JFKWHA-020.

1 I use "secret" in quotation marks to denote the critical unsettling condition of secrets that highlights how they get produced, for whom they are meant to withhold information, and whether such information is necessarily unknowable.

2 This document was not the first one known to discuss U.S. military aid to Laos, but it was my first encounter with such heavy redactions which shaped my analysis that secrets are as much about hiding content as they involve the processing of government documents. I analyze it as an example to ground my analytic of the missing and to develop my argument that secrets structure knowledge. This document has since been released in its unredacted version by the U.S. Department of State Office of the Historian, but it reinforces my argument that the mundane acts of marking things secret and

removing sensitive content reflect the secrecy of state governance and knowledge. See *Foreign Relations of the United States, 1961–1963*, volume 24, Laos Crisis, February–May 1962: U.S. Sanctions Against Phoumi Nosavan and the Nam Tha Crisis, available online at the website of U.S. Department of State Office of the Historian, accessed January 7, 2020, https://history.state.gov/historicaldocuments/frus1961-63v24/d329.

3   The idea of "open secrets" follows anthropologist Michael Taussig's notion of the "public secret," in which something is generally known but cannot easily be articulated.

4   Matthew S. Hull, *Government of Paper: The Materiality of Bureaucracy in Urban Pakistan* (Berkeley: University of California Press, 2012), 5.

5   Hull, *Government of Paper*, 1.

6   Andrew Friedman, *Covert Capital: Landscapes of Denial and the Making of U.S. Empire in the Suburbs of Northern Virginia* (Berkeley: University of California Press, 2013), 10–11.

7   Friedman, *Covert Capital*, 14.

8   Ann Laura Stoler, "Colonial Archives and the Arts of Governance," *Archival Science* 2 (2002): 91.

9   Davorn Sisavath has noted the difficulties of accessing records on U.S.-Laos relations at the National Archives because some were destroyed in the transferring process and many remain classified. Her research, instead, examines military waste in Laos as an archive by tracing the remains of bombs dropped on Laos. See "The US Secret War in Laos: Constructing an Archive from Military Waste," *Radical History Review*, no. 133 (2019): 103–16, https://doi.org/10.1215/01636545-7160089.

10 Antoinette Burton, "Introduction: Archive Fever, Archive Stories," in *Archive Stories: Facts, Fictions, and the Writing of History* (Durham, NC: Duke University Press, 2005), 7.

11 Joan M. Schwartz and Terry Cook, "Archives, Records, and Power: The Making of Modern Memory," *Archival Science* 2 (2002): 2.

12 Stoler, "Colonial Archives and the Arts of Governance," 100.

13 Stoler, "Colonial Archives and the Arts of Governance," 101.

14 Anjali Arondekar, *For the Record: Sexuality and the Colonial Archive in India* (Durham, NC: Duke University Press, 2009), 4.

15 Stoler, "Colonial Archives and the Arts of Governance," 103.

16 Stoler, "Colonial Archives and the Arts of Governance," 107–8.

17 Stoler, "Colonial Archives and the Arts of Governance," 108.

18 Schwartz and Cook, "Archives, Records, and Power," 5.

19 Lisa Lowe, *The Intimacies of Four Continents* (Durham, NC: Duke University Press, 2015), 1, 4, 2.

20 Lowe, *Intimacies of Four Continents*, 2.

21 Lowe, *Intimacies of Four Continents*, 4.

22 Martin E. Goldstein, *American Policy toward Laos* (Rutherford, NJ: Fairleigh Dickinson University Press, 1973), 24.

23 On the north–south route, see Goldstein, *American Policy toward Laos*, 35–36. On "geographic frontiers," see Shiri Pasternak, "The Shifting Spatial Requirements for Indigenous Genocide in Canada" (paper presented at the Critical Ethnic Studies Association Conference, University of California, Riverside, March 10–12, 2011).

24 *The Story of Laos: The Problem for a U.S. Foreign Policy*, John F. Kennedy National Security Files on Asia and the Pacific: 1961–1963, Vietnam Center and Archive, Texas Tech University.

25 Thomas L. Ahern Jr., *Undercover Armies: CIA and Surrogate Warfare in Laos, 1961–1973* (Washington, DC: Center for the Study of Intelligence, 2006), 4. This major military effort "took the form of a military assistance and advisory program," called the Program Evaluation Office (PEO), to circumvent the provisions of the Geneva Accords, which prohibited foreign military presence except for a "residual French mission." Part of the economic aid program, the PEO "equipped and trained regular units of the Forces Armées Royals [Royal Lao Armed Forces]."

26 See Arnold R. Isaacs, Gordon Hardy, MacAlister Brown, et al., *Pawns of War: Cambodia and Laos* (Boston: Boston Publishing, 1987). From a U.S. personnel perspective on Laos as a pawn, see Milliard Graham, *Laotian Pawn* (Bloomington, IN: 1st Books Library, 1996).

27 *Twelve Years of U.S. Imperialist Intervention and Aggression in Laos* (Laos: Neo Lao Haksat Publications, 1966), 11.

28 Chalmers Johnson, *The Sorrows of Empire: Militarism, Secrecy, and the End of the Republic* (New York: Metropolitan Books, 2004), 8.

29 The quotes in this paragraph came from the document in the Kennedy Files titled "Memorandum of Conversation," April 29, 1961, Foreign Relations of the United States, 1961–63, vol. 24, Laos Crisis, John F. Kennedy National Security Files on Asia and the Pacific, Vietnam Center and Archive, Texas Tech University.

30 Martin Dodge, Rob Kitchin, and Chris Perkins, "Introductory Essay: Power and Politics of Mapping," in *The Map Reader: Theories of Mapping Practice and Cartographic Representation*, ed. Martin Dodge, Rob Kitchin, and Chris Perkins (Oxford: John Wiley and Sons, 2011), 388.

31 Friedman, *Covert Capital*, 12.

32 Dodge, Kitchin, and Perkins, "Introductory Essay," 390.

33 Dodge, Kitchin, and Perkins, "Introductory Essay," 390.

34 Jodi Kim, *Ends of Empire: Asian American Critique and the Cold War* (Minneapolis: University of Minnesota Press, 2010), 30.

35 The discussion in this paragraph comes from the letter from Lucian W. Pye (Department of Economics and Social Science at MIT) to Walt W. Rostow (Deputy Assistant to the President for National Security Affairs), March 20, 1961, President John F. Kennedy's National Security Council Files and Foreign Relations documents from 1961–1963 prepared by the John F. Kennedy Presidential Library and Museum and held at the Vietnam Center and Archive at Texas Tech University, accessed September 6–10, 2010. Also see John F. Kennedy National Security Files, John F. Kennedy Presidential Library and Museum, box 130, folder 10 (JFKNSF-130-010).

36 K. T. Young, "A New Look at Laos," February 3, 1961, Kennedy Files.

37 Young, "New Look at Laos."

38 Richard Slotkin, *Gunfighter Nation: The Myth of the Frontier in Twentieth-Century America* (New York: Atheneum, 1992), 3–4.

39 Kenneth L. Hill, "President Kennedy and the Neutralization of Laos," *Review of Politics* 31, no. 3 (1969): 354.

40 Hill, "President Kennedy and the Neutralization of Laos," 357. Because Laos was considered a test case, its value existed in its political viability.
41 Pye, letter to Rostow, March 20, 1961.
42 Ahern, *Undercover Armies*, 50.
43 Ahern, *Undercover Armies*, xv.
44 The quotes in this paragraph came from "Memorandum of Conversation," April 29, 1961.
45 Seth Jacobs, "Laos," in *A Companion to John F. Kennedy*, edited by Marc J. Selverstone (Chichester, West Sussex, UK: John Wiley, 2014), 250.
46 Jacobs, "Laos," 250.
47 Gregory A. Olson, *Mansfield and Vietnam: A Study in Rhetorical Adaptation* (East Lansing: Michigan State University Press, 1995), 94, quoted in Jacobs, "Laos," 250.
48 Ahern, *Undercover Armies*, 74.
49 Ahern, *Undercover Armies*, 56; on the Plain of Jars, see 66–67.
50 Ahern, *Undercover Armies*, 41.
51 Ahern, *Undercover Armies*, xv.
52 Hill, "President Kennedy and the Neutralization of Laos," 364.
53 Here I've quoted from *Story of Laos*.
54 In comparison to Vietnam and Cambodia, Laos was seen as a failed colony due to its centralized government's inability to govern and incorporate the ethnic minorities distant from Vientiane and Luang Prabang, the centers of government and of royal power, respectively.
55 "Chronology of Events in Laos," President John F. Kennedy's National Security Council Files and Foreign Relations documents from 1961–1963 prepared by the John F. Kennedy Presidential Library and Museum and held at the Vietnam Center and Archive at Texas Tech University (n.d.), accessed September 6–10, 2009; italics in original. The original document is a secret Pentagon paper, "The Situation and Short-Term Outlook in Laos," Justification of the War. Internal Documents. The Eisenhower Administration. Volume IV: 1956 French Withdrawal—1960, available online at website of the National Archives, Pentagon-Papers-Part-V-B-3d (National Archives Identifier 5890524), accessed June 10, 2020, https://www.archives.gov/research/pentagon-papers.
56 "Memorandum of Meeting: Meeting with the President, Harriman, Forrestal, Representatives of AID, and DCI," July 27, 1962, Central Intelligence Agency, DCI-McCone Files, drafted by John A. McCone, held in Foreign Relations of the United States, 1961–1963, vol. 24, Laos Crisis, document 412; available online at website of the U.S. Department of State Office of the Historian, https://history.state.gov/historicaldocuments/frus1961-63v24/d412.
57 "Memorandum of Conversation: Meeting with Prince Souvanna Phouma," July 27, 1962, Department of State, Central Files, 751J.00/7–2762, held in Foreign Relations of the United States, 1961–1963, vol. 24, Laos Crisis, document 413 (drafted by Koren); available online at website of the U.S. Department of State Office of the Historian, https://history.state.gov/historicaldocuments/frus1961-63v24/d413.
58 Bill Lair had been in Thailand since the early 1950s to organize and train the elite Thai police group called the Police Air Reconnaissance Unit. From Richard L. Holm, "Recollections of a Case Officer in Laos, 1962–1964: No Drums, No Bugles," CIA Center for the

Study of Intelligence, accessed June 15, 2017, https://www.cia.gov/library/center-for-the-study-of-intelligence/csi-publications/csi-studies/studies/vol47no1/article01.html.

59 Quotation from Goldstein, *American Policy toward Laos*, 32.
60 Ahern, *Undercover Armies*, 34.
61 Ahern, *Undercover Armies*, 36.
62 Ahern, *Undercover Armies*, 34.
63 Similarly, Brao in southern Laos near the Lao-Cambodian border were recruited for their strategic geopolitical location to aid U.S. bombings, patrol the Ho Chi Minh Trail, and stop North Vietnamese Army advances in the region. See Ian G. Baird, "The US Central Intelligence Agency and the Brao," *Aséanie* 25 (2010): 23–51.
64 Ahern, *Undercover Armies*, 35.
65 Ahern, *Undercover Armies*, 35.
66 Ahern, *Undercover Armies*, xv.
67 Mai Na Lee, *Dreams of the Hmong Kingdom: The Quest for Legitimation in French Indochina, 1850–1960* (Madison: University of Wisconsin Press, 2015). Some of these early Hmong leaders included Lo Pachay, Lo Blia Yao, and Touby Lyfoung, of whom Vang Pao was a protégé.
68 M. Lee, *Dreams of the Hmong Kingdom*, xii.
69 Geoffrey C. Gunn, *Political Struggles in Laos (1930–1954): Vietnamese Communist Power and the Lao Struggle for National Independence* (Bangkok, Thailand: Duang Kamol, 1988), 216.
70 Gunn, *Political Struggles in Laos*, 215.
71 Gunn, *Political Struggles in Laos*, 216.
72 Ahern, *Undercover Armies*, 29. I use "General Vang Pao" in general references to him and instead use "Vang Pao" when discussing him in historical context.
73 Ahern, *Undercover Armies*, 31.
74 Ahern, *Undercover Armies*, 31.
75 Ahern, *Undercover Armies*, 41.
76 John Prados, *Presidents' Secret Wars: CIA and Pentagon Covert Operations from World War II through the Persian Gulf* (Chicago: Ivan R. Dee, 1986), 266.
77 The quotes here are from Ahern, *Undercover Armies*, 30.
78 Ahern, *Undercover Armies*, 58.
79 Richard Secord with Jay Wurts, *Honored and Betrayed: Irangate, Covert Affairs, and the Secret War in Laos* (New York: John Wiley and Sons, 1992), 75.
80 Ahern, *Undercover Armies*, 43.
81 Ahern, *Undercover Armies*, 44. In addition, Secord and Wurts, in *Honored and Betrayed*, reiterate the perception of Hmong as naturalized guerrilla fighters whose soldiers usually escape unscathed because nobody expected them to "stand fast" under the pressure of heavy infantry and artillery since that is not how guerrillas fight. In doing so, they broke up into squads and "melted into the jungle" only to "reappear magically" at a different site (87).
82 Ahern, *Undercover Armies*, 44.
83 Ahern, *Undercover Armies*, 36.
84 See Jane Hamilton-Merritt, *Tragic Mountains: The Hmong, the Americans, and the Secret Wars for Laos, 1942–1992* (Bloomington: Indiana University Press, 1993); and

Gayle Morrison, *Sky Is Falling: An Oral History of the CIA's Evacuation of the Hmong from Laos* (Jefferson, NC: McFarland, 1999), for discussions of the CIA's coordination of General Vang Pao and his officials' evacuations from Long Cheng, leaving thousands of Hmong soldiers and civilians on the airstrip. This group, along with Hmong from other parts of Laos who feared Pathet Lao retribution, escaped by car and on foot to the Mekong River to cross into Thailand. Many Hmong lost their lives during this dangerous and tragic escape.

85 Lionel Rosenblatt, "The History behind the Hmong Refugee Exodus," panel organized by the *Hmongstory 40 Project*, Fresno City College, August 22, 2015.

86 Thomas P. Conroy, "Highland Lao Refugees: Repatriation and Resettlement Preferences in Ban Vinai Camp, Thailand," Bridgette Marshall Collection, Southeast Asian Archive Special Collections, Langson Library, University of California, Irvine, 46–60.

87 Quotation from Mishuana Goeman, "(Re)Mapping Indigenous Presence on the Land in Native Women's Literature," *American Quarterly* 60, no. 2 (2008): 300.

88 Goeman, "(Re)Mapping Indigenous Presence," 301.

89 Christopher Woon, dir., *Among B-Boys*, CRS1UN Productions, 2011, DVD.

90 I would like to thank Adria Imada for suggesting that I consider the CIA ID cards as a counter-use of documents.

91 Interview with Dan Moua, Merced, CA, October 2015.

CHAPTER 3

A significant portion of chapter 3 has been published as "The Refugee Soldier: A Critique of Recognition and Citizenship in the Hmong Veterans' Naturalization Act of 1997," in "Southeast Asian/American Studies," special issue, *positions: east asia cultures critique* 20, no. 3 (2012): 685–712.

1 Lisa Lowe and Elaine Kim contend that an engagement with the racialization of Asians in the United States must be attentive to the context in Asia. Elaine H. Kim and Lisa Lowe, introduction to "New Formations, New Questions: Asian American Studies," special issue, *positions* 5, no. 2 (1997): v–xiv.

2 As I mention in the introduction, I hesitate to name the formation of Hmong racial difference as subjects who do not have geographic borders as stateless because it negates them as lacking nation, history, and belonging. However, my discussion in this chapter will draw on the term *stateless* as a useful analytic to analyze the process of state recognition, which deems Hmong as stateless and primitive in order for the U.S. to include them as citizens.

3 Oftentimes the usage of *racialization* misses the fact that modern subjects emerge as either racial "I" or racial "other" and are coconstitutive of each other. See Denise Ferreira da Silva, *Toward a Global Idea of Race* (Minneapolis: University of Minnesota Press, 2007). I employ the term here to describe the constant ideological work necessary to maintain racial difference.

4 Yến Lê Espiritu, "The 'We-Win-Even-When-We-Lose' Syndrome: U.S. Press Coverage of the Twenty-Fifth Anniversary of the 'Fall of Saigon,'" *American Quarterly* 58, no. 2 (2006): 330.

5 The war's paradox constitutes the dual production of soldier and refugee, signifying the U.S. imperialist project of using the local population as valorized figures and subjecting them to political persecution.
6 I employ the term *moral political* as an analytical descriptor of the simultaneous military and humanitarian projects in U.S. wars that produced the "new friend."
7 Amy Kaplan, "Violent Belongings and the Question of Empire Today: Presidential Address to the American Studies Association, October 17, 2003," *American Quarterly* 56, no. 1 (2004): 1–18.
8 Yến Lê Espiritu, "Toward a Critical Refugee Study: The Vietnamese Refugee Subject in U.S. Scholarship," *Journal of Vietnamese Studies* 1, nos. 1–2 (2006): 410–33.
9 The Hmong Veterans' Naturalization Act of 1997—sponsored by U.S. Representative Bruce Vento (D-Minn.)—was introduced to the Immigration and Claims Subcommittee of the 105th Congress on June 26, but it was not signed into Public Law 106–207 until May 26, 2000, designating citizenship to forty-five thousand eligible refugees. In its passage, the legislation benefited hundreds of Hmong veterans and their families who would otherwise experience a more difficult process in naturalizing. My analysis, although attentive to this reality, examines what this legislation actually does or opens up for those of us investigating a history that was not supposed to exist and with state departments ensuring that it is forgotten. I am less interested in the ethics of state recognition through the legislation than in excavating the power strategies of the state.
10 U.S. Congress, *Hmong Veterans' Naturalization Act of 1997; and Canadian Border Boat Landing Permit Requirements: Hearing on H.R. 371 before the Subcomm. on Immigration and Claims*, 105th Cong., June 26, 1997 (Washington, DC: Government Printing Office, 1997), 3.
11 U.S. Congress, *Hearing*, 2, 15.
12 Here, I do not suggest an apolitical singularity to the immigrant figure but rather contend that its context of contact with the United States is different from that of the refugee figure. Thus, a conflation between the two situates both in an assimilationist paradigm that is not attentive to their different circumstances.
13 The title of section 3 of the bill calls attention to the veterans' "service in a special guerrilla unit" as their eligibility for naturalization, again, citing the Immigration and Nationality Act's specifications for "naturalization through active-duty service in the armed forces" while "an alien or a noncitizen national of the United States" (U.S. Congress, *Hearing*, 5).
14 In doing so, the title of section 2 of the bill proposes to waive the "English language requirement" for these "alien" soldiers (U.S. Congress, *Hearing*, 4), under the stipulations of the Immigration and Nationality Act that requires an understanding of English, and knowledge and understanding of the "fundamentals of the history, and of the principles and form of government, of the United States" (U.S. Congress, "Hmong Veterans' Naturalization Act of 2000: Report to accompany H.R. 371," 106th Cong., 2nd Session, April 6, 2000, 8, U.S. Congress website, accessed June 11, 2020, https://www.congress.gov/106/crpt/hrpt563/CRPT-106hrpt563.pdf). I use the term *alien soldier* to refer to those living outside the United States and recruited to fight for U.S. causes as in the case of the Hmong soldiers.

15 I borrow the phrase *politics of recognition* from the works of Glen S. Coulthard and Patchen Markell to indicate the legislative process's inability to acknowledge or address the central issues of war, violence, and displacement through this naturalization bill. The "politics of recognition," Coulthard contends, refers to the expansive range of recognition-based models of liberal pluralism with state agencies as key mediators that reproduce unequal relations of power, and, for Indigenous communities, reproduce colonial power. Furthermore, relations of recognition are constitutive of subjectivity, which requires the "self-determining" agent to be recognized by another self-conscious subject (Glen S. Coulthard, "Subjects of Empire: Indigenous Peoples and the 'Politics of Recognition' in Canada," *Contemporary Political Theory* 6 [2007]: 440). Patchen Markell renames recognition as "misrecognition" because it fails to "acknowledge" the fundamental conditions of one's own situation. He argues that the "politics of recognition" inevitably constitutes a failed project because it compounds relations of subordination, the desire for sovereignty, and its reliance on temporality, the separation of what was in the past from the present. He proposes a "politics of acknowledgment" to rethink an emancipatory project that is attentive to the underlying structures of desire. See Patchen Markell, *Bound by Recognition* (Princeton, NJ: Princeton University Press, 2003). Also see Glen S. Coulthard, *Red Skin, White Masks: Rejecting the Colonial Politics of Recognition* (Minneapolis: University of Minnesota Press, 2014) for a broader discussion of the politics of recognition as a structure of settler colonialism.
16 Chandan Reddy, "Asian Diasporas, Neoliberalism, and Family: Reviewing the Case for Homosexual Asylum in the Context of Family Rights," *Social Text* 84–85 (2005): 103, 115.
17 U.S. Congress, *Hearing* (statement of Bruce Vento), 12.
18 Elaine Scarry, *The Body in Pain: The Making and Unmaking of the World* (Oxford: Oxford University Press, 1985), 112.
19 Scarry, *Body in Pain*, 113.
20 Diana Taylor, *The Archive and the Repertoire: Performing Cultural Memory in the Americas* (Durham, NC: Duke University, Press, 2003), 19.
21 U.S. Congress, *Hearing*, 20; italics added.
22 I introduce the term *archive on refugees* to refer to the process in which Representative Vento discusses "refugee processing," camps, and so on. Refugee processing through the management and documentation of refugee health and livelihood to applications for resettlement constitutes an inadequate archiving of the refugee condition of statelessness.
23 U.S. Congress, *Hearing* (statement of Louis D. Crocetti Jr.), 22; italics added.
24 U.S. Congress, *Hearing* (statement of Lamar Smith), 35.
25 U.S. Congress, *Hearing*, 17. This excerpt comes from Colonel Wangyee Vang's submitted statement to the congressional committee that became a part of the hearing's printed record.
26 Hannah Arendt, "We Refugees," in *The Jew as Pariah*, ed. Ron H. Feldman (New York: Grove Press, [1943] 1978), 57.
27 Giorgio Agamben, "We Refugees," trans. Michel Rocke, *Symposium: A Quarterly Journal in Modern Literatures* 49, no. 2 (1995): 114–19. Accessed June 11, 2020, https://doi.org/10.1080/00397709.1995.10733798.

28 Hannah Arendt, "Statelessness" (lecture, April 22, 1955), 3; available online at The Hannah Arendt Papers at the Library of Congress: Speeches and Writings File, 1923–1975, accessed March 15, 2012, https://memory.loc.gov/cgi-bin/ampage?collId=mharendt_pub&fileName=05/052290/052290page.db&recNum=2&tempFile=./temp/~ammem_4O3c&filecode=mharendt&prev_filecode=mharendt&itemnum=2&ndocs=2.
29 For these quotations, see, respectively, U.S. Congress, *Hearing*, 20, 31, 69, 9.
30 Denise Ferreira da Silva, "Tale of Two Cities: Saigon, Fallujah, and the Ethical Boundaries of Empire," in "Thirty Years AfterWARd: Vietnamese Americans and U.S. Empire," special issue, *Amerasia* 31, no. 2 (2005): 125.
31 da Silva, "Tale of Two Cities," 125.
32 U.S. Congress, *Hearing* (statement of Bruce Vento), 11.
33 The U.S. government's "promise" of safe haven to Hmong soldiers and their families is an often-cited "deal" between the United States and Hmong during the war. U.S. Congress, *Hearing*, 18.
34 U.S. Congress, *Hearing* (statement of Ron Kind), 11.
35 Takashi Fujitani, "Right to Kill, Right to Make Live: Koreans as Japanese and Japanese as Americans during WWII," *Representations* 99 (2007): 13–39.
36 U.S. Congress, *Hearing* (statement of Patrick J. Kennedy), 68.
37 U.S. Congress, *Hearing* (statement of Scott L. Klug), 71.
38 In both "We Refugees" and *Homo Sacer*, Agamben foregrounds the refugee as a *political* figure that brings the fiction of sovereignty into crisis—this fiction is constituted in the link between birth and nation, the rights of man and citizen. In *Homo Sacer*, Agamben states, "If refugees represent such a disquieting element in the order of the modern nation-state, this is above all because by breaking the continuity between man and citizen, nativity and nationality, they put the originary fiction of modern sovereignty in crisis." See Giorgio Agamben, *Homo Sacer: Sovereign Power and Bare Life*, trans. Daniel Heller-Roazen, ed. Werner Hamacher and David E. Wellbery (Stanford, CA: Stanford University Press, 1998), 131; and Agamben, "We Refugees."
39 Anna Yeatman, "The Subject of Citizenship," *Citizenship Studies* 11, no. 1 (2007): 105–15.
40 Michael Ignatieff, "The Myth of Citizenship," in *Theorizing Citizenship*, ed. Ronald Beiner (Albany: State University of New York Press, 1995), 57.
41 U.S. Congress, *Hearing*, 38.
42 U.S. Congress, *Hearing* (statement of Susan Haigh), 26.
43 U.S. Congress, *Hearing* (statement of Bruce Vento), 14.
44 U.S. Congress, *Hearing*, 12.
45 U.S. Congress, *Hearing*, 12, 14.
46 U.S. Congress, *Hearing*, 1.
47 U.S. Congress, *Hearing*, 17, 19.
48 U.S. Congress, *Hearing* (statement of National Asian Pacific American Legal Consortium), 18.
49 Ernest Renan, "What Is a Nation?," in *Nations and Identities: Classic Readings*, ed. Vincent P. Pecora (Malden, MA: Blackwell, 2001), 166.
50 U.S. Congress, *Hearing* (statement of Ron Kind), 69.
51 U.S. Congress, *Hearing* (statement of Gary A. Condit), 70.

52 U.S. Congress, *Hearing* (statement of Louis D. Crocetti Jr.), 23.
53 Taylor, *Archive and the Repertoire*, 24.
54 Taylor, *Archive and the Repertoire*, 34.
55 U.S. Congress, *Hearing* (statement of Calvin M. Dooley), 15.
56 This discussion on language offers a critique of formulations of nation and nationalism that privilege the written language. See Benedict Anderson, *Imagined Communities: Reflections on the Origin and Spread of Nationalism* (New York: Verso Books, 1991). In line with my points about the expendability of Hmong bodies to perpetuate U.S. militarism and the refugee soldier figure who does not have a place in the law and nation, Hmong language, rendered "preliterate," does not have a place in the national culture. This predicament sheds light on the lack of Hmong-language courses offered as a national, foreign language for those interested in Southeast Asia area studies but more so as "Hmong-language" heritage classes or for non-Hmong who wish to work with Hmong communities.
57 da Silva, "Tale of Two Cities," 123–27.
58 U.S. Congress, *Hearing* (statement of Bruce Vento), 13.
59 The issue of Hmong linguistic insufficiency as racial difference elides the fact that a segment of Hmong soldiers were students who studied Lao and French prior to enlisting in the "secret army." More importantly, Hmong refugees/veterans actively refute the claim of their illiteracy and delayed intelligence by citing they could not have been pilots, radio operators, scouts, nurses, medics, etc., without a command of English, Lao, or French. The technologies of warfare, indeed, operated in English and Western epistemologies.
60 U.S. Congress, *Hearing* (statement of Louis D. Crocetti Jr.), 21.
61 U.S. Congress, *Hearing* (statement of Susan Haigh), 25.
62 U.S. Congress, *Hearing* (statement of National Asian Pacific American Legal Consortium), 18. This echoing of the reasons already espoused from a pan-Asian advocacy group illustrates how organizations such as this one must adopt the language of difference in advocating for Hmong.
63 U.S. Congress, *Hearing* (statement of General Vang Pao), 17.
64 U.S. Congress, *Hearing* (statement of Lamar Smith), 1.
65 U.S. Congress, *Hearing* (statement of National Asian Pacific American Legal Consortium), 18. There are discrepancies in which the pan-Asian group advocated for Hmong first using the language of difference, and then addressing the abject conditions of war that contribute to their difficulties in learning English.
66 U.S. Congress, *Hearing* (statement of Louis D. Crocetti Jr.), 21.
67 da Silva, "Tale of Two Cities," 123.
68 For the phrase *subject-in-becoming*, see da Silva, "Tale of Two Cities," 125.
69 I borrow this point from Agamben, who contends that the fiction of sovereignty is that "*birth* immediately becomes *nation*" (Agamben, "We Refugees," 117; italics in original). Therefore, centering the refugee (a marginal figure) as the figure of political history throws into crisis the original fiction of sovereignty. My discussion of the Hmong refugee soldier figure brings into crisis questions of citizenship, sovereignty, and war/imperialism.

70 U.S. Congress, *Hearing* (statement of Mark Krikorian), 33.
71 Yến Lê Espiritu, *Home Bound: Filipino American Lives across Cultures, Communities, and Countries* (Berkeley: University of California Press, 2003), 67.
72 U.S. Congress, *Hearing* (statement of Mark Krikorian), 32.
73 This assertion does not negate the struggles of Mexican Americans and immigrants and their colonial relationship with the United States but highlights how the work of soldiering and sacrifice become an organizing principle for citizenship. Indeed, the logic of cultural difference characterizes Mexican immigrants as "unwilling" to attain citizenship, whereas Hmong refugees are "unable" to do so.
74 An unsettling immigration and citizenship trend is the U.S. State Department stripping passports from primarily Mexican Americans so that they are either trapped in the U.S. or outside its borders. Hundreds of citizens have been accused of possessing fraudulent birth certificates provided by midwives in Texas in the Trump administration's quest to revoke U.S. Americans of their citizenship. See Bethania Palma, "Is the Trump Administration Revoking Passports of U.S. Citizens?," *Snopes*, August 30, 2018, https://www.snopes.com/news/2018/08/30/revoking-passports-us-citizens/.
75 U.S. Congress, *Hearing*, 32–33.
76 Under the Real ID Act of 2005, a provision of the USA Patriot Act of 2001, anyone providing "material support" to "terrorist" organizations is named a terrorist. Hmong fall under this category, ironically, for helping the United States during the war by bearing arms against their government, Laos. Those seeking refugee or asylee status are vulnerable to this law because it prevents them from resettling in the United States.
77 General Vang Pao was arrested along with nine other Hmong community leaders and a former U.S. National Guard lieutenant for the intent to purchase $9.8 million in illegal weapons and for their plot to overthrow the Communist Laotian government. The eighteen-page blueprint with details of the plot titled "Operation Popcorn" (Political Opposition Party's Coup Operation to Rescue the Nation) confiscated and filed in court outlined "exactly how Laos could be transformed into an *American-style democracy* with free elections, freedom of speech, a new constitution and judiciary, and a congress including the Hmong and other ethnic minorities" (Stephen Magagnini, "Hmong Coup Details Unveiled," *Sacramento Bee*, June 16, 2007, A1. *NewsBank: Access World News*, https://infoweb.newsbank.com/apps/news/document-view?p=AWNB&docref=news/119D2FBCC476D280; italics added). Mass community mobilizations in California and other large Hmong communities across the United States protested General Vang's arrest, citing it as a second act of betrayal by the federal government. The first betrayal, still an unresolved issue, was U.S. abandonment of Hmong after the "fall of Saigon."
78 "Dedicated to the U.S. Secret Army in the Kingdom of Laos 1961–1975," Arlington National Cemetery website, accessed July 8, 2019, http://www.arlingtoncemetery.net/laosmem.htm.
79 Representative Jim Costa, quoted in Agnes Constante, "'Secret War' Veterans Ask Congress for National Cemetery Burials," *NBC News*, January 12, 2018, https://www.nbcnews.com/news/asian-america/secret-war-veterans-ask-congress-national-cemetery-burials-n837296.

80 Letter of support for Hmong veterans' burial at Arlington Cemetery, circulated at General Vang Pao's funeral services in Fresno, CA, February 4–9, 2011. For additional stories on the request for the General's burial at Arlington, see Josh Gerstein, "Army Still Waiting for Hmong General's Arlington Burial Request," Politico, January 12, 2011, accessed June 11, 2020, https://www.politico.com/blogs/under-the-radar/2011/01/army-still-waiting-for-hmong-generals-arlington-burial-request-032302; and Frederick Melo, "Hmong Veterans Ask for Burial Rights in US Veterans Cemeteries," Military News, July 15, 2019, accessed June 11, 2020, https://www.military.com/daily-news/2019/07/15/hmong-veterans-ask-burial-rights-us-veterans-cemeteries.html. For information on approval of Hmong burial and memorial benefits, see "Hmong Burial and Memorial Benefits," VA Benefits Eligibility for Hmong Individuals factsheet, U.S. Department of Veterans Affairs, National Cemetery Administration website, accessed June 11, 2020, https://www.cem.va.gov/cem/docs/factsheets/Hmong_Burial_Memorial_Benefits_Factsheet.pdf.

81 Author interview with Yer Vang on September 8, 2009. *Txiaj ntsim* is something that Hmong soldiers and civilians have given the U.S. for saving U.S. lives and bodies from the enemy line. Rescue was a gift bestowed upon U.S. Americans, and the statue represents this exchange.

82 Author interview with Yer Vang on September 8, 2009.

CHAPTER 4

1 The ten defendants include Lo Cha Thao (34 years old), a former aide to former Wisconsin State Senator Gary George (D-Milwaukee), and resident of Clovis, CA; Lo Thao (53), president of the United Hmong International (a.k.a., Supreme Council of the Hmong Eighteen Clans) based in Sacramento County, CA; Youa True Vang (60), founder of Hmong International New Year in Fresno; Hue Vang (39), a former Clovis, CA, police officer and director of the United Lao Council for Peace, Freedom and Reconstruction; Chong Vang Thao (53), a chiropractor from Fresno; Seng Vue (68), a resident of Fresno and a clan representative in United Hmong International; Chue Lo (59), a resident of Stockton, CA, and a clan representative in United Hmong International; Nhia Kao Vang (48), a resident of Rancho Cordova, CA; Dang Vang (48), a resident of Fresno, CA; and Harrison Ulrich Jack (60), a resident of Woodland, CA, a former U.S. Army officer and lieutenant colonel with the California National Guard, and a 1968 graduate of West Point who served in Southeast Asia. Wameng Moua, "Leader in Trouble: 77-Year-Old General Vang Pao Arrested," *Hmong Today*, June 20, 2007, http://www.tcdailyplanet.net/article/2007/06/19/leader-trouble-77-year-old-general-vang-pao-arrested.html. Also see the press release for the arrests, "'Operation Tarnished Eagle' Thwarts Plot to Overthrow the Government of Laos," Press Release, June 4, 2007, web archive website, accessed June 11, 2020, https://web.archive.org/web/20080216032118/http://www.usdoj.gov/usao/cae/press_releases/docs/2007/06-04-07JackPressRls.pdf. While the Hmong men, especially General Vang Pao, were portrayed as backward and irrational in their plot to overthrow the government of Laos, Jack, a white U.S. American, was depicted in the news and even by ATF agents as a

decorated military hero with a distinguished background as a West Point graduate. He served on California's strategic committee on terrorism, so his arrest and involvement were out of character and came as a shock to family and friends. He was hired by the Hmong men because he had contacts in the U.S. defense, homeland security, and defense contractor communities. Therefore, the case was less about a violation of the U.S. neutrality act by U.S. citizens and more concerned with refugee former-U.S.-allied soldiers and their precarious political positions. See Demian Bulwa, "Why Ex-Soldier Got Involved with Hmong / 'I Owe Them My Life,' Says Suspect in Alleged Plot," *SF Gate*, June 6, 2007, http://www.sfgate.com/news/article/Why-ex-soldier-got-involved-with-Hmong-I-owe-2573280.php.

2 Rich Connell and Robert J. Lopez, "U.S. Accuses 10 of Plotting Coup in Laos," *Los Angeles Times*, June 5, 2007; italics added.

3 Stephen Magagnini, "Hmong Coup Details Unveiled," *Sacramento Bee*, June 16, 2007, A1. *NewsBank: Access World News*, https://infoweb.newsbank.com/apps/news/document-view?p=AWNB&docref=news/119D2FBCC476D280; italics added.

4 Jeffrey Brody, "Betraying an Old Friend," *Los Angeles Times (1996-Current)*, June 18, 2007, https://search.proquest.com/docview/2212483809?accountid=14515/opinion/commentary/la-oebrody18jun18,1,2851826,print.story?ctrack=6&cset=true.

5 Court documents reveal that retired Lt. Col. Harrison Ulrich Jack and other members of the group met repeatedly with an undercover agent for the ATF to "discuss battle tactics and the logistics of secretly moving mercenaries, as well as machine guns, anti-tank missiles and plastic explosives into Laos." See Robert J. Lopez and Rich Connell, "Alleged Coup Plotters Sought CHP Training," *Los Angeles Times*, June 6, 2007, http://articles.latimes.com/2007/jun/06/local/me-laos6.

6 For the term *an/archive*, see Akira Mizuta Lippit, "The Shadow Archive: From Light to Cinder," *Tympanum* 4, no. 1 (2000), https://web.archive.org/web/20090226074638/http://www.usc.edu/dept/comp-lit/tympanum/4/lippit.html.

7 Jasbir Puar, *Terrorist Assemblages: Homonationalism in Queer Times* (Durham, NC: Duke University Press, 2007), 205.

8 Laura Hyun Yi Kang, *Compositional Subjects: Enfiguring Asian/American Women* (Durham, NC: Duke University Press, 2000).

9 Mimi Thi Nguyen, *The Gift of Freedom: War, Debt, and Other Refugee Passages* (Durham, NC: Duke University Press, 2012).

10 Puar, *Terrorist Assemblages*, xx.

11 Monica Davey, "Arrest Uncovers Divide in Hmong-Americans," *New York Times*, June 14, 2007, http://www.nytimes.com/2007/06/14/us/14hmong.html?pagewante=2&_r=1.

12 Chai Soua Vang was depicted in the mainstream news media and in court as a trespasser, which obscured the racial tensions between Hmong and white hunters in Minnesota and Wisconsin. For a full discussion of the occulting of race, see Louisa Schein and Va-Megn Thoj, "Occult Racism: The Masking of Race in the Hmong Hunter Incident: A Dialogue between Anthropologist Louisa Schein and Filmmaker/Activist Va-Megn Thoj," *American Quarterly* 59, no. 4 (2007): 1051–95. After the arrests and during the trial, Vang admitted to the killings but explained that it was in self-defense because white hunters threatened him with racial epithets and surrounded him.

13 Mai Der Vang, "A Bright Hmong Future after Vang Pao," *New America Media*, June 4, 2009, https://web.archive.org/web/20121119104041/http://news.newamericamedia.org/news/view_article.html?article_id=f7c3b6284371c6cea63d20b5de3f20ec.

14 Although there were numerous immediate disavowals about Hmong as terrorists, for the U.S. public and Hmong community to read the general's arrest as an isolated case, I make a rhetorical move to connote the shift in U.S. global politics which required that former allies become enemies or terrorists. My use of the term *terrorism* is not how it has usually been understood within the age of terror, but instead as a moment for Hmong to contest the erasure of their history and "blast" the past into the present. I explore how Hmong refugees/Americans displaced by war and the absence of a nation-state articulate their histories in relation to the present.

15 Lisa Yoneyama, "Liberation under Siege: U.S. Military Occupation and Japanese Women's Enfranchisement," *American Quarterly* 57, no. 3 (2005): 885–901.

16 Ashley Powers, "Battle's Not Over When They Come to the U.S.," *Los Angeles Times*, June 7, 2007, http://articles.latimes.com/2007/jun/07/local/me-overthrow7.

17 Denny Walsh and Bill Lindelof, "Judge Orders Vang Pao Released on Bail," *Sacramento Bee*, July 12, 2007, https://www.mcclatchydc.com/news/nation-world/national/article24466486.html.

18 Stephen Magagnini and Denny Walsh, "Hmong Rally for 'The General,'" *Sacramento Bee*, June 19, 2007, http://www.sacbee.com/101/v-print/story/229794.html.

19 Louisa Schein and Va-Megn Thoj, "*Gran Torino*'s Boys and Men with Guns: Hmong Perspectives," *Hmong Studies Journal* 10, no. 1 (2009): 5, 7.

20 The combined properties of their families and friends were used as collateral: thirty homes, an apartment complex, and a family trust. The general was released on bail and placed under house arrest in his Southern California home on July 12, 2007, after significant pressure from Hmong protest rallies.

21 Mai Der Vang, "Gen. Vang Pao's Release Momentous for Young Hmong Americans," *New America Media*, September 21, 2009, https://web.archive.org/web/20121119104038/http://news.newamericamedia.org/news/view_article.html?article_id=7f6cdeb868f27f5b174a062df5d8099d.

22 Lila Abu-Lughod, "Locating Ethnography," *Ethnography* 1, no. 2 (2000): 265.

23 In reflecting on anthropological studies of social media, Jolynna Sinana explains that it is about relationships. Social media presents a lens to paint a picture of the place and its people as well as how people's posts reveal the sense of identity about the place. Social media is a point of entry to examine a "participant's actions" rather than focusing on it as an object of study. See Jolynna Sinana, *Social Media in Trinidad: Values and Visibility* (London: University College London Press, 2017), 200.

24 Kang, *Compositional Subjects*, 217.

25 For a longer discussion on new media online comments, specifically blogs, and their mediated and less mediated form, see Kit Myers, "'Real' Families: The Violence of Love in New Media Adoption Discourse," *Critical Discourse Studies* 11 (2013): 175–93, https://doi.org/10.1080/17405904.2013.852983. In *Social Media in Trinidad*, anthropologist Jolynna Sinana also makes the claim that from an anthropological approach,

social media "takes into account the context in which individuals are embedded" and a reflection of society (200, 206). For a discussion of race and online comments, see Heather Hensman Kettrey and Whitney Nicole Laster, "Staking Territory in the 'World White Web': An Exploration of the Roles of Overt and Color-Blind Racism in Maintaining Racial Boundaries on a Popular Web Site," *Social Currents* 1 (2014): 257–74.

26 Lisa Yoneyama has problematized how the post-1990s culture of redress shows the state's inability to provide or protect rights to reparations. She argues that redress and the broader discourse on violence and justice are inseparable from reconstitutions of self, sociality, and history. Yoneyama's critique of redress reinforces my argument that Hmong mobilizations represent efforts to contend with history as much as to protest the charges of terrorism. See Lisa Yoneyama, *Cold War Ruins: Transpacific Critique of American Justice and Japanese War Crimes* (Durham, NC: Duke University Press, 2016), 7.

27 Lippit, "Shadow Archive," 7.

28 Akira Mizuta Lippit, *Atomic Light (Shadow Optics)* (Minneapolis: University of Minnesota Press, 2005), 30.

29 Walter Benjamin, "Theses on the Philosophy of History," in *Illuminations*, ed. Hannah Arendt (New York: Schocken Books, 1968), 255.

30 Jasbir K. Puar and Amit S. Rai, "Monster, Terrorist, Fag: The War on Terrorism and the Production of Docile Patriots," *Social Text* 20, no. 3 (2002): 117.

31 Puar and Rai, "Monster, Terrorist, Fag," 119–20.

32 Puar, *Terrorist Assemblages*, 37.

33 Puar, *Terrorist Assemblages*, 38.

34 Puar, *Terrorist Assemblages*, 39. Here, we are reminded of Abu Ghraib and other scandals that perpetuate homonationalisms.

35 Iris Marion Young, "Logic of Masculinist Protection: Reflections on the Current Security State," *Signs: Journal of Women in Culture and Society* 29, no. 1 (2003): 3.

36 Young, "Logic of Masculinist Protection," 4. Gina Marchetti also analyzes this masculinist logic as the "white knight complex" in which chivalry defined the white knight's superiority through his enlightened and moral treatment of the "weaker sex," and by extension that of European nations, compared to nonwhite peoples and non-Western places. See Gina Marchetti, *Romance and the "Yellow Peril": Race, Sex, and Discursive Strategies in Hollywood Fiction* (Berkeley: University of California Press, 1994), 114.

37 Young, "Logic of Masculinist Protection," 4.

38 Young, "Logic of Masculinist Protection," 5.

39 Kang, *Compositional Subjects*, 215.

40 Kang, *Compositional Subjects*, 217.

41 John J. Lumpkin, "CIA's Paramilitary Force a Cross between Spies and Soldiers," Associated Press, December 3, 2001; repr. in *Hmong Times*, December 16, 2001.

42 Michael Doyle, "WikiLeaks Cables Bare Secrets of U.S.-Laotian Relations," *The Wichita Eagle*, April 22, 2011, accessed June 11, 2020, https://www.kansas.com/news/politics-government/article1192757.html.

43 These three quotes came from "Lao Government Cautiously Welcomes U.S. Arrests," cable from the American Embassy in Vientiane to the Secretary of State and Department of Justice, June 25, 2007, WikiLeaks website, accessed June 11, 2020, https://wikileaks.org/plusd/cables/07VIENTIANE525_a.html.

44 Carol A. Stabile and Carrie Rentschler, "States of Insecurity and the Gendered Politics of Fear," *NWSA Journal* 17, no. 3 (Autumn 2005): ix.

45 I would like to thank Lisa Yoneyama for suggesting this elaboration on the "global odd couple."

46 Kang, *Compositional Subjects*, 3.

47 Powers, "Battle's Not Over." This is another example of the pathologized refugee belatedness to History.

48 Powers, "Battle's Not Over."

49 This sentiment is not necessarily unique toward former soldiers and refugees from Southeast Asia because it has also shaped the narrative about John McCain, a Vietnam veteran and prisoner of war. He is considered somewhat marginal as a political figure, but his whiteness makes his backward-looking stance not pathologized but righteous. I would like to thank Lisa Yoneyama for helping make this connection.

50 Tim Weiner, "Gen. Vang Pao's Last War," *New York Times*, May 11, 2008.

51 In informal conversations with Hmong American colleagues and acquittances over the course of the rallies and hearings, the sentiment was two-fold: acknowledgment of General Vang Pao's brutal methods as a military leader and his problematic promises to bring Hmong refugees back to Laos, coupled with the observation, which I noted, to situate his arrest as a part of the U.S. mission to capture terrorists around the world.

52 Kong Pha, "Queer Refugeeism: Constructions of Race, Gender, and Sexuality in the Hmong Diaspora" (PhD diss., University of Minnesota, 2017).

53 W. Moua, "Leader in Trouble"; and "Thousands Protest at Vang Pao Hearing," *Bangkok Post*, June 20, 2007, 2bangkok.com forum, http://2bangkok.com/forum/showthread.php?2455-Hmong-Still-a-Secret-War!/page2.

54 "US Judge Releases Alleged Coup Plotter Vang Pao to House Arrest," Associated Press, July 12, 2007.

55 Chong Jones, "Vang Pao and the U.S. Government, Marriage and Betrayal," *Hmong Today*, July 15, 2007, https://www.tcdailyplanet.net/vang-pao-and-u-s-government-marriage-and-betrayal/; italics added.

56 Paraphrased from Jones, "Vang Pao and the U.S. Government."

57 Jones, "Vang Pao and the U.S. Government."

58 Rebecca Sommer, dir., *Hunted Like Animals* (SommerFilms, 2008), DVD.

59 I would like to thank Lisa Yoneyama for helping to articulate this point.

60 Anonymous comment in W. Moua, "Leader in Trouble"; capitalization in original.

61 For a discussion of the transnational formation of Hmong political activism, see Nengher N. Vang, "Political Transmigrants: Rethinking Hmong Political Activism in America," *Hmong Studies Journal* 12 (2011): 1–46.

62 danny, "Buble Burst," comment in Wameng Moua, "General Vang Pao, Hero," *Hmong Today*, June 18, 2007, http://www.tcdailyplanet.net/article/2007/06/18/general-vang-pao-hero.html?print=1.

63 Early news media coverage of the protest rallies emphasized the peaceful and clean coordination of Hmong demonstrations because they picked up after themselves (no trash left behind) and did not block traffic or official business at the capital.
64 Christina Jewett, "Hmong Rally at Capitol," *Sacramento Bee*, June 18, 2007, *NewsBank: Access World News*, https://infoweb.newsbank.com/apps/news/document-view?p=AWNB&docref=news/119DD627A87C9020.
65 Quoted in W. Moua, "Leader in Trouble."
66 Comment on published press release, "Press Release: Hmong American Ad Hoc Rally on April 22, 2011, in Sacramento, CA," Suab Hmong News website, accessed February 1, 2012, http://www.shrdo.com/index.php/suabhmong-news/hmong-news/905-press-release-hmong-american-ad-hoc-rally-on-april-21-2011-in-sacramento-ca.
67 Quoted in Steve Chawkins, "Arrest Greeted by Disbelief," *Los Angeles Times*, June 6, 2007, http://articles.latimes.com/2007/jun/06/local/me-hmong6.
68 Anonymous comment in W. Moua, "Leader in Trouble."
69 Amanda Perez, "Patriot Act Classifies Hmong as Terrorists," abc30.com, February 18, 2007.
70 Phoung Tran Nguyen, "The People of the Fall: Refugee Nationalism in Little Saigon, 1975–2005" (PhD diss., University of Southern California, 2009), 119. In his book, Nguyen explores how Little Saigon became home to anti-Communist insurgency in the 1980s and examines how Vietnamese refugees created their own version of the Viet Cong. See Phoung Tran Nguyen, *Becoming Refugee American: The Politics of Rescue in Little Saigon* (Urbana: University of Illinois Press, 2017).
71 Quoted in Richard Wanglue Vang, "SuabHmong News: Exclusive Interview Wameng Xiong, Hmong American AD HOC Committee," YouTube video, July 19, 2011, http://www.youtube.com/watch?v=nZ4PyZlaMME.
72 Quoted in R. Vang, "SuabHmong News."
73 See Yến Lê Espiritu, "The 'We-Win-Even-Though-We-Lose' Syndrome: U.S. Press Coverage of the Twenty-Fifth Anniversary of the 'Fall of Saigon,'" *American Quarterly* 58, no. 2 (2006): 329–52.
74 Quoted in Eric Bailey, "Hmong Want Leader Freed: Thousands Demonstrate against the Jailing of a General Who Aided the U.S. in the Vietnam War," *Los Angeles Times*, June 19, 2007, http://articles.latimes.com/2007/jun/19/local/me-hmong19.
75 W. Moua, "General Vang Pao, Hero."
76 The statements "son of Laos" and "key U.S. ally" were made at his funeral service in Fresno, California, on February 4, 2011.
77 Keith Comacho, *Cultures of Commemoration: The Politics of War, Memory, and History in the Mariana Islands* (Honolulu: University of Hawaii Press, 2011), 37. In addition, as Espiritu notes in commemorating South Vietnam's war dead, it "is not the same as valorizing them; rather it is acknowledging that they are worthy of remembrance." See Yến Lê Espiritu, *Body Counts: The Vietnam War and Militarized Refugees* (Berkeley: University of California Press, 2014), 106.
78 Dr. Nhia Lue Vang, speech at Hmong American rally in Sacramento, California, on October 15, 2010; available online at Chong Vang, "Hmong Protest/Rally at Sacramento Federal Court House 10/15/10 Part 4," October 22, 2010, YouTube video, 9:58, https://www.youtube.com/watch?v=bue1tlbWTS0.

79 Russell Berman, "Can Terrorists Really Infiltrate the Syrian Refugee Program?," *Atlantic*, November 18, 2015, https://www.theatlantic.com/politics/archive/2015/11/can-terrorists-really-infiltrate-the-syrian-refugee-program/416475/.
80 Berman, "Can Terrorists Really Infiltrate the Syrian Refugee Program?"
81 The executive order halted all refugee admissions for 120 days and banned Syrian refugees indefinitely. It also temporarily barred people from seven Muslim-majority countries (Iran, Iraq, Syria, Yemen, Somalia, Sudan, and Libya) from entering the U.S.

CHAPTER 5

1 Kao Kalia Yang, *The Latehomecomer: A Hmong Family Memoir* (Minneapolis: Coffee House Press, 2008). I will use in-text citations whenever I quote from the memoir.
2 Jenny Edkins conceptualizes an alternative mode to contending with the trauma of the political, that of "*encircling the trauma.*" Encircling is a Žižekian way to mark the trauma to keep open the space for political challenge and resist reinscribing trauma in memory and memorialization. Jenny Edkins, *Trauma and the Memory of Politics* (Cambridge: Cambridge University Press, 2003), 15. Thank you to Mai-Linh Hong for helping extend this point about encircling.
3 Aylwyn Walsh, "Fugitive Knowledge: Performance Pedagogies, Legibility and the Undercommons," *Applied Theatre Research* 6, no. 2 (2018): 121–37.
4 Mark Rifkin, *Beyond Settler Time: Temporal Sovereignty and Indigenous Self-Determination* (Durham, NC: Duke University Press, 2018), 17.
5 King-Kok Cheung, *Articulate Silences: Hisaye Yamamot, Maxine Hong Kingston, Joy Kogawa* (Ithaca, NY: Cornell University Press, 1993), 4.
6 Cheung, *Articulate Silences*, 3.
7 Here, I borrow from Rifkin's usage of "Indigenous orientations" in *Beyond Settler Time* to discuss Indigenous peoples' varied conceptions of time that are about "being-in-time" rather than that of settler time. Orientations suggest the divergent process of becoming and inhabiting time, the regeneration of continuity, and the pluralization of time. Collective modes of orientations, therefore, function as "temporal formation" (Rifkin, *Beyond Settler Time*, 1–5).
8 Ma Vang, "Writing on the Run: Hmong American Literary Formations and the Deterritorialized Subject," in "Refugee Cultures: Forty Years after the Vietnam War," special issue, *MELUS: Multi-Ethnic Literature of the United States* 41, no. 3 (2016): 90, https://doi.org/10.1093/melus/mlw031. See Hmong American Writers' Circle, *How Do I Begin?: A Hmong American Literary Anthology* (Berkeley, CA: Heyday Press, 2011); and Mai Neng Moua, ed., *Bamboo among the Oaks: Contemporary Writing by Hmong Americans* (St. Paul: Minnesota Historical Society Press, 2002).
9 M. Vang, "Writing on the Run," 2.
10 Aline Lo, "Writing Citizenship: Flexible Forms of Belonging in Kao Kalia Yang's *The Latehomecomer*," *Hmong Studies Journal* 12 (2011): 13.
11 Lo, "Writing Citizenship," 2.
12 HighBridge, "Giving Voice to *The Latehomecomer*," April 18, 2011, YouTube video, 10:27, http://www.youtube.com/watch?v=2xPeLYfD3Nk.

13 Minnesota Original (MN O), "Kao Kalia Yang," May 11, 2010, available online at website of Minnesota Original, accessed May 8, 2011, https://www.tpt.org/mn-original/resource/kao-kalia-yang-writer/.
14 MN O, "Kao Kalia Yang."
15 MN O, "Kao Kalia Yang."
16 Michel Foucault, *The History of Sexuality*. Vol. 1: *An Introduction*, trans. Robert Hurley (New York: Pantheon Books, 1978), 27.
17 Jenny Edkins, *Trauma and the Memory of Politics* (Cambridge: Cambridge University Press, 2003), 8.
18 Michel Foucault, *The Archaeology of Knowledge and the Discourse on Language*, trans. A. M. Sheridan Smith (New York: Pantheon Books, 1972), 26.
19 Foucault, *Archaeology of Knowledge*, 25.
20 Foucault, *Archaeology of Knowledge*, 25.
21 Foucault, *Archaeology of Knowledge*, 25. Instead, Foucault explains that discourse should be treated as and when it occurs in its sudden irruption "that enables it to be repeated, known, forgotten, transformed, utterly erased, and hidden, far from all view" (25).
22 Elizabeth Freeman, *Time Binds: Queer Temporalities, Queer Histories* (Durham, NC: Duke University Press, 2010), 62.
23 Freeman, *Time Binds*, 59, 62.
24 Freeman, *Time Binds*, 62.
25 Freeman, *Time Binds*, xxi.
26 Lisa Yoneyama, *Hiroshima Traces: Time, Space, and the Dialectics of Memory* (Berkeley: University of California Press, 1999), 146.
27 Carole McGranahan, *Arrested Histories: Tibet, the CIA, and Memories of a Forgotten War* (Durham, NC: Duke University Press, 2010), 19.
28 The 2010 U.S. census data shows that Hmong elders make up only 3 percent of the Hmong refugee/American population.
29 HighBridge, "Giving Voice to *The Latehomecomer*."
30 Thanks to Mai-Linh Hong for helping emphasize this point.
31 MN O, "Kao Kalia Yang."
32 Aline Lo, "Fanciful Flights: Reimagining Refugee Narratives of Escape in Kao Kalia Yang's *The Latehomecomer: A Hmong Family Memoir*," *a/b: Auto/Biography Studies* 32, no. 3 (2017): 644, https://doi.org/10.1080/08989575.2017.1339452.
33 Lo, "Fanciful Flights," 646.
34 Dipesh Chakrabarty, *Provincializing Europe: Postcolonial Thought and Historical Difference* (Princeton, NJ: Princeton University Press, 2000), 8.
35 See McGranahan, *Arrested Histories*.
36 HighBridge, "Giving Voice to *The Latehomecomer*." In this context, it was important to Yang "that [the book] would be one of the first to be published in America from the Hmong perspective."
37 Shoshana Felman and Dori Laub, *Testimony: Crises of Witnessing in Literature, Psychoanalysis, and History* (New York: Routledge, 1992), xx.
38 M. Vang, "Writing on the Run," 4–6.

39 Mishuana Goeman, *Mark My Words: Native Women Mapping Our Nations* (Minneapolis: University of Minnesota Press, 2013), 10.
40 Walsh, "Fugitive Knowledge," 128.
41 Goeman, *Mark My Words*, 9.
42 See *Gran Torino* DVD "Special Features." Indeed, the DVD's special features emphasize cars as symbolic of "manning the wheel" where both the actors and filmmakers nostalgically recount their first and dream cars. *Gran Torino*, dir. Clint Eastwood (2008; Burbank, CA: Warner Home Video, 2009), DVD.
43 For a discussion of Detroit as a postindustrial frontier in which stories produced about the city enable the erasure of white privilege and systemic racism, see Rebecca J. Kinney, *Beautiful Wasteland: The Rise of Detroit as America's Postindustrial Frontier* (Minneapolis: University of Minnesota Press, 2016).
44 Louisa Schein and Va-Megn Thoj, "*Gran Torino*'s Boys and Men with Guns: Hmong Perspectives," *Hmong Studies Journal* 10 (2009): 28. The film, as Ly Chong Thong Jalao describes, recycles the theme of redemption for the benevolent white individual and repackages it for our era of change and racial transition. See Ly Chong Thong Jalao, "Looking *Gran Torino* in the Eye: A Review," *Journal of Southeast Asian American Education and Advancement* 5 (2010): 2.
45 Thank you Mai-Linh Hong for emphasizing this double-edged representation of Asian American women.
46 Adia and Jessie, "'Gran Torino,' White Masculinity and Racism," *Racism Review*, January 17, 2009, http://www.racismreview.com/blog/2009/01/17/gran-torino-white-masculinity-racism/.
47 See William Petersen, "Success Story, Japanese-American Style," *New York Times*, January 9, 1966, http://inside.sfuhs.org/dept/history/US_History_reader/Chapter14/modelminority.pdf; and David Brand, "The New Whiz Kids: Why Asian Americans are doing so well, and what it costs them," *Time*, August 31, 1987, http://content.time.com/time/subscriber/article/0,33009,965326,00.html.
48 Schein and Thoj contend that these unsubtitled lines conspire to mute Hmong speech in alignment with the narrative of Walt's slurs of "screaming" and "jabbering" gooks ("*Gran Torino*'s Boys and Men with Guns," 34).
49 The possibility of a Hmong reading stems from the decision to cast all Hmong "nonactors," with the exception of Doua Moua (who plays the gang member Spider), which compelled Eastwood to "let them go with the flow" and capture performances in a much more improvisational fashion than he would have done with trained actors. Author interview with Cedric Lee, "Hmong cultural consultant" for *Gran Torino*, August 1, 2011.
50 Cedric Lee explains that *Gran Torino*'s producer brought him to Warner Brothers studio to translate the Hmong lines during the film's postproduction stage. Lee and his wife spent a few days translating every Hmong line, whether or not they were scripted. However, the producers made the final decision on which lines to subtitle.
51 Author interview with Cedric Lee, August 2011.
52 Hmong viewers excitedly anticipated a Hmong story to emerge from this Hollywood motion picture, especially in the efforts to cast Hmong actors for the Hmong characters through auditions in heavily Hmong-concentrated areas such as Fresno, St. Paul/

Minneapolis, and Detroit. In discussions on social networks such as Facebook, Hmong Americans debate whether *Gran Torino* is about Hmong or just another movie about Eastwood and the character he portrays in light of the absence of Hmong in the film's promotion. Such heated conversations, especially about the misrepresentations of Hmong culture, underpin a desire for the film to be about Hmong, too.

53 Schein and Thoj state in "*Gran Torino*'s Boys and Men with Guns" that "with Eastwood's directorial style of no rehearsals and almost no coaching or direction, [the actors] stepped up to fashioning their characters largely on their own" (8). They note in their analysis of the celebration by a Hmong gang member (Elvis Thao) after shooting Walt that the actors want us to attend to the "careful artifice of the actors' creative process." Hence, *Gran Torino* is fashioned in part by the "hands of its artisans" (35).

54 Schein and Thoj, "*Gran Torino*'s Boys and Men with Guns," 37. In a published interview with Hmong media scholar Louisa Schein, Bee Vang recounts his intentions to continue auditioning for the role of Thao to "try to improve on the script and the ways Hmong were portrayed" and make him a more "complex and credible" character. Even when he got the part and had to portray an effeminate and subordinated teenager, "he did it with more attitude." Louisa Schein and Bee Vang, "*Gran Torino*'s Hmong Lead: Bee Vang on Film, Race and Masculinity," *Hmong Studies Journal* 11 (2010): 4.

55 Jalao, "Looking *Gran Torino* in the Eye," 4.

56 "Hmong Speak Out on *Gran Torino*: A Discussion with the Hmong Actors at University of Minnesota, February 20, 2009," producer/director Louisa Schein, screened on Crossings TV Sacramento/Fresno, June 7 and 14, 2009, accessed July 31, 2011, author's translation, video.

57 I thank Mai-Linh Hong for helping articulate this point in her reading of the chapter.

58 Thank you Aline Lo for helping articulate this point about the erasure of Black auto workers.

59 Francesca Tognetti, "*Gran Torino*: A Foreign Neighbourhood," *Other Modernities* 10, no. 2 (2009): 380.

60 Cathy Caruth, *Unclaimed Experience: Trauma, Narrative, and History* (Baltimore: John Hopkins University Press, 1996), 46.

61 Caruth, *Unclaimed Experience*, 51. Caruth's consideration of the question of translation in her analysis of *Hiroshima mon amour* highlights the untranslatability of French dialogue memorized and recited by Eiji Okada, the film's Japanese actor who plays the Japanese architect Lui who has an affair with the Frenchwoman Elle, because he performs the lines. She asserts, therefore, that this act of recitation does not represent but rather "voices his difference quite literally, and untranslatably."

62 See Gayatri Chakravorty Spivak, "Can the Subaltern Speak?," in *Marxism and the Interpretation of Culture*, ed. Cary Nelson and Lawrence Grossberg (Urbana: University of Illinois Press, 1988), 271–313.

63 "Hmong Speak Out on *Gran Torino*"; author's translation.

64 Author interview with Cedric Lee, August 2011.

65 I thank Aline Lo for emphasizing this point about situating Grandma's lines within the scenes and other witnesses.

66 I would like to thank Yến Espiritu for helping with this phrasing to characterize the exchanges between Grandma and Walt.

67 Caruth, *Unclaimed Experience*, 9.
68 Quotation from Caruth, *Unclaimed Experience*, 9.
69 Jalao, "Looking *Gran Torino* in the Eye," 4.

EPILOGUE

1 I borrow this phrase from Katherine McKittrick's title to the introduction to her book *Demonic Grounds* on conceptualizing Black women's geographies in the Black diaspora. Her work brings together Black studies and human geography to rethink the "interplay between domination and black women's geographies" (xi). McKittrick shows how Black women imagine "new geographic stories" (ix). I draw from her idea to connect Hmong refugee histories to human geography, and read Hmong American poetry as a way to imagine refugee histories' production of space. See Katherine McKittrick, *Demonic Grounds: Black Women and the Cartographies of Struggle* (Minneapolis: University of Minnesota Press, 2006).
2 Mishuana Goeman, *Mark My Words: Native Women Mapping Our Nations* (Minneapolis: University of Minnesota Press, 2013), 119.
3 Personal communication with Mai See Thao about the project of Hmong American studies scholarship, April 25, 2019.
4 On the plig as an ontological starting point for understanding return migrations, see Mai Thao, "Bittersweet Migrations: Type II Diabetes and Healing in the Hmong Diaspora" (PhD diss., University of Minnesota, 2018), 92.
5 M. Thao, "Bittersweet Migrations," 31, 125.
6 Goeman, *Mark My Words*, 3.
7 Jo Ellen Fair and Lisa Parks, "Africa on Camera: Television News Coverage and Aerial Imaging of Rwandan Refugees," *Africa Today* 48, no. 2 (2001): 37. Fair and Parks's analysis of televised video footage of U.S. news and aerial images of Rwandan refugee movements show that the news organizations' "on-the-ground" images represented "refugees as a deterritorialized mass unanchored from the historical realities that unfolded in Rwanda in 1994" (37). These visual depictions allowed viewers to keep a safe distance from the genocide and refugees. Visual representations become maps of disconnected refugee movements.
8 Yến Lê Espiritu and Lan Duong, "Feminist Refugee Epistemology: Reading Displacement in Vietnamese and Syrian Refugee Art," *Signs: Journal of Women in Culture and Society* 43, no. 3 (2018): 590.
9 M. Jacqui Alexander, *Pedagogies of Crossing: Meditations on Feminism, Sexual Politics, Memory, and the Sacred* (Durham, NC: Duke University Press, 2005), 297.
10 Mai Der Vang, "Transmigration," in *Afterland* (Minneapolis: Graywolf Press, 2017), line 1.
11 M. D. Vang, "Transmigration," lines 5, 7.
12 M. D. Vang, "Transmigration," lines 8, 10–11, 13–14, 18.
13 Alexander, *Pedagogies of Crossing*, 2, 289.
14 Alexander, *Pedagogies of Crossing*, 292.
15 Alexander, *Pedagogies of Crossing*, 7.
16 Goeman, *Mark My Words*, 158.

17 Mai Der Vang, "Afterland," in *Afterland* (Minneapolis: Graywolf Press, 2017), lines 7, 11.
18 M. D. Vang, "Afterland," lines 19–22, 35, 38, 40.
19 M. D. Vang, "Afterland," lines 50–63.
20 Goeman, *Mark My Words*, 157. Goeman explains that the narratives of the past are colonial writings such as historic almanacs, diaries, and travel journals that write Indigenous peoples as a part of the global economy in which "they mark the settler colonial narrative as the constant present absence" (157).
21 Goeman, *Mark My Words*, 170.
22 M. D. Vang, "Afterland," lines 64–76.
23 M. Thao, "Bittersweet Migrations," 4.
24 Mai Der Vang, "Your Mountain Lies Down with You," in *Afterland* (Minneapolis: Graywolf Press, 2017), lines 2–6.

BIBLIOGRAPHY

PRIMARY SOURCES

Ahern, Thomas L. *Undercover Armies: CIA and Surrogate Warfare in Laos, 1961–1973*. Washington, DC: Center for the Study of Intelligence, 2006. Available online at National Security Archive (NSA), "The CIA's Vietnam Histories," National Security Archive website, accessed October 1, 2010. https://nsarchive2.gwu.edu//NSAEBB/NSAEBB284/6-UNDERCOVER_ARMIES.pdf.

Arendt, Hannah. "Statelessness." Lecture, April 22, 1955. Available online at Hannah Arendt Papers at the Library of Congress, Speeches and Writings File, 1923–1975, accessed March 15, 2012. https://memory.loc.gov/cgi-bin/ampage?collId=mharendt_pub&fileName=05/052290/052290page.db&recNum=2&tempFile=./temp/~ammem_4O3c&filecode=mharendt&prev_filecode=mharendt&itemnum=2&ndocs=2.

Bailey, Eric. "Hmong Want Leader Freed: Thousands Demonstrate against the Jailing of a General Who Aided the U.S. in the Vietnam War." *Los Angeles Times*, June 19, 2007. http://articles.latimes.com/2007/jun/19/local/me-hmong19.

Brody, Jeffrey. "Betraying an Old Friend," *Los Angeles Times (1996–Current)*, June 18, 2007. https://search.proquest.com/docview/2212483809?accountid=14515.

Chawkins, Steve. "Arrest Greeted by Disbelief." *Los Angeles Times*, June 6, 2007. http://articles.latimes.com/2007/jun/06/local/me-hmong6.

"Chronology of Events in Laos." Undated. President John F. Kennedy's National Security Council Files and Foreign Relations documents from 1961–1963. Prepared by the John F. Kennedy Presidential Library and Museum. Held at the Vietnam Center and Archive at Texas Tech University. Accessed on September 6–10, 2009.

Connell, Rich, and Robert J. Lopez. "U.S. Accuses 10 of Plotting Coup in Laos." *Los Angeles Times*, June 5, 2007.

Conroy, Thomas P. "Highland Lao Refugees: Repatriation and Resettlement Preferences in Ban Vinai Camp, Thailand." Bridgette Marshall Collection, Southeast Asian Archive Special Collections. Langson Library, University of California, Irvine.

Davey, Monica. "Arrest Uncovers Divide in Hmong-Americans." *New York Times*, June 14, 2007. http://www.nytimes.com/2007/06/14/us/14hmong.html?pagewante=2&_r=1.

Doyle, Michael. "WikiLeaks Cables Bare Secrets of U.S.-Laotian Relations." *The Wichita Eagle*. April 22, 2011. Accessed June 11, 2020. https://www.kansas.com/news/politics-government/article1192757.html.

Dulles, John Foster. "Indochina—Midway in the Geneva Conference: Address by the Secretary of State, May 7, 1954." Website of The Avalon Project: Documents in Law, History and Diplomacy (Yale Law School). Accessed March 13, 2015. http://avalon.law.yale.edu/20th_century/inch022.asp.

Eastwood, Clint, dir. *Gran Torino*. 2008; Burbank, CA: Warner Bros. Productions, 2009. DVD.

Gerstein, Josh. "Army Still Waiting for Hmong General's Arlington Burial Request." *Politico*, Under the Radar blog, January 12, 2011. Accessed June 11, 2020. https://www.politico.com/blogs/under-the-radar/2011/01/army-still-waiting-for-hmong-generals-arlington-burial-request-032302.

HighBridge. "Giving Voice to *The Latehomecomer*." April 18, 2011. YouTube video, 10:27. http://www.youtube.com/watch?v=2xPeLYfD3Nk.

"Hmong Burial and Memorial Benefits." VA Benefits Eligibility for Hmong Individuals Factsheet. Available online on website of U.S. Department of Veterans Affairs National Cemetery Administration. Accessed June 11, 2020. https://www.cem.va.gov/cem/docs/factsheets/Hmong_Burial_Memorial_Benefits_Factsheet.pdf.

"Hmong Speak Out on Gran Torino: A Discussion with the Hmong Actors at the University of Minnesota, February 20, 2009." Producer/director Louisa Schein. Screened on Crossings TV Sacramento/Fresno, June 7 and 14, 2009. Video.

Holm, Richard L. "Recollections of a Case Officer in Laos, 1962–1964: No Drums, No Bugles." CIA Center for the Study of Intelligence. Accessed June 15, 2017. https://www.cia.gov/library/center-for-the-study-of-intelligence/csi-publications/csi-studies/studies/vol47no1/article01.html.

Jewett, Christina. "Hmong Rally at Capitol." *Sacramento Bee*, June 18, 2007. *NewsBank: Access World News*. https://infoweb.newsbank.com/apps/news/document-view?p=AWNB&docref=news/119DD627A87C9020.

Jones, Chong. "Vang Pao and the U.S. Government, Marriage and Betrayal." *Hmong Today*, July 15, 2007. https://www.tcdailyplanet.net/vang-pao-and-u-s-government-marriage-and-betrayal/.

Kennedy, John F. "Press Conference, March 23, 1961." President John F. Kennedy's National Security Council Files and Foreign Relations documents from 1961–1963. Prepared by the John F. Kennedy Presidential Library and Museum. Held at the Vietnam Center and Archive, Texas Tech University. Also available on website of John F. Kennedy Presidential Library and Museum. Accessed January 10, 2020. https://www.jfklibrary.org/asset-viewer/archives/JFKWHA/1961/JFKWHA-020/JFKWHA-020.

"Lao Government Cautiously Welcomes U.S. Arrests." June 25, 2007. American Embassy in Vientiane cable to the Secretary of State and Department of Justice. Available on website of WikiLeaks. Accessed June 11, 2020, https://wikileaks.org/plusd/cables/07VIENTIANE525a.html.

Leary, William M. "CIA Air Operations in Laos, 1955–1974: Supporting the 'Secret War.'" Central Intelligence Agency Library. Accessed June 15, 2017. https://www.cia.gov/library/center-for-the-study-of-intelligence/csi-publications/csi-studies/studies/winter99-00/art7.html.

Legacies of War. "Secret War in Laos." Legacies of War website. Accessed September 15, 2017. http://legaciesofwar.org/about-laos/secret-war-laos/.

Lopez, Robert J., and Rich Connell. "Alleged Coup Plotters Sought CHP Training." *Los Angeles Times*, June 6, 2007. http://articles.latimes.com/2007/jun/06/local/me-laos6.

Lumpkin, John J. "CIA's Paramilitary Force a Cross between Spies and Soldiers." Associated Press, December 3, 2001. Reprinted in *Hmong Times*, December 16, 2001.

Magagnini, Stephen. "Hmong Coup Details Unveiled." *Sacramento Bee*, June 16, 2007. *NewsBank: Access World News*. https://infoweb.newsbank.com/apps/news/document-view?p=AWNB&docref=news/119D2FBCC476D280.

Magagnini, Stephen, and Denny Walsh. "Hmong Rally for 'The General.'" *Sacramento Bee*, June 19, 2007. *NewsBank: Access World News*. https://infoweb.newsbank.com/apps/news/documentview?p=AWNB&docref=news/119E29FA169BC3F8.

Melo, Frederick. "Hmong Veterans Ask for Burial Rights in US Veterans Cemeteries." *Military News*, July 15, 2019. Accessed June 11, 2020. https://www.military.com/daily-news/2019/07/15/hmong-veterans-ask-burial-rights-us-veterans-cemeteries.html.

"Memorandum of Conversation." April 29, 1961. Foreign Relations of the United States, 1961–63. Vol. 24, Laos Crisis. John F. Kennedy National Security Files on Asia and the Pacific, Vietnam Center and Archive, Texas Tech University.

"Memorandum of Conversation: Meeting with Prince Souvanna Phouma." July 27, 1962. Department of State, Central Files, 751J.00/7–2762. Drafted by H. L. T. Koren. Held in Foreign Relations of the United States, 1961–1963. Vol. 24, Laos Crisis. Document 413. Available online at website of the U.S. Department of State Office of the Historian. https://history.state.gov/historicaldocuments/frus1961-63v24/d413.

"Memorandum of Meeting: Meeting with the President, Harriman, Forrestal, Representatives of AID, and DCI." July 27, 1962. Central Intelligence Agency, DCI-McCone Files. Drafted by John A. McCone. Held in Foreign Relations of the United States, 1961–1963. Vol. 24, Laos Crisis. Document 412. Available online at website of the U.S. Department of State Office of the Historian. https://history.state.gov/historicaldocuments/frus1961-63v24/d412.

Minnesota Original (MN O). "Kao Kalia Yang." May 11, 2010. Available online at website of Minnesota Original. Accessed May 8, 2011. https://www.tpt.org/mn-original/resource/kao-kalia-yang-writer/.

Moua, Wameng. "General Vang Pao, Hero." *Hmong Today*, June 18, 2007. http://www.tcdailyplanet.net/article/2007/06/18/general-vang-pao-hero.html?print=1.

Moua, Wameng. "Leader in Trouble: 77-Year-Old General Vang Pao Arrested." *Hmong Today*, June 20, 2007. http://www.tcdailyplanet.net/article/2007/06/19/leader-trouble-77-year-old-general-vang-pao-arrested.html.

"'Operation Tarnished Eagle' Thwarts Plot to Overthrow the Government of Laos." June 4, 2007. Press Release. Available on website of Web Archive. Accessed June 11, 2020. https://web.archive.org/web/20080216032118/http://www.usdoj.gov/usao/cae/press_releases/docs/2007/06-04-07JackPressRls.pdf.

Perez, Amanda. "Patriot Act Classifies Hmong as Terrorists." abc30.com, February 18, 2007.

Powers, Ashley. "Battle's Not Over When They Come to the U.S." *Los Angeles Times*, June 7, 2007. http://articles.latimes.com/2007/jun/07/local/me-overthrow7.

Pye, Lucian W. Letter to Walt W. Rostow. March 20, 1961. President John F. Kennedy's National Security Council Files and Foreign Relations documents from 1961–1963. Prepared by the John F. Kennedy Presidential Library and Museum. Held at the Vietnam Center and Archive at Texas Tech University. Accessed September 6–10, 2010. Also available at John F. Kennedy Presidential Library and Museum. John F. Kennedy National Security Files. Box 130, folder 10 (JFKNSF-130-010).

"Press Release: Hmong American Ad Hoc Rally on April 22, 2011 in Sacramento, CA." Available on website of Suab Hmong News. Accessed February 1, 2012. http://www.shrdo.com/index.php/suabhmong-news/hmong-news/905-press-release-hmong-american-ad-hoc-rally-on-april-21-2011-in-sacramento-ca.

"The Situation and Short-Term Outlook in Laos." December 6, 1960. Pentagon Paper. Secret. Justification of the War. Internal Documents. The Eisenhower Administration. Volume IV: 1956 French Withdrawal—1960. Pentagon-Papers-Part-V-B-3d (National Archives Identifier 5890524). Available online at website of The National Archives. Accessed June 10, 2020. https://www.archives.gov/research/pentagon-papers.

The Story of Laos: The Problem for a U.S. Foreign Policy. John F. Kennedy National Security Files on Asia and the Pacific: 1961–1963. Vietnam Center and Archive, Texas Tech University.

U.S. Congress. *Hmong Veterans' Naturalization Act of 1997; and Canadian Border Boat Landing Permit Requirements: Hearing on H.R. 371 before the Subcomm. on Immigration and Claims.* 105th Cong. June 26, 1997. Washington, DC: Government Printing Office, 1997.

U.S. Congress. *Hmong Veterans' Naturalization Act of 2000: Report to accompany H.R. 371.* 106th Cong., 2nd Session. April 6, 2000. Available at website of the U.S. Congress. Accessed June 11, 2020. https://www.congress.gov/106/crpt/hrpt563/CRPT-106hrpt563.pdf.

Vang, Mai Der. "A Bright Hmong Future after Vang Pao." *New America Media*, June 4, 2009. https://web.archive.org/web/20121119104041/http://news.newamericamedia.org/news/view_article.html?article_id=f7c3b6284371c6cea63d20b5de3f20ec.

Vang, Mai Der. "Gen. Vang Pao's Release Momentous for Young Hmong Americans." *New America Media*, September 21, 2009. https://web.archive.org/web/20121119104038/http://news.newamericamedia.org/news/view_article.html?article_id=7f6cdeb868f27f5b174a062df5d8099d.

Vang, Richard Wanglue. "SuabHmong News: Exclusive Interview Wameng Xiong, Hmong American AD HOC Committee." July 19, 2011. YouTube video, 14:54. http://www.youtube.com/watch?v=nZ4PyZlaMME.

Walsh, Denny, and Bill Lindelof. "Judge Orders Vang Pao Released on Bail." *Sacramento Bee*, July 12, 2007. https://www.mcclatchydc.com/news/nation-world/national/article24466486.html.

Weiner, Tim. "Gen. Vang Pao's Last War." *New York Times*, May 11, 2008. http://www.nytimes.com/2008/05/11/magazine/11pao-t.html?pagewanted=all.

Woon, Christopher, dir. *Among B-Boys*. CRS1UN Productions, 2011. DVD.

Yang, Kou. "The Deadly, Horrible Mess We Made Still Plagues Indochina." *Modesto Bee*, March 5, 2015. http://www.modbee.com/opinion/opn-columns-blogs/community-columns/article17237951.html.

SECONDARY SOURCES

Abu-Lughod, Lila. "Locating Ethnography." *Ethnography* 1, no. 2 (2000): 261–67.
Agamben, Giorgio. "Beyond Human Rights." *Open* 15 (2008): 90–95.
Agamben, Giorgio. *Homo Sacer: Sovereign Power and Bare Life*. Translated by Daniel Heller-Roazen. Edited by Werner Hamacher and David E. Wellbery. Stanford, CA: Stanford University Press, 1998.
Agamben, Giorgio. *State of Exception*. Chicago: University of Chicago Press, 2005.
Agamben, Giorgio. "We Refugees." Translated by Michel Rocke. *Symposium* 49, no. 2 (1995): 114–19. https://doi.org/10.1080/00397709.1995.10733798.
Aldrich, Richard J., and Ming-Yeh Rawnsley. *The Clandestine Cold War in Asia, 1945–65: Western Intelligence, Propaganda and Special Operations*. London: Routledge, 2013.
Alexander, M. Jacqui. *Pedagogies of Crossing: Meditations on Feminism, Sexual Politics, Memory, and the Sacred*. Durham, NC: Duke University Press, 2006.
Anderson, Benedict. *Imagined Communities: Reflections on the Origins and Spread of Nationalism*. London: Verso Books, [1983] 1991.
Appy, Christian G., ed. *Cold War Constructions: The Political Culture of United States Imperialism, 1945–1966*. Amherst: University of Massachusetts Press, 2000.
Arendt, Hannah. "The Decline of the Nation-State and the End of the Rights of Man." In *The Origins of Totalitarianism*, 147–82. New York: Harcourt, Brace, and World, 1951.
Arendt, Hannah. "We Refugees." In *The Jew as Pariah*, edited by Ron H. Feldman, 55–66. New York: Grove Press, [1943] 1978.
Arondekar, Anjali. *For the Record: Sexuality and the Colonial Archive in India*. Durham, NC: Duke University Press, 2009.
Arvin, Maile, Eve Tuck, and Angela Morrill. "Decolonizing Feminism: Challenging Connections between Settler Colonialism and Heteropatriarchy." *Feminist Formations* 25, no. 1 (2013): 8–34.
Baird, Ian G. "Colonialism, Indigeneity and the Brao." In *The Concept of Indigenous Peoples in Asia: A Resource Book*, edited by Christian Erni, 201–21. Copenhagen: International Work Group for Indigenous Affairs (IWGIA) and Asia Indigenous Peoples Pact Foundation (AIPP), 2008.
Baird, Ian G. "Indigeneity in Asia: An Emerging But Contested Concept." *Asian Ethnicity* 17, no. 4 (2016): 501–5.
Baird, Ian G. "The US Central Intelligence Agency and the Brao." *Aséanie* 25 (2010): 23–51.
Barret, David M. *The CIA and Congress: The Untold Story from Truman to Kennedy*. Lawrence: University Press of Kansas, 2005.
Behera, Navnita Chadha, ed. *Gender, Conflict and Migration*. New Delhi: SAGE, 2006.
Beiner, Ronald, ed. *Theorizing Citizenship*. Albany: State University of New York Press, 1995.
Benjamin, Walter. "Theses on the Philosophy of History." In *Illuminations*, edited by Hannah Arendt, 253–64. New York: Schocken Books, 1968.
Bertrais, Fr. Yves. "About Us." Hmong RPA website. Accessed March 15, 2018. http://www.hmongrpa.org/aboutus.html.
Bhabha, Homi. *The Location of Culture*. New York: Routledge, 1994.

Bijleveld, Anne Willem, ed. *The State of the World's Refugees 2006: Human Displacement in the New Millennium*. Oxford: Office of the United Nations High Commissioner for Refugees, 2006.

Birchall, Clare. "An Introduction to 'Transparency': The Politics of Opacity and Openness." *Theory, Culture and Society* 28, nos. 7–8 (2012): 7–25. https://doi.org/10.1177/0263276411427744.

Birchall, Clare. "'There's Been Too Much Secrecy in This City': The False Choice between Secrecy and Transparency in US Politics." *Cultural Politics* 7, no. 1 (2011): 133–56. https://doi.org/10.2752/175174311X12861940861905.

Bradley, Mark P. *Imagining Vietnam and America: The Making of Postcolonial Vietnam*. Chapel Hill: University of North Carolina Press, 2000.

Brocheux, Pierre, and Daniel Hemery. *Indochina: An Ambiguous Colonization, 1858–1954*. Translated by Ly Lan Dill-Klein with Eric Jennings, Nora Taylor, and Noemi Tousignant. Berkeley: University of California Press, 2009.

Bui, Long T. "Suspended Futures: The Vietnamization of South Vietnamese History and Memory." PhD dissertation, University of California, San Diego, 2011.

Burton, Antoinette. "Introduction: Archive Fever, Archive Stories." In *Archive Stories: Facts, Fictions, and the Writing of History*, 1–24. Durham, NC: Duke University Press, 2005.

Camacho, Keith. *Cultures of Commemoration: The Politics of War, Memory, and History in the Mariana Islands*. Honolulu: University of Hawaii Press, 2011.

Camp, Stephanie M. H. Introduction to *Closer to Freedom: Enslaved Women and Everyday Resistance in the Plantation South*, 1–11. Chapel Hill: University of North Carolina Press, 2004.

Camp, Stephanie M. H. "A Geography of Containment: The Bondage of Space of Time." In *Closer to Freedom: Enslaved Women and Everyday Resistance in the Plantation South*, 12–34. Chapel Hill: University of North Carolina Press, 2004.

Canetti, Elias. *Crowds and Power*. New York: Farrar, Straus and Giroux, 1984.

Carey, Jane Perry Clark. "Some Aspects of Statelessness since World War I." *American Political Science Review* 40, no. 1 (1946): 113–23.

Caruth, Cathy. *Unclaimed Experience: Trauma, Narrative, and History*. Baltimore: John Hopkins University Press, 1996.

Castle, Timothy N. *At War in the Shadow of Vietnam: U.S. Military Aid to the Royal Lao Government, 1955–1975*. New York: Columbia University Press, 1993.

Castle, Timothy N. *One Day Too Long: Top Secret Site 85 and the Bombing of North Vietnam*. New York: Columbia University Press, 1999.

Center for Southeast Asian Studies. "The Father Yves Bertrais Collection." Hmong Studies Consortium website. Accessed September 15, 2017. https://hmongstudies.wisc.edu/wp-content/uploads/sites/420/2019/02/Bertrais-Collection-Boxes-Guide-Chong.pdf.

Central Intelligence Agency (CIA). "About CIA: Timeline." Central Intelligence Agency website. Last updated April 26, 2016. https://www.cia.gov/about-cia/cia-museum/experience-the-collection/text-version/timeline.html.

Chakrabarty, Dipesh. *Provincializing Europe: Postcolonial Thought and Historical Difference*. Princeton, NJ: Princeton University Press, 2000.

Chan, Sucheng, ed. *Hmong Means Free: Life in Laos and America*. Philadelphia: Temple University Press, 1994.

Chanson, Philippe. "Father Yves Bertrais, An Essential Figure in the History of Hmong Christianity." *Exchange* 22, no. 1 (1993): vii–17. https://doi.org/10.1163/157254393X00092.

Chatterjee, Partha. *The Nation and Its Fragments: Colonial and Postcolonial Histories.* Princeton, NJ: Princeton University Press, 1993.

Cheng, Cindy I-Fen. *Citizens of Asian America: Democracy and Race during the Cold War.* New York: New York University Press, 2013.

Cheung, King-Kok. *Articulate Silences: Hisaye Yamamot, Maxine Hong Kingston, Joy Kogawa.* Ithaca, NY: Cornell University Press, 1993.

Chuh, Kandice, and Karen Shimakawa. *Orientations: Mapping Studies in the Asian Diaspora.* Durham, NC: Duke University Press, 2001.

Coulthard, Glen. "Place against Empire: Understanding Indigenous Anti-Colonialism." *Affinities: A Journal of Radical Theory, Culture, and Action* 4, no. 2 (2010): 79–83.

Coulthard, Glen. *Red Skin, White Masks: Rejecting the Colonial Politics of Recognition.* Minneapolis: University of Minnesota Press, 2014.

Coulthard, Glen. "Subjects of Empire: Indigenous Peoples and the 'Politics of Recognition' in Canada." *Contemporary Political Theory* 6 (2007): 437–60.

Creak, Simon. *Embodied Nation: Sport, Masculinity, and the Making of Modern Laos.* Honolulu: University of Hawaii Press, 2015.

Crock, Mary, Ben Saul, and Azadeh Dastyari, eds. *Future Seekers II: Refugees and Irregular Migration in Australia.* Leichhardt, NSW: Federation Press, 2006.

Culas, Christian, and Jean Michaud. "A Contribution to the Study of Hmong (Miao) Migrations and History." *Bijdragen tot de Taal-, Land- en Volkenkunde* 153, no. 2 (1997): 211–43.

Cullather, Nick. *The Hungry World: America's Cold War Battle against Poverty in Asia.* Cambridge, MA: Harvard University Press, 2013.

Dahl, Jens. *The Indigenous Peoples and Marginalized Spaces at the United Nations.* New York: Palgrave Macmillan, 2012.

Daniel, E. Valentine, and John Chr Knudsen, eds. *Mistrusting Refugees.* Berkeley: University of California Press, 1995.

da Silva, Denise Ferreira. "Tale of Two Cities: Saigon, Fallujah, and the Ethical Boundaries of Empire." In "Thirty Years AfterWARd: Vietnamese Americans and U.S. Empire." Special issue, *Amerasia* 31, no. 2 (2005): 121–34.

da Silva, Denise Ferreira. *Toward a Global Idea of Race.* Minneapolis: University of Minnesota Press, 2007.

Day, Iyko. *Alien Capital: Asian Racialization and the Logic of Settler Colonial Capitalism.* Durham, NC: Duke University Press, 2016.

Dean, Jodi. "Publicity's Secret." *Political Theory* 29, no. 5 (2001): 624–50.

Derrida, Jacques. *Archive Fever: A Freudian Impression.* Chicago: University of Chicago Press, 1996.

Derrida, Jacques. *Geneses, Genealogies, Genres, and Genius: The Secrets of the Archive.* Translated by Beverley Bie Brahic. New York: Columbia University Press, 2003.

Derrida, Jacques. *The Gift of Death.* 2nd edition. Translated by David Wills. Chicago: University of Chicago Press, 1995.

Derrida, Jacques. *Literature in Secret.* Translated by David Wills. Chicago: University of Chicago Press, 2008.

Derrida, Jacques, and Maurizio Ferraris. *A Taste for the Secret.* Translated by Giacomo Donis. Edited by Giacomo Donis and David Webb. Malden, MA: Polity Press, 2001.

Dodge, Martin, Rob Kitchin, and Chris Perkins. "Introductory Essay: Power and Politics of Mapping." In *The Map Reader: Theories of Mapping Practice and Cartographic Representation*, edited by Martin Dodge, Rob Kitchin, and Chris Perkins, 388–94. Oxford: John Wiley and Sons, 2011. Accessed November 1, 2011. http://onlinelibrary.wiley.com/book/10.1002/9780470979587.

Donnelly, Nancy. *Changing Lives of Refugee Hmong Women.* Seattle: University of Washington Press, 1997.

Dunbar-Ortiz, Roxanne. *An Indigenous Peoples' History of the United States.* Boston: Beacon Press, 2014.

Edkins, Jenny. *Trauma and the Memory of Politics.* Cambridge: Cambridge University Press, 2003.

Espiritu, Augusto. "Inter-Imperial Relations, the Pacific, and Asian American History." *Pacific Historical Review* 83, no. 2 (2014): 238–54.

Espiritu, Yến Lê. *Body Counts: The Vietnam War and Militarized Refuge(es).* Berkeley: University of California Press, 2014.

Espiritu, Yến Lê. *Home Bound: Filipino American Lives across Cultures, Communities, and Countries.* Berkeley: University of California Press, 2003.

Espiritu, Yến Lê. "Rethinking 'Collateral Damage' in the Vietnam War: The Other Others in the Circuits of U.S. Empire." In "(Re)Collecting the Vietnam War." Special issue, *Asian American Literary Review* 6, no. 2 (2015): 133–39.

Espiritu, Yến Lê. "Thirty Years AfterWARd: The Endings That Are Not Over." In "Thirty Years AfterWARd: Vietnamese Americans and U.S. Empire." Special issue, *Amerasia* 31, no. 2 (2019): xiii–xxiii.

Espiritu, Yến Lê. "Toward a Critical Refugee Study: The Vietnamese Refugee Subject in U.S. Scholarship." *Journal of Vietnamese Studies* 1, nos. 1–2 (2006): 410–33.

Espiritu, Yến Lê. "The 'We-Win-Even-When-We-Lose' Syndrome: U.S. Press Coverage of the Twenty-Fifth Anniversary of the 'Fall of Saigon.'" *American Quarterly* 58, no. 2 (2006): 329–52.

Espiritu, Yến Lê, and Lan Duong. "Feminist Refugee Epistemology: Reading Displacement in Vietnamese and Syrian Refugee Art." *Signs: Journal of Women in Culture and Society* 43, no. 3 (2018): 587–615.

Essed, Philomena, Georg Frerks, and Joke Schrijvers, eds. *Refugees and the Transformation of Societies: Agency, Policies, Ethics and Politics.* New York: Berghahn Books, 2004.

Faderman, Lillian. *I Begin My Life All Over: The Hmong and the American Immigrant Experience.* Boston: Beacon Press, 1998.

Fadiman, Anne. *The Spirit Catches You and You Fall Down: A Hmong Child, Her American Doctors, and the Collision of Two Cultures.* New York: Farrar, Straus and Giroux, 1997.

Fair, Jo Ellen, and Lisa Parks. "Africa on Camera: Television News Coverage and Aerial Imaging of Rwandan Refugees." *Africa Today* 48, no. 2 (2001): 35–57.

Faist, Thomas, and Peter Kivisto, eds. *Dual Citizenship in Global Perspective: From Unitary to Multiple Citizenship.* New York: Palgrave Macmillan, 2007.

Felman, Shoshana, and Dori Laub. *Testimony: Crises of Witnessing in Literature, Psychoanalysis, and History.* New York: Routledge, 1992.

Ferguson, Roderick. *Aberrations in Black: Toward a Queer of Color Critique.* Minneapolis: University of Minnesota Press, 2004.

Foucault, Michel. *The Archaeology of Knowledge and the Discourse on Language.* Translated by A. M. Sheridan Smith. New York: Pantheon Books, 1972.

Foucault, Michel. *The History of Sexuality, Vol. 1: An Introduction.* Translated by Robert Hurley. New York: Pantheon Books, 1978.

Freeman, Elizabeth. *Time Binds: Queer Temporalities, Queer Histories.* Durham, NC: Duke University Press, 2010.

Friedman, Andrew. *Covert Capital: Landscapes of Denial and the Making of U.S. Empire in the Suburbs of Northern Virginia.* Berkeley: University of California Press, 2013.

Fujikane, Candace, and Johnathan Y. Okamura. *Asian Settler Colonialism: From Local Governance to the Habits of Everyday Life in Hawai'i.* Honolulu: University of Hawaii Press, 2008.

Fujitani, Takashi. "Right to Kill, Right to Make Live: Koreans as Japanese and Japanese as Americans during WWII." *Representations* 99 (2007): 13–39.

Fujitani, Takashi, Geoffrey M. White, and Lisa Yoneyama. "Introduction: Remembering and Dismembering the Asia-Pacific War(s)." In *Perilous Memories: The Asia-Pacific War(s),* edited by Takashi Fujitani, Geoffrey M. White, and Lisa Yoneyama, 1–29. Durham, NC: Duke University Press, 2001.

Geiger, Danilo. "Some Thoughts on 'Indigeneity' in the Context of Migration and Conflicts at Contemporary Asian Frontiers." In *The Concept of Indigenous Peoples in Asia: A Resource Book,* edited by Christian Erni, 183–98. Copenhagen: International Work Group for Indigenous Affairs (IWGIA) and Asia Indigenous Peoples Pact Foundation (AIPP), 2008.

Ghandhi, Leela. *Affective Communities: Anticolonial Thought, Fin-de-Siècle Radicalism, and the Politics of Friendship.* Durham, NC: Duke University Press, 2006.

Gibney, Matthew J. "Liberal Democratic States and Responsibilities to Refugees." *American Political Science Review* 93, no. 1 (1999): 169–81.

Gilkey, Robert. "Laos: Politics, Elections and Foreign Aid." *Far Eastern Survey* 27, no. 6 (1958): 89–94.

Goeman, Mishuana. *Mark My Words: Native Women Mapping Our Nations.* Minneapolis: University of Minnesota Press, 2013.

Goeman, Mishuana. "(Re)Mapping Indigenous Presence on the Land in Native Women's Literature." *American Quarterly* 60, no. 2 (2008): 295–302.

Goldberg, David Theo. *The Racial State.* Malden, MA: Blackwell, 2002.

Goldstein, Martin E. *American Policy toward Laos.* Rutherford, NJ: Fairleigh Dickinson University Press, 1973.

Gordon, Avery. *Ghostly Matters: Haunting and the Sociological Imagination.* Minneapolis: University of Minnesota Press, 1997.

Graham, Milliard. *Laotian Pawn.* Bloomington, IN: 1st Books Library, 1996.

Greenstein, Fred I., and Richard H. Immerman. "What Did Eisenhower Tell Kennedy about Indochina? The Politics of Misperception." *Journal of American History* 79, no.2 (1992): 568–87.

Gunn, Geoffrey C. *Political Struggles in Laos, 1930–1954: Vietnamese Communist Power and the Lao Struggle for National Independence.* Bangkok, Thailand: Duang Kamol, 1988.

Halberstam, Jack. "The Wild Beyond: With and for the Undercommons." Introduction to *The Undercommons: Fugitive Planning and Black Study*, by Stefano Harney and Fred Moten, 4–12. New York: Minor Compositions, 2013.

Hamilton-Merritt, Jane. *Tragic Mountains: The Hmong, the Americans, and the Secret Wars for Laos, 1942–1992*. Bloomington: Indiana University Press, 1993.

Hammer, Ellen Joy. *The Struggle for Indochina, 1940–1955*. Stanford, CA: Stanford University Press, 1967.

Hardt, Michael, and Antonio Negri. *Empire*. Cambridge, MA: Harvard University Press, 2000.

Harney, Stefano, and Fred Moten. *The Undercommons: Fugitive Planning and Black Study*. New York: Minor Compositions, 2013.

Hartman, Saidiya. "Venus in Two Acts." *Small Axe* 12, no. 2 (2008): 1–14.

Hein, Jeremy. *From Vietnam, Laos, and Cambodia: A Refugee Experience in the United States*. New York: Twayne, 1995.

Hill, Kenneth L. "President Kennedy and the Neutralization of Laos." *Review of Politics* 31, no. 3 (1969): 353–69.

Hittinger, John P. "The Soldier and the Citizen: Lessons from Plato and Aristotle." International Society for Military Ethics website, accessed January 10, 2020. http://isme.tamu.edu/JSCOPE95/Hittinger95.html.

Hmong American Writers' Circle. *How Do I Begin? A Hmong American Literary Anthology*. Berkeley, CA: Heyday Press, 2011.

Hobsbawm, Eric. *Nations and Nationalism since 1780*. Cambridge, MA: Harvard University Press, 1990.

Hull, Matthew S. *Government of Paper: The Materiality of Bureaucracy in Urban Pakistan*. Berkeley: University of California Press, 2012.

Hundleby, Catherine. "The Epistemological Evaluation of Oppositional Secrets." *Hypatia* 20, no. 4 (2005): 44–58.

Hyndman, Jennifer. "The Geopolitics of Migration and Mobility." *Geopolitics* 17 (2012): 243–55.

Hyndman, Jennifer. "Introduction: The Feminist Politics of Refugee Migration." *Gender, Place and Culture* 17, no. 4 (2010): 453–59.

Hyndman, Jennifer. *Managing Displacement: Refugees and the Politics of Humanitarianism*. Minneapolis: University of Minnesota Press, 2000.

Ignatieff, Michael. "The Myth of Citizenship." In *Theorizing Citizenship*, edited by Ronald Beiner, 53–78. Albany: State University of New York Press, 1995.

Isaac, Allan Punzalan. *American Tropics: Articulating Filipino America*. Minneapolis: University of Minnesota Press, 2006.

Isaacs, Arnold R., Gordon Hardy, MacAlister Brown, et al. *Pawns of War: Cambodia and Laos*. Boston: Boston Publishing, 1987.

Jacobs, Seth. "Laos." In *A Companion to John F. Kennedy*, edited by Marc J. Selverstone, 249–68. Chicester, West Sussex, UK: John Wiley and Sons, 2014.

Jacobs, Seth. *The Universe Unraveling: American Foreign Policy in Cold War Laos*. The United States in the World. Ithaca, NY: Cornell University Press, 2012.

Jalao, Ly Chong Thong. "Looking *Gran Torino* in the Eye: A Review." *Journal of Southeast Asian American Education and Advancement* 5, no. 1 (2010): 1–4.

James, Leslie, and Elisabeth Leake, eds. *Decolonization and the Cold War: Negotiating Independence*. London: Bloomsbury, 2015.

Jeffreys-Jones, Rhodri. *The CIA and American Democracy*. New Haven, CT: Yale University Press, 1989.

Johnson, Chalmers. *The Sorrows of Empire: Militarism, Secrecy, and the End of the Republic*. New York: Metropolitan Books, 2004.

Johnson, Paul Christopher. *Secrets, Gossip, and Gods: The Transformation of Brazilian Candomblé*. New York: Oxford University Press, 2002.

Kang, Laura Hyun Yi. *Compositional Subjects: Enfiguring Asian/American Women*. Durham, NC: Duke University Press, 2002.

Kaplan, Amy. "'Left Alone with America': The Absence of Empire in the Study of American Culture." In *Cultures of United States Imperialism*, edited by Amy Kaplan and Donald E. Pease, 3–21. Durham, NC: Duke University Press, 1993.

Kaplan, Amy. "Manifest Domesticity." In *The Futures of American Studies*, edited by Donald E. Pease and Robyn Wiegman, 111–34. Durham, NC: Duke University Press, 2002.

Kaplan, Amy. "Violent Belongings and the Question of Empire Today: Presidential Address to the American Studies Association, October 17, 2003." *American Quarterly* 56, no. 1 (2004): 1–18.

Keating, Neal B. "Kuy Alterities: The Struggle to Conceptualize and Claim Indigenous Land Rights in Neoliberal Cambodia." In "Indigeneity and Natural Resources in Cambodia." Special issue, *Asia Pacific Viewpoint* 54, no. 3 (2013): 309–22.

Kelly, John D., and Martha Kaplan. "Nation and Decolonization: Toward a New Anthropology of Nationalism." *Anthropological Theory* 1, no. 4 (2001): 419–37.

Kerber, Linda. "History of the Statelessness." *American Quarterly* 57, no. 3 (2005): 727–49.

Kerber, Linda. "Presidential Address: The Stateless as the Citizen's Other: A View from the United States." *American Historical Review* 112, no. 1 (2007): 1–34.

Kerber, Linda. "Toward a History of Statelessness in America." *American Quarterly* 57, no. 3 (2005): 727–49.

Kettrey, Heather Hensman, and Whitney Nicole Laster. "Staking Territory in the 'World White Web': An Exploration of the Roles of Overt and Color-Blind Racism in Maintaining Racial Boundaries on a Popular Web Site." *Social Currents* 1 (2014): 257–74.

Kim, Elaine, and Chungmoo Choi, eds. *Dangerous Women: Gender and Korean Nationalism*. New York: Routledge, 1998.

Kim, Elaine H., and Lisa Lowe. Introduction to "New Formations, New Questions: Asian American Studies." Special issue, *positions* 5, no. 2 (1997): v–xiv.

Kim, Jodi. *Ends of Empire: Asian American Critique and the Cold War*. Minneapolis: University of Minnesota Press, 2010.

Kinney, Rebecca J. *Beautiful Wasteland: The Rise of Detroit as America's Postindustrial Frontier*. Minneapolis: University of Minnesota Press, 2016.

Kivisto, Peter, and Thomas Faist. *Citizenship: Discourse, Theory, and Transnational Prospects*. Malden, MA: Blackwell, 2007.

Klein, Christina. *Cold War Orientalism: Asia in the Middlebrow Imagination, 1945–1961*. Berkeley: University of California Press, 2003.

Koehn, Peter H. *Refugees from Revolution: U.S. Policy and Third-World Migration.* Boulder, CO: Westview Press, 1991.

Kurlantzick, Joshua. *A Great Place to Have a War: America in Laos and the Birth of a Military CIA.* New York: Simon and Schuster, 2017.

Kushner, Tony. *Remembering Refugees: Then and Now.* Manchester, UK: Manchester University Press, 2006.

Lai, Paul, and Lindsey Claire Smith. Introduction to "Alternative Contact: Indigeneity, Globalism, and American Studies." Special issue, *American Quarterly* 62, no. 3 (2010): 407–36.

Lau, Albert. Introduction to *Southeast Asia and the Cold War.* Edited by Albert Lau, 1–12. New York: Routledge, 2012.

Lee, Mai Na. *Dreams of the Hmong Kingdom: The Quest for Legitimation in French Indochina, 1850–1960.* Madison: University of Wisconsin Press, 2015.

Lee, Mai Na. "The Women of 'Dragon Capital': Marriage Alliances and the Rise of Vang Pao." In *Claiming Place: On the Agency of Hmong Women*, edited by Chia Youyee Vang, Faith Nibbs, and Ma Vang, 87–116. Minneapolis: University of Minnesota Press, 2016.

Lee, Steven Hugh. *Outposts of Empire: Korea, Vietnam and the Origins of the Cold War in Asia, 1949–1954.* Montreal: McGill-Queen's University Press, 1995.

Li, Tanya Murray. "Indigeneity, Capitalism, and the Management of Dispossession." *Current Anthropology* 51, no. 3 (2010): 385–414.

Lim, Bliss Cua. *Translating Time: Cinema, the Fantastic, and Temporal Critique.* Durham, NC: Duke University Press, 2009.

Lippit, Akira Mizuta. *Atomic Light (Shadow Optics).* Minneapolis: University of Minnesota Press, 2005.

Lippit, Akira Mizuta. "The Shadow Archive: From Light to Cinder." *Tympanum* 4, no. 1. (2000). https://doi.org/10.2752/175174311X12861940861905.

Lischer, Sarah Kenyon. "Collateral Damage: Humanitarian Assistance as a Cause for Conflict." *International Security* 28, no. 1 (2003): 79–109.

Lo, Aline. "Fanciful Flights: Reimagining Refugee Narratives of Escape in Kao Kalia Yang's *The Latehomecomer: A Hmong Family Memoir*." *a/b: Auto/Biography Studies* 32, no. 3 (2017): 643–48. https://doi.org/10.1080/08989575.2017.1339452.

Lo, Aline. "Writing Citizenship: Flexible Forms of Belonging in Kao Kalia Yang's *The Latehomecomer*." *Hmong Studies Journal* 12 (2011): 1–15.

Loescher, Gil, and John A. Scanlan. *Calculated Kindness: Refugees and America's Half-Open Door, 1945 to the Present.* New York: Free Press, 1986.

Lowe, Lisa. "Epistemological Shifts: National Ontology and the New Asian Immigrant." In *Orientations: Mapping Studies in the Asian Diaspora*, 268–76. Durham, NC: Duke University Press, 2001.

Lowe, Lisa. *Immigrant Acts: On Asian American Cultural Politics.* Durham, NC: Duke University Press, 1996.

Lowe, Lisa. "The Intimacies of Four Continents." In *Haunted by Empire: Geographies of Intimacy in North American History*, edited by Ann Laura Stoler, 191–212. Durham, NC: Duke University Press, 2006.

Lowe, Lisa. *The Intimacies of Four Continents*. Durham, NC: Duke University Press, 2015.

Lui, Robyn. "Governing Refugees 1919–1945." *borderlands e-journal* 1, no. 1 (2002). Accessed November 16, 2005. http://borderlands.net.au/vol1no1_2002/lui_governing.html.

Macekura, Stephen. "'For Fear of Persecution': Displaced Salvadorans and U.S. Refuge Policy in the 1980s." *Journal of Policy History* 23, no. 3 (2011): 357–80. https://doi.org/10.1017/S0898030611000145.

Mackenthun, Gesa, and Andreas Beer, eds. *Fugitive Knowledge: The Loss and Preservation of Knowledge in Cultural Contact Zones*. Münster: Waxmann Verlag, 2015.

Magnette, Paul. *Citizenship: The History of an Idea*. Colchester, UK: European Consortium for Political Research, 2005.

Malkki, Lisa H. "Refugees and Exile: From 'Refugee Studies' to the National Order of Things." *Annual Review of Anthropology* 24 (1995): 495–523.

Man, Simeon. *Soldiering through Empire: Race and the Making of the Decolonizing Pacific*. Berkeley: University of California Press, 2018.

Marchetti, Gina. *Romance and the "Yellow Peril": Race, Sex, and Discursive Strategies in Hollywood Fiction*. Berkeley: University of California Press, 1994.

Marfleet, Philip. *Refugees in a Global Era*. New York: Palgrave Macmillan, 2006.

Markell, Patchen. *Bound by Recognition*. Princeton, NJ: Princeton University Press, 2003.

Martin, Susan Forbes. *Refugee Women*. Atlantic Highlands, NJ: Zed Books, 1992.

Massey, Doreen B. *For Space*. London: SAGE, 2005.

Massey, Doreen B. "Power-Geometry and a Progressive Sense of Place." In *Mapping the Futures: Local Cultures, Global Change*, edited by J. Bird, B. Curtis, T. Putnam, G. Robertson, and L. Tickner, 59–69. New York: Routledge, 1993.

McAlister, Melani. *Epic Encounters: Culture, Media, and U.S. Interests in the Middle East since 1945*. Berkeley: University of California Press, 2001.

McCoy, Alfred. *The Politics of Heroin in Southeast Asia*. New York: Harper and Row, 1972.

McGehee, Ralph. "Bombing Laos." Hartford Web Publishing website. October 9, 1995. Accessed March 12, 2015. http://www.hartford-hwp.com/archives/54/057.html.

McGranahan, Carole. *Arrested Histories: Tibet, the CIA, and Memories of a Forgotten War*. Durham, NC: Duke University Press, 2010.

McKittrick, Katherine. *Demonic Grounds: Black Women and the Cartographies of Struggle*. Minneapolis: University of Minnesota Press, 2006.

Michaud, Jean. *"Incidental" Ethnographers: French Catholic Missions on the Tonkin-Yunnan Frontier, 1880–1930*. Leiden: Brill Press, 2007.

Miles, Tiya. *Ties That Bind: The Story of an Afro-Cherokee Family in Slavery and Freedom*. Berkeley: University of California Press, 2005.

Miller, Bruce Granville. *Invisible Indigenes: The Politics of Nonrecognition*. Lincoln: University of Nebraska Press, 2003.

Morrison, Gayle. *Sky Is Falling: An Oral History of the CIA's Evacuation of the Hmong from Laos*. Jefferson, NC: McFarland, 1999.

Mote, Sue Murphy. *Hmong and American: Stories of Transition to a Strange Land*. Jefferson, NC: McFarland, 2004.

Moua, Chai Charles. *Roars of Traditional Leaders: Mong (Miao) American Cultural Practices in a Conventional Society*. Lanham, MD: University Press of American, 2012.

Moua, Mai Neng, ed. *Bamboo among the Oaks: Contemporary Writing by Hmong Americans*. St. Paul: Minnesota Historical Society Press, 2002.

Myers, Kit. "Love and Violence in Transracial/National Adoption." Master's thesis, University of California, San Diego, 2009.

Myers, Kit. "'Real' Families: The Violence of Love in New Media Adoption Discourse." *Critical Discourse Studies* 11 (2013): 175–93. https://doi.org/10.1080/17405904.2013.852983.

Nackerud, Larry G. *The Central American Refugee Issue in Brownsville, Texas: Seeking Understanding of Public Policy Formulation from within a Community Setting*. San Francisco: Mellen Research University Press, 1993.

Ngai, Mae M. *Impossible Subjects: Illegal Aliens and the Making of Modern America*. Princeton, NJ: Princeton University Press, 2004.

Nguyen, Mimi Thi. *The Gift of Freedom: War, Debt, and Other Refugee Passages*. Durham, NC: Duke University Press, 2012.

Nguyen, Phoung Tran. *Becoming Refugee American: The Politics of Rescue in Little Saigon*. Urbana: University of Illinois Press, 2017.

Nguyen, Phoung Tran. "The People of the Fall: Refugee Nationalism in Little Saigon, 1975–2005." PhD dissertation, University of Southern California, 2009.

Nguyen, Viet Thanh. *Nothing Ever Dies: Vietnam and the Memory of War*. Cambridge, MA: Harvard University Press, 2016.

Nguyen, Viet Thanh. "Representing Reconciliation: Le Ly Hayslip and the Victimized Body." *positions: east asian cultures critique* 5, no. 2 (1997): 605–42.

Nguyen-Vo, Thu Huong. "Forking Paths: How Shall We Mourn the Dead?" In "Thirty Years AfterWARd: Vietnamese Americans and U.S. Empire." Special issue, *Amerasia* 31, no. 2 (2005): 137–49.

Norindr, Panivong. "On Photography, History, and Affect: Re-Narrating the Political Life of a Laotian Subject." *Historical Reflections* 34, no. 1 (2008): 89–103.

North, Liisa, and Alan B. Simmons. *Journeys of Fear: Refugee Return and National Transformation in Guatemala*. Montreal: McGill-Queen's University Press, 1999.

Olson, Gregory A. *Mansfield and Vietnam: A Study in Rhetorical Adaptation*. East Lansing: Michigan State University Press, 1995.

Ong, Aihwa. *Buddha Is Hiding: Refugees, Citizenship, the New America*. Berkeley: University of California Press, 2003.

Ong, Aihwa. *Flexible Citizenship: The Cultural Logics of Transnationality*. Durham, NC: Duke University Press, 1999.

"Our Secret Army." Narrated by Mike Wallace. Produced by Barry Lando. *60 Minutes*. CBS, 1975. Television. Available online at Sheena Kalies, "Hmong Our Secret Army CBS 60 Minutes," August 13, 2015, YouTube video, 16:15. https://www.youtube.com/watch?v=L4U2P7tsOAQ.

Parker, James E., Jr. *Covert Ops: The CIA's Secret War in Laos*. New York: St. Martin's, 1995.

Pasternak, Shiri. "The Shifting Spatial Requirements for Indigenous Genocide in Canada." Paper presented at the Critical Ethnic Studies Association Conference, University of California, Riverside, March 10–12, 2011.

Perera, Suvendrini. "What Is a Camp . . . ?" *borderlands e-journal* 1, no. 1 (2002). Accessed November 16, 2005. http://borderlands.net.au/vol1no1_2002/perera_camp.html.

Pha, Kong. "Queer Refugeeism: Constructions of Race, Gender, and Sexuality in the Hmong Diaspora." PhD dissertation, University of Minnesota, 2017.

Pickering, Sharon. *Refugees and State Crime*. Leichhardt, NSW: Federation Press, 2005.

Prados, John. *Presidents' Secret Wars: CIA and Pentagon Covert Operations from World War II through the Persian Gulf*. Chicago: Ivan R. Dee, 1986.

Puar, Jasbir. *Terrorist Assemblages: Homonationalism in Queer Times*. Durham, NC: Duke University Press, 2007.

Puar, Jasbir K., and Amit S. Rai. "Monster, Terrorist, Fag: The War on Terrorism and the Production of Docile Patriots." *Social Text* 20, no. 3 (2002): 117–48.

Publiese, Joseph. "Penal Asylum: Refugees, Ethics, Hospitality." *borderlands e-journal* 1, no. 1 (2002). Accessed November 16, 2005. http://borderlands.net.au/vol1no1_2002/pugliese.html.

Quincy, Keith. *Harvesting Pa Chay's Wheat: The Hmong and America's Secret War in Laos*. Spokane: Eastern Washington University Press, 2000.

Ramos, Efren Rivera. "The Legal Construction of American Colonialism: The Insular Cases (1901–1922)." *Revista Juridica Universidad de Puerto Rico* 65 (1996): 225–328.

Reddy, Chandan. "Asian Diasporas, Neoliberalism, and Family: Reviewing the Case for Homosexual Asylum in the Context of Family Rights." *Social Text* 84–85 (2005): 101–19.

Renan, Ernest. "What Is a Nation?" In *Nations and Identities: Classic Readings*, edited by Vincent P. Pecora, 162–76. Malden, MA: Blackwell, 2001.

Reynolds, Henry. *Aboriginal Sovereignty: Reflections on Race, State, and Nation*. St. Leonards, NSW: Allen and Unwin, 1996.

Rifkin, Mark. *Beyond Settler Time: Temporal Sovereignty and Indigenous Self-Determination*. Durham, NC: Duke University Press, 2017.

Robinson, W. Courtland. *Terms of Refuge*. London: Zed Books, 1998.

Rosenblatt, Lionel. "The History behind the Hmong Refugee Exodus." Panel organized by the *Hmongstory 40 Project*, Fresno City College, August 22, 2015.

Rostow, Walt W., with Richard W. Hatch. *An American Policy in Asia*. New York: John Wiley and Sons, 1955.

Rubin, Barry. *Secrets of State: The State Department and the Struggle over U.S. Foreign Policy*. New York: Oxford University Press, 1985.

Sahara, Ayako. "Operations New Life/Arrivals U.S. National Project to Forget the Vietnam War." Master's thesis, University of California, San Diego, 2009.

Samaddar, Ranabir, ed. *Refugees and the State: Practices of Asylum and Care in India, 1947–2000*. New Delhi: SAGE, 2003.

Samito, Christian G. *Becoming American under Fire: Irish Americans, African Americans, and the Politics of Citizenship during the Civil War Era*. Ithaca, NY: Cornell University Press, 2009.

Savada, Andrea Matles, ed. *Laos: A Country Study*. Washington, DC: GPO for the Library of Congress, 1994. Available online at Library of Congress Country Studies website. Accessed March 12, 2015. http://countrystudies.us/laos/.

Savina, François Marie. *Histoire des Miao*. Paris: Société des missions-étrangères, 1924.

Scarry, Elaine. *The Body in Pain: The Making and Unmaking of the World*. Oxford: Oxford University Press, 1985.

Schein, Louisa, and Bee Vang. "*Gran Torino*'s Hmong Lead: Bee Vang on Film, Race and Masculinity." *Hmong Studies Journal* 11 (2010): 1–11.

Schein, Louisa, and Va-Megn Thoj. "*Gran Torino*'s Boys and Men with Guns: Hmong Perspectives." *Hmong Studies Journal* 10, no. 1 (2009): 1–52.

Schein, Louisa, and Va-Megn Thoj. "Occult Racism: The Masking of Race in the Hmong Hunter Incident: A Dialogue between Anthropologist Louisa Schein and Filmmaker/Activist Va-Megn Thoj." *American Quarterly* 59, no. 4 (2007): 1051–95.

Schlund-Vials, Cathy. "Collateral + Damage." Special issue, *Asian American Literary Review* 6, no. 2 (2015): 122.

Schmitt, Carl. *The Concept of the Political*. Chicago: Chicago University Press, 1996.

Schwartz, Joan M., and Terry Cook. "Archives, Records, and Power: The Making of Modern Memory." *Archival Science* 2 (2002): 1–19.

Scott, James C. *The Art of Not Being Governed: An Anarchist History of Upland Southeast Asia*. New Haven, CT: Yale University Press, 2009.

Scott, James C. "Hill and Valley in Southeast Asia . . . or Why the State is the Enemy of People who Move Around . . . or . . . Why Civilizations Can't Climb Hills." In *The Concept of Indigenous Peoples in Asia: A Resource Book*, edited by Christian Erni, 161–82. Copenhagen: International Work Group for Indigenous Affairs (IWGIA) and Asia Indigenous Peoples Pact Foundation (AIPP), 2008.

Seckler-Hudson, Catheryn. *Statelessness: With Special Reference to the United States (A Study in Nationality and Conflict of Laws)*. Washington, DC: Digest Press, 1934.

Secord, Richard, with Jay Wurts. *Honored and Betrayed: Irangate, Covert Affairs, and the Secret War in Laos*. New York: John Wiley and Sons, 1992.

Shigematsu, Setsu, and Keith Camacho. Introduction to *Militarized Currents: Toward a Decolonized Future in Asia and the Pacific*. Edited by Setsu Shigematsu and Keith Camacho, xv–xlviii. Minneapolis: University of Minnesota Press, 2010.

Shils, Edward A. *The Torment of Secrecy: The Background and Consequences of American Security Policies*. Glencoe, IL: Free Press, 1956.

Simpson, Audra. *Mohawk Interruptus: Political Life across the Borders of Settler States*. Durham, NC: Duke University Press, 2014.

Simpson, Audra. *To the Reserve and Back Again: Kahnawake Mohawk Narratives of Self, Home and Nation*. Montreal: McGill University Press, 2003.

Sinana, Jolynna. *Social Media in Trinidad: Values and Visibility*. London: University College London Press, 2017.

Sisavath, Davorn. "The US Secret War in Laos: Constructing an Archive from Military Waste." *Radical History Review*, no. 133 (2019): 103–16. https://doi.org/10.1215/01636545-7160089.

Slotkin, Richard. *Gunfighter Nation: The Myth of the Frontier in Twentieth-Century America*. New York: Atheneum, 1992.

Soguk, Nevzat. *States and Strangers: Refugees and Displacements of Statecraft*. Minneapolis: University of Minnesota Press, 1999.

Sommer, Rebecca, dir. *Hunted Like Animals*. SommerFilms, 2008. DVD.

Spivak, Gayatri Chakravorty. "Can the Subaltern Speak?" In *Marxism and the Interpretation of Culture*, edited by Cary Nelson and Lawrence Grossberg, 271–313. Urbana: University of Illinois Press, 1988.

St. Cartmail, Keith. *Exodus Indochina*. Auckland: Heineman, 1983.

Stabile, Carol A., and Carrie Rentschler. "States of Insecurity and the Gendered Politics of Fear." *NWSA Journal* 17, no. 3 (autumn 2005): vii–xxv.

Stoler, Ann Laura. *Along the Archival Grain: Epistemic Anxieties and Colonial Common Sense*. Princeton, NJ: Princeton University Press, 2010.

Stoler, Ann Laura. "Colonial Archives and the Arts of Governance." *Archival Science* 2 (2002): 87–109.

Stoler, Ann Laura, ed. *Haunted by Empire: Geographies of Intimacy in North American History*. Durham, NC: Duke University Press, 2006.

Strand, Paul J., and Woodrow Jones Jr. *Indochinese Refugees in America: Problems of Adaptation and Assimilation*. Durham, NC: Duke University Press, 1985.

Stuart-Fox, Martin. *A History of Laos*. Cambridge: Cambridge University Press, 1997.

Tang, Eric. *Unsettled: Cambodian Refugees in the New York Hyperghetto*. Philadelphia: Temple University Press, 2015.

Taussig, Michael. *Defacement: Public Secrecy and the Labor of the Negative*. Stanford, CA: Stanford University Press, 1999.

Taylor, Diana. *The Archive and the Repertoire: Performing Cultural Memory in the Americas*. Durham, NC: Duke University Press, 2003.

Tepper, Elliot L., ed. *Southeast Asian Exodus: From Tradition to Resettlement— Understanding Refugees from Laos, Kampuchea and Vietnam in Canada*. Ottawa: Canadian Asian Studies Association, 1980.

Thao, Mai See. "Bittersweet Migrations: Type II Diabetes and Healing in the Hmong Diaspora." PhD dissertation, University of Minnesota, 2018.

Thao, Yer J. "Culture and Knowledge of the Sacred Instrument Qeej in the Mong-American Community." *Asian Folklore Studies* 65, no. 2 (2006): 249–67.

Todd, Molly. *Beyond Displacement: Campesinos, Refugees, and Collective Action in the Salvadoran Civil War*. Madison: University of Wisconsin Press, 2011.

Tognetti, Francesca. "*Gran Torino*: A Foreign Neighbourhood." *Other Modernities* 10, no. 2 (2009): 378–81.

Trouillot, Michel-Rolph. *Silencing the Past: Power and the Production of History*. Boston: Beacon Press, 1995.

Tuck, Patrick J. N. *French Catholic Missionaries and the Politics of Imperialism in Vietnam, 1857–1914: A Documentary Survey*. Liverpool: Liverpool University Press, 1987.

Tuitt, Patricia. *False Images: Law's Construction of the Refugee*. London: Pluto Press, 1996.

Tuitt, Patricia. *Race, Law, Resistance*. London: GlassHouse, 2004.

Twelve Years of U.S. Imperialist Intervention and Aggression in Laos. Laos: Neo Lao Haksat Publications, 1966.

Um, Khatharya. *From the Land of Shadows: War, Revolution, and the Making of the Cambodian Diaspora*. New York: New York University Press, 2015.

Um, Khatharya. "The 'Vietnam War': What's in a Name?" In "Thirty Years AfterWARd: Vietnamese Americans and U.S. Empire." Special issue, *Amerasia* 31, no. 2 (2005): 151–55.

Van Hear, Nicholas, and Christopher McDowell, eds. *Catching Fire: Containing Forced Migration in a Volatile World*. Lanham, MD: Lexington Books, 2006.

Vang, Chia Youyee. *Fly until You Die: An Oral History of Hmong Pilots in the Vietnam War.* New York: Oxford University Press, 2019.

Vang, Chia Youyee. *Hmong American: Reconstructing Community in Diaspora.* Urbana: University of Illinois Press, 2010.

Vang, Chong. "Hmong Protest/Rally at Sacramento Federal Court House 10/15/10 Part 4." October 22, 2010. YouTube video, 9:58. http://www.youtube.com/watch?v=bue1tlbWTS0&feature=endscreen.

Vang, Ma. "Rechronicling Histories: Toward a Hmong Feminist Perspective." In *Claiming Place: On the Agency of Hmong Women,* edited by Chia Youyee Vang, Faith Nibbs, and Ma Vang, 28–55. Minneapolis: University of Minnesota Press, 2016.

Vang, Ma. "The Refugee Soldier: A Critique of Recognition and Citizenship in the Hmong Veterans' Naturalization Act of 1997." In "Southeast Asian/American Studies." Special issue, *positions: east asia cultures critique* 20, no. 3 (2012): 685–712.

Vang, Ma. "Writing on the Run: Hmong American Literary Formations and the Deterritorialized Subject." In "Refugee Cultures: Forty Years after the Vietnam War." Special issue, *MELUS: Multi-Ethnic Literature of the United States* 41, no. 3 (2016): 89–111. https://doi.org/10.1093/melus/mlw031.

Vang, Mai Der. *Afterland.* Minneapolis: Graywolf Press, 2017.

Vang, Nengher N. "Political Transmigrants: Rethinking Hmong Political Activism in America." *Hmong Studies Journal* 12 (2011): 1–46.

Volpp, Leti. "The Citizen and the Terrorist." *UCLA Law Review* 49 (2002): 1575–600.

Voutira, Eftihia, and Giorgia Dona. "Editorial Introduction: Refugee Research Methodologies: Consolidation and Transformation of a Field." *Journal of Refugee Studies* 20, no. 2 (2007): 163–71.

Vwj Zoov Tsheej nrog Yaj Ntxoov Yias thiab Txiv Plig Nyiaj Pov. *Haiv Hmoob Li Xwm.* Quezon City, Philippines: Association Patrimoine Cultural Hmong, 1997.

Walker-Moffat, Wendy. *The Other Side of the Asian American Success Story.* San Francisco: Jossey-Bass, 1995.

Walsh, Aylwyn. "Fugitive Knowledge: Performance Pedagogies, Legibility and the Undercommons." *Applied Theatre Research* 6, no. 2 (2018): 121–37.

Warner, Roger. *Back Fire: The CIA's Secret War in Laos and Its Link to the War in Vietnam.* New York: Simon and Schuster, 1995.

Warner, Roger. *Shooting at the Moon: The Story of America's Clandestine War in Laos.* South Royalton, VT: Steerforth Press, 1998.

Warrior, Robert Allen. *Tribal Secrets: Recovering American Indian Intellectual Traditions.* Minneapolis: University of Minnesota Press, 1995.

Webb, Billy. *Secret War.* Bloomington, IN: Xlibris, 2010.

Weis, Paul. "The Convention Relating to the Status of Stateless Persons." *International and Comparative Law Quarterly* 10, no. 2 (1961): 255–64.

Weld, Kirsten. *Paper Cadavers: The Archives of Dictatorship in Guatemala.* Durham, NC: Duke University Press, 2014.

White, James D., and Anthony J. Marsella, eds. *Fear of Persecution: Global Human Rights, International Law, and Human Well-Being.* Lanham, MD: Lexington Books, 2007.

Wolf, Eric R. *Europe and the People without History*. Berkeley: University of California Press, 1982.

Wolfe, Patrick. "Settler Colonialism and the Elimination of the Native." *Journal of Genocide Research* 8, no. 4 (2006): 387–409.

Wright, Michelle. *Becoming Black: Creating Identity in the African Diaspora*. Durham, NC: Duke University Press, 2004.

Yang, Dao, and Jeanne L. Blake. *Hmong at the Turning Point*. Minneapolis: Woodbridge, 1993.

Yang, Kao Kalia. *The Latehomecomer: A Hmong Family Memoir*. Minneapolis: Coffee House Press, 2008.

Yeatman, Anna. "The Subject of Citizenship." *Citizenship Studies* 11, no. 1 (2007): 105–15.

Yoneyama, Lisa. *Cold War Ruins: Transpacific Critique of American Justice and Japanese War Crimes*. Durham, NC: Duke University Press, 2016.

Yoneyama, Lisa. *Hiroshima Traces: Time, Space, and the Dialectics of Memory*. Berkeley: University of California, 1999.

Yoneyama, Lisa. "Liberation under Siege: U.S. Military Occupation and Japanese Women's Enfranchisement." *American Quarterly* 57, no. 3 (2005): 885–901.

Young, Iris Marion. "Logic of Masculinist Protection: Reflections on the Current Security State." *Signs: Journal of Women in Culture and Society* 29, no. 1 (2003): 1–26.

Zetter, Roger. "Preface: Celebrating the 25th Anniversary of the Refugee Studies Centre and the 20th Anniversary of the Journal of Refugee Studies." *Journal of Refugee Studies* 20, no. 2 (2007): 161–62.

Zolberg, Aristide R., Astri Suhrke, and Sergio Aguayo. *Escape from Violence: Conflict and the Refugee Crisis in the Developing World*. New York: Oxford University Press, 1989.

INDEX

Page numbers followed by f indicate figures.

Abadie, Clarence "Chuck," 80–81
Abu Ghraib scandal, 221n34
Abu-Lughod, Lila, 122
"affirmative action citizenship," 110–11
Afghanistan, 128, 131
Afterland (Mai Der Vang), 182–87
Agamben, Giorgio, 20, 215n38, 217n69
Ahern, Thomas, Jr., 42–44, 204n64; on Hmong fighters, 83–84; *Undercover Armies*, 59, 72, 74, 75f, 78f, 79–81
Akha people, 12, 19
Alcohol, Tobacco, Firearms and Explosives, Bureau of, 117, 219n5
Alexander, M. Jacqui, 14, 183
"alien soldier," 214n14
Al Qaeda, 119
Among B-Boys (film), 89–90
Anderson, Benedict, 216n56
Angola, 128
Arbenz, Jacobo, 41
"archival memory," 22–23
archive(s), 61–62; "anarchive" or "antiarchive" and, 123–27; Derrida on, 34; of Guatemalan police, 38, 202n43; legal, 98–102; of liberalism, 63; missing elements in, 33, 59–63, 84–91, 160–61; refugee, 22–25, 84–91, 99–100, 214n22. *See also* historiography
Arendt, Hannah, 20, 21, 198n93
Arondekar, Anjali, 61

Arvin, Maile, 193n39
autonomy, 18, 81–82; cultural, 20; "limited," 51; political, 29–30, 49, 52, 54
Autry, Alan, 113

Baird, Ian G., 12, 293n39
Bandung conference (1955), 51
Barney, Linwood, 19
Beer, Andreas, 14
Benjamin, Walter, 124
Bertrais, Yves, 19, 196n82
bin Laden, Osama, 125, 131–32
biopolitics, 39, 119
Birchall, Clare, 35, 36
Black diaspora. *See* slave trade
"boat people crisis," 139
Bono, Sonny, 104
Boston Marathon bombing (2013), 142
Boun Oum, 51, 54
Bradley, Mark P., 44
Brao people, 5, 12, 29; nationalism of, 45–46; U.S. military service by, 211n63
Brown, Lawrence, 122
Brown, Winthrop G., 80
Burke, Arleigh, 72
Burma, 11, 12, 47, 195n76; Golden Triangle of, 63; languages of, 49
Burton, Antoinette, 61
Bush, George W., 127, 134–35

Camacho, Keith, 44, 141
Cambodia, 5, 48, 118, 210n54; refugees from, 27, 42, 130, 194n53; Vietnam War and, 41–42
Candomblé, 36, 202n37
Canetti, Elias, 35
Caruth, Cathy, 174, 227n61
Central Intelligence Agency (CIA), 5; establishment of, 40–41, 203n56; ID cards of, 84, 90–91, 212n90; opium trade and, 195n77; Special Activities Division of, 128; USAID and, 30–31, 58, 79, 91
Chakrabarty, Dipesh, 16
Chamorro people, 141
Chan, Sucheng, 196n78
Chanthalangsy, Yong, 129
Cheung, King-Kok, 148
Chin, Vincent, 165
China, 46, 63, 76; Hmong homeland in, 10–12, 63, 76, 193n36, 196n78; opium trade of, 18, 195n77
Choi, Chungmoo, 44
citizenship, 95–106; "affirmative action," 110–11; contractual, 102, 109–10; contradictions of, 97–98, 215n38, 217n69; English test for, 97, 105–10, 147, 213n14, 216n65; social contract theory and, 103–4; of stateless persons, 21
Cold War, 38–42, 59–89, 119, 129–31; cartography of, 63–74, 66–68f, 80, 88–89; China and, 46; crimes of, 133–34; decolonization and, 44–47, 51–52, 204n70; secret documents of, 62; U.S. imperialism during, 33, 38. *See also* Korean War
colonialism, 29; archives of, 61–62; in French Indochina, 5, 47–53, 58, 81–83; Japanese, 44, 141; late capitalism and, 183; militarism and, 13, 44–46, 52; as modernization project, 39; "secret war" as, 28, 30; slave trade and, 9, 63. *See also* decolonization; imperialism
"compositional subject," 6, 119, 127
concealment codes, 62
Consolidated Appropriations Act (2018), 112–13
Cook, Paul, 113
Cook, Terry, 61
Costa, Jim, 113
Coulthard, Glen S., 214n15
Creak, Simon, 46, 47, 51
Critical Refugee Studies Collective, 180
Crocetti, Louis D., Jr., 100–101
Cuba, 70, 204n65
Culas, Christian, 18, 195nn76–77

Dahl, Jens, 197n85
Damrell, Frank, 122
Daniels, Jerry, 190n11
da Silva, Denise Ferreira, 102
Day, Iyko, 29
Dean, Jodi, 35
Decker, George H., 69
decolonization: Cold War and, 44–47, 51–53, 204n70; feminist praxis of, 14–15; of Laos, 28–30, 47–55; "secret war" and, 28, 30
democracy, 95, 118, 137, 217n77; secrecy and, 35, 41; "totalitarianization" of, 35–36
Derrida, Jacques, 34–36
diabetes mellitus, 13, 186
Dien Bien Phu, 52. *See also* French Indochina
Donovan, William J., 203n56
Doyle, Michael, 128–29
"drag," as gender performativity, 154
"dragging histories," 147–56
Dulles, John Foster, 52–53

Eastwood, Clint, 23, 126, 163–64, 176, 227n53
Edkins, Jenny, 151, 224n2
Eisenhower, Dwight D., 52–54
El Salvador, 28, 200n5
English language skills, 88, 147–48, 150–51, 166, 176–77, 189n11; literacy and, 106–11, 213n14, 216n56, 216n59
English test for citizenship, 97, 105–10, 147, 213n14, 216n65
epistemology, 59; definition of, 192n23; of secrecy, 33–38
Espiritu, Augusto, 200n10
Espiritu, Yến Lê, 42

Fa Ngum, 47
Fair, Jo Ellen, 228n7
Fang, Jesse, 40
Faydang, Lo, 82
Felman, Shoshana, 158
feminisms, 4, 8, 36, 154, 194n54; biopolitics and, 119; colonial archives and, 61, 88–89; *Gran Torino* and, 163, 166, 174; refugee geopolitics and, 14–15, 124, 180–81; transnational, 14, 183, 192n24. *See also* gender
Ferguson, Roderick, 192n23
Foucault, Michel, 124–25, 151, 153, 225n21; biopolitics of, 39, 119

252 Index

Franco-Lao Treaty of Amity and Association (1953), 51
"freedom fighters," 120–22, 130, 139; war memorial to, 113–15, 114f
Freeman, Elizabeth, 124, 153–54
French Guiana, 193n82
French Indochina, 5, 47–49, 51–53, 58, 81–83
Friedman, Andrew, 60, 69
Fujitani, Takashi, 39
funeral ritual (*Qhuab Ke*), 11, 155, 184

Gaddis, John Lewis, 45
gender, 154; race and, 120, 125, 164–78, 221n36, 228n1. *See also* feminisms
Geneva Accords: of 1954, 5, 31, 51–54, 58, 66–67; of 1962, 31, 51, 58, 77
"geographic domination," 15
"geographic stories," 179–87
Goeman, Mishuana, 88–89, 179–80; *Mark My Words*, 16, 194n63, 229n20; on "narrative mapping," 184; on Silko, 185
Goldberg, David Theo, 198n96
Golden Triangle, 63
Goldstein, Martin E., 65
Gran Torino (film), 23, 126, 146–47, 156, 163–78
Guam, 70
Guatemala, 28, 38, 41, 202n43
guerrilla fighters, 96–98, 100–103, 105, 213n13. *See also* "freedom fighters"
Gunn, Geoffrey, 82
Gutman, Harvey E., 54

Habermas, Jürgen, 37–38
Haigh, Susan, 104, 108
Harney, Stefano, 14
Hartman, Saidiya, 25
Hayes, Sharon, 154
healers, 13, 149, 186
Hill, Kenneth L., 71–72
hip-hop culture, 89–90
historical erasure, 6, 63–65, 118–19
histories on the run, 122, 146, 148–49
historiography, 28, 37, 165; secrets and, 24–25, 58–63, 148, 150–51. *See also* archives
history(ies), 24–25; "arrested," 158; deferred, 22–25; "dragging," 147–56; fugitive, 8, 10–14, 26, 158, 191n17; normalization of, 63
Hmong American AD HOC (organization), 139–40

Hmong people, 45–46, 193n36, 199n3; Chinese homeland of, 10–12, 63, 76, 193n36, 196n78; Communist faction of, 81, 82; as ethnic group, 28, 106–8, 170, 198n97; histories of, 11–12, 18–19, 49–50; language of, 11, 19, 108, 196n82; literacy among, 106–11, 213n14, 216n56, 216n59; names for, 189n4, 196n78; opium trade and, 195n77, 205n102; oral traditions of, 11–12; as pilots, 5, 31–32, 32f, 216n59; "primitivism" of, 20, 84, 94, 106–9, 212n2; U.S. military service by, 8–9, 38–44, 74–76, 83–84; after Vietnam War, 85–86, 134, 157, 168, 170
Hmong refugees, 62; assimilation of, 94, 97, 108; demographics of, 27; Thailand and, 11, 39, 85–86, 161–62, 195n76
Hmong veterans, 27–28, 95–106, 112–15, 114f, 181–82
Hmong Veterans' Naturalization Act (2000), 90, 94, 97–98, 106, 110–12, 213n9
Hmong Veterans' Service Recognition Act (2018), 112–13
Ho Chi Minh Trail, 5, 78f, 113, 142
homosexuality, 125, 132, 221n34
honor (*txiaj ntsim*), 114–15, 218n81
Hull, Matthew S., 60
humanitarianism, 79; militarism and, 30–31, 96, 213n6
human rights, 20, 21, 134–35
Hundleby, Catherine, 36
hu plig (soul-calling), 4, 182–83, 189n9
Hussein, Saddam, 125, 131, 132
Hyndman, Jennifer, 15, 194n54

Immigration and Nationality Act (1965), 213nn13–14
Immigration and Naturalization Service (INS), 98–106
Immigration History and Research Center, 1, 86, 189n1
Immigration Reform and Control Act (1986), 100
imperialism, 95–98, 111, 146, 200n10. *See also* colonialism; liberal imperialism
"imperial time," 17
Indigenous peoples, 16, 88–89, 194n63; ethnicity and, 12, 28, 193n39; literacy of, 107–9; nationalism among, 18, 45–46
Indochina. *See* French Indochina
International Control Commission (ICC), 53

Index 253

International Institute of Minnesota, 2, 189nn1–2
Iran, 41
Iraq, 203n54, 221n34
Islamophobia, 110, 119
Iu Mien people, 49

Jack, Harrison Ulrich, 218n1, 219n5
Jacobs, Seth, 46
Jalao, Ly Chong Thong, 167, 226n44
Japan, 33, 39, 44, 68, 141, 176
Jobs, Sebastian, 191n17
Johnson, Chalmers, 68
Johnson, Paul Cristopher, 36–37, 202n37
Jones, Chong, 133, 134

Kang, Laura, 122–23, 190n15
Kaplan, Amy, 96
Kaplan, Martha, 30
Kaysone Phomvihane, 54
Keker, Jon, 132–33
Kelly, John D., 30
Kennedy, John F.: Bay of Pigs Invasion and, 204n65; on Laos, 57–59, 62, 64f, 65–76, 93; "New Frontier" policies of, 71, 80
Kennedy, Patrick J., 103
Kerber, Linda, 198n97
Kha people, 5, 29; geographic distribution of, 83; nationalism of, 45–46; Pathet Lao and, 82
Khmer Rouge, 42
Khmu people, 5, 29, 75f
Kim, Elaine, 44, 212n1
Kim, Jodi, 33, 38, 201n22
Klug, Scott L., 103
knowledge, 61; "ancestral," 180; embodied, 107, 147, 159–63; fugitive, 6–19, 146–47, 191n17, 194n52; "nonreproducible," 23; secret structuring of, 27–28, 30–33, 208n2; "uncertain," 14
Korean War, 41, 44, 126, 164, 170. *See also* Cold War
Kowalski, Walt, 126
Krikorian, Mark, 110–11

Lair, Bill, 79, 80, 82, 83, 211n58
Lam, Tony, 165
Lamet people, 75f
Lan Xang kingdom, 47
Lao Hmong American War Memorial, 113–15, 114f

Lao Issara (Free Lao) movement, 49, 50
Lao people, 28–29, 62; divisions of, 48–49; geographic distribution of, 74–75, 75f
Laos, 28–30, 50–55, 134–35; Communist areas of, 65–68, 66–68f, 180; Eisenhower policies on, 53–54; ethnic groups of, 28, 74–76, 75f, 210n54; history of, 47–50; independence of, 5, 50–52, 58, 93; Kennedy policies on, 57–59, 62, 64f, 65–74, 93; languages of, 49; maps of, 66–68f, 75f, 78f; natural resources of, 65; U.S. bombing of, 5, 31–32, 39, 118, 200n14; U.S. military aid to, 58, 73, 74; U.S. neutrality toward, 29, 53, 67, 71–73, 118, 133; Vang's attempted coup in, 117–18, 217n77. *See also* Royal Lao Armed Forces
Lao Veterans of America, Inc., 90, 101, 112, 114
Latehomecomer, The (Yang), 145–63, 176–78
Lau, Albert, 46
Laub, Dori, 158
Le, Kong, 55
Lee, Cedric, 166–67, 175, 176, 226n50
Lee, Lue, 190n13
Lee, Mai Na, 11, 12, 20, 81, 192n25, 206n109
Lee, Steven Hugh, 45
Legacies of War website, 200n14
liberal imperialism, 4, 7–9, 12–13, 42, 61, 68; Lao "neutrality" and, 29, 53, 67, 71–73, 118, 133; strategies of, 44–45, 119. *See also* decolonization
Lim, Bliss Cua, 17, 18
Lima Sites (airstrips), 69
Lippit, Akira Mizuta, 123–24
Lisu people, 12, 19
literacy, 106–11, 213n14, 216n56, 216n59. *See also* English language skills
Lo, Aline, 149
Lo, Chue, 218n1
Lo, Pa Chay, 49, or Lo, Pachay, 211n67
Lobliayao, Faydang, 48
Lolo people, 195n77
Lowe, Lisa, 63, 199n108, 212n1
"loyal ally," 90, 120–23, 135
Lundestad, Geir, 45
Lyfoung, Touby, 39–40, 49, 211n67

Mackenthun, Gesa, 14
Man, Simeon, 9, 29
Marchetti, Gina, 221n36

Markell, Patchen, 214n15
Massey, Doreen, 15, 16
McCain, John, 222n49
McCoy, Alfred, 195n77
McGranahan, Carole, 23, 158
McKittrick, Katherine, 15, 179, 194n57, 228n1
memory, 24–25; Benjamin on, 124; collective, 61; crafting of, 160; mediation of, 169–72; writing and, 107
Méo. *See* Hmong people
Methven, Stu, 79, 82–84
Mexican immigrants, 110–11, 217nn73–74
Michaud, Jean, 18, 195nn76–77, 196n80
Mien people, 5, 29
militarism, 38, 95, 102, 216n56; colonialism and, 44–46, 52; humanitarianism and, 96, 213n6; Islamophobia and, 119; after 9/11 attacks, 131
Miller, Bruce Granville, 197n86
modernization, 48, 70–71; colonialism and, 39; literacy and, 107–11, 216n56; "political," 43–44
"modern time consciousness," 17
Mossadeq, Mohammed, 41
Moten, Fred, 14
Moua, Dan, 91
Moua, Doua, 226n49
Moua, Palee, 13, 190n9
Moua, Wameng, 123, 140
Mountz, Alison, 180–81
Myanmar. *See* Burma

National Asian Pacific American Legal Consortium, 105–6, 108
National Security Act (1947), 40
nation-building, 45–46, 82, 206n124; Agamben on, 215n38, 217n69; decolonial, 8, 16, 29; "limited autonomy" and, 51; Scarry on, 99; U.S. views of, 70–71, 74–76
Native Americans. *See* Indigenous peoples
Neo Lao Hak Xat (Lao People's Front), 55
Neutrality Act (U.S.), 118, 133
"New Frontier" policies, 71, 80
Nguyen, Mimi Thi, 17, 45, 119, 191n17
Nguyen, Phoung Tran, 139, 223n70
Nicaragua, 128, 131
9/11 attacks, 112, 118, 119, 126–28, 131
Noriega, Manuel, 131–32
Norindr, Panivong, 25
ntsuj plig (spirit), 3–4, 155, 180, 182–84, 190n9

Obama, Barack, 142
Okinawa, 195n64
"Operation Popcorn," 118, 217n77
"Operation Tarnished Eagle," 131
opium trade, 18, 48, 195n77, 205n102

Pakistan, 60, 98
Panama, 131–32
Paris conference (1954), 32
Paris Peace Accords (1973), 32, 85
Parks, Lisa, 228n7
Pathet Lao, 49, 53–55, 96; Hmong and, 81, 82; Kha and, 82; Kha people and, 82; Soviet support of, 55, 71–73, 76; on U.S. intervention, 67–69
Patriot Act (2001), 112, 134, 217n76
Pavie, August, 205n96
Pha, Kong, 132
Phetsarath Rattanavongsa, 50
Philippines, 52, 68
Phoumi Nosavan, 55, 57–58, 208n2
Plain of Jars (Plaine des jarres), 55, 67f, 73–79, 75f, 78f, 83
Police Air Reconnaissance Unit, 211n58
Pol Pot, 42
posttraumatic stress disorder (PTSD), 109
Powers, Ashley, 130
"primitivism," 20, 84, 94, 106–9, 212n2
Programs Evaluation Office (PEO), 53–55, 209n25
Project Waterpump, 31–32
Puar, Jasbir K., 119, 124, 125, 132
Puerto Rico, 70
Pye, Lucian W., 70–72, 76

Qhuab Ke (funeral ritual), 11, 155, 184

race: ethnicity and, 12, 28, 45–46, 193n39; gender and, 120, 125, 164–78, 221n36, 228n1
racialization, 95, 101, 102, 106–11, 213n3
Rai, Amit S., 124
Rambo (film), 121
rape, 162, 173, 177
Raymond, Jean de, 50
Real ID Act (2005), 112, 217n76
recognition, politics of, 95–98, 106, 109, 169–72, 214n15
Reddy, Chandan, 98

Index 255

refugees, 4, 21; Agamben on, 215n38, 217n69; archives of, 22–25, 84–91, 99–100, 214n22; definition of, 193n37; "economic migrants" versus, 101; as "loyal allies," 120–23, 135; mapping of, 180–82; Rwandan, 228n7; stateless persons versus, 20–21, 198n93; temporality of, 16–22, 106–7, 156–60

refugee grandmother: in *Gran Torino*, 146–47, 156, 163–78; in *The Latehomecomer*, 145–63, 176–78

"refugee secrecy," 37–38

refugee soldier figure, 27–28, 94–102, 113–15, 181–82; Agamben on, 215n38, 217n69; Anderson on, 216n56

refugee studies, 14–15, 180, 189n1

Rentschler, Carrie, 129

Rifkin, Mark, 17–18, 146, 195n67, 224n7

Romanized Popular Alphabet (RPA), 19, 108

Roosevelt, Franklin D., 203n56

Rosenblatt, Lionel, 85, 190n11, 196n78

Rostow, Walt W., 70–71, 76

Royal Lao Armed Forces, 28–29, 51, 55, 73–76, 84; Eisenhower aid to, 52–54; Program Evaluation Office and, 209n25; U.S. pilots in, 31, 32, 201n16

Ruiz, Raul, 113

Rwandan refugees, 228n7

Savang Vatthana, 53

Savina, François Marie, 19

Scarry, Elaine, 99

Schein, Louisa, 167, 227n54

Schwartz, Joan M., 61

Scott, James C., 19–20

Secord, Richard, 84

secrets, 36–38, 202n37; definition of, 207n1; Derrida on, 34–36; epistemology of, 33–38; historiography and, 24–25, 58–63, 148, 150–51; knowledge structured by, 27–28, 30–33, 208n2; "oppositional," 36; "public," 34–36, 208n3; Taussig on, 34–35

"secret war" in Laos (1961–75), 5–10, 27–44, 85, 100–101; definition of, 33; effects on Hmong of, 13; literature on, 199n3; memorials to, 112–15, 114f; "success" of, 204n65

self-determination, 18, 30, 39, 54. See also autonomy

Seneca people, 194n63

September 11th attacks. See 9/11 attacks

settler colonialism, 29

Shigematsu, Setsu, 44

Silko, Leslie Marmon, 185

Sinana, Jolynna, 220n23

Sisavang Vong, 50

Sisavath, Davorn, 208

slave trade: colonialism and, 9, 63; transatlantic, 15, 25, 183, 202n37

Slotkin, Richard, 71

Smith, Lamar, 99–101

social contract theory, 103–4

Somali refugees, 142

soul-calling (*hu plig*), 4, 182–83, 189n9

Souphanouvong, 49, 50; on Hmong, 77; nationalism of, 54, 82

Souvanna Phouma, 31, 50, 54, 55; on Hmong, 77; nationalism of, 82

Souvannarath, 51

Special Guerrilla Units, 96–98, 100–103, 105, 213n13. See also "freedom fighters"

"spirit." See *ntsuj plig*

Stabile, Carol A., 129

stateless persons, 180; Hmong as, 11–12, 16–22, 28, 94–95, 212n2; nomadic movements of, 19, 21; "primitiveness" of, 20, 94, 106–9, 212n2; refugees versus, 20–21, 198n93; timelessness of, 16–22, 106–7

Steeves, John, 72

Stoler, Ann Laura, 8, 61, 198n100

Story Maps project, 180

Syrian refugees, 39, 142, 223n81

Tai language, 49

Tang, Eric, 194n53

Taussig, Michael, 34–35, 208n3

Taylor, Diana, 22–23, 106–7

terrorism, 9, 112, 133, 142–43, 217n76; definition of, 220n14

"terrorist ally," 119, 122–27, 142, 180–81

Thailand, 29, 68, 72; Hmong in, 11, 39, 85–86, 161–62, 195n76; "secret war" pilots from, 5, 32, 42

Thao, Chee, 166, 168, 175

Thao, Chong Vang, 218n1

Thao, Lo Cha, 132, 218n1

Thao, Mai See, 3–4, 13, 186, 190n9

Thao, Sai Kua, 17

Thoj, Va-Megn, 167
Tibetan refugees, 23
timelessness, 119; statelessness and, 16–22, 106–7, 156–60
Todd, Molly, 200n5
Tognetti, Francesca, 172
"totalitarianization of democracy," 35–36
traditional healers, 13, 149, 186
transparency, politics of, 34–36, 38
Trouillot, Michel-Rolph, 37
Trump, Donald, 110, 217n74, 224n81
Twiss, Robert, 121
txiaj ntsim (honor), 114–15, 218n81

Um, Khatharya, 42, 203n62
Union of Soviet Socialist Republics (USSR), 29, 46, 51–53; Pathet Lao support by, 55, 71–72, 76. *See also* Cold War
United States Agency for International Development (USAID): CIA and, 30–31, 58, 79, 91; Programs Evaluation Office and, 54
United States Immigration and Citizenship Service (USICS), 98–106
USA Patriot Act (2001), 112, 134, 217n76

Vang Pao, 5, 32, 82–88, 117–43; arrest of, 21–22, 112, 115, 117, 134–35; attorney of, 132–33; CIA handler of, 190n11; coup attempt by, 117–18, 217n77; death of, 122; as "freedom fighter," 120; funeral of, 218n80; judicial council of, 17; Lao nationalists and, 81–83; Lyfoung and, 39–40; mentor of, 211n67; military base of, 79, 85; opium trade and, 195n77; protests in support of, 136–39, 138f, 222n51; recruitment efforts by, 40; U.S. military support of, 77–79; war crimes of, 122
Vang, Bee, 164, 227n54
Vang, Chai Soua, 120, 126, 219n12
Vang, Dang, 218n1
Vang, Hue, 218n1
Vang, Mai Der, 182–87
Vang, Nhia Lue, 141

Vang, Wangyee, 101, 215n25
Vang, Yang Cheng, 11
Vang, Yer, 114–15
Vang, Youa True, 218n1
Vento, Bruce, 98–100, 103–7, 213n9, 214n22
Vietnam, 72, 118; as French colony, 47–49, 51–53, 58, 81–83; independence of, 5, 52
Vietnamese refugees, 27, 39, 130, 223n70
Vietnam War, 5, 41–42, 73; end of, 85, 135; Hmong refugees after, 85–86, 157, 168; Hmong soldiers in, 11, 27, 195n76; Um on, 42, 203n62; Viet Cong of, 81
Village Promotion Program, 71
Vinai, Ban, 150
Vincent Who? (film), 165
Vue, Seng, 218n1
Vwj, Zoov Tsheej, 12

Walsh, Aylwyn, 194n52
Warner, Roger, 201n17
Weiner, Tim, 131
Weis, Paul, 197n90
Weld, Kirsten, 38, 202n43
WikiLeaks, 128–29
World War I, 21
World War II, 33, 39–40, 141, 176, 203n56

Xiong, Wameng, 139–40

Yang, Dao, 196n78
Yang, Kao Kalia, 145–63, 176–78
Yang, Kay, 138
Yao, Lo Blia, 211n67
Yao people, 195n77
Yawm Xaiv Kuam, 17
Yoneyama, Lisa, 24, 45, 192n20, 195n64, 221n26
Young, Don, 113
Young, Iris Marion, 126–27
Young, K. T., 71, 76

Žižek, Slavoj, 224n2

Index 257

www.ingramcontent.com/pod-product-compliance
Lightning Source LLC
Chambersburg PA
CBHW072020290525
27270CB00018BA/282